Forbidden Science 3

Also by Jacques Vallee

In English:

Anatomy of a Phenomenon
Challenge to Science (with Janine Vallee)
Passport to Magonia
The Invisible College
Messengers of Deception
The Edge of Reality (with Dr. J. A. Hynek)
Dimensions
Confrontations
Revelations
The Network Revolution
Electronic Meetings (co-author)
Computer Message Systems
A Cosmic Samizdat
Forbidden Science 1
Forbidden Science 2
The Four Elements of Financial Alchemy
FastWalker (novel)
The Heart of the Internet
Stratagem (novel)
Wonders in the Sky (with C. Aubeck)

In French:

Le Sub-Espace (novel)
Le Satellite Sombre (novel)
Alintel (novel)
La Mémoire de Markov (novel)
Les Enjeux du Millénaire (essay)
Au Coeur d'Internet
Stratagème (novel)

Forbidden Science 3

On the Trail of Hidden Truths

The Journals of
Jacques Vallee
1980-1989

ANOMALIST BOOKS
San Antonio * Charlottesville

Forbidden Science 3: On the Trail of Hidden Truths
 ISBN: 978-1-938398-78-0
Second Edition

This book was originally published as *Forbidden Science Volume Three* by Documatica Research, LLC in 2012.

Cover image: Godruma/iStock

Cover design by Seale Studios

The author can be contacted at:
P.O. Box 641650
San Francisco, CA. 94164

The author's website: www.jacquesvallee.com

For information about Anomalist Books, go to AnomalistBooks.com or write to: Anomalist Books, 5150 Broadway #108, San Antonio, Texas 78209-5710

Contents

Figures

Introduction

> We didn't start the fire
> It was always burning
> Since the world's been turning
> We didn't start the fire
> No we didn't light it
> But we tried to fight it
>
> Billy Joel, 1989

The French call it *Devoir de mémoire*, the duty of memory: anyone who lives through exceptional times, or has the privilege to work with exceptional people, should preserve the recollection of the thoughts, the deeds and even the feelings that characterized the era in question. It is only in this way that future researchers will be able to assess the testimony of contemporaries and verify key facts.

This third volume of *Forbidden Science* covers the decade of the Eighties, during which this research took me from the United States to Europe and other places (Argentina, Brazil) in search of first-hand information on anomalous phenomena. In the process the reader will discover how several Intelligence agencies pursued a high level of interest in the subject, including much collaboration between French and U.S. services in secret studies: their research on UFOs had little to do with space Aliens and a lot to do with microwave weapons.

In the previous decades (covered by Volumes One and Two of these Journals) I had concluded that the UFO phenomenon was real in a physical sense but also in a spiritual and paranormal sense, a fact that did not sit well with many fellow researchers. The Intelligence agencies exploited the belief systems created in the wake of the phenomenon: they injected spurious data and manipulated opinion for their own purposes, which ranged from psychological warfare and "active measures" to the disguising of high-tech prototypes. The next step in my own analysis, then, had to be taken privately in the field, in dialogues with trustworthy witnesses who had first-hand data or physical samples, away from such government interference.

Unfortunately the context for rational research deteriorated rapidly during this period as the field of ufology took a devastating turn towards delusional patterns. While an unknown physical phenomenon continued to be reported, the media debate moved to breathless stories of abductions by short gray Aliens. Thousands of claims of such intimate contacts, promoted by dozens of amateur hypnotists filled the airwaves with lurid tales of coverup and pointless torture aboard flying saucers. I believe many abduction reports describe genuine experiences, yet to be understood, but the indiscriminate use of hypnosis promoting a narrow "E.T." interpretation represents a violation of ethical and scientific practice.

Rather than joining that parade I remained guided by the model of consciousness I had first encountered as a young scientist and cultivated through the spiritual literature.

The Eighties were also a pivotal time in the development of venture capital, leading to a financial infrastructure to support innovation throughout the western world. Here I found my professional passion, working with financiers, entrepreneurs, scientists and physicians, and private researchers who left their mark on history by creating real value for the world. I found new mentors. While my wife Janine and I made friends in many countries, willing to help in our investigations, we were also saddened by the loss of admired partners in research, notably Dr. J. Allen Hynek, who had tried to educate scientists and the public about the world's mysteries.

Nowadays much of the research in the paranormal field, like the pivotal *Star Gate* project at SRI of which I was a part, remains behind a double fence of secrecy and misinformation. I have tried to strip this confusion from the historical record.

I have often admired the epitaph on William Saroyan's black granite tombstone: "In the time of your life, live—so that in that wondrous time you will not add to the misery and sorrow of the world but shall smile to the infinite delight and mystery of it."

I present this volume as an application of that excellent principle.

Jacques Vallee – Douvres-la-Délivrande – June 2011
San Francisco – September 2013

Part Nine

DEALS AND ORDEALS

1

Palo Alto. Sunday 20 January 1980.

From my office at InfoMedia, the software networking and social collaboration company I founded four years ago, the domes of Lick observatory look like two white marbles some giant toddler might have forgotten after playing on the top ridge. To the west, the coastal range is green and blue with dark pine trees precisely drawn over the sky. The sunshine has returned, crackling fresh.

Our stresses of last year have gone away with the latest windstorm. Venture capitalists experienced with Silicon Valley have agreed to finance our startup, leaving 70% of the company in our hands as founders and staff (**1**). As part of the deal an experienced businessman joins me as executive vice-president, bringing increased credibility. I will stay on as chairman, devoting my time to my main interest, the next level of technology development.

Last week my mother flew back to Paris; our life settled down to suburban family routine. Our children grow up so fast! Olivier now borrows my three-quarter ton Cheyenne truck whenever he visits friends; my daughter practices karate, rides her bike, delivers the paper around the neighborhood.

Palo Alto. Saturday 26 January 1980.

Over lunch with college teacher Tom Gates today I met television journalist Renwick Breck who told me about his experiences in Australia where he was to report on the re-entry of Skylab. His adventures centered on Pine Gap, an American national security facility that controls the orbital trajectories of spy satellites over the Southern hemisphere. The story of Chris Boyce has already revealed how TRW was transmitting satellite data back from Pine Gap to CIA and NSA in Washington (**2**). Sentenced for giving information to the Russians, Boyce has just escaped from Lompoc penitentiary.

"Pine Gap does all sorts of other things!" Ren said. "I found out it directed the Polaris submarines and ran experiments with particle beam weapons and Star Wars platforms."

Ren believes that a new phase of the discreet "cold" war in space has begun between the Soviets and us; their Soyouz craft are suspected of carrying anti-satellite weapons. But there's more: "Pine Gap is hosting disk-shaped drones that may be used to direct particle beams towards specific targets," he told us, drawing donut-like objects on his napkin. "They're often mistaken for flying saucers. They may be nothing more than big magnets, powered from the ground by an energy beam. Such weapons would change the balance, the nuclear stalemate, making atom bombs obsolete."

"So, whatever happened to Skylab?" I asked. He laughed: "The damn thing came down in the middle of a news blackout. Imagine that! The communications workers of Australia went on strike just at the critical period. Guess who controls the Unions down there?"

I had no idea.

"The CIA, that's who! It was a very convenient strike. They did make one exception, to allow the broadcasting of the Miss World Pageant from Perth. For four days all you could see on TV from Australia was a bunch of bimbos in bathing suits. In the meantime Skylab crashed down, right smack on the highway to Pine Gap after narrowly missing two airliners Nasa hadn't bothered to warn. The world had been told that the final trajectory was unpredictable. What a joke! Tom here had computed it at the public planetarium in San Jose. The main safe from Skylab was picked up near the front door of the secret Pine Gap facility. Heaven knows what was inside. Nasa served as a cover for military experiments once again."

One of the rumors spread by New Age guru Ira Einhorn (and denied by Dr. Christopher "Kit" Green at CIA) claims that the Russians have destroyed one of Pine Gap's facilities by "Tesla vibration," whatever that means. Commonwealth Secretary Christian de Laët tells me that he can't get his Australian friends to comment on the issue. Pine Gap is a major target for Soviet intercontinental missiles, so Kit's denials leave me unconvinced. I am also skeptical of his comments about the continuing mystery of cattle mutilations. He sides with ex-FBI investigator Ken Rommel in denying their reality, but I see Rommel playing the same role as Professor Ed Condon ten years ago in debunking UFOs, with white-washing arguments that have no relationship to the facts.

Palo Alto. Thursday 31 January 1980.

A nasty cold virus makes me miserable. Forced to stay home, I read Brad Ayers' book about the anti-Castro operations conducted by the CIA since the Bay of Pigs (**3**). It reinforces my impression that the Intelligence community is out of control, acting for its own interests rather than those of the citizenry.

Palo Alto. Saturday 9 February 1980.

Kit keeps saying that we should be sending sociologists and psychologists, not biologists, to study mutilation reports. Well, I just flew back from a series of investigations in Arkansas, where I interviewed seven witnesses in one day. I walked through the mud of a pasture where the jaws and vertebrae of a decomposing cow were waiting for someone to ponder their silence. When I went into the farmhouse I saw a loaded rifle leaning against the wall next to the door in anticipation of another intrusion by strange flying machines.

At my request the rancher took a piece of paper and drew the "helicopter" he has repeatedly seen in connection with mutilations on his land. The craft comes over at night, without any lights. I can imagine what would happen to the unlucky psychologist who would stumble onto this scene, a stack of Minnesota Multiple Personality Inventory questionnaires under his arm.

Palo Alto. Monday 18 February 1980.

Fabio Zerpa, a respected investigator of the paranormal in South America, surprises me with a long letter inviting me to conduct a lecture tour in Argentina under the auspices of his "Onife" organization, as an opportunity to study cases in the field. I have dreamed of this for a long time. I will agree, provided Janine can come with me. The financing of InfoMedia should close in another week. The professional burden will be lifted from my shoulders then.

My plan is to go to Argentina in mid-April, with a stop in Brazil. Janine and I discussed all this under a powerful series of Pacific storms as we drove up to our ranch at Spring Hill, the truck moving like a ship in heavy squalls.

Palo Alto. Monday 25 February 1980.

Janine and I left on Saturday, eager to get away from the city, if only for a couple of days. We drove along the Mendocino coast to Timber Cove. We slept with the sound of the waves breaking against the rocks, stayed in bed all day Sunday listening to the wind and the rain: we returned through Point Reyes. In our absence our children had gone shopping for us and cleaned the whole house. A bit of melancholy lingers, under the spell of the North Coast's majestic isolation. I must let this impression mature: it holds a message I don't know how to decipher.

My poet friend Robin Rule wrote to me she'd seen me on Telegraph Avenue, and I hadn't said hello: Was I upset at her? But it wasn't me, I hadn't set foot in Berkeley. Last week she wrote again, sending along a book she'd found in a friend's attic. She was helping him move his library when a volume fell into her hands. It is entitled *Doppelgangers*, a science-fiction novel by H. F. Heard.

Palo Alto. Tuesday 26 February 1980.

Janine and Catherine have gone off to a Yehudi Menuhin concert, so I dined with my son at a local restaurant. The car parked next to mine had a license plate that read 963KIT. Then Kit called: he was in San Francisco; he'll come see us tomorrow.

This afternoon my associates and I signed the closing documents for InfoMedia's financing. We should be getting checks for $250,000 from our investors within a day.

Psychologist Blue Harary, a colleague from the SRI psychic project, explained to me that a crisis was rocking the Human Freedom Center, leading to a split in this support group created by the families of converts to sects such as Jim Jones' People Temple. Some members of this cult-fighting organization want to preserve religious freedom at all cost, while others don't hesitate to kidnap the victims to de-program them. The Center, where he serves as a counselor, has difficulty collecting dues, even from grateful parents. Harary shares my concern about the new cults, which proliferate.

Palo Alto. Wednesday 27 February 1980.

Al and Jeanie Mills, former leaders of Jim Jones' People's Temple, were coldly assassinated last night at the Human Freedom Center. Over lunch with Brendan O'Regan, who is growing a beard like psychic Ingo Swann, we discussed this event and another recent murder of a noted researcher, Wilbur Franklin, who was about to go to Alma-Ata for a year along with a psychiatrist friend from New York. Is that why he was killed? And why did the Mills have to die?

Palo Alto. Thursday 28 February 1980.

Details are starting to come in about the Mills murder. All three victims (their daughter Daphne was assassinated as well) died of a bullet in the forehead. Isn't that the signature of a professional assassin? Their son, watching television in another room, claims he heard nothing.

I had a busy afternoon at InfoMedia. One of our clients, a Utility company, experienced safety problems with a nuclear plant in Florida and was anxious to use our online collaboration conferencing software to link their experts together. While Rich Miller and the staff handled the computer network I went over to the office of our attorney who gave me three checks from our investors. I deposited the sum and was back at the office in time to meet Kit. We spent the evening discussing the Ira Einhorn affair and cattle mutilations. After he left I spent a bad night, with pains in my stomach in revulsion at all these murders, the senseless, sudden bloodshed. The New Age was supposed to be about meditating, holding hands, enjoying lofty philosophy, not discussing bullets shot from a silent .22, or bodies stuffed into trunks.

Palo Alto. Saturday 1 March 1980.

This novel, *Doppelgangers*, which fell into Robin Rule's hands, is an intriguing spy story set in 1995. It involves a paternalistic dictator named Alpha who has created a régime based on the principle of Bishop Berkeley, "to be perceived is to exist" (*percipi est esse*). He applies it to the citizenry: "Never give them a toy they have to assemble by themselves..." becomes his rule.

Alpha ends up committing suicide and is replaced by his double, who is soon contacted by a mysterious scientific genius. The visitor describes himself as "an elevator man," sent by his superiors from a higher level of existence to restore order on Earth. The ultimate secret, he reveals, rests in three words: "freedom, faith, and anonymity."

In the real world Al, Jeannie, and Daphne are dead. Did they stumble on some hot scandal of American politics? They were about to testify before Congress in Washington, yet they weren't afraid of Jim Jones' followers. Does that mean they were killed by someone outside the cult? A government agent? The assassin must have come on foot, and left the same way. No weapon has been found.

Palo Alto. Sunday 9 March 1980.

The heavy winter rains continue. I spend all my spare time on a new manuscript about the coming impact of computers on society, entitled *The Network Revolution*. The media have dropped the Mills murder--as if it never happened.

Palo Alto. Thursday 13 March 1980.

A local journalist has written a critique of my book *Messengers of Deception.* In the process he interviewed many ufologists to get their opinion of me. Stanton Friedman is sure I was paid by the CIA to write the book. "We need a little more time before we reveal the reality of the Aliens," they are supposed to have told me as an inducement! A local investigator for Mufon, Paul Cerny, told the reporter I was a thorn in the side of "serious UFO researchers" like him. For good measure he insinuated the odious rumor that I was an opium addict. Honest Tom Gates said he was unconvinced by my arguments but interested in my research. As for skeptic Bob Shaeffer, he said I wrote books to make money, "like all the other charlatans who believe in that crap."

After hearing this I felt thoroughly disgusted and ready to drop this research. To my surprise, Janine had a different opinion. She would be sorry to see me give up as Aimé Michel had done, she said.

On Wednesday I had lunch with the SRI psi team, among them Hal Puthoff, Russell Targ, and Hella Hammid. They felt discouraged too, running out of money again. Their military sponsors plan to bring the remote viewing project in-house. This is an election year; the government is scared of political exposure.

On Saturday I drove up to Spring Hill, our country retreat in Mendocino County, accompanied by Catherine, who asked me why we cared so much about the ranch. I spoke to her about the importance of nature in our lives—real nature, not the expensive flowers of suburban Palo Alto—and of seeing the stars, and exploring the uncharted realms of the mind.

Palo Alto. Friday 28 March 1980.

Many individuals who claim contact with Aliens also exhibit pathological symptoms that psychiatrists quickly label with terms like "paranoia" and "schizophrenia," so I continue to educate myself about what these words mean. Over dinner with Rosalie Ritz, an artist who specializes in courtroom scenes and portraits of assassins, we discussed these diagnoses in the context of the criminal mind. She has followed every local trial for murder on behalf of Associated Press over the last 20 years. This led us to talk about discarnate voices, which played such an important role in some murder cases like Sirhan's plot to assassinate Robert Kennedy.

Rosalie stressed her impression that the many psychiatric experts she had seen in courtrooms used such terms as "paranoid schizophrenic" when they didn't know what to say about a particular individual, just as skeptics use them in reference to paranormal experiences for which they have no context in their education or in their textbooks.

The first meeting of the new Board of InfoMedia took place this morning. Our investors of the Page Mill Group, which includes integrated circuit co-inventor Robert Noyce, were represented by Paul Ely, a senior vice-president at Hewlett-Packard, and Herb Dwight, a highly respected local businessman, CEO of Spectraphysics.

The economy is marked by an alarming increase in inflation. I am reminded of the Fifties in France, when prices flared up and the government was unable to control them. Jimmy Carter seems equally helpless. Inflation is good news for those who own real estate but it bodes ill for new companies like Infomedia, making our financial stability very fragile: the interest rates demanded by our banks are appalling: 20% and up.

My daughter often speaks of living in France some day. She reads the novels of the *Comtesse de Ségur* and dreams of long walks in Normandy. Life in Bayeux represents her idea of paradise, and I find it hard to argue with her.

Washington. Tuesday 8 April 1980.

In the plane I read Jeannie Mills' book about Jim Jones (**4**). What it reveals about the cults of Northern California is staggering. Once again I am struck by the convergence of so many well-meaning people towards a small corner of the world where a special level of spirituality seemed within reach. Jim Jones and his followers selected the Ukiah area for the same reasons we did: its natural beauty, its relative remoteness away from major conflicts. But the conflicts were inside, eventually driving them to Guiana and death.

I walked around Washington in the rain all evening. The cherry trees are in bloom. Jimmy Carter has forced the closure of the Iranian Embassy. This is an election year; government flexes its muscle. Television news show Marine troops repainting their tanks in desert colors. The U.S. budget is being balanced through new taxes disguised as a means to finance novel energy research. As soon as the money is collected, these projects get cancelled; the funds go to the military.

Washington. Thursday 10 April 1980.

Absurd theories continue to clash around the animal mutilations topic. Ken Rommel, whom I suspect to be funded by Kit at the CIA, has told *Science Digest* that all the cases were explainable through predators: coyotes, vultures, mice or snakes. Then I spoke to Peter Jordan, a researcher who believes the government is responsible for the death of cattle: he claims its biologists use the organs of cows as concentrators of mineral substances for which it needs to test. Both ideas seem equally unlikely in the cases I studied: predators hadn't had time to reach the carcasses. As for the government, it could use cows on federal lands if it ever had a need for bovine tissue samples.

What is so striking about the mutilation mystery is precisely that it is designed to be obtrusive, not secret at all. Ken Rommel threatens legal action against those who might propagate rumors of unnatural death. No wonder the ranchers are keeping the best cases quiet.

This weekend we fly to South America, where I will have a chance to find out first-hand what the situation is with these phenomena.

Today an associate and I presented our network communications system in the conference room of the NRC, the Nuclear Regulatory Commission. It was like a scene from some bad *film noir* about the waste and dread of Washington bureaucracy. The elderly guard who gave us our badges was cleaning his .45 with shaking fingers. The rooms were dirty and cluttered.

Flying over the Bermuda Triangle. Saturday 12 April 1980.

Now Janine and I are on the way to Argentina, with a stop in Brazil. Olivier took the wheel of the white Ford and drove us to catch the flight, a new experience for all of us. We found Miami airport noisy and dark, with only the occasional light of duty-free shops; then Varig swept us up with a group of passengers in white shirt sleeves.

Sao Paulo, Brazil. Sunday 13 April 1980.

We saw nothing of the Amazon. The black sky was starless. Good Brazilian coffee woke us up. Yesterday we had a brief stopover in Rio, a glimpse of white dawn over the silver wing, shredded cloud layers, white sky and the white city as in an overexposed photograph. Taking off again, we flew over the hill in Niteroi where two men wearing lead masks in anticipation of a saucer contact were found dead fourteen years ago. I plan to return there in two weeks.

The plane veered over Santos harbor, blue lakes in dark green forests at the edge of a steep plateau, canals feeding turbines. A few more miles, and all we were seeing were factories.

Today we slept, with interludes for coffee with luscious Brazilian pastries and a walk in the nearby park. Twice we were awakened by women who evidently ring hotel rooms at random, offering sex. From our window we see four hookers in miniskirts dancing under the rain at the corner of Bento Freitas, hoping a client's car will stop.

Sao Paulo reminds me of Chicago by its noise, its giant size, and its greedy skyscrapers. We indulged in a Champagne dinner while watching a thunderstorm roll over the city.

Sao Paulo. Monday 14 April 1980.

We spent the day discussing telecom investments with associates of the Churchill Group at Brasilinvest and visited the facilities of the local telephone company, Telesp. At night the traffic never stops; people keep singing in the streets. We breathe the pollution from endless processions of Volkswagens.

Sao Paulo. Tuesday 15 April 1980.

All efforts to connect my terminal to the net have been unsuccesful. The noisy phone line could barely get through to the Tymshare server in the States but I couldn't login. The sky remains low and gray. In this part of the country people tend to be dark-haired, and their speech sings in colorful tones. The city is a mass of huge buildings adorned by clothes drying out, draped over balconies. Long walls are topped by flowering trees, palms, tall branches. Sao Paulo is bigger than Paris or even Rio; the smell of gasoline is everywhere.

Buenos Aires, Argentina. Thursday 17 April 1980.

The illiterate Brazilian cabbie who took us to Sao Paulo airport this morning couldn't read the road signs. I had to tell him which turn to take to reach the terminal. We flew among clouds for an hour before seeing small villages and a vast swampy plain, the meanders of Rio Negro and the mouth of the Parana that separates Uruguay from Argentina.

Fabio Zerpa and his wife Bettina were waiting for us at Buenos Aires airport. The day was spent giving interviews in Spanish, then going from one café to another. We had a long talk about Men in Black (*Hombres de Negro*), evidently a major factor in recent South American cases. All night the wind—the *Pampero*—blew around us.

Buenos Aires. Friday 18 April 1980.

The sun rises in the East but climbs to the North. We're trying to get used to it. More interviews, articles about us in the press. We visited the offices of the Onife research group where Fabio's daughter works. Over dinner we began discussing specific paranormal cases. Their knowledge of foreign events is sparse: they had never heard of the Lead Mask incident, for example, which happened near Rio in August 1966 and involved the well-documented death of two researchers of the paranormal. But they were well aware of the

Spanish Ummo hoax, which has repercussions in Argentina. We also discussed Lopez Rega. His book on esoteric astrology, a big treatise on black magic, is banned in Argentina. Rega, who has had to leave the country, makes his home in Spain. He is said to be a homosexual with influence over the Peron family, especially young Isabella.

"He even became minister of social affairs," said Bettina.

"And head of the *Hand of Fire*, the secret police," added Fabio. (*)

Mar del Plata. Saturday 19 April 1980.

We caught up with lost sleep this afternoon, soothed by the waves splashing over concrete piers. Last night we had dinner *Chez Régine* in Buenos Aires with an American businessman, Mr. Oks and his wife. This afternoon we drove through insane traffic to interview a witness in San Isidro, regarding a remarkable visitation by a shining being. We also spent time discussing the details of a UFO crash that is supposed to have happened at the Bolivian border. Fabio believes there may be an underground UFO base in the Andes.

Mar del Plata. Sunday 20 April 1980.

A raging wind blew all night but the morning was calm enough for us to have lunch on the beach. Following my lecture the public asked the same questions North Americans always do, except that people here are not shocked by the concept of other dimensions, which puzzles audiences in the physically provincial U.S. I tried to get direct information on events I had heard about. One of the classic South American cases involves the Vidal family, rumored to have been abducted from their car by Aliens. A young woman told me she knew a couple who had driven on the same road as the Vidals on the date of their mysterious disappearance (**5**). Fabio laughed: he has met numerous people like her, who *knew someone who knew* the

----

(*) Note that in this period CIA director William Casey had reportedly begun farming out Argentina's death squad commanders as trainers for the Contras in Nicaragua.

Vidals. But in six years of active research his organization has never been able to actually verify the existence of the Vidals. This has taken on the characteristics of a myth. There is even a rumor that the unfortunate couple and their car are sequestered by Nasa in the U.S.! Mar del Plata bears witness to the past grandeur of Argentina, with enormous hotels (ours is as cavernous as an Egyptian ruin) and the world's biggest casino. We spent a studious Sunday visiting the sites of several UFO observations. Near Pier Five, two medical students spoke of a confrontation with black beings that came from the water, like the Kappas of Japanese legend. Similar creatures were reported in Punta Arenas in Chile a year ago. Such black beings were said to take the blood of their victims. As in some U.S. cases, this happened near a naval base. Were they commandos in combat training? Punta Arenas is also a magical center, according to Bettina, which harbors numerous cults and quite a few ex-Nazi. (+)

The Vidal case turns out to be more complicated than first reported. Perhaps Fabio never found the witnesses because their real name isn't Vidal at all! They may have avoided publicity with the help of Cide, the Army's intelligence unit. Fabio once reviewed the case with the head of that group, who told him the car had indeed been confiscated and taken to the U.S., "not by Nasa, of course, but by another agency." So the mystery continues.

Buenos Aires. Monday 21 April 1980.

Storms and rain, the city noisier than ever. Drivers play a fascinating death-defying game, straddling the white lines to squeeze out the next car. The result is chaos, bent fenders and frayed tempers.

Fabio is an extraordinary man. We spent the afternoon in his office, discussing a remarkable case in Venado Tuerto and various abduction reports. He had all the facts clear in his memory, a skill he attributes to his earlier training as a history teacher. A generous, charismatic and energetic man, he reminds me of the father character

- - - - - - - - -

(+) The Argentina junta-mafia power structure did not collapse until 1982.

in the Western series *La Ponderosa*: a wise white-haired figure giving instruction and inspiration to a team of young bucks. Under his direction his sons load up the loudspeakers, the projectors and the special lectern they've built for us, and we hit the road again.

In Argentina as everywhere else, students of the paranormal are split among dozens of small chapels. One local character, a former assistant to Fabio, is particularly colorful. He stole some of the files when they broke up. He called up other researchers in the middle of the night, disguising his voice, pretending to be from Ummo! Prevented from meeting us, he proffered various threats, painted black triangles on Bettina's door and kept pestering her.

Buenos Aires. Tuesday 22 April 1980.

At one intermission I had the pleasure of meeting Father Reyna, an elderly Jesuit theologian who was the first Argentinian researcher of the UFO subject. The public is enthusiastic and friendly, rushing to meet us, always ready to help, eager to shake hands and to tell us stories. We just had coffee with Mario Ujvari and his girlfriend Martha.

When I confessed I had never heard of Jose Hernandez, a great national literary figure here, Mario rushed out and came back with a leather-bound copy of *Martin Fierro*, his Gaucho epic, as a present for us.

Bahia Blanca. Wednesday 23 April 1980.

We left the noise and smog of Buenos Aires for a trip to the edge of the pampa near Patagonia, its open spaces and its dynamic people. During a live radio interview a journalist brought us news of an incident that took place just last night. A man driving his Chevy Impala near Santa Rosa lost power as he met two luminous beings on the road. They “squeezed his head,” he said, and he lost consciousness. He regained control of his senses 20 minutes later and 10 blocks away. He remains in shock, in a local hospital.

Bahia Blanca. Thursday 24 April 1980.

Full lecture hall, standing room only, many questions from a sophisticated audience. We spoke with a local psychiatrist until 2 am He gave us a brilliant overview of his personal theories of schizophrenia. Now we're flying over the *Pampa de las Salinas* on the way to Mendoza. We continue to hear of current cases all over South America: last Saturday two people in Uruguay saw a luminous object. They reportedly saw 13 beings with large heads, but we have no opportunity to follow up, or verify any of this.

Cordoba. Grand Hotel Dora. Saturday 26 April 1980.

This is a high-class town, an academic center with fine tree-lined streets and a massive Jesuit fortress. We are all tired, even Fabio the human dynamo. When we left Mendoza we caught a wonderful view of the glaciers on the slopes of Aconcagua in the pink rising sun. It has rained all night; the airport is closed. Bettina tells us we will have to drive all the way to Rosario, our next stop.

Rosario. Hotel Libertador. Later the same day.

We hear that back in the United States all the talk is about Jimmy Carter and the Iranian hostage situation. An attempt to rescue them has failed, a helicopter collided with a U.S. plane over the desert, and the White House seems helpless in the debacle.

Now I am ready for my last lecture of the tour. We had an insane car trip from Cordoba, driven by a woman reporter who repeatedly brought us within inches of disaster in a cloud of black smoke. The landscape of woods and farms was luxurious and friendly. We had lunch (an *asado* of well-cooked meats) near Oncativo. During the long drive Bettina told us the story of her own sighting, and the strange beings who contacted her: in 1968 she was approached by men with big eyes and long blond hair wearing white turtleneck sweaters. "What a pity, that you're not ready!" they told her.

Buenos Aires. Hotel Bauen. Sunday 27 April 1980.

We left Rosario early. A team of young researchers from the CIC group took us to Venado Tuerto in their Chevy truck. The main witnesses are a 12-year old boy of Inca lineage and his Gaucho father, his belt proudly adorned with silver pesos, a flat felt hat on his head, blue scarf around his neck.

The experience they described to us was profoundly complex. By a foggy morning on the forsaken plain the father sent the boy out to gather the horses. He came face to face with two incredible beings, a short robot and a tall "man" wearing large gray-silver gloves. A landed saucer was nearby. The boy recalls the robot cutting up a cow's leg over what looked like a plastic table. The father, a few days before, had found a decomposing cow with a leg missing.

A child's fantasy? Then how does one explain the series of cases independently observed in the area? (**6**) And what about the injuries sustained by the child's horse? The animal became nearly blind after the incident and bore scars at the place where Oscar swears it kicked the saucer's metallic ladder. The giant gave the kid one of his gloves, but it was very heavy, so Oscar tied it up to his horse's bridle as he rode home. Two craft flew out of the sky and chased him, he said.

Two lights emerged, a square one and a round one. They merged, came closer and *pulled the glove through the air*, so hard that the bridle broke. The most striking aspects of the story are the boy's simple beauty, the quiet nobility of his father, the cheer in evidence around the big family table where we were treated to grilled steaks and sausages, and the flat country with its wide marshes. The waters come and go, overflowing during the rainy seasons.

On the way back to Rosario our driver showed us an immense lake covering the horizon. It had begun as a mere pond, he said. Nobody seems to know if the ground is sinking or if the lake's level rises through infiltration. The water is salty.

As we kept driving the lake was soon on both sides of us, the road becoming just a thin straight ribbon. We could see the top branches of drowning trees emerging from the gloom, the roofs of old estancias and even the white structure of a three-story hotel turned

Fig.1. Mar del Plata: planning our trip with Fabio Zerpa and Bettina

Fig.2. At the site of the Venado Tuerto close encounter, April 1980.

into an incongruous island. It was a landscape worthy of Poe, with the setting sun at one end of the road, the full Moon rising at the other, and a few Argentinian peasants fishing for blind fish in the acrid waters.

Buenos Aires. Hotel Bauen. Monday 28 April 1980.

We are packing our suitcases again. The noise of cars on Avenida Corrientes is like rolling thunder and a heat wave has turned the city into a gas chamber. In Argentina we have witnessed how constant the features of the phenomenon could be in different cultures, and that is important to note. The behavior of reported lights, the pattern of waves, interferences with motors, reports of abductions, the appearance of luminous beings, all that is consistent with events elsewhere. The difference is in the witnesses, so courteous and friendly here, with none of the suspicious coldness often found in the U.S. Local research is enthusiastic, practical and well-organized, even if various chapels create unavoidable tensions.

Having said all this, the deeper nature of the phenomenon still escapes analysis. The murky role of government remains a big question: Fabio Zerpa has suffered three burglaries. Each time his archives were the only target.

Another remarkable factor in Argentina is the prevalence of "Men in Black" reports. But the case that made the greatest impact on us is the Venado Tuerto episode. I can't believe the boy was physically transported into the craft. The experience seems similar to that of an aborigine of New Guinea, for example, who might be captured by a commando, flown to Hollywood, exposed to *Star Wars* and later returned to his village (7). Such a witness could never distinguish between the real and the imaginal part of his journey: both would have been experienced at the same emotional and sensory level.

But what about the wounds to the horse, the broken bridle, the dead cow, the independent sightings? Did the boy lie, make up a story to hide some mistake he made, and injuring his horse? Would he have invented the two lights that merged and extracted the gray glove? Is it mere coincidence that the horse is going blind?

Flying to Rio de Janeiro, later the same day.

We stopped in Sao Paulo and now we continue our flight along the coast. We have taken leave of Bettina, who told us to be careful in Rio and not to trust the Brazilians. Fabio took us to Ezeiza airport after one last crisis as the car ran out of gas.

Rio, Copacabana. Tuesday 29 April 1980.

As soon as we arrived I called researcher and writer Irene Granchi, not really expecting to find her at home, but an hour later we were in her living room with a distinguished group of investigators including Sr. Soares from Rio Grande do Sul and a woman psychiatrist who studies UFOs. We spent most of the time talking about the 1966 Lead Mask mystery (in which two electronic technicians on a "contact" expedition died in suspicious circumstances). We made an appointment to meet with the pathologist who conducted the autopsies and a journalist who has researched the case for years.

The weather is warm, the Atlantic air a bit sticky, which seems to raise the ambient noise level. Across the way the beach is infinite in the haze of the waves. We had to call room service three times in three different languages to order breakfast but when it finally arrived we found ourselves in front of an elegant table with a white tablecloth loaded with fruits, honey, an assortment of croissants and breads, a variety of jams and preserves and of course, fragrant hot Brazilian coffee. As we ate on the balcony we could see kids playing soccer on the beach and a fishing boat lumbering to the horizon.

Copacabana, later the same day.

We have just driven back from the *Morro do Vintèm*, literally the "Hill of the Coin of 20 Cruzeiros," where we have spent the day. When we arrived this morning at the home of Dr. Lago we were introduced to the detective who had been in charge of the Lead Mask case; with them was a French professor who served as our interpreter and two journalists who had investigated the case. The library of Dr.

Lago is lined with books on magic and parapsychology in French, English, and Portuguese. He pulled out file after file, and we reviewed all the relevant data on the case until the early afternoon when we climbed into two cars to drive over to Niteroi. We stopped on the way to pick up a witness, the first man who saw the bodies on that fateful day when children who were playing on the hillside discovered the deaths. We followed him up the hill along the steep trail that was occasionally lost in the grass, and we finally reached the top. He led us to the place where the bodies of Manuel and Miguel had been found. Along the way we made notes about changes in the vegetation that had taken place since the event.

The meeting we had at the home of Dr. Sylvio Lago was unprecedented, even in the heady atmosphere of Brazil's fascination with UFOs: for the first time, parapsychologists and UFO specialists were speaking directly with the detectives and witnesses who had seen the two bodies back in August 1966. The policeman in charge, Detective Saulo, told me that his unit still had no conclusion about the case. He agreed that the explanation published two years ago, based on the confessions of a jailed con man, did not fit the facts. Since then a new piece of information has surfaced: Saulo found a handkerchief near the site, with the initials ANS matching the name of a spiritualist who calls himself "The Marahana." This man was interrogated but wasn't arrested, for lack of evidence.

The police assumes that Miguel and Manuel swallowed curare capsules in an attempt to enhance a spirit trance. There is no question that they were searching for this kind of experience. They had twice conducted such experiments with a civilian pilot named Elcio. Witnesses spoke of mysterious explosions and of an attempt to invoke a higher entity. Everything points to a hidden chief with authority over the victims. He may be the man who convinced them to go to Niteroi. Is the story of their journey to Sao Paulo and the large sum of money they carried, only a red herring designed to draw attention away from the real trip? They had confided to a cousin of theirs that the goal was a different one: "When I get back I'll tell you whether or not I believe in spiritism."

Detective Saulo has reconstructed their itinerary, only losing their trace once in the vicinity of a house that serves as a spiritualist center. The next thing they do is to buy raincoats and a bottle of mineral water, keeping the receipt with them. They climb up the Morro do Vintèm under the rain. They make a sort of shelter using vines and leaves and lie down, the lead masks next to them. The instructions they carry say to "ingest the capsules, cover the eyes and wait for the agreed-upon signal."

From the site we saw, the signal could have been a sound, or a light coming from Rio or from Niteroi. Were the capsules improperly measured? Saulo believes they died of a curare overdose. Oddly enough, the bodies did not smell (contrary to what the press wrote) and were not attacked by birds. The investigation has left many questions unanswered, especially the nature of the large orange disk that many witnesses reported, hovering over the Morro do Vintèm at the approximate time when the two men were lying there.

Lima, Peru. Wednesday 30 April 1980.

We have a short stopover at Lima airport, and will not see the city. I had planned to do a lot of writing before we left Brazil but we were seduced by the atmosphere of the gorgeous city of Rio and we ended up riding the cable car to the top of the Sugarloaf like all the tourists. Now we have lost our sense of time and are so tired that space itself is getting murky. We left Rio an hour late but flew back to the coast when the pilot realized over the Matto Grosso that he had lost his radar! After dumping kerosene all over the jungle and refueling back in Rio we finally left at midnight. All I could see through the window was a milky mass of clouds in the light of the full Moon.

Flying over Mexico. Thursday 1 May 1980.

Still the white clouds below us. Janine remarks with a smile that we have seen no sign of extraterrestrials. Yet we must have flown slightly to the north of Cuzco where contactee G. H. Williamson once assured me that the Monastery of the Seven Rays was located.

Palo Alto. Saturday 3 May 1980.

We found everything in order at home. Olivier came to pick us up in the truck. Our friend Missie had kept the house in impeccable order. A letter from Aimé Michel: the Russians have issued a positive assessment of the UFO question, he wrote, and now they are sweeping up documents from every source. Indeed I had another letter at the office, coming from Sanarov in Novosibirsk. He wanted my latest book, and copies of the most obscure old reports.

Palo Alto. Sunday 11 May 1980.

On Thursday the weather was gray, and in the mysterious ambiance of the rain I felt so much love for Janine, such a tender fervor that I started crying. Our Brazilian friend Irene Granchi had looked at her with keen admiration in Rio, comparing her to a Spanish painting.

Time, thought, and everything else changes. The rhythm of my research, too. On my latest trip to Redding my son and I spoke like old friends, all the way. We took the truck up the hillside in four-wheel drive to install the newest version of our automated camera to take pictures over the canyon. The mountains were still covered with snow, the air sharp and cold as a knife. We had to shake ice from our hair as we walked under the frozen trees.

On the way back I plunged into a very strange case, which made me wonder whether my hypothetical Control System was indeed playing with us. Four women (a mother, three daughters) had reported to researcher Bill Murphy being engulfed in a luminous cloud as they were driving outside Redding. While inside the cloud they couldn't hear any sound from the road and lost their sense of time. Once they emerged from it they stopped to buy soft drinks and drove back without seeing any trace of the cloud. They went to a friend's home, only to realize it was 40 minutes later than it "should've been."

The next day there were suspicious marks on the arms of two girls, a spot behind the ear of the youngest one. The mother called police, who put her in touch with a ufologist in Seattle, who called Coral Lorenzen of Apro, who called Bill. That was Thursday evening.

The mother showed us the place where it happened, and then Bill and I grilled her skeptically for four hours. There is a striking element in all this, an *intersign* again that hits me at a personal level: They report being surprised at finding *a gray glove* by the side of the road that night. One of the girls keeps dreaming about that glove. It is worn, in her dream, by a tall man in an armor of gray nylon. Yet I haven't told anyone, not even Bill, about the case at Venado Tuerto, where the dramatic scene of the gray glove occurred.

Douglass Price-Williams, who teaches anthropology at UCLA, has been urging me to pay attention to such coincidences and mythopoietic aspects, as he does in working with Carlos Castañeda.

Palo Alto. Tuesday 13 May 1980.

Today at InfoMedia I turned over the CEO's duties to the executive we have recruited, with whom I get along well.

I have been running the company during the four years of the start-up phase. We have established the technical feasibility and the business reality of computer-based conferencing, the funding and initial sales. Now it is up to him to put the company on a path to break-even operation while I work on expanding foreign contacts, starting with a marketing trip to England and France in ten days.

Palo Alto. Wednesday 21 May 1980.

Bad sleep, shaken by allergies: everything is always blooming here. There is a hedge of rosebushes along our fence, and jasmine at the corner. Over lunch with Hal Puthoff at SRI, I told him I no longer believed the government had an ongoing UFO project. He has reached similar conclusions. I added I had no intention to be used by the Intelligence folks. The more I know them, the more I have the feeling they play stupid games. “No,” Hal replied, “but as soon as they get promoted they only respond to political signals.”

“That's the same thing as playing stupid games,” I said, “I can't afford to share UFO data with them—what if I happened to expose some of their own games?”

"We have the same problem," Hal said. "Our successes with remote viewing are a threat to the satellite folks. Some big budget organizations want to shut us down, so they spread false rumors about us. Even the White House is having trouble finding out the truth. In our war game simulation we succeeded in pinpointing the position of MX missiles in one of 10 hidden silos on a random basis. We did it 12 times in a row, no misses—a result with odds of one in a trillion! But the budget for the projected MX is 55 billion dollars. How can we fight against that?"

London. Hotel Russell. Monday 26 May 1980.

The direct PanAm flight takes ten hours to reach London. I used them to read Jimmy Guieu's book about the Cergy-Pontoise abduction of 26 November last year **(8)**, filled with tales of hypnosis and predictions of imminent contact with Aliens. The experience of the main witness, Franck Fontaine, does emerge from all this as a genuine mystery. This young man vanished among a ballet of lights that remind me of the "spirogyres" I had invented in *Sub-Espace*, my 1961 novel. Unlucky witnesses: Guieu describes how they were harassed, first by the Gendarmes, and later by scientists from Gepan. Everybody handled them from the beginning as if they were crooks, not witnesses or victims of an unknown phenomenon.

I landed in London in the afternoon and went to the British Museum to see the show about the Vikings. I like this unpretentious area with its little shops, the Theosophical Editions, the Atlantis bookstore. I called the University of Birmingham, which is buying our software in support of a British Library project, the first electronic journal in the world. Then I spoke to my friend Simonne Servais, who has the rank of Ambassador and can see through the bureaucracy: "All right," she said laughing, "We'll drive to YOUR Pontoise!" She thinks the witnesses won't talk: "There's nothing to expect from Gepan," she assures me.

From London I called my mother, her voice young and strong. She warned me that "things are going very badly in France," a complaint I have heard for 40 years.

On Thursday we had Ray and Carol Williams as dinner guests at her apartment on *Rue de la Clef*. Carol asked how our life would change if InfoMedia made millions of dollars. How can I explain that everything would remain the same? I only dream of the forests of Mendocino, fine books, life with Janine, and the love of our children.

Brussels. Galerie Stéphanie. Thursday 29 May 1980.

In Belgium for meetings with Sligos, a big software company. My room is impeccable, silent, and boring. In London I signed our contract to install computer conferencing at the British library. Here I am negotiating for European representation.

Reading Jeannie Mills' book carefully I find it has the acutely painful tone of truth. Holsinger, a staffer to Congressman Leo Ryan who was killed in Guyana, has accused the CIA of mind control manipulation of the People's Temple. It is clear that the government was aware of Jones' slightest move. So why was he allowed to export weapons and poisons? Why did he die of a bullet in the head? Why was Larry Layton set free? All troubling questions about the destiny of such a cult and its paranoia.

I had breakfast with information expert Tony Judge, who understands the far-reaching consequences of network conferencing. We spoke of the confusion that surrounds Ira Einhorn. Christian de Laët told him someone had started a rumor that I was a KGB agent! So now I have heard everything, since Stanton Friedman says I must have written *Messengers* on behalf of the CIA. I am surprised nobody has yet picked up on the rumor that I am the *Comte de Saint Germain!*

Paris. Rue de la Clef. Friday 30 May 1980.

Walking around the Latin Quarter with Maman, I found that the Pope had picked the same day for a visit; most of the bridges over the Seine were cordoned off. At *Square Viviani* the crowd was intoning "O Lord, I am not worthy of receiving you." I looked at them: tired old women leaning against the retaining wall of the park, serious French gentlemen in three-piece suits with the frozen faces of faith, the glazed eyes. They did not have the look of crazed cultists or stoned hippies; they were not illuminated by some delusion: Simply, they conformed to an inner voice that spoke of something beyond. There was a mystical wind over the Seine but mixed with it was the political exploitation, riot police in deep lines, blue uniforms among the white of the priests, the sabers alongside the *goupillons*, as the second Christian millennium comes to a close. At the Jussieu metro station someone has scribbled: "Pope go Rome!"

Paris. Rue de la Clef. Saturday 31 May 1980.

A long evening with Simonne discussing parapsychology. Physicist Yves Rocard, who remembers meeting me with Aimé Michel, is doing dowsing experiments with Simonne. He plans to build detection instruments for Esterle at Gepan. He is the father of Michel Rocard, head of a socialist group and presidential candidate against Giscard d'Estaing. Unfortunately the two great tenors of French psychic research, Rocard and Costa de Beauregard, cannot get along. Costa is a strict Catholic, unwilling to question church dogma. The only new approach uses medical methods at DGRME, a French military research agency studying "electromagnetic influences on the balance of the human body," according to what Simonne told me.

The Gepan group also has a secretive medical unit directed from the Invalides. But Alain Esterle is said to be sidetracked: Curien, the current director of Cnes is deeply skeptical and the whole thing is simply political insurance. As for Claude Poher, he has faded away.

Paris. Rue de la Clef. Sunday 1 June 1980.

I wake up early. I don't mind. It allows me to read, write, or call Janine. I speak to her softly, not to wake up my mother. The only sounds are from the sparrows of Paris who sing in the gray dawn.

I met Simonne in Neuilly as icy sheets of morning rain hit her little Peugeot, and we went to Pontoise. The weather would have made a lesser man feel suicidal. I thought I would recognize the road so often traveled in my youth but I only saw sad tenements, gray buildings, the freeway and huge earthworks that hide what little charm is left in *Ile-de-France*. The suburbs had become maudlin and unappealing as the bourgeois influence swept them after the war, but the latest urban "improvements" under Pompidou have turned them into an ugly zone that cannot even boast the poisonous beauty of industrial wasteland or the primitive savagery of a swamp.

The curious little town of St.Ouen l'Aumône where the White Queen used to make her retreat at Maubuisson has fallen victim to the same orderly destruction under a nest of freeway ramps and concrete arches.

In Pontoise, the town congested and shiny with rain, I went up *Rue Thiers* and escaped on foot for a glimpse of the public park. Some day I will have a meeting there with my old self, outside time, for a serious accounting of my sins and shortcomings. I alone know the secrets of that place, the aspirations and fears of childhood.

There is only one way in life: total honesty with oneself, a mystical integrity which must become an obsession, or surely fails.

We drove on to the *Purple Justice* apartment building where Franck Fontaine is said to have been abducted last November. What a site! Over the vast plain swept by high winds, good lands with sticky mud producing abundant cabbages and beets, the Planners have erected massive towers for the sub-proletariat of modern France. Plain cement walls, fabricated plates hastily stapled together. Satan smiles here: Rational Man has been tricked into conceiving, drafting and implementing the destruction of his own soul.

A road has been thrown over the ancient fields turned into parking lots, and the concrete towers have been painted in "quality of life" tones: orange, grey and finally *Purple Justice*. Across the road is a giant utility substation where high-tension lines converge, antennas and transformers and spidery towers scratching the low rain clouds.

We take a little path; it leads us to a road. People have dumped old cardboard boxes and trash there; the wind has scattered the debris around. It rains hard. The plain stinks with the smell of mud, beets, and garbage. The gray sky drips with horror.

I think I am beginning to understand what really happened to Franck Fontaine. We drove back to Paris under the rain and I spoke for a long time with the curious lady who once gave orders to all the French science attachés around the world to assemble information on paranormal research.

Rue de la Clef. Monday 2 June 1980.

I miss Janine and my kids. I even think of canceling New York to get home early. Lots of phone calls: London University, the British Library. Tomorrow I set up our French subsidiary.

Dr. Hubert Larcher runs the *Institut Métapsychique*, the oldest and most serious parapsychology research group in France. Simonne and I had a most courteous meeting with him. He spoke enthusiastically of a technique called micro-plysmography. He applied a discovery by a Dr. Vittox about pulsing capillaries, used in equipment testing for schizophrenia. The idea is to test it for nervous system effects related to psychic functionning. We also spoke of Dr. Barron's research, under contract with the French military.

When we left the *Institut Métapsychique* Simonne and I sat down at a nearby café and spoke of politics. Her vision of French society is sharp as a laser beam, a sober but pessimistic assessment of its future. I watch Paris becoming encircled by increasingly ugly suburbs where the State allows an entire generation to grow without any vision of its future, without even the terrible poetry of genuine poverty. In the current phraseology they become *les Autonomes*, unpredictable and ungovernable, who hold the streets of the suburbs as anguish holds the hearts of the bourgeois in wealthier areas. I feel like an "Autonome" myself, creating my own structures as I step through the garbage.

In the plane to New York. Wednesday 4 June 1980.

Garbage indeed: the strikes at Charles de Gaulle airport began with the cleaning service. I watched the Concorde take off gracefully over an area littered with refuse. Inside the terminals trashcans were full,

Fig. 3. Gendarmes at the site of the Cergy-Pontoise "abduction" case.

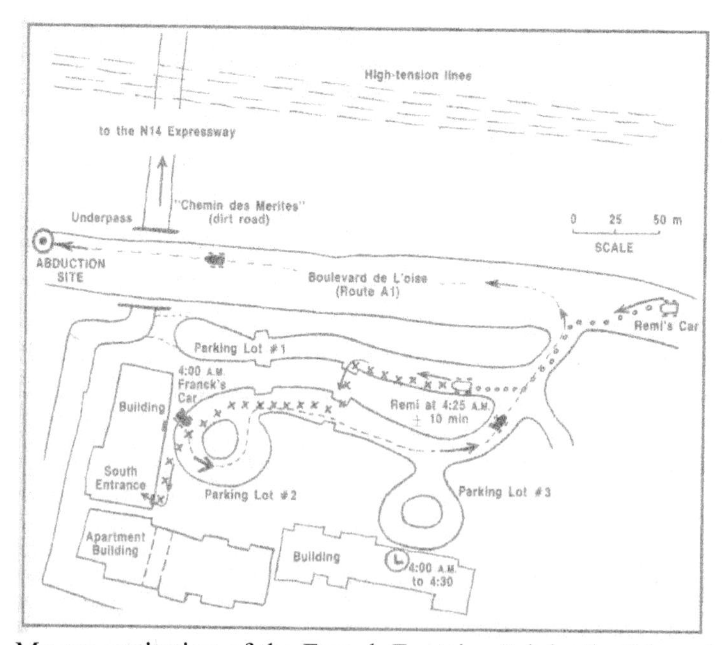

Fig. 4. My reconstitution of the Franck Fontaine "abduction" based on the testimony of independent witnesses challenged prevalent theories, showing the event could have been staged as a psychological warfare test.

nobody was picking up Coke bottles and old newspapers; spilled coffee made sticky swamps in the hallways.

I boarded my plane with mixed emotions; sadness at leaving my old mother behind, although well cared for and with frequent visitors in a sunny apartment in her beloved Paris; eagerness to find Janine again, and Catherine who teaches me so much through her new eyes and bubbly conversation, Olivier who told me the other day he felt I was always with him, even in class. When he took a test he sensed I was there, spoke to me. He reproached me for not realizing how much I counted, how important I was for him.

France drags along too many ancient problems. The Pontoise case bothers me for many reasons, including the similarities with my 1961 novel *Sub-Space*. In my book was a scene where an alien light abducted a young couple and spoke to them telepathically.

I have written to Fontaine, advising him not to allow himself to be hypnotized either by the ufologists or by doctors from Gepan.

New York. Thursday 5 June 1980.

New York University has asked me to give a seminar about networking. I feel tiredness drawing pressure down my spine, my jaws, my eyebrows. As important as InfoMedia is in my life, I must detach myself to relinquish the sense of power that comes with running a company. The life of CEOs driven by such fleeting illusions is an empty waste.

This has been one of those rare, glorious Manhattan days, with chamber orchestras at street corners and friends sipping coffee at outdoor bistrots. I had dinner with a team of communications consultants from London, and went to see the *Star Wars* sequel.

Thinking about Fatima and the impact of the paranormal in religion, one could formulate the following hypothesis: "For every creative, spontaneous action of mankind there arises an equal manipulative reaction that exploits it." The most blatant example is Christianity: Jesus' spiritual effort to free the downtrodden has been hijacked by the power structures of churches. Marxism is another example: an intense attempt to cure the causes of exploitation and war has been turned into massive bureaucratization of the State and, inevitably, another channel for social exploitation and war.

We now have another example in psychical research. Paranormal phenomena, instead of being studied objectively and rationally as they could be (ignorant "rationalists" notwithstanding) are pigeon-holed into convenient categories to promote traditional ideas. Similarly the facts of ufology are distorted to support the extraterrestrial ideology. It is impossible to argue for the reality of UFO observations without being exploited by cultists. And anyone analyzing paranormal phenomena or alleged miracles runs the danger of being vilified by academics or captured by fanatical sects. This represents a weakness in the human intellect, detestable to me.

Palo Alto. Saturday 28 June 1980.

My creative life is awake again, after being stifled by the hard business work of InfoMedia these last few years. The French electrical utility company, EDF, has just signed a contract with the subsidiary I have setup in Paris.

I have finished writing *Network Revolution*. Janine likes the book. Now I'm reviewing the proofs of the Bantam edition of *Messengers of Deception*, a more sober and coherent text than the And/Or original. I feel I have emerged from my studies of cults and mutilations with a sharper understanding of the subject.

The Peninsula was in the throes of a heat wave today. We drove up to the City to look at houses, with the idea that we might move again next year. I don't quite understand my current creative phase, working on three books at the same time, except that our trip to South America has had refreshing effects.

Palo Alto. Thursday 10 July 1980.

Hal is about to hire a consultant physicist, Rucker, who has written *Geometry, Relativity, and the Fourth Dimension*. We spoke about Uri and Puharich. The former is in New York, borrowing an apartment from the producer of *Grease* and *Jesus Christ Superstar*.

This producer has bought the rights to his autobiography after a big fight with Puharich who gets a percentage of the deal. "Andrija still believes those Hoova stories," says Uri with contempt. About Puharich there are very differing views. Some people treat him like a national hero; others spread the absurd rumor that he set fire to his own house in Ossining in order to get insurance money.

Hal, with Rucker, is pursuing the 4-dimensional theory of UFOs. His psychic project is back on solid footing, with Dr. Edwin May and a staff on a full-time basis. They invited me to SRI for a PK test, which went well. The secret lab is equipped with Dick Shoup's painting machine, borrowed from Xerox Parc. On the largest wall of the electronically secured room: a huge map of the USSR.

Palo Alto. Saturday 12 July 1980.

Olivier and I just drove back from Mount Shasta, having spent the night in Redding. This morning we met with Bill Murphy and climbed up the Blue Hill, from which we could see Whiskeytown Lake and a snowy ridge to the North.

We buried our well-camouflaged camera designed to monitor the canyon for UFOs, then drove on to Shasta City and up to 8,500 feet. From there the eye is level with the top of the volcano, shrouded in grey white fog with purple tints like cotton puffs. We joked they were blown over by the Lemurians to hide their mysteries.

Palo Alto. Sunday 20 July 1980.

The weather was hot and terribly humid in Washington where I just spent three days: thunder, lightning, hellish rain every night. I saw Kit the first evening. He has determined that Ron Hubbard's son died of carbon monoxide poisoning. We discussed researcher Len Stringfield's repeated claims about Alien bodies captured by the government. Stringfield is PR director for Dubois Chemical, a division of Cyanamid. At a recent Mufon meeting he showed so-called humanoid photos to a small group of selected ufologists, but the bodies had none of the details one would need in order to prove anything. The photos are so bad one wonders why anyone would go to the trouble of pulling such a hoax. Rumor has it that a man named Jean-Pierre Calmet, who works with Esterle, knows a French scientist who saw Alien bodies in the U.S. **(9).** But two American specialists, Tom Deuley of NSA and John Schuessler, a manager at McDonnell Douglas say that Stringfield's photos are crude fakes.

Kit and Deuley have access to reconnaissance satellite data. They can now check for the presence of objects within 10 days of a sighting. The satellites of VELA-10 type have repeatedly caught what experts call "FastWalkers," erratic sources of energy. These may represent previously unknown electrical phenomena, or perhaps UFOs. My clearance is still active, so I could see these images if the need arises. Kit, who somehow gets all the data from Gepan, has shown me two recent reports from Esterle. But they only consist in a hodge-podge of uninteresting statistics.

Kit ran an electrocardiogram on me, using a new device being tested by his medical colleagues. He reassured me about my heart murmur. My blood pressure is consistently excellent, he said. **(10)**

The main purpose of my trip was to attend an OTA meeting about the future impact of electronic mail on American labor patterns **(11).** A body of experts has been asssembled, drawn from government and industry. The organizer is Bob Chartrand, of the Congressional Research Service, a senior analyst with considerable background in intelligence, assisted by RuAnn Pengov. As we sat in his office at the library of Congress, he pulled down a well-thumbed copy of *Challenge to Science* and asked me to inscribe it. He introduced me to Marcia Smith, who once wrote a summary of the UFO literature for the Library. He also told me about his time at TRW when he worked on a remarkable project called "Slavia," a simulation of the USSR that cost $20M a year and served to train analysts in the interpretation of satellite imagery.

Chartrand is an old friend of the legendary Tom Belden, a veteran intelligence analyst, a pioneer in computer applications in the federal government and author with his wife of *The Lengthening Shadow*, about Watson of IBM. He also wrote a classified study of the Japanese and American messages from the Pear Harbor crisis. Bob

Chartrand has promised to introduce me to Arthur Lundahl, another close friend of his **(12)**. Lundahl is the man who analyzed the Cuban missile photographs and took them to John Kennedy. Earlier he'd analyzed the Mariana (Great Falls, Montana) UFO film, but he never saw the first frames of it: someone had cut them off.

After lunch I met with Kit again at his house in Reston. He gave me a copy of Ken Rommel's report about mutilations, so I confronted him about the work. The main effect of his report is to discredit the honest cops, veterinarians and ranchers who try to find out what is going on. Again, I am left wondering what game is being played.

It felt good to return to California after three days in the stifling oven of Washington. Janine and Catherine had many stories for me and Olivier had built a new circuit for his electronic drums.

Palo Alto. Monday 28 July 1980.

Although exhausted with another asthma crisis, and preoccupied with preparing the business trip that will take me to Australia next week, I went back to Redding to work on the French Gulch case where an old couple keep seeing an egg-shaped object on their land.

On the way we visited Mount Lassen, geologically more interesting than Shasta by its dramatic heaps of rocks, its chilly lakes, sulphur vapors, and eternal snows up on top. We drove back at 3 am in the warm night, Olivier at the wheel.

Beverly Hills. Thursday 31 July 1980.

Columbia Pictures, which is hosting a two-day party at the Beverly Wilshire for the release of the new version of *Close Encounters,* has invited me to Hollywood. I just saw Allen on TV, more charismatic than ever, solid behind his white goatee. Unfortunately Janine is not with me, which nullifies all the luxury that surrounds me.

While in Beverly Hills I had lunch and dinner with Allen. We got along well and the press conference showed it. Allen told me his plans to get industrial partners to finance Cufos were going nowhere: "I managed to get some businessmen interested," he told me, "but they can't convince their own boards." These companies give money to charity but UFOs are too controversial for them.

Allen agreed with me about Len Springfield: someone is using him as a naïve conduit to feed crappy pictures of alleged dead ufonauts to credulous ufologists. In the meantime, he said, the real phenomenon is quiet, and Cufos is not getting any interesting reports.

Sydney, Australia. Hotel Wentworth. Wednesday 6 August 1980.

If some day I am asked what I was doing on Tuesday 5 August I will be at pains to answer, because that day fell off the calendar as I flew over the dateline. In the plane as I watched new constellations south of the Equator I found my old inspiration again.

First impressions of Australia: good-natured greetings, friendly open faces. The uncomplicated feeling comes with an impression of general indifference: The desk girl at Quantas can't take information down properly, our bus takes a wrong turn into a one-way street, people get dropped off blocks away from their destination, but there is no ill-will and no intent to harm behind all these mistakes. From a high window, a worker throws down sacks of plaster into an open truck; they shatter and bounce, covering the street with trash. People pick this up and clean it quietly. From my window I see the cranes of Wooloomooloo Bay and part of the harbor.

Breakfast in mid-afternoon, bright sun. My waiter is French, from Lyon! He dreams of California. Salaries are too low in Australia, he complains, and people too coarse. I called home, spoke to Olivier. He had finished the box for his computer and earned $20 by painting the staircase at a friend's house. Now I feel suspended beyond time, beyond the world, in a large city where no one knows me, and I enjoy it. There is a current that scoops me along, seemingly transcending life itself.

Sydney. Sunday 10 August 1980.

Every day I communicate with Janine and the children through the Infomedia message system. I had several meetings with a potential

Australian representative for us. Now I am waiting for him and his friends; a picnic is planned outside the city. Tomorrow morning we fly to Melbourne, and on Wednesday I can go home.

South Pacific. Wednesday 13 August 1980.

I am flying towards the Fiji Islands on the way back. Melbourne was quiet, wet, hospitable, a city as easy to appreciate as a familiar pair of slippers: uncomplicated, no snobbery, no pretense. My friends there believe strongly in the future of Australia, including the probability of its survival in case of nuclear war. I am reading Peter Watson's book *War on the Mind.*

Palo Alto. Tuesday 19 August 1980.

During the long wait to board the plane for the return trip I toyed with ideas for a novel in which an oil-drilling platform would be taken over by terrorists. On the flight between Sydney and Fiji the airline showed the movie *Foulks*, the story of an oil drilling platform taken over by terrorists: cryptomnesia or precognition? An *intersign*?

My old Chicago friend Fred Beckman tells me about a book called *Carl Jung Speaking* that mentions a meeting between Lindberg and Jung. Lindberg was a friend of Donald Keyhoe. He went to Switzerland to discuss UFOs with Jung.

Palo Alto. Monday 1 September 1980.

We found a depressing spectacle at Spring Hill last week-end: debris piled up in the yard, a partially collapsed retaining wall, a power line destroyed by a careless backhoe driven by a local crook sentenced to "community service." After every such disappointment I talk of selling everything, then the beauty of the place re-asserts itself. We decided to keep the ranch and find a house in San Francisco.

Few things are more interesting than looking for real estate in California. We drove from the grayness of the Cliff House into the fog of Twin Peaks, from the tourist spots of Ghirardelli Square to the cliffs of Telegraph Hill. I looked at no less than 14 houses today: an imposing structure in Haight-Ashbury; an apartment building with a gorgeous view of the waterfront; a fake castle painted green, overlooking the Pacific.

That last property was the most picturesque. It belonged to an old Russian couple. It was filled with religious icons and one of the tenants was a pope in black garb. The flats were made interesting by uneven floors, slanted walls and an accumulation of Russian antiques, books, musical instruments, old carpets, flower pots, and at the top a very old man piously painting a golden image while a group of unruly dogs played, fought and defecated on the stairwell.

Palo Alto. Monday 8 September 1980.

I love Janine to distraction. Whether in the fog of the harbor, or the blatant flatness of Palo Alto sunshine, quietly she takes hold of my heart and mind. We haven't found our dream house yet, but we are beginning to know the City well, with its wonderful microclimates and microcultures.

Palo Alto. Saturday 13 September 1980.

We are making an offer on an old Victorian on Hyde Street, a couple of blocks up from the Pier, the Cannery and the cable car turnaround. We had lunch in San Francisco while Olivier helped his buddy Bob Rich move his belongings and my daughter played with her friend Rhea. Next month Janine will undergo surgery, exploration for a possible breast tumor that terrifies us, so she will have to stay home for three weeks.

I spoke to our former friend Don (Brian) Hanlon yesterday and was pleased to find him a bit more settled. He had just become a happy father: his girlfriend has given birth to a boy, Aleister Salomon.

Local ufologist Jim McCampbell is telling everybody that the French government has isolated Claude Poher and me from other researchers, to enable us to "solve the final mystery." How do such wonderful tales get started? Now Kit has sent me an offer of support for my research from the newly formed Fund for UFO research, a group filled with government people he knows well. It's too late for all that, and I don't trust them anyway. The offer reinforces my impression that government agencies plan to use that Fund as an information channel, now that the old Nicap vacuum cleaner is dead.

Flight Dallas—San Francisco. Monday 15 September 1980.

I was supposed to work here with an investigator who had good data (notably about mutilation cases). He did meet me in Dallas last night. Unfortunately he arrived half drunk and brought a local mathematician who was in the same state. They sat in the bar and ordered one whisky after another, so I quickly gave up on the research I had hoped to plan with them. Today I made my scheduled presentation on computer networking before the Edison Institute and I boarded an earlier flight home without seeing them again.

Arthur Koestler, Colin Wilson, and others have mentioned an interesting theory, according to which evolution has produced the human brain as an incomplete, even abnormal and dysfunctional organ. Man, they suggest, is fundamentally insane. Could a higher intelligence suffer from the same problem?

Now I fly over Lake Powell; I look at the orange sandstone towers that rise from the desert and contemplate the next phase of my work: drawing lessons from my failures.

Palo Alto. Saturday 20 September 1980.

Yesterday I had lunch with Blue Harary. He confirmed that Eddie, the Mills' son, was under suspicion of killing his parents. However he was not arrested, nor has the murder weapon been found. The investigation of the People's Temple in Guyana appears to be stalled as well: the few living witnesses won't talk. Blue himself has had to move and change his phone number.

We drank Champagne tonight, because Janine's brother Alain came over and Olivier, barely 17, landed his first job as an electronics assembler at Nestar, a microcomputer company.

We were also celebrating the Victorian house; our offer has been accepted, so we will soon move to San Francisco.

Palo Alto. Sunday 28 September 1980.

On Friday evening we drove to Ukiah, listening along the way to songs by Jacques Douai, Brel and Gilbert Bécaud; the chronology of Bécaud's songs shows the slow decline of the French spirit. The early ones are powerful, like *The Matador*. Later they turn to petty sentimentality and maudlin conformity.

Along the way we discussed Colin Wilson, who doesn't seem to have understood Casanova. Janine says that Casanova is one of history's most unappreciated characters, because he achieved so many things others dream about in vain, and not only in the bedroom. They reduce him to a mere seducer of virgins. Wilson, a fine analyst of the paranormal, should have seen the man's qualities.

We had work to do at Spring Hill. A neighbor of ours, a developer, wants to cut the ancient redwoods on his property. We don't know how to stop him.

Palo Alto. Thursday 2 October 1980.

Is it the apprehension that Janine will soon be under the surgeon's knife? Or the hot weather that drapes stifling brown smog over the Peninsula? Is it the sad spectacle of the streets of San Francisco, fat men in ugly shorts, stoned waifs lost, drifters in tattered clothes, and the debris of the failed New Age? Is it the old people who sit in doorsteps with nothing in their eyes but a stunned vacuum? Is it the unsteady growth of my company? I feel disoriented, and watch the similar disorientation of society in those little groups that surprise, amuse and occasionally enlighten me.

Palo Alto. Monday 6 October 1980.

Routine defines reality. As soon as the usual flow of small every day actions is broken, one traverses the mirror, then the cavernous world of cables and strings that manipulate appearances becomes revealed. So I drove Janine to the hospital this morning after a too short night, a night of love, deep and tender, that tore at our hearts.

"If something happens to me," she said, "You should let the children do whatever they want in life. If Catherine wants to live in France, let her."

"You know that I adore them, they will always be free."

"And I adore you."

"So why are you making me cry?"

Later the same day.

Going through the motions all day. Pretending to do my job, while Janine is unconscious, back there in the operating room.

I saw her this evening. She opened one eye, her cheek trembling with cold, her face drawn. I kissed her, and then spoke to the surgeon. There was no tumor, he said, only a precancerous condition that was cured by the operation.

I walked out of the room on tiptoes while she went back to sleep. Everything else, the bustle that seemed to define my life, has become an uninteresting backdrop. I put away letters and reports of sightings, theories and magazines, without reading them.

Hynek has taken part in a Smithsonian symposium where he debated arch-skeptic Philip Klass: nobody won that argument. Now someone claims again to have "uncovered" the fact that the U.S. government is hiding little Alien cadavers. I am invited to a "secret" gathering of researchers in Colorado (yet they want to bring their tape recorders, "is that all right?")

I declined.

I fail to see what I could contribute at the moment, beyond the basic challenge I posed in *Messengers of Deception*. It seems the phenomenon only increases in complexity as we gather more data from more cultures, as I did in Argentina and Brazil. Tonight I only want to think of our life, the new phase that opens up.

2

Palo Alto. Tuesday 14 October 1980.

Science teacher Tom Gates called me yesterday on behalf of Allen Hynek who was in the area, having breakfast with Paul Cerny, a local director for the Mutual UFO Network (Mufon). He wanted me to setup a network conference open to selected ufologists. He plans to meet with me, but only after he visits the site of a new close encounter case in Happy Camp with Cerny. I wish him luck: a six-hour drive under the rain, and Cerny such a royal bore.

Washington. Sunday 19 October 1980.

A shaky plane, overheated bus, heavy suitcases. I travel with Ruthie Smith, a new recruit at Infomedia who brings her dynamic salesmanship to the team as well as her bubbly humor. We will demonstrate Notepad before Nasa and the French embassy.

Yesterday was my 20th wedding Anniversary. Janine wore a white dress, white shoes, and bought us a hilarious white cake with two angels kissing under a moon crescent. Olivier found this extremely ridiculous; we spent the whole evening in giggles.

Washington. Monday 20 October 1980.

At Bob Chartrand's house in Chevy Chase I just spent two interesting hours with his friend Tom Belden, currently on the staff of the DCI (**13**). We spoke of the history of computing, network conferencing, and aerial photography in the Intelligence world. Both Tom and Bob remember Art Lundahl explaining the Cuban missile photographs at the White House: neither John nor Robert Kennedy could see what he meant at first, untrained as they were in the interpretation of such imagery. Tom now works for the Air Force on "detection errors."

Bob Chartrand told me an amusing story from Naval Intelligence days, aboard a carrier that was a base for photo-reconnaissance missions over Red China during the Korean War.

"Even today, the existence of such missions is denied," Bob told me, "but the fact is, we did fly them, and our Admiral always insisted on getting the photos before anyone else. He fancied himself as a better expert than the specialists, so one day we decided to play a joke on him. We used a photograph of a U.S. battleship at the proper scale, and pasted it with appropriate water currents around its hull onto a fine picture of the Yellow River the planes had just brought us. We re-photographed it and inserted the print in the still-wet stack of new images. I'll never forget the Admiral's voice, bellowing over the intercom, summoning us to the map room. 'The Chinese are building a battleship!' he said, all excited. We looked and pondered his discovery. 'Remarkable, Sir, and they're doing it 200 miles away from the sea!' we said in unison."

Tom spoke of his interest in collaboration systems, going back to the time when he tried to setup a telephone conference with 16 countries during the Berlin crisis, and of the simulation games he designed for the Pentagon, notably a clever hierarchical chess game.

As we got into a discussion of strategic decisions, Tom gave me an analogy: "Running foreign policy is like playing billiards. There are many balls whose position at a given time is known. Each ball is a country or a world leader. Predicting their trajectory is a problem in seventeenth century physics, easily solved. The difficulty is that you are not playing in a stable room, but aboard a ship at sea, rising and plunging in a storm. Furthermore, any player has the right to kick the table at any moment!"

Einstein wrote to Roosevelt about the feasibility of an atom bomb in the late summer of 1939. Tom Belden thinks the letter would have elicited no interest if war had not started a few weeks later. Tom also made a very important observation, that all information systems in existence move data from the base to the top. Yet what is essential is to be able to move from the top to the base. Given today's information systems, any question such as: "Are there UFOs?" will necessary elicit a negative answer, because there is no available data that can go up the channel.

At least Kennedy had the good sense to summon Art Lundahl himself into his office to get a full briefing about Cuba. To Tom's knowledge, no president has felt the same need about UFOs.

Flying back from Cincinnati. Wednesday 22 October 1980.

The Procter & Gamble computer staff received us politely. We have convinced them to start using Notepad, our latest conferencing and group collaboration system.

The first application will link together scientists doing research on toxic shock syndrome.

On my way through D.C. I spoke to Kit at length at the Marriott in Dulles. He told me that UFO contactee Valerie Ransone was in La Jolla after some sort of crisis. Kit seemed blasé, fed up with government.

Palo Alto. Sunday 26 October 1980.

Among a gathering of Berkeley intellectuals I struck a conversation with writer Marian Kester about American politics. She told me I should pay attention to the convergence of the extreme left and the extreme right in the paranoid worldview of Lyndon LaRouche, about whom I knew nothing.

I am increasingly convinced the universe should be explored as an associative information structure, not as a physical continuum.

Occultists use a Latin formula that can be written into a square: *Sator Arepo Tenet Opera Rotas*, "The plowman carefully maintains the plow in the furrow." In my own interpretation, the Control System is the plowman. The fact that the Latin formula can be spelled either forward or backward indicates that the Present is over-determined, both from the past and from the future. Yet contemporary physics doesn't recognize this aspect of time.

Palo Alto. Thursday 6 November 1980.

Just back from SRI. I had taken my daughter with me. She sat down at one of the project's computers and went through a psychokinetic test for Dr. Ed May while I spoke to Ingo Swann, who now explains his work in terms of levels of remote viewing. We discussed the characteristics of the signal that controls it, and the role of time.

Palo Alto. Sunday 9 November 1980.

One of the wonderful contradictions of the United States is found in religious attitudes. Once indoctrinated in the Protestant worldview of the first European settlers, Americans now rediscover mystical impulses that translate into the best and worst in reform movements.

The most obvious result is a smattering of sects, from Christian fundamentalists, contactee ufologists, and survival fanatics. The UFO belief feeds their convergence, away from scientific analysis. The New Age has recently taken on a new aspect, murkier than ever.

The "Two" (Marshall Applewhite, Bonnie Nettles and their followers) are an example of the new movements. Other groups take the position that UFOs should not be studied at all, either because God has secretly sent them here, or because they are tools of Lucifer.

Palo Alto. Monday 17 November 1980.

We spent the weekend at Lake Tahoe on a company retreat. We now have 14 people on the staff of InfoMedia, so the idea was to get to know each other better, to build up team spirit, to bring our families. The lake was magnificent, but that fine area where wealthy families have their second homes was filled with vicious barking dogs.

Janine and I enjoy each other's company in the most mundane activities: a cup of coffee at some roadside coffee shop, a stroll in the boring streets of Palo Alto. It's a small happiness: a very important small happiness in total disregard of the world's panache and pomp, of grand events. It's happiness that goes into the depth of our hearts and minds, the roots of life.

Palo Alto. Thursday 20 November 1980.

I read two things so well written I could not put them down: *Le Pays où l'on n'arrive jamais* (**14**) and an essay by Marian Kester on love: "My friend and I may feel a bit orphaned now and then, but we live like ladies in the splendid genteel shabbiness bequeathed us by our mothers," she writes elegantly.

San Diego, where I just attended a computer education conference, seemed charmingly incomplete.

As I walked around in search of a restaurant in the moist ocean air I heard a voice calling me: it was Kit, in the company of a doctor in physiology from Florida. The three of us had dinner on the harbor where the big trawlers were swinging in the waves, loaded with tuna nets and helicopter platforms. Of course we disagreed about the continuing mutilation problem.

Later Kit told me he had seen an NSA intercept: a Russian ship off Gibraltar had sent a report to the oceanography institute in Moscow. The crew had observed a flying cigar with a searchlight, in full daylight. It split into two objects that maneuvered overhead. One object flew away, the other went on rolling and circling, and then melted on the spot.

Palo Alto. Sunday 30 November 1980.

Yesterday I wrote a prototype program for a new electronic mail system I call Jenny. It felt good to work with code again rather than managing, planning, raising money.

Today the weather has turned gray. El Camino looked sad, even the toyshops crowded with robots and video games. The Peninsula felt empty.

I called Professor Douglass Price-Williams at UCLA. He agreed to hypnotize me next month, to try to fill in the details of my 1955 sighting in Pontoise. He told me he'd recently had lunch with Carlos Castañeda (**15**) who complained he had trouble finding a publisher for his newest book.

Palo Alto. Wednesday 3 December 1980.

The stereo plays Vivaldi. The wind has brought sheets of rain, tearing off the golden leaves from our big tree, a Ginkgo Biloba, gluing them to the concrete sidewalk. Olivier is 17 today, top of his class in physics at Menlo College, a year ahead of his peers in math. Every afternoon Catherine gets on her bike and distributes the *Palo Alto Times* in the neighborhood. We compute the receipts together. I wouldn't give those moments for any wealth in the world.

On Monday we saw a movie biography of Gertrude Stein and Anaïs Nin. This kind of artistic memoir leaves me puzzled. Such celebrity rests upon a tiny coterie of those who have won the battle of media promotion, obsessively feeding their own notoriety.

It is the hidden geniuses I admire most deeply. Not Picasso but Arthur-Maria Rener (**16**). Not Carl Sagan but Aimé Michel. Those who are misunderstood by their contemporaries are more likely to be close to important secrets. Stein and Nin and their friends simply drifted in a tiny circle of elegant folks. Couturier Pierre Balmain, interviewed in the movie, explains the hardships of the *Exode* in 1940, when the German army overran France: Gertrude Stein was forced to escape to Aix-en-Provence, where he "made a few skirts" for her while Anaïs Nin meditated on the detachment of Art in the house Frank Lloyd Wright had designed for her, unaware there was a world war in progress...

Palo Alto. Monday 29 December 1980.

Curious mental transformations, those of winter and idleness, brief holiday musings. My mother is back with us again; she likes to sit and read near the tall Christmas tree with its red ornaments. I have started to review old UFO files, to classify them. Madame de Castéja has visited us with her husband, now French ambassador to Chile. We took them to Infomedia and had a pleasant dinner with them.

Two weeks ago in Los Angeles I stretched out in professor Price-Williams' studio as he hypnotized me to help analyze my own observation in Pontoise, back in 1955 (**17**).

I still cannot recall how the object left. My mother clearly saw it fly away, leaving white puffs. When Douglass brought me back to the time of the sighting I was taken with dizziness, and then felt as if my arms were caught in cement, from the fingertips to the shoulder. Janine attended the whole session.

Palo Alto. Sunday 4 January 1981.

As an original beginning for the New Year I broke my collarbone while playing basketball with neighborhood kids. This gives me an excuse to stay home for a few days and work on a novel entitled *Alintel* that links UFOs to the paranormal (**18**).

Tonight I spoke to Allen Hynek, who was happy to compare notes. He went to Argentina recently and spent two hours with Captain Lima who heads up the Argentine equivalent of Project Blue Book.

Palo Alto. Monday 19 January 1981.

Ronald Reagan has just become President with less than 25% of the country voting for him. There were nearly 66% non-voters in California (versus only 26% in 1960).

Every night I wake up several times, my collarbone still hurting. On Thursday I took my mother to her flight in Los Angeles airport, an ugly plastic world of display screens and remote terminals. As this modern world imposes its constraints on us, more and more complex information systems become interposed between physical reality and us. Who is responsible for the status screens? Do they give correct data? To whom do they report? Our reference system slips away. We have no way of knowing what is really true any more.

The great crises of the future will be information crises, like Three Mile Island, where the operators of the nuclear plant had no way of knowing that their displays were lying to them, and that the plant would have safely shut itself down if everyone had just gone home.

My mother's departure leaves us sad, yet relieved. Her concerns centered on family details, illnesses and divorces back home. She either disregarded her California environment or disparaged it entirely, unaware of all our efforts to please her. She criticized the children for everything they did. She often brought my daughter and Janine to tears. This stubborn attitude surprised us all, although the kids handled it with remarkable maturity.

Olivier's application is accepted at the University of California, Berkeley or San Diego. He has a preference for the latter. In the last year, equipped with his own car and a job in an electronics firm, he has shown tremendous self-reliance for a 17-year old.

Last night in San Francisco, a movie with Janine: *Arabian Nights* by Pasolini. Tomorrow Reagan will be inaugurated in Washington.

Palo Alto. Tuesday 20 January 1981.

This historic day has been gray, sad and weird, unforgiving like a great river under the rain, its banks thick with mud. With an exquisite sense of timing, the Ayatollah Khomeini stole the show with the dramatic liberation of his 52 hostages in Iran. Their plane landed in the rain in Algiers.

It rained, too, in San Francisco. The city seemed bored, empty, as if people had gone off on some holiday, or had left, *en masse*, for some foreign war.

Palo Alto. Thursday 29 January 1981.

At night, when my sore shoulder wakes me up, I savor the quiet pause, Janine sleeping softly next to me. We are getting ready for some changes, the term of our existence as a complete family. Olivier will soon leave for San Diego, and we'll move to the City. So I wonder about our own set of values.

Could we live at the ranch, Janine and I, when both children are grown up? Or should we go back to Europe? America is becoming tougher and meaner. It has acquired a brutal face, giving gun merchants its highest honors. America keeps looking for a fight. In Northern California and other places survivalists buy rifles, ammunition, and dry food for their shelters.

Lake Tahoe. Saturday 7 February 1981.

Dr. Haines considers leaving Nasa whose budget has been reduced by Reagan. He has made progress in his analysis of the case of Valentich, a pilot who disappeared on the way to Tasmania. One of the hypotheses he pursues is that of an accident: the unfortunate pilot may have been hit not by a UFO but by an American test of a new weapon, perhaps a particle beam.

Saber rattling has dominated television news since the return of the hostages. The orchestration of the imagery is obvious: generals are being interviewed; they request a return to obligatory military service; "documentaries" show warplanes and tanks, destroyers and cruisers under steam. Even the advertisements follow the same trend.

Here at Lake Tahoe we are stealing one day from the world, watching the sun over the quiet snow. Janine is reading Henry Miller, her favorite author. I write and dream. I think of Anton who used to say he felt alienated, in the sense of "alien," the foreigner. I do not feel alienated but—like Janine—a traveler on this Earth.

Palo Alto. Sunday 15 February 1981.

We went back to visit our old house in Belmont. It was empty, our tenants having moved away. Janine prepared some sandwiches; the kids helped me setup the redwood table on the patio. All the plants have grown tall. The small pine tree of our first California Christmas now hides the neighbor's house.

Some confused emotions: I went downstairs to my former study, now a big white empty room. Nostalgia, sadness, some bitterness welled up inside. What became of the hopes and the visions that went through this place? The gestures, the words, the pains, and the laughter? Olivier thinks it is bad to become attached to a location: "That restricts your freedom," he says. He feels no roots here.

My mother sends me a clipping from *Le Matin* (29 January 81) entitled "Physicist Costa de Beauregard Crowned King of the Magi." French rationalists are accusing him of using his position to cover pseudo-scientific fantasies. They are trying to ridicule him "to call attention to the danger of fostering belief in these phenomena among the public." His crime? He has argued that theoretical physics validates parapsychology.

Palo Alto. Sunday 22 February 1981.

Kit came to see us last night. We had dinner at Ming's and spoke of UFOs. Little has changed: news of contactee Valerie Ransone, Dr. Puharich who now lives in Mexico, astronaut Gordon Cooper who has left Disney and Tom Bearden who believes the Russians are deploying a psychotronic system over radar waves. We spoke about Richard Niemtzow, an M.D. who is a friend of both Kit and Poher. Niemtzow, who is also close to John Schuessler, serves in the Air Force at Travis AFB near Sacramento. Gepan regularly calls him about close encounter cases in France. He advises them about appropriate tests, proposing to fly over to study the cases, but Gepan calls back every time to tell him it was a hoax after all.

"So why don't they find a doctor in France?" asks Kit. "And isn't it strange that it always turns out to be a hoax?"

Speaking of hoaxes, a strange one has taken place in San Francisco. A man who is said to be a "rich Texan" has set up an organization calling itself Millennium. They had a big party and called for research proposals in parapsychology. Expecting riches, many people responded with their best ideas...and never heard from the group again. It looks like a setup by some shadowy service to vacuum up information about current research in America.

Our conversation turned to the new technology of remotely piloted vehicles. Kit confirmed the persistent rumors that his agency was working on small devices that could carry on reconnaissance missions, flying discreetly in graceful circles over foreign military installations, particularly those in the Soviet Union.

This afternoon Olivier drove me to San Bruno in his green Ford station wagon. My office in the new facilities of Infomedia will be located there. I have some forebodings about the future of the company, and new doubts about the direction set up by our CEO. We have grown, however, now with 20 employees, a contract with EDF in France and the subsidiary I setup in Australia. My concerns come from our financial situation: our receivables line is pegged well above the prime rate, now over 20%. The strategy set by the Board discourages efforts at increasing international revenues, yet I believe that in the primitive state of computer networking, the cost of our system is best justified for business interaction that bridges time zones and geography. My Board (including Paul Ely of HP and Herb Dwight of Spectraphysics) insists that the company should first establish itself locally, and I think that is a strategic mistake.

Tonight I showed our children a series of slides of our future house on Hyde Street, a classic Victorian. From the top of the hill the view of Alcatraz and the Golden Gate Bridge takes one's breath away.

New York. Sunday 1 March 1981.

On the way to New York I stopped in Toronto to discuss plans for an Infomedia Canada, after which I did some research at the New York public library. I found Manhattan quiet, with a certain haughty charm under the cold rain. I kept running into amusing numerical coincidences, multiples of 23, which Anton Wilson considers as a magical number. I had dinner at *Auctions* with researcher Lee Spiegel, who told me that Major Keyhoe was a Rosicrucian. In his investigations of the paranormal Lee believes he has witnessed levitation: someone actually hovering above the cushions where he had been meditating. Hynek believes the same thing.

What does it mean when someone says, "I believe I have witnessed levitation?" You should be able to state that you did see it, or did not. Where are the photographs? Then this afternoon, in Greenwich Village, I bumped into Ingo Swann, so we stopped for coffee.

New York. Monday 2 March 1981.

The conference on Information Utilities has begun, very boring as usual. I had dinner with Shel Gordon after meeting him at his fine office at Lehman Brothers. We went to Harry of Hanover Square, a famous Wall Street establishment.

Shel is intrigued by Ira Einhorn's disappearance. He has a reliable source in Philadelphia who assures him the police knows perfectly well where Ira is. Shel remembers Ira visiting his home and baking cookies for his kids, in the days of their friendship.

As the cab followed the East River on the way to Wall Street, with the statue of Liberty rising above the buildings and warehouses, I was seized by a familiar feeling: the piers of New York harbor, the streets strewn with debris, the elevated rail line: this was our very first view of America 18 years ago. We were a bit sick, Janine and I, recovering from the acrid smells and random heaving of the Queen Mary. We dragged our suitcases after hours of humiliation at the hands of U.S. Customs people. My darling Janine, the road covered together...

This morning I met Eugenia Macer-Story, a perceptive analyst of the paranormal with whom I have corresponded. She was waiting for me on 18th Street in front of a theater; a serious figure dressed in jeans, graying hair, a plastic jacket, fragile and smart like all Greenwich Village. We spent an hour at a nearby coffee shop discussing her experiences and my own work. She believes there is a criminal psychic network that employs gifted subjects, and may be involved in the cattle mutilations. Eugenia made a strong impression on me. Once she took off her plastic smock, her New York slick armor, she was a good friend, a colleague in a puzzling field where we both have more intuitions and speculations than hard facts.

When I look in the mirror, who am I seeing? In my youth I was an idealist fed on a diet of lofty traditions and hard science. Today the image has changed; I see a fellow with clear eyes, tough graying hair over the forehead, a narrow face that cuts into the wind. I have plenty of energy, enough to tackle any rough creature arising from inner space. I do not have a need to belong to any group, school, chapel, Order or party because I feel equipped with the necessary tools to transcend the information matrix, with access to the knowledge left by earlier researchers of the tradition. I can only count on my own work to put that knowledge to use.

All that is speculation, however, on the far side of my mirror. On this, the real side, there is hard work ahead. Before my talk at the computer conference the organizers showed a documentary entitled *Fast Forward*, shot a year ago by Ontario TV: computers, the information revolution, the new networks. Suddenly Ira was on screen wearing a light blue sweater, using the terminal I gave him, explaining InfoMedia's conferencing system. He was relaxed and used the right words, precise and concise in his demonstrations. The screen went dark and, eerily, it was my turn to speak.

Ukiah. Saturday 7 March 1981.

This town, silly and forlorn in its wonderful valley between two rows of splendid hills, seems to be finally growing up. Janine has even discovered a coffee shop that sells spices and fresh croissants. At Spring Hill, we found the rain and fog dressed in white, draped around the tall pines, and we heard threatening news from the loggers in the area, but our morale remained high. The Daytons regaled us with country stories.

Palo Alto. Monday 9 March 1981.

Last night Janine and I had dinner with Richard Niemtzow and his wife Jacqueline at a Chinese restaurant at the Cannery. A major difference between us is that he searches for extraterrestrial life with passionate idealism and relies on ufology as a path to discover it. His image of extraterrestrial life is of beings similar to us, another big trap in my opinion. Along with John Schuessler, he is sure there is a Big Secret hidden by the government. Another trap? I suspect the truth is more mysterious, less simple, and far less romantic.

Niemtzow once met René Hardy, who told him: "If you want to solve the UFO problem, take a region 100 km in diameter... the phenomenon is everywhere. Statistically you should be able to observe it yourself."

I found Niemtzow smart but curiously impatient, looking around nervously, his eyes darting right and left as if he expected to detect spies, or sudden danger.

Palo Alto. Saturday 21 March 1981.

Things I can live without: vacations in the idle sun, tropical beaches, cocktails, luxury, Hawaiian trips, cruises to Mexico. All that encapsulates the highest kind of boredom for me. I feel most happy walking in city streets in the rain, or inventing games for my kids: Sometimes we simply sit in the car in the driveway, and we pretend to travel somewhere. I am happy writing in bed. I am happy in my truck on Highway 101 listening to a tape of baroque brass, or some electronic music Olivier has selected for me. At InfoMedia I delegate most of my current duties, thinking of the next step. On Thursday, lunch with Clayton Carlson, chief editor for Harper & Row: an eye-opening view of the publishing world.

Palo Alto. Sunday 29 March 1981.

We spent another weekend in Tehama near lake Tahoe, with Professor Bruce Lusignan, our friend “Aunt Helen” and her daughter Rhea, many kids. We went cross-country skiing. On the way back Janine and I spoke nostalgically of Europe: should we go back? I could transfer my research there, look for financing and launch an effort to expand computer networking. But we would deprive my daughter of excellent schools in San Francisco. Besides, all technical progress is taking place here; my books are published here, and I am in love with this region where my soul lives free.

What does Europe offer? Obsolete chapels and ideologies, endless quarrelling; old wealthy families ruthlessly grabbing power, ruling the economy; Poland defenseless before Russian tanks; Belgium torn in hateful divisions; France stumbling ahead like a drunkard, the State handing over contracts and subsidies to major industrial powers and corrupt promoters trampling individual creativity; strikes everywhere.

French reality is a lie, behind all the sweet appeals and easy sentiments. In contrast American reality is too obvious. It doesn't cover itself up in layers of politeness and pretenses of Art. It is rough and plain: Is this the price one pays for authenticity?

London. Hotel Russell. Monday 6 April 1981.

On the way to London I stopped in New York again for two days to launch InfoMedia's applications at Lehman Brothers. This hotel is convenient on the rail line from Heathrow airport, close to my train to Birmingham. The BBC plays melancholy dance tunes.

My great pleasure is to observe people young and old, and briefly to be a part of their existence. I want to pass lightly. Perhaps I am misinterpreting as detachment what really amounts to shyness. I do need human contact. My books prove it; my lectures are an important part of my life. Isn't that just another way to intrude into the lives of others and, through this device, to define my own?

In the train to Birmingham. Tuesday 7 April 1981.

England is gray and green, wet, still hoping for spring. The train follows a canal; names file into a blur: Rugby, Stafford, Creve, Runcorn in Cheshire. A faithful user of Notepad conferencing named Dennis Loveridge who works at Pilkington Glass was waiting for me at the station. I spent the night at his house in a cold, drafty room, newly decorated. Bird songs woke me up. Lancashire reminds me of Normandy: You feel the moisture through the walls. Dennis drove along the *mosses*, lands stolen from the lakes, below sea level.

In the plane to San Francisco. Thursday 9 April 1981.

At the University of Birmingham I had a long meeting with a British Library representative and the Computing Center director, Professor Brian Shackel and his staff. The outcome is an agreement to install our Notepad system as the basis of the first electronic Journal in Europe, a $69,000 contract for Infomedia with the British Library.

Palo Alto. Sunday 12 April 1981.

Under a glorious sun the four of us went to see the Hyde street Victorian house yesterday. We made all sorts of plans and signed a thick stack of papers. Our daughter likes the house but Olivier finds it cramped and complicated.

The USC business school has offered me to join their Faculty. They are launching a project in teleconferencing. I still don't see us moving to Los Angeles, however.

Jay Levey, who has read *Alintel*, points out my style is typical "right brain," dream-like, non-linear, nonrational. The effect on people is either to charm them completely or to lose them altogether, he points out wisely, advising a rewrite.

Lunch with Allan Lundell, publisher of *Infoworld* and former neighbor of Puharich at Ossining. He says Andrija's house was set afire by arsonists from a Christian sect, the *Children of God*, who believed that parapsychology research was evil. Hal Puthoff observes that if I haven't found a key to the UFO problem after all the time I have invested and the high level of contacts I have reached, the problem may be unsolvable. I pointed out to him that he had studied Geller for years and still couldn't bend a teaspoon.

In reality I do know something about UFOs now: the phenomena operate in a space for which our every day spacetime continuum is only a subset. I also think the phenomenon is physical, but it integrates psychic functioning. Contact is possible but irreversible. In fact contact must be possible in several ways, just as we can travel to Australia by boat, by plane, in a balloon... But those who gain the contact become deviants. I am in no hurry to become a toy of incomprehensible entities. I am more interested in mapping the space where they dwell. So far I have compiled 55 detailed dossiers with witness interviews, maps and pictures, weather reports and sometimes hard samples. I hope this work will get me closer to the phenomenon. My impression is that the greater domain is not a continuum and can't be described with the current physics of energy.

Palo Alto. Monday 27 April 1981.

Tonight Wenjie Li came over for dinner with us. He is a Chinese scientist from the Academy of Space Technology who is spending two years in the satellite study program at Stanford. Olivier has now

Fig.5. The Infomedia startup team in 1981 in Palo Alto, California.

Fig.6. My mother at 81, in her apartment on *Rue de la Clef* in Paris.

taught him how to drive an American car, the dream of his life. He asked me many pointed questions about UFOs.

Richard Niemtzow is actively corresponding with Alain Esterle, the current head of Gepan. Richard believes that Kit doesn't have access to what the U.S. military is really doing. After his latest trip to France Richard told Kit about Gepan's interest in cooperating with the U.S. Kit wrote an official memo that reached the level of the president's science adviser, but nothing happened. Richard also told me he had seen a copy of Franck Fontaine's medical file.

Paris. Sheraton Montparnasse. Sunday 3 May 1981.

Paris is cold. I am here to implement a special version of our software for *Electricité de France*. The sun is rarely seen, barely credible. Montparnasse is a hideous emulation of American modernity. The French are about to vote for Mitterrand over Giscard, one can feel it: not to change the system, as socialistic promotion claims, but to perpetuate it. Mitterrand will institutionalize the concept of the State as a paternalistic boss, allowing every trick of the corrupt bureaucracy to blossom, covering up all the little turpitudes. The French public's dominant posture is shameful apathy.

Midnight: a storm has been unleashed, scraping the windows of my green room on the 20th floor. My friend, writer Elisabeth Antébi speaks of herself as "the typical spinster with her cat, her books, and her little flowerpot." She likes Neuilly because nothing happens there. The publisher Tchou tells her, "What I find interesting in you is that you're a *quiet* adventurer," a remark that could apply to me.

From this ugly tower I don't recognize Paris. This jumble of roofs could be Milwaukee or Sao Paulo. The low meaningless sky made me sad, so sad I cried softly, for no reason, suddenly aware of the muscles in the face that are used when we cry, long idle.

My mother tells me she constantly argues with my brother about politics. She is passionately interested in space technology, which he despises. "Those leftist politicians of his, they've talked enough about silly old stuff," she says, "we need to build new things."

She runs through the streets and the shops, full of energy, wondering if she's really 81 years old. In her building people call her *la Dame aux Fleurs*, the lady with the flowers. When she is not gardening on her balcony she spends her afternoons copying masterworks in pastel. I find her copies more fun, inspired and vibrant than the too-perfect originals.

Paris. Sheraton Hotel. Wednesday 6 May 1981.

On a visit to Simonne Servais I almost fell asleep on her sofa, sick with jet lag, while watching a political debate between Mitterrand and Giscard. There was a curious incident when she walked near the speakers of her stereo system: a sudden high pitch sound, clearly a case of feedback. Was she wearing a microphone? I asked with carefree laughter about bugs in her apartment. She laughed too, replying that was quite possible. An interesting, smart lady.

I have spoken to Esterle, first to relay a request by Niemtzow to become an official consultant (he does have this position on an individual basis, but not in his role with the Air Force) and to discuss *Messengers*. Esterle takes the manipulation idea seriously. Esoteric writer René Guénon had made a similar suggestion about the spirit phenomena of the 19th century. It is Esterle who recommended his book to me.

During the night of 18/19 May 1981.

I had a vivid dream about seeing a flying saucer in a setting that was reminiscent of the Pontoise event I witnessed in my youth.

I was inside a house with several people, including Janine and my mother. We saw a blue light moving in the sky, attached to a multi-faceted object. After it disappeared we went out to see if we could observe it again. We stepped on the terrace and the light came back (from the opposite direction where I had seen the object in 1955) and the craft landed next to us. It had the appearance of a bright aluminum kitchen instrument, was highly reflective and bathed everything in blue light.

A small being came out next to it, its appearance disappointingly ordinary. There was some symbolic exchange of gestures with this being, then the dream stopped. I was left with a deep impression that lasted all day, of a mystical awakening tantalizingly close, very personal. This feeling may illustrate what witnesses try to express.

Palo Alto. Saturday 30 May 1981.

Every night I wake up and worry about InfoMedia, measuring the little progress we have made. I must write to the Board about what I perceive as our management errors. I have built this company, cajoled the early users, defined the initial strategy, but now it is veering off-course. Whatever solution I choose has to be worthy of what we did before.

Olivier finished high school yesterday. He didn't bother to attend the graduation. I am not in a good position to urge him to go there. I have never spent much time on social events or ceremonies. Janine did go, all by herself, feeling very sad.

Palo Alto. Sunday 31 May 1981.

InfoWorld Magazine gave a party in San Rafael today. Allan Lundell received us by the pool. Many guests were already in the hot tub while a handful of scientists debated the merits of various methods for allotropic liquefaction of silver. A woman in a loose swimming suit that barely contained her pendulous breasts introduced us to a naked hacker who was arguing with a group of Pleiadian contactees and a bearded fellow from Chicago who said he was followed everywhere by invisible saucers that gave him instructions. An engineer with the Grateful Dead and several special effects artists from the nearby George Lucas facility completed the party.

We were soon tired of hearing Pleiadian gobbledygook and of breathing marijuana smoke, so we went into the house where a supposed expert in physics tried to convinced me that Kelley, the inventor, had built a true perpetual motion machine. Stanley Krippner arrived. General discussion followed about Bob Beck,

Puharich, Einhorn. Silly rumors circulated of Beck being paid by the CIA, and Krippner by the Russians.

Someone from Apple plugged a computer into a TV set to demonstrate a barely intelligible text editor of his invention. Couples started drifting to various bedrooms.

As we left, Brendan O'Regan was just driving up in his Porsche. There isn't much warmth or friendship in such gatherings in spite of all the polite affected spirituality and freedom of the New Age, the exposed skin, the superficial smiles, and the fake comraderie of high tech.

Palo Alto. Wednesday 10 June 1981.

Troubled time. The Board has told our "businessman president" to resign and asked me to run the company again. I made the announcement today in a very difficult speech to my staff. I lost my voice in the middle of it. Afterwards I had a quiet dinner with Olivier at Sam's, our favorite bistrot.

Janine and our daughter have flown off on a visit to France.

Palo Alto. Monday 29 June 1981.

Rod Fredrickson, my old boss at Stanford, came over last week. I was delighted to see him. On Thursday I was in Atlanta, at the Institute for Nuclear Power Operations, which now uses Notepad to link 72 nuclear plants in twelve countries in their safety collaboration network (**19**).

The next day I studied a UFO event reported by one of my investigators, another poltergeist case mixed with strange lights and the alleged disappearance of five people.

Yesterday I drove Olivier to the airport for his first orientation at UC San Diego, so I found myself alone and useless, in empty space. My friend Ginger, whom I hadn't seen for two years, took pity on me and dragged me to see *Raiders of the Lost Ark*. She was funny and lively. We had dinner at Coffee Cantata on Union Street.

Palo Alto. Saturday 4 July 1981.

Kids run all over the street, blowing up firecrackers. The weather is heavy, close without being hot. The sky is striated with wide streaks of pink and silver. Ginger and I went to listen to a Jazz band at the Sea Witch in Ghirardelli Square. I was silent. Ginger said, "You're thinking about Janine. You miss her."

Yes, I do miss her. She writes that Paris is sad, empty, people unpleasant. "A vacation without you is not a real vacation." Love with Janine beyond pleasure sends my mind sliding into a slow discovery of unlimited worlds, a revelation of hidden powers. On June 25, from Normandy: "winter weather," she writes, "full time rain, gray sky from horizon to horizon... We visit all the little villages Mamie knows so well. Write to me that you love me."

Of course I do. Today Olivier and I went to the Hyde Street house and began the enormous job of cleaning up the debris in the basement. We drove away with a full truck of rusty pipes, old plasterboards, mildewed carpets, and rotten timbers. We laughed through the whole thing, my boy and I, and drove up Russian Hill where the view was a glimpse of Paradise. I feel enormous enthusiasm when I think of the future; I wait for you. A lone cricket unafraid of firecrackers keeps complaining with an acrid song.

Palo Alto. Sunday 19 July 1981.

Janine came back in time for us to celebrate *Bastille Day* at Montmartre café with Ginger. We went over to Dr. May's house for dinner. The same day I had lunch with Ingo, who suggested he should train me in remote viewing to test his new technique, once I obtain the required secret clearance.

One of our favorite outings is a leisurely garbage run to the Marsh street dump where the truck climbs over a hill of debris along a mountain road behind our comrades, a long line of old Fords and Chevies carrying overflowing trash cans. Workers in blue overalls direct traffic among the stinking piles. Behind them is the quiet bay, sunshine over the eastern hills. We back up to a spot where the previous driver has vomited a cargo of purple sofas. We strike the back panel and throw out a load of old things from Hyde Street: cardboard hearts, yellowed books, broken mirrors, metal tablets. Watchful seagulls circle; they follow the lazy bulldozers. The smell is indescribable, so acrid and rancid that it goes beyond disgust; it lifts the soul as it turns the stomach.

We drive back to San Francisco to taste our first coffee in the upstairs kitchen. The used car Olivier had insisted on buying lost its radiator on the freeway at midnight. So I drove back to pick him up and we managed to have a fight and yell at each other. I love him so much that such friction makes me ashamed and miserable for days.

Palo Alto. Sunday 16 August 1981.

It's our last weekend in Palo Alto. I will be happy to leave, although in the morning the landscape seems new and shiny; there is a beautiful softness around us; the sun caresses the roses obliquely, like a shy lover. But the rest of the day is flat. Palo Alto is for electronic experts locked in their labs, hackers at their consoles, and financial wizards who scheme and trade to buy ever-more expensive houses in the hills. At Hyde Street the other day, waiting for the phone company, I was looking towards the Bay through the dusty glass pane. I saw a cable car climbing through gray fog, a restaurateur hosing down the sidewalk, shop owners wishing good morning to each other. All that from my little window as I sat at a wooden desk, my new center of operations.

The fog lifted about 10 o'clock. First came a sort of false light, a medieval illumination that fell on Alcatraz. It was a sacred vision, like *Mont Saint Michel* greeting the Archangel. A few sailboats were already out, leaning in the wind toward the Golden Gate.

3

Hyde Street. Sunday 23 August 1981.

A cable car clanks its way up the hill, bells ringing. San Francisco is a city of unique sounds. All night the foghorns sounded lugubriously, deliciously, and the seals barked in the harbor. The move has left us with trembling limbs, shaken minds, bruised arms and thighs. We live among boxes and open drawers. In a few weeks Olivier will move to San Diego, but he will keep his mad scientist room here. Our daughter who has just enlisted at the French-American school will be living with us for five more years. Janine has already found a job downtown at the Bank of America's massive computing facility.

The UFO mystery goes on: Dick Haines told me last week about a pilot sighting over Lake Michigan. I listen to such stories and follow up on a few choice cases privately sent by readers or close friends like him, but I have distanced myself from the topic, letting my last magazine subscriptions lapse. By turning away from old hypotheses about "Aliens" (little more than reminiscences of monster movies from the fifties), I hope to gain a fresh perspective on the problem's fundamental contradictions, which I had highlighted in *Messengers*.

This move to the old heart of San Francisco feels like another transformation, a distillation.

Hyde Street. Sunday 30 August 1981.

We drove up to Ukiah yesterday. Spring Hill had almost burned down: the old wires started smoking; the dry boards in the attic were ready to burn when our tenants grabbed a fire extinguisher. Now we have a new electrical system and a stack of bills.

At home in San Francisco I have liberated old treasures, too long in storage, like Uncle Maurice's telescope. Working in the basement, I lift away the old insulation from the Victorian era, nailed there long before modern plasterboard was invented. Underneath are two layers of faded wallpaper with a flower motif, as well as leaky pipes and ancient wires. I sit among the debris, wondering how to rebuild the place. Then I hear the screeching cable cars pulling their way up Russian Hill, and I feel blessed to live here; as if we had reached a harbor at last, like those big cargo ships we watch through the telescope as they glide past Alcatraz with their stacks of brightly colored containers.

Hyde Street. Monday 7 September 1981. Labor Day.

Janine will soon take up her new work as a software specialist at the Bank of America technology center. Olivier called from San Diego where he has found a room. He left us on Friday afternoon after loading his big green car. We made a feeble attempt at a joke: "All right, so I give you my paternal blessing," I said, secretly troubled.

He drove off. Janine went shopping. Alone in the house I looked at my son's room, his bed unmade as if he was coming back tonight, and the electronic clock he'd built, his books.

I saw his original, funny inventions, measured all he meant to me, and started crying. I am proud he has gone away and is independent. I just thought I was ready for him to leave, and found I was wrong.

Washington, Hotel Shoreham. Wednesday 23 September 1981.

A typical conference: federal computer systems, Air Force majors in uniform watching tracing tables and color terminals. Bad breakfast for us speakers. Everyone tries to look bright.

Gordon Wells and I are on the same panel. He is a friendly Texan, founding his third company to develop voice mail, which he demonstrates with gusto. Later, over dinner with Connie McLindon at a Hungarian restaurant, he bragged about his racing cars.

Hyde Street. Saturday 26 September 1981.

Kit came to pick me up at Dulles. In Thailand recently he befriended a paramilitary guy, a mercenary. Over a long train journey, eating rice and drinking beer, the man told him about a job he'd done in the Midwest at the instigation of high level Pentagon people. The mission was to infiltrate a nuclear installation. They took several quiet helicopters, disguised them as flying saucers, and were able to get very close to the missile silos.

We also spoke of the Cash-Landrum case in Texas that John Schuessler keeps studying: Three witnesses were exposed to radiation from a hovering object. For the first time a real medical study has been conducted. Kit is afraid two of the witnesses may die from the experience (**20**). We discussed the possibility that a secret project existed somewhere, either in France or here. Kit remains skeptical. "The only time in history when scientists were made to disappear was when Los Alamos was built. For most of the Manhattan project, scientists were left where they were."

On Thursday—my 42nd birthday—I landed in Chicago where the Center for UFO Studies was planning a major conference. Fred Beckman was already there; Allen Hynek arrived from New York a short while later. "It's good to see you both!" He laughed: "It's like our Troïka, in the old days!"

We went to lunch in Skokie. Allen's gray and pink house in Evanston hasn't changed: It remains hospitable, open, littered with every electronic gadget, the stairs piled up with magazines and letters, two upstairs bedrooms filled with Cufos papers repatriated from the old office in Chicago: the Center can no longer afford to pay rent or a secretary, so it is Mark Rodeghier, a quiet tall fellow, well organized, who maintains order. Mimi seems more subdued than in previous years, reconciled with all that activity.

Allen suddenly told us he had to drive off to the airport to pick up someone from Sweden. I will sleep at Fred's place. Another fellow arrived, also from Sweden. Discussion turned to UFO interference with car engines, a priority study of Rodeghier. This went on until mid-afternoon, when Fred suggested it was time to leave. Mimi was disappointed because a dinner was planned with local ufologists who wanted to discuss "my theories."

As we drove down Lakeshore Drive (Edgewater Beach, Bryn Mawr, how familiar these names sound!) Fred and I marveled at Allen's eternal youth. He attributes his energy to vitamins and L-Dopa, a medication recommended to him by Dirk Pearson who researches the aging process. A big dumb dog named Afshar was waiting for us at the apartment, where Fred showed me his portfolio of art photographs. I slept well, charmed by the sounds of the rain.

We went back to Evanston in mid-morning and met Roberto Pinotti, a dynamic Italian researcher. He had just seen Peter Sturrock in Toulouse, where Peter told Esterle there was a discreet group of would-be ufologists at Nasa. Claude Poher is back in Paris working for Cnes again.

Other researchers arrived for the Cufos conference, notably Marc Chesney, Bertil Kuhlemann and kindly John Timmerman. Sherman Larsen seemed surprised to see me. Allen had stayed up until 4 am writing a keynote speech. He finally came downstairs, with a worried look: Dick Haines had cancelled. Then the group got up for a Board of directors meeting.

Since Fred and I weren't members we didn't feel welcome and left for a drive, during which I learned a great deal about the life of Sir Thomas Beecham. Fred plans to resign from the scientific advisory board of Cufos, because "it doesn't do very much," he said.

Hyde Street. Saturday 3 October 1981.

My daughter invited me to dinner at Ghirardelli Square for my birthday, a great pleasure, but we have new financial worries: this move to the City has been expensive, with workers to pay and Olivier in college. Infomedia has turned a corner, however: business is picking up. On Thursday night the whole company (twenty people) attended the wedding of "Nif" Lear at Julius Castle, on top of the City's steepest hill. It was a fine autumn night, the Bay scincillating from horizon to horizon.

Hyde Street. Monday 12 October 1981.

Ingo Swann has requested that I formally join the classified remote viewing program at SRI as a consultant to *Grill Flame*. He called me on Thursday to tell me the project monitor would contact me.

Olivier has connected a modem to his computer, so he now communicates with us through Notepad from San Diego. We don't feel so sad any more at being separated.

I am very tired with bronchitis and asthma; my reflexes are shot, I cough all the time. I have trouble getting to sleep, unused to street noise. Then I wake up at 3 am in complete silence and can't go back to sleep. Janine is in Pasadena for a Bank computer project.

The federal monitor on Ingo's project, Jim Salyer, called me at work. We made an appointment for lunch tomorrow. This has been a curious day, psychically intense, as I often experience when I am at the extreme edge of tiredness.

In the plane to Tulsa. Thursday 15 October 1981.

Jim Salyer is a sad-looking federal bureaucrat who seems very bored; he wears an open shirt with pink stripes, a gray sweater. He doesn't say much. Over lunch at TGIF in San Bruno we discussed "the program." I asked him if he worked for the same company as Kit. He said no, Kit is a civilian while Jim belongs to DIA. His role is to monitor how project funds are spent. I tried to introduce the topic of UFOs and drew a blank. He did express a lot of interest in the psychic computer conference I organized a few years ago (**21**).

Hot Springs, Arkansas. Sunday 18 October 1981.

A six-hour drive from Tulsa, with a stop in Russelville, in the Ozarks. A fine autumn day. The landscape is American wealth, blue and green, with a Southern atmosphere.

San Francisco is beautiful and intense but it acts as a lens, presenting an unreal view of the world. I love traveling because it enables me to see reality up close. In Tulsa, my friend Barbara

Bartholic was eloquent about her latest field research. She knows the country people well; they're her true family. She cares for them, and shares their emotions with enthusiasm and talent. We drove on to Joplin and Picher to gather data on several recent cases.

Hyde Street. Tuesday 27 October 1981.

On Friday I met Blue Harary for lunch, at his request. He wanted to warn me against involvement in the SRI project, which he sees as driven by an urgent need to provide quick results.

"But the method does work," I pointed out.

"It works because the ability is genuine, but other methods might work even better."

The project also suffers from internal disagreements about the nature of psychic functioning. As for the classified aspects of the work, they're too often compromised. At a recent party in New York someone told him casually, "So, you're the latest student of Ingo? How interesting!"

Since Dr. Harary has well-established credentials in parapsychology he resents being seen as someone's student. The deeper question has to do with the ability itself. One interpretation, which he supports, argues that it is widespread in the general population. The other view is that of the government, looking for exceptional subjects, so-called "psychics," treated as gifted. Military secrecy absurdly reinforces that view. Jim Salyer told me that no other laboratory in the United States had the unique intellectual resources and the well rounded engineering and scientific experience of SRI.

All my books will soon be out of storage at last. I have built myself a meditation space, an "information discontinuity" where I can read or write, conduct experiments with the necessary detachment.

Hyde Street. Saturday 31 October 1981.

Another trip to the storage shack to load the truck with the essential books: Stanislas de Guaita my precious friend, Sédir and Serge Hutin, Randolph...

Halloween in San Francisco seemed sad this year. After midnight all we saw along Market Street were revellers thowing up and cops lining up rowdy kids along the walls.

My friend Bill Murphy has written from Redding:

> The leaves on my backyard mulberry tree are beginning to yellow. After the fall there will be an almost unobstructed view of the mountain horizon from slightly West of Mount Shasta to slightly South of Mount Lassen. The county library has ordered microfiches of Yreka newspapers for me. I believe it was in 1898 that the airship was seen in the Sacramento River valley and Oakland. Red Bluff is as far north as I've read reports of it being seen.

A phone conversation with Ingo disclosed that the newest phase of the SRI project was about to start; he told me pleasantly he'd consider it an honor to work with me, and the feeling is mutual.

Hyde Street. Sunday 8 November 1981.

Allen Hynek has sent me a guarded letter that vacillates between friendship and bitterness: he is coming over in ten days, he writes, but he has to see Dr. Jim Harder, Paul Cerny, Brad Sparks and many other people: not much time to talk to me, he says. He does want to consult me about two abduction cases I have been studying.

Hyde Street. Sunday 15 November 1981.

Rainy Sunday, after violent windstorms that forced us to suspend our computer service on Friday. Our life is active again: we spent an evening with our old friend Hans, reminiscing about Chicago days. We learn about the city's wonderful restaurants, its quirky streets. Most delightfully we are in love, out of the world or in it.

Tomorrow I join the SRI remote viewing project. The secret clearance I already have can serve for the occasion. Hal Puthoff is just back from China.

Hyde Street. Monday 16 November 1981.

There was a curious ambiance at SRI today as I had lunch with Jim Salyer, Hal, and Ingo. Sitting at the next table, Russell Targ never said a word to us. It was his last day at the Institute. Thus in 10 years I have witnessed the whole cycle of the association between Hal and Russell. The primary goal of the project now is to discover from a distance, with high precision, the nature of Soviet sites whose coordinates are known. Ingo gave me the formal briefing, which mentioned four earlier subjects: photo analyst Gary Langford, Hella Hammid, Blue Harary, and a woman who lives in New York.

Ingo made it clear he regarded the course material as his intellectual property: SRI is only "evaluating it" and he wants to keep it from prying eyes, but his office at the Institute had been burglarized. Ingo also told us he believed that normal psi perception was 20% signal and 80% noise.

Ingo claimed that his technique led to 95% signal and 5% noise. It is based on the theory that a stimulus or address (such as site coordinates) triggers psychic impressions that can be acquired in a formal series of phases, the first of which represents a gestalt best expressed in ideograms, the second physical sensations, the third aesthetic impact. The training program covers all three phases.

The higher ones would be: (4) quantitative information, (5) qualitative information, (6) sounds and words and (7) change of state. The "noise" comes from what he calls analytical overlays. These may be detected and corrected because they are expressed in analogies or allegories, he says.

Hyde Street. Tuesday 17 November 1981.

Nights are tough for me, with more coughing and asthma. I went to SRI where I met Ingo, project monitor Richard Griess and Hal for a second lesson that covered the distinction between the objective and the subjective in parapsychology.

Ingo feels that the mistake of most researchers in the field is to amplify simple rèverie with a high degree of noise, because modern parapsychology has evolved from spiritualism and the wanderings of mediums. We spent the time learning to write out analytical overlays and classifying ideograms.

Hyde Street. Wednesday 18 November 1981.

Allen Hynek, in town today, showed me some UFO pictures over lunch. The Board of Nicap, facing bankruptcy, has suggested a merger with Cufos, selling their files for $3,000. Allen himself is wondering about the future:

"I don't know what will happen to the Center, Jacques, when I go on to my next assignment," he tried to joke. He would like to hand over the reins to someone with a PhD. So would I accept that responsibility? He asked.

"I am not so much an organizer as an explorer at the frontier," I replied. "I am not the man to manage the Center."

"What would you do, if you were in my shoes?"

"Disband Cufos. You've earned the right to conduct your own research without bending to the requirements of any group."

We spoke of what really interests him: Rudolph Steiner the precursor, and building new models for science. I left him at the Hyatt on Union Square, asking the concierge about buying a ticket for a show. I drove down to SRI for another training session in remote viewing.

Ingo's experiments take place in a white rectangular room with a stand for an atlas and files. Two knobs control the light intensity. Ingo has perfected an interesting technique and his codification of it into discrete phases is brilliant.

We explored three sites: the Cascades range, Los Angeles, Paris, limiting ourselves to ideograms.

Hyde Street. Thursday 19 November 1981.

Another remote viewing lesson with Ingo: Mount Fuji and the middle of the Atlantic. Now I understand clearly what he means by "catching the signal line," a remarkable process indeed.

Hyde Street. Thursday 26 November 1981. Thanksgiving.

Hewlett-Packard proposes to integrate Notepad with their software, with the right to buy our company. This would be a welcome exit. Janine and I have new financial worries, because I only draw half of a small salary and our house payments are high.

Boarding a plane in Washington on Tuesday, I bumped into Ed May at Dulles with the SRI team including Beverly Humphrey, coming to D.C. for a high-level briefing. I was in town for Congressional Hearings on the use of information technology for crisis management, at the instigation of Al Gore and Bob Chartrand (**22**). Tom Belden was with us, as well as participants from intelligence agencies and the Atomic Energy Commission, characters straight out of a novel. On Tuesday I met Kit at the CIA; he drove me back to Dulles airport, which gave us some time to catch up.

I have received a message from Henry Gris, the author of a book about UFOs in the Soviet Union: "Do you want to make an old man happy?" he asked. "Alexander Kazantsev would so much like to hear from you!" Kit told me Gris had been authorized to visit Soviet parapsychology labs and may have been used by the Russians to give a slanted view of the research there: "His book is a hodge-podge of old stuff about clairvoyance and telekinesis," he pointed out.

Janine and I went out to see *Montenegro*, the movie by Makarejev.

Hyde Street. Friday 4 December 1981.

Over a brief vacation I'm having fun writing about computers. For pure physical activity I continue to work on the basement apartment, tearing down and rebuilding the walls. Reading Daumal, *L'Evidence Absurde*. Something has changed in me: because of Ingo's teachings?

News from France: Mitterrand has created a computer science institute, hiring Alan Kay and Terry Winograd. Their pet project is a pocket computer (vocal input, no keyboard) designed to save the third world from technical decadence: Utopia in a well-meaning, high-tech wrapping, ignoring real problems. Such projects can just as easily widen the technical gap.

I keep rediscovering simple things: Waking up in the middle of the night next to Janine, guarding her sleep; opening the wooden shutters in the morning over a view of the cable car line and the three masts of the *Thayer*, that old ship softly floating at the Hyde Street Pier: small moments of unique beauty in the city I admire, with people I love.

Over dinner with Blue and his friend Pat we discussed parapsychology and cults. Again, conversation turned to the unsolved murder of Al and Jeanie Mills. Who was the assassin? I remain skeptical of the theory that their teen-age son killed them. The murder weapon was never found, and the crime looks like a very professional affair. Was the government behind it?

Hyde Street. Sunday 6 December 1981.

Physicist Jack Sarfatti reports that his address book and all his notes on frontier topics, which he had left in the trunk of his car, have been stolen in San Francisco. Such incidents force me to think in new ways about what happened to the Mills, because "someone" seems to have an interest in monitoring the activities of such people—someone above the law, who doesn't care if traces are left.

Completing the esoteric library, I have retrieved more books from storage, notably a box full of Rosicrucian rituals and a sci-fi novel in French, *Bureau de l'Invisible* by Jean-Gaston Vandel, badly written but full of ideas, in the legendary *Fleuve Noir* collection.

Hyde Street. Thursday 10 December 1981.

I am very tired but happy because Olivier called this evening on his way up from San Diego, so the family will be together for the holidays. We have a nasty wet wind. Walking through the city, I sought refuge at *Café Flore*. A punk kid with blond hair coiffed straight up, green shirt, green striped pants and red scarf, was holding court, talking about literature. The new fashion is all male; girls are erased in non-descript blacks and browns, short hair, an occasional purple sock the only note of fantasy.

4

Hyde Street. Friday 1 January 1982.

Raindrops splattered by the storm constellate the black windows. The whining of the street cable mixed with the wind give us the illusion that this old Victorian, built like an upside-down ship by a naval architect who came over with the miners of the Gold Rush, rides on furious waves. It creaks and groans. I wonder when the old wooden stairs that lead to our front porch, soaked by the rain, will finally give way.

Olivier will drive back to San Diego tomorrow, his car loaded with electronics, notebooks, and many dreams. He was patient with me these two weeks, only winking at me with a smile whenever I launched into some diatribe for his benefit.

My work, too, is getting better organized; thanks to the emergence of new computer networks like Tymnet that are more competent, available, affordable and reliable, I can work from home part of the time and maintain far-flung business contacts. I do need to fight hard in a world of egotistical programmers, uncertain clients, impatient backers, and ambitious associates.

Tonight the family was together again, like old times, Janine in my arms. Catherine had made herself a throne with a mound of cushions where she sat like a princess, reading *Tintin*; the tall white tree glowed with blinking colors; Olivier played space music and *Tangerine Dream*. We spoke of the New Year, our hopes and plans.

Atlanta. Thursday 14 January 1982.

Ice and snow, an unusual setting for Georgia. The networking conference at the Hyatt has been turned into chaos by the storm. I had flown in on Sunday, met our sales director Ruthie and our marketing VP at the hotel amidst icy desolation, crowds stranded by blocked roads and numerous accidents. In spite of all that we set up our stand, established the computer connections, and yesterday I chaired a technical panel on collaboration systems.

The same evening an airliner crashed into the 14th Street Bridge in Washington. We watched in horror, as the whole country did, television cameras showing survivors trying to catch safety lines, hanging from helicopters, unable to grasp them, falling back into the icy water, the deadly Potomac.

Ukiah. Saturday 16 January 1982.

Sitting at Denny's. The round light fixtures reflected on the windows simulate a squadron of flying saucers in the blue sky of Mendocino County. In the orchards workers are pruning the pear trees for the new season. The year started with a series of regional disasters. Heavy rains, mud slides in Marin, the Golden Gate Bridge closed for two days, bulldozers cleaning up access roads, pushing trees from the highway. Santa Rosa was drowned in white fog. The sun came out later as we drove by Squaw Rock and the Russian river.

On the first workday of the New Year my chief financial officer came into my office. He is a well trained, trustworthy Catholic, intelligent and direct. He saw the company on the verge of a difficult test, he said, because we lack the resources to implement our ideas and our marketing efforts are still unfocused. His career plans would be better served if he went to work for a larger company...

Through the windows I see the back roads of San Bruno, the rain over naked trees, big planes leaving SFO forcing their way into the sky. I hadn't planned to start the year this way, but perhaps he is right, it's time to sell the company and let someone else try to turn network conferencing into industrial reality.

Between Christmas and New Year I had an interesting lunch with RuAnn Pengov (**23**) who heads up office automation at Hewlett-Packard. We met at *The Fisherman*, near the Bay, under intense rain. She drew a picture on a napkin: human interfaces will define the future of computing. My team's expertise in achieving elegant interaction with user communities is well recognized. RuAnn proposed a merger. My treasurer agreed to stay for a while. If HP acquired InfoMedia he would leave with a nice bundle of shares.

The rain went on falling. There is a thick carpet of eucalyptus leaves and bark all around the building. One day we lost power and our computer was idled seven times in a row.

Our old Victorian house, sturdy on the rock of Russian Hill, loves this weather as water cascades down its redwood boards. Along the coast, that's another story. Houses built hurriedly at the edge of slippery canyons crash into one another in torrents of mud. Some roads simply vanish, leaving emergency vehicles stranded on the lip of chasms. The flimsy California dream meets the storm of reality.

Hyde Street. Tuesday 19 January 1982.

When I went to SRI to work with Ingo today we ran another series of remote viewings. Ingo was happy with my ideograms and graduated me to the second stage: Sensations, tastes, colors. In the first stage ideograms are non-visual, graphic characterizations of the signal.

On the phone, Simonne Servais describes to me the Gepan booth at the recent Bourget airshow: four simple panels illustrating various kinds of optical illusions. She spoke with two fellows from Toulouse who confessed that two unexplained sightings had taken place in 1981 in Carcassonne and Draguignan: in both cases the witnesses' story was quite precise. Gepan is "elaborating a methodology that will process recorded phenomena," they told her, "in such a way that it will challenge current basic ideas in biology," a worthless statement in the absence of any solid objective.

Hyde Street. Sunday 24 January 1982.

Janine and I spent a long quiet weekend alone, lovers amidst a busy world. I am sending the manuscript of *Network Revolution* to publishers. The city has gone crazy because the Forty-niners have won the Superbowl: people are yelling, cars honking.

Ingo and his friend Julia came over for another of Janine's fine dinners. Ingo was relaxed. He told us anecdotes about the early days of the project and the experiments that led the government to fund SRI: The first big success had to do with a certain structure, a large crane near a landing strip in Russia, never seen before, and was confirmed by spy photographs; the second time, the remote viewers successfully described an underground room covered with green tiles that turned out to be a biological weapon lab.

Hyde Street. Monday 25 January 1982.

Tabulating unique editions of my books, I listed 45. There are probably some pirated translations, in Italy or South America. Jay estimates the total number of copies must be well beyond a million.

At SRI this afternoon Ingo argued with Jim Salyer about the Cold War. Ingo said he was sure that the Soviets would attack the U.S. some day. Jim disagreed, pointing to the advanced age of the soviet leaders, the looming economic crisis in Russia. The U.S., he said, can force the Soviets to overspend on armaments until their system gets exhausted. As for all the shelters that each side is building against an attack, they are useless. If it came to a nuclear exchange everything would be overwhelmed: both sides now realize it.

Hyde Street. Wednesday 27 January 1982.

Ingo's lab is a windowless room on the third floor of a nondescript SRI building. When I came in this afternoon he was presiding over a group composed of Jim Salyer, Hal Puthoff, Ed May, Beverly Humphrey, Julia, two secretaries, and an old geologist. He joked, "We're the ghosts of the third floor," amused by the fact that most SRI scientists protect their sacrosanct reputation by studiously ignoring the classified paranormal project among them.

Seattle. Sunday 31 January 1982.

A joyful reunion amidst wind and fog, flags and androids, robots, and alien monsters at the Space Needle: I have been invited to serve as a judge at the Star Trek science-fiction convention. We had dinner

Fig.7. With "Scotty" at a Star Trek convention, Seattle, Jan.1982.

Fig. 8. The small tower I built at the Spring Hill Ranch.

with Allen Hynek and Mimi, and spent Saturday evening at *Place Pigalle* in the Old Market with Jimmy Doohan ("Scotty" on *Star Trek*) who came with his daughter and friends.

I slept poorly, suffering from asthma, and discovered that, like an idiot, I had forgotten Janine's birthday. I am tired of such wasted moments, all the more painful because I love her so much, and feel such happiness just beyond the grasp of my clumsy hands. She is my partner in the life I want, and she reads me like a book, but why is she so quiet, leaving me lost in the labyrinth of her silence?

Hyde Street. Monday 1 February 1982.

Tired by asthma, lack of sleep, and medication that induces its own torpor, we had a good day nonetheless: one of InfoMedia's salesmen has obtained the first contract for the Jenny electronic mail software, Ruthie has signed an agreement with Memorex, and McGrawHill is interested in my book on computer message systems.

I went home and got on the network to send messages to my son and update the sightings database. I have much hope now, so many projects...

Modern literature puzzles me. Susan Sontag writes about Paul Goodman, Artaud, and Roland Barthes. I read this and I feel as if she had thrown me back on a school bench, parsing discourses of authors who analyse the discourses of other authors.

Their pages are full of gratuitous assertions that are supposed to define an era:

> Breton was attracted by the hope of reconciling the demands of individual freedom with the need to expand and balance the personality through generous corporate emotions.

That is supposed to mean something? I am incapable of those convolutions modern intellectuals find so admirable. My daily diet is made up of irrational facts assailing me, beyond classification and "the hope of reconciling" anything, anything at all.

Hyde Street. Tuesday 2 February 1982.

In the heart of Silicon Valley my lieutenants and I had lunch with RuAnn and another HP executive to discuss the sale of InfoMedia. There was a funny moment when a man got up from another table and shook my hand warmly: he was an engineer with Bell Northern Research, he said, interested in UFOs. He had just bought one of my books at the airport in Riyadh, in Saudi Arabia.

HP seems serious about this merger. I would stay on as a director of one of their software laboratories. We wouldn't be wealthy, but life would be easier; we could breathe more freely and Janine wouldn't need to work so hard.

Hyde Street. Sunday 7 February 1982.

The flu makes a cotton universe, noises muted. We went to Spring Hill anyway. The ranch was like a great beast crouching in easy silence. Water was everywhere. In San Francisco the house emerges from ages of dust and neglect. I contemplate with pleasure the work yet to be done. Secret joy, Sunday work, piecing together dreams and visions. I feel awed by the complexity of the paranormal reports I receive, evidently genuine, plain challenges to our pitiful knowledge.

Hyde Street. Saturday 13 February 1982.

Framed by our wooden windows, the aircraft carrier Enterprise is steaming into port, escorted by the spray of fireboats that seem a bit incongruous in the rain. It's a beautiful sight as it passes Alcatraz, punching holes in the grey clouds with the wails of its sirens.

Last night I joined a circle of people at the home of a woman named Sandra to discuss Marilyn Ferguson's *Aquarian Conspiracy*. There was a warm atmosphere of well-meaning spirituality, punctuated by references to astrology and psychic awareness. Other trendy concepts like “synergy” and intimate networks were mixed in with space vistas. I can only hope these people are right and a more humane world will come soon, erasing our self-imposed boundaries.

Hyde Street. Monday 15 February 1982.

Winter has unleashed another storm. The windowpanes are impacted by big drops that reflect the city, with shards of red and green from the corner streetlight. Janine and Catherine had driven off to visit Olivier in San Diego. Janine came back depressed, finding him tired, malnourished, disoriented. We need to trust and support him as best we can as he sets a direction for his life.

Unique sounds of San Francisco: The foghorn has howled all night. Now, the noise is of tires screeching across the cable car rails.

Victor Hugo writes: "For each one of us there are certain parallels between our intelligence, our moral behavior, and our character, which develop smoothly. They only break upon the major perturbation of life." Our move to this house and the end game at InfoMedia spell an imminent perturbation and new experiences. I want to be ready.

Hyde Street. Wednesday 24 February 1982.

Life has gotten harder. Janine works at night, on-call at the Bank, so I lose sleep altogether, and asthma has gotten worse. InfoMedia keeps losing money; today I must lay off another programmer. At 2 o'clock in the morning Janine called from a phone booth: her car had stalled in the middle of Market Street. Winos and derelicts were hovering around, scaring her. I called a tow truck and the cops. This is too absurd.

Hyde Street. Sunday 28 February 1982.

Ingo is pleased with my progress in remote viewing, yet I am impatient to move on. Reading Pollack's book about the remarkable Dutch psychic Croiset (**24**) I find this passage:

> Another way in which Croiset differs from less gifted mortals is that he tends to think in pictures instead of words. Like other paragnosts, he sees images before his eyes....

> Sometimes these pictures are "run off" at great speed....His mind leaps forward so quickly that the pencil cannot always keep up with his images. When I questioned him about the accuracy of these images he shrugged, asserting: 'the pictures I get are always correct. But, of course, I sometimes make mistakes in trying to interpret them'."

Such is precisely the process described by Ingo's teaching. Many gifted psychics have not understood how it was possible to slow down the signal in order to analyze it, and to decode it in layers.

Hal has become fascinated with the so-called Roswell incident, which is suddenly being promoted as the main topic of interest among ufologists. A saucer and its occupants are alleged to have crashed in the desert there, back in July 1947.

Hyde Street. Sunday 14 March 1982.

We woke up late. Janine dreamed of a village called Cressida she wasn't able to reach. Friends kept giving her incomplete directions: "It's very close, you will find it easily," then "Is it near Santa Cruz?" The answer: "Not exactly, but you won't have any trouble." She went to several towns: they were deserted.

Yesterday our company held a retreat at Fort Mason. I told my staff about our difficult acquisition negotiations with HP. Now Janine has managed to get a new work assignment, so she won't work at night any more. She says she loves me. It's my whole life.

Hyde Street. Sunday 21 March 1982.

Cheryl Weiner, a clever woman with a PhD in communications who has taken an interest in publishing *Computer Message Systems*, came over for the West Coast computer faire. She said she'd cried when she read *Network Revolution*. She gave me Milan Kundera's *Book of Laughter and Forgetting*. Olivier and his friend Bob Rich were at the conference, too, buying a printer. So we all went out for a pizza, ice cream, a game of electronic centipede. The dentist has removed

Catherine's braces; her smile now brightens every room when she walks in.

Hyde Street. Sunday 4 April 1982.

At Hewlett Packard a polite manager called to tell me they wouldn't pursue the idea of buying our company after all. To acquire InfoMedia would imply that their own internal effort—a rather ineffective and ponderous electronic mail project managed from England—was inadequate. The “not-invented-here” syndrome strikes again; no one in authority at HP dares to impose a new vision.

When I told my staff we all felt the blow, rejection, disappointment, then a reaction: why don't we restart our own company, with our own resources? Yet I felt very tired. It has rained all week, in wide penetrating salvos.

Our friend Elizabeth Antébi has arrived from Paris, touring Silicon Valley, intending to write about technology and its emotional gaps.

Hyde Street. Tuesday 6 April 1982.

Another office automation conference is in session. I know everybody here, it's a bad sign. InfoMedia is mentioned as a technical success, but we keep losing money.

Dick Haines told me about a recent visit to Vandenberg Air Force base. He came back certain there was a secret government project to study UFOs. On the base it was obvious the personnel knew about these objects. They channeled all sighting information to higher-ups, he said. Dick continues to favor the extraterrestrial hypothesis. I am not so sure: In two recent close encounter investigations I have found bundles of fiber at the site, possible indication of human trickery. I am hiring a forensic lab to analyze them.

Hyde Street. Monday 12 April 1982.

Mamie, Janine's mother, writes: “It's the anniversary of the end of the Algerian war, twenty years…you left that same year, and Alain was in the Army. What a year! It was raining hard the day you went away, as it does today."

We did get some good news, a check from publisher Albin Michel, a contract with And/Or in Berkeley for *Network Revolution*, and *Messengers* is ready to be published in France, writes Simonne Servais, adding some comments of her own about French politics under Mitterrand:

> The unavoidable mistakes made during their first year by people who have been away from power for 23 years are forgivable. I know from experience the weight of political supporters, thanks to whom organized Parties are able to cross that desert. They bark at their leaders' feet, demanding rewards for long waits and old promises. Between 1958 and 1968 *Le Général* used up three men as different as Debré, Pompidou, and Couve. During the war in Algeria until 1963, and later under the stabilization plan, things weren't very rosy for the Gaullist power; I can attest to it as the former spokesperson. In one word, the Left is here but the civic sense of the French, as usual, is absent.

She adds her observations on French parapsychology:

> People now dare to say that the optical experiments at Orsay on the non-separability of photons from a single source, moving in opposite directions, seem to support Chauvin's and Costa's theories against the intellectual safety lock of the "rationalists" like Pecker, Kastler, and Vigier, who are furious, ready to commit murder! It's a good thing that we don't burn people alive anymore. It'd be great to publish *Messengers* in the middle of this epic battle.

Hyde Street. Saturday 24 April 1982.

Our company has bounced back with a new sales team in place, a sense of trust in our product, anticipation of success.

Last night I spoke to Sandra over dinner on Clement Street. She shares my interest in hermetic societies, in the honest seekers at the frontier, and my concerns about the dangerous roots the Nazi movement shares with modern sects. Her own theory is that the world is now emerging from the "Me" phase of egotism and greed at last, to enter an altruistic period. I hope she's right.

This is a quiet time, with sunshine and wind over the City hills, gray waves over the blue of Alcatraz waters. Hyde Street climbs to the sky in glory. I work on the house, carpentry the best therapy for stress. Later Janine and I walk up and down Polk Street rummaging through antique shops. We went all the way to the Tenderloin, passing young punks and little old ladies, gay couples in leather jackets and Indian families in exquisite attire of colorful silk. We came back with the tourists, on the cable car that stops at our door.

Hyde Street. Monday 3 May 1982.

Over breakfast in San Carlos, RuAnn told me she still had hopes of negotiating a purchase of our company by HP. My board will have to agree about a new price. At SRI Ingo is back from New York. We started 'Level Two' training. Perhaps because I was so tired, I did well. Later this week I will visit my son in San Diego.

San Diego. Saturday 8 May 1982.

Midnight. Olivier has gone downstairs with his sleeping bag, letting me use his comfortable bed with the golden fake fur spread. Yet I can't sleep, bothered with allergies to the canyon grass.

This afternoon we went to Tijuana like tourists, my boy and I. Mexicans assailed us with offers of leather bags and fake jewelry. We just wanted a place to relax and talk. San Diego seems plastic, everything new and shiny along the steep hills. We played videogames. Olivier let me read his essays; they show an attractive style, touching observations, a deep sense of reality.

Staying at his place I look at his world around me tonight: the chest of drawers, the blue desk, his stereo. I think he's happy, but so fragile he makes me realize my own vulnerability. His car, an old monstrosity he bought in L.A., betrays his anguish, and the fear of living, which I feel within myself too.

San Diego is humorless. We went to see the Unarius Society in El Cajon, where elderly contactees are waiting for their saucers in a plastic temple of interplanetary kitsch. The decor is so absurd that it ends up providing a fair impression of transcendence, cultist obsession with other worlds of equal platitude and reincarnated silliness, cardboard saucers. But why shouldn't a parallel universe hold the same measure of stupidity as our own?

Olivier has kept his own standards. He fights well. There is a special passion in him. He won't be able to feed it in San Diego. I hope he will go and take his intense drive to Europe, where there are durable reasons to love and suffer. My own sadness comes from loving my son who fights to grow in this world, and not being able to help him much. A father's love is not an answer, at best a guide, a faraway glow, a faint spot of light in the storm.

Hyde Street. Sunday 16 May 1982.

We are moving our bedroom to the back of the house, away from the rumble of the street. We expect to sleep better there. There is a fireplace in this big room. While InfoMedia waits for HP to make a decision we have had new visitors from Thomson-CSF: Jacques Johnson, his boss and two managers. We gave them a scintillating presentation; now they have to go back to Paris and think about what they've seen. The French can never delegate investment decisions. Anything that involves money is political for them.

At Stanford, Peter Sturrock has founded the Society for Scientific Exploration, a dream we conceived together ten years ago when I worked for him.

Hyde Street. Sunday 23 May 1982.

Sleep does improve in our new bedroom, to a deep silent slumber. Reading *Holy Blood, Holy Grail* (**25**) makes me think of the Ummo hoax, a slick mixture of real events and silly inventions. I have long thought that hoaxes could hide deeper truths than all the candor of scientific fact. It is to jokester George Adamski that we owe the first mass recognition of the UFOs' reality, and to the pseudo-archeology of Eric Von Daniken that we owe the realization that prehistory is full of holes academic pundits are at pains to patch up.

It reminds me of fairy tales describing the relativity of time, centuries before Einstein: dreamers, insane folks, poets, and hoaxers are sometimes able to grasp the essence of a problem precisely because they don't bother with the analytical steps (**26**). George Adamski lied about flying to the moon and Venus, but his story contained the elements of future space exploration. All the details were wrong, yet he forced us to dream in a novel way.

On Wednesday Ingo gave a party in the third floor lab at SRI, attended by Beverly Humphrey, Marcia Adams, and other staff members who kept telling dirty jokes. They formed an interesting group, with a mixture of academic jealousy, conspiratorial aura, the awareness that foreign spies circle around our results, and an ever-present financial uncertainty. Hal, who supervises all this like a benign father, told us about an interesting physical principle based on Dicke's work at Princeton, possibly a serious step toward true interplanetary travel.

Hyde Street. Saturday 5 June 1982.

InfoMedia is now reduced to a small company at the edge of failure, an agony. My awareness of it swings from despair to hope, because we are expecting a $400,000 contract in July, but HP has decided not to go through with an acquisition, for reasons of their own internal politics this time. We pursue other contacts: Bob Metcalfe, the inventor of Ethernet, has suggested we merge our two companies.

Hyde Street. Sunday 27 June 1982.

A quiet life now, much work, including trips to Berkeley to edit *Network Revolution* at And/Or Press. We took a camping trip to Big

Sur, had little dinners in Noe Valley, and bought records of Jean-Michel Jarre's music. Executives from Thomson keep calling us and visiting us, suggesting either an investment or an acquisition of InfoMedia.

I am reading Michael Murphy's *An end to Ordinary History* (**27**) that delves into the strategic and political aspects of parapsychology.

Lake Powell. Friday 16 July 1982.

Taking a short vacation alone: from the Wahweap Marina, ochre canyons border the deep blue lake, a sight I had often admired from the air and vouched to explore at more leisure. Las Vegas, last night: superficially amusing, but I find the desert far more stimulating and alive than the city. I had lunch in Kanab in the ineffable vastness of Utah, and drove on to Page, listening to sparse radio reports and a religious show. Mormon pioneers in quest of their surrealistic God have undeniably found a match here, between the turmoil of their faith and a mystical landscape that seems to have been designed by Salvador Dali.

Hyde Street. Wednesday 21 July 1982.

I drove back from Lake Powell through Zion National Park, all cliffs and tunnels, and went on to L.A. through Death Valley, an inspiring landscape of cacti, rocky walls, and grottoes, with an oddly sensual wind that makes people a bit crazy. Back at InfoMedia, I found more problems. Interest rates are going through the ceiling: our bank now demands over 20% per year for its loans.

Hyde Street. Tuesday 27 July 1982.

Janine is in Los Angeles again for a technology project at the bank. I miss her, body and mind. Walking through North Beach I passed *Café Trieste* where Jack Sarfatti was engaged in some passionate argument. He saw me and ran to catch me, so we ended up at *Café*

Puccini next door, where I ordered a prosciutto sandwich and a cup of coffee, and listened to his theories.

Sarfatti's ideas are full of color, short on proofs. He "confided" to me, as he does with everyone within earshot, that people close to Reagan, Meese, and Caspar Weinberger support him; he hints he is close to Bechtel. The wife of the American ambassador in Paris keeps calling him at Café Trieste and political pundit Bill Buckley listens to him. It is impossible to separate the real from the imaginary in all this. Jack's life is a tapestry of stunning coincidences and romantic episodes. It is undeniable that he was a child prodigy. In 1953, age 15 (we are the same age) he was sitting in the Brooklyn library reading a math book on switching functions when he received a phone call from a mechanical voice that plunged him into a quasi-hypnotic state. He only remembers one phone call but his mother states there was a series of them, always from the same bizarre voice.

The phone calls changed his life, he said. They led him to theorize about the energy of the vacuum and faster-than-light propulsion. He cites all the right authors, such as Coxeter, whose work I recently read. And he is certainly right when he says Einstein's theory is only a special case of a wider physics.

Hyde Street. Sunday 1 August 1982.

I haven't felt so much energy in a long time, climbing stairs a dozen times to fetch hammer and nail, repair my daughter's window and build a bookcase for her while Janine paints the desk. Sandra came over for a pleasant dinner and a long talk about California, the New Age, and changing lifestyles.

The other day Sarfatti assured me Ira Einhorn had been caught in Ireland and would soon be returned to the United States to face trial. Sarfatti also believes that Charlie Rose has intervened in Ira's favor and stated he had worked for him. Rose is a congressman involved in oversight of the Intelligence Community. He has a keen interest in parapsychology.

On Thursday I gave a lecture at the Stanford institute on computer science applications to pedagogy, followed by a private discussion at the Faculty Club. Russell Targ told me he was researching dowsing and precognition applied to precious metal markets, working with two SRI gifted subjects who had worked with Ingo, namely Hella Hammid and Blue Harary (**28**). Russell is only half time at SRI and no longer holds a clearance. He also said that the son of Ed and Jeanie Mills has been set free without a trial.

A shopping trip looking for furniture across the Bay brought us to Berkeley, in the middle of a giant Hare Krishna parade complete with floats, flowers, cupolas, red and gold streamers, perfumed hippies, floating robes, strident music, and chants.

Hyde Street. Thursday 12 August 1982.

Anton and Diane, whom we hadn't seen for years, came over for dinner yesterday. We commiserated about the state of our respective homes, as owners of old San Francisco Victorians regularly do. The conversation expanded to computers, movies, the Telluride festival, and crazy new sects. We gave them a demonstration of the Adventure game on the InfoMedia machine. I had a feeling that their life had settled into a more bourgeois pattern since our last meeting. Their daughter Karla now lives in Amsterdam, Zeena in Sacramento with her son Stanton, and Anton spends much of his time building a video collection of film noir and horror movies. He hadn't heard of *Montenegro* or *Das Boot,* which surprised me. Anton seems to have lost much of his charisma and power. He reminded me of Allen Hynek, still magnetic, a living legend, and warmly human, but the higher inspiration has evaporated.

Hal Puthoff tells me that Poher has contacted him officially through the French Embassy. He was in the U.S. with his wife.

"I've done research on UFOs," he said.

"I know your work through Jacques Vallee, who is a friend of mine," answered Hal.

Poher did not try to see me, but he insisted to visit SRI. He clearly was aware of the secret nature of the research and specifically asked if he would be allowed to see Puthoff's lab. This is in line with what Pignolet told me, that Poher was in charge of "prospective," advanced propulsion, and proposals to dispose of radioactive byproducts in space. But his interests are obviously wider. Are the French using him for a bit of friendly intelligence gathering?

Hyde Street. Monday 23 August 1982.

Hal called me, puzzled about Poher's visit. Claude came to SRI accompanied by his wife, and immediately asked direct questions: "Is it true that you've been working under government funding for ten years? And what's your annual budget?"

Hal said yes to the first question and $100,000 to the second, which is far below the truth. Suspecting that Poher was reporting to French Intelligence, he took Claude through his office but didn't show him the remote viewing lab where we work on the third floor. Afterwards the two couples went out to dinner.

Poher didn't have much to say about UFOs. Hal did mention his relativistic theory, including truncated light beams (the refraction index being such that the atmosphere behaves as an optical fiber). Then he inquired about the magnetic action effect we had mentioned in our 1975 AIAA paper (**29**). Poher said he no longer believed the measurements were significant: he found the same correlation with apparitions of the Virgin! Hal was not surprised at that: if a craft flew over a site, creating local conditions of zero gravity, witnesses might feel it as a mystical state. In a Catholic country like France they might hallucinate the Virgin. Poher hadn't thought of that.

Claude said he no longer worked on UFOs, there was nothing to expect from new sightings, and new ideas were lacking. Poher and his wife spoke of their current passion, sophrology, a psychological practice that places subjects in a sleep-like suggestive state. Poher's wife, a physician, has experienced precognitive visions on several occasions. They tried to turn sophrology into a business, without success. She went back to medicine and he returned to Cnes. I do find it curious that Poher didn't try to see me. By coincidence (?) another Frenchman, Guy Pignolet came by one week earlier, and insisted to quiz me about my work.

Hyde Street. Tuesday 24 August 1982.

My correspondent Linda Strand and her boyfriend were in town today. They took me to a Buddhist ceremony in the Mission district. I was impressed by the chanting and amused by the motivations expressed by those in attendance. When they stated their goal in the endless repetition of their mantra, it generally had to do with a material objective. One member, a guitar salesman, hoped his prayers would enable him to meet his quota for the month. A gay man was looking for the perfect mate. Then Linda assured me that otherworldly entities had instructed her to read my books - even before they were published. "They" told her she must write to me.

Hyde Street. Monday 13 September 1982.

The "Us Festival" organized by Steve Wozniak, co-founder of Apple, assembled 200,000 rock music lovers near Colton under a hot sky, 113 degrees, loud music in the desert. I gave a lecture there and had a chance to speak with Stewart Brand.

This morning at SRI Hal and I attended a training session by Ingo along with Marcia Adams, Martha Thomson, and Tom McNear. Ingo described stage two: sensations, external stimulation, excited interest, subconscious effects creating physiological responses.

Hyde Street. Saturday 18 September 1982.

I worked hard at InfoMedia today, as I do most weekends, elaborating a new marketing plan. Within two weeks we need to lay off half of the staff, unless Thomson does decide to invest, or we can achieve a merger with Tymshare. Messages from Olivier via Notepad: he feels lonely in San Diego—lonely and sad.

Hyde Street. Wednesday 29 September 1982.

Whenever InfoMedia seems about to die it bounces back to life and new contracts get signed, but our venture investors cannot support us, they have their own problems. Jack Melchor is closing his Fund, so we have no support to expect from our leading investor. Thomson makes no decision. When I come home in the evening, close to despair, Janine and I have a big cup of coffee together, then I often walk over to the arcades of Fisherman's Wharf to play electronic games, trying to shake my dark mood by shooting at robots.

I am proud of Olivier, who has found a technical job at a company that specializes in deep-water imagery.

Later the same day.

Lunch with Hal at the Bay Window near the Menlo Park train station, a quiet restaurant with the finest cuisine on the Peninsula, frequented by wealthy matrons. One of SRI's clients, an intelligence agency, has slipped the coordinates of Pat Price's four mountains among a test list for remote viewers. One site in Australia is well known locally for peculiar lights. The remote viewers correctly identified all four places as mountains and described underground installations. One of them said: “I am surrounded with leading-edge technology... like a prehistoric man sitting in an automobile. This site has something to do with transportation.”

We went on to draw up specifications for a computer program that would analyze Ingo's sessions. Then we left the restaurant and oncc we were alone Hal told me about an incident that bothered him.

It concerned a friend of his, a physicist with Sandia. This man is married to the niece of an older physicist who is said to have studied a crashed saucer in the fifties. Allegedly he analyzed the propulsion system and duplicated an antigravity device. Now this man, the uncle, has been found hanged, his hands tied behind his back, his lab in a shambles. The uncle was a careful man: all his plans were in a secret bank safe. In case of death, someone in the family would receive a letter with instructions to retrieve the documents. The letter did arrive but the bankers said that government men bearing official identification had opened the box and confiscated the contents.

Now Hal's friend is panicking. His house has been burglarized several times. He was studying an alleged energy machine,

"Johnson's motor." All his models have been taken apart by visitors who made no effort to be discreet. Neighbors have seen the men driving away. The scientist is afraid the murderers of the uncle may threaten him, assuming the secret was passed on to him.

Hal is now certain Poher was sent to SRI to gather intelligence: "When he arrived he spent the first 15 minutes asking me a series of precise questions as if he was going down a list he had memorized: how long the project had been in business, who was paying for it, how much... Having exhausted the list he relaxed and the conversation changed to a normal interchange between scientists..."

Hyde Street. Monday 15 November 1982.

Professor Price Williams was waiting for us tonight in front of the Buena Vista bar, looking very British and dignified in a big coat. We took him to the Cannery for dinner. We spoke of mythology, of Linda Strand's experiences and of Castañeda. He told us of an astonishing observation, mixing reality and fiction in grotesque proportions: Inspired by the success of Castañeda's books (which Douglass regards as pure fiction), Mexican Indians have started to rename their Elders, calling them Don Juan or Don Gennaro for the edification of wealthy U.S. New-Agers traveling South in search of spiritual wisdom. The other day Douglass received a call at UCLA from an Indian with a message for Carlos: his presence was required at the funeral of Don Gennaro!

"There are at least a dozen old Indians calling themselves by that name now," said Douglass. "What if Carlos really went to such a funeral? The myth would suddenly become fact. I wonder if most of our historical beliefs don't have a similar origin, especially the facts of early Christianity."

Hyde Street. Tuesday 16 November 1982.

Another cold day, a transition, a rusty hinge that squeaks in the wind. Over lunch at the Sundeck Peter Wolken gave me a good overview of venture capital in Silicon Valley. He gave me high marks, throughout the InfoMedia affair, for keeping my emotions in check. Afterwards I drove to the office to tell Ruthie it was time for her to resign. She cried but felt a heavy weight lifted. It was the opportunity to work with me that made the job interesting, she said. She realizes I'm on the way out, too. Before any decision Janine and I feel the need to travel as far away as we can from Silicon Valley. We have decided to spend the next ten days in Haïti.

Port-au-Prince. Friday 19 November 1982.

The waiters argue in Créole. I'm the only customer in the hotel coffee shop. The wind shakes the palm trees. Night falls quickly.

There are few visitors to Haïti these days. As we walked by the Palace, guards sternly ordered us to cross the street, bayonets at the ready. At the end of the square one gets caught in the narrow streets: sidewalks filled with derelicts, sleeping bodies, squatting kids with baskets trying to sell some incongruous goods, pastries and ribbons. Small trenches serve as sewers; the stench is overpowering.

Closer to the harbor we passed the French Institute and the American Embassy, the smell getting worse. In the seaside park lives a transient population; they defecate behind every palm tree. Newspapers complain in vain, quoting the increasing death toll among young intellectuals, due to an undiagnosed new disease. They suspect the polluted water, unfit to drink (**30**). The sweet Caribbean wind blows over all this. The well-sugared coffee is a delight, as is the smile of the women, their inquisitive gaze.

On 18 November 1803 the former slaves of Santo Domingo kicked out the French Army and founded the world's first Black republic. I do not recall being taught that chapter of French history in college: "*Ce siècle avait trois ans*," as Victor Hugo could have written, and Napoleon's navy sailed home in defeat away from the Caribbean Sea.

Port-au-Prince. Monday 22 November 1982.

We walked through the main cemetery today, observing that the dead had obtained better accommodations from *Baron Samedi* than the living did from Baby Doc. One reaches the cemetery by a bridge over a swamp that reeks of urine and rotten things. Beyond that horrible place rise the tombs and the monuments, white and bright blue, with their metal flowers. One spectacular mausoleum features a stairway to a platform. An old man in a wheelchair spends the afternoon there. Who has lifted him all the way to the top?

In every street, every gate, every doorway, human forms lie in odd positions. Some still have strength to beg; others have gone beyond such concerns. In the mud of the street they rest, ill-formed limbs, bent legs, crippled arms. They ask nothing, expect nothing.

The wide boulevard bordering the shore is named Avenue Truman. We walked all the way, passing municipal "projects" advertised in tall billboards that rise amidst piles of trash. Eminent politicians have inaugurated the site in great fanfare and left in a hurry, the money in their pocket and a handkerchief over their nose, never to return.

Between Truman Avenue and the sea lie stagnant ponds and mountains of debris. Girls rummage through this horrible place, looking for some usable object to bring home while black pigs dig happily into the smelly mess. The sea sparkles beyond, blue under the quiet sky. We climbed along the tracks of a tramway that has long ceased to function, reaching the outskirts of Jacmel. Kids smiled at us, women walked over to Janine to touch her blue dress and her shoes. People are well dressed here, and fashion conscious, which makes the contrast with their surroundings even crueler.

Climbing higher along the lane we passed groups of boys playing soccer, and we reached a high wall: *L'habitation Leclerc* sat in luxury on the hillside, with its Gobelins tapestries and a bust of Bonaparte. We saw businessmen there, seated at clean tables under the trees. Two blocks away kids are dying of tuberculosis in rat-infested hovels.

Joe Namphy, an eminent figure here, laments that Haïti is misunderstood by France, despised by the United States and detested by its Caribbean neighbors. The French élite is responsible for a series of recent scandals involving real estate deals, failed resorts, and the promoting of nonexistent tourism facilities that have bilked investors and left Haïti even poorer than before.

Cap Haïtien. Wednesday 24 November 1982.

Our hotel, *Brises de Mer*, has an appropriate name. The storm that threatened to burst since our arrival here has finally exploded as we were having dinner on the terrace, under the touching accents of a Créole orchestra (*Haïti, Haïti chérie...*) Lightning illuminated the bay as we came back to our room, and waves crashed over the sea wall across the street, bordered in blue and ultraviolet. We made love watching all this, leaning against the parapet. I cannot find sleep: rain is unleashed; palm trees rub their huge leaves with a hissing sound, as if tons of fish were being fried in enormous pans. The waves keep coming back and crashing. It's as hot as ever.

I think about what we have seen on the island. On Monday a pretty black girl named Maria took us to a voodoo ritual, merely a tourist performance. Yesterday we rented a small Japanese car, 85000 km old with bad shock absorbers. It danced and rushed over the ill-paved roads as we drove along the North coast all the way to Kyona Plage, where we swam in warm, very salty water. On the way back we had dinner with a local friend who told us about real voodoo.

Today we climbed over the central mountain chain and drove down to the curious town of Cap Haïtien, the former *Cap Français*. Northwest of here, an impossible rocky road climbs yet another mountain and drops you to the sea at Cormier Plage where indigenous shacks leave room for the bungalows of a bizarre hotel, lost on a marvelous beach. Nearby is the Bay of Labadie where pirates from *île de la Tortue* used to come spend their gold with Haïtian whores. Foolishly, we took the rocky, scary road at dusk, with the feeling we had reached the end of the world. An atmosphere of haunted night hangs over this isolated gulf.

Port-au-Prince. Friday 26 November 1982.

Thinking back over this year, when InfoMedia could have been acquired by HP or Thomson-CSF, I have an ambiguous feeling. It would have been a logical step, and a satisfactory exit to sell the company, although nobody would have gotten very rich. But I would have ended up as a manager within a traditional organization where our technology would probably have died, and I might have felt even unhappier than I am now.

We drove back from Cap Haïtien today. It rained in the central mountains, black women shielding their heads with banana leaves. Villages have French names: Plaisance, Varennes. Kids in clean uniforms walk out of the schools. The girls wear pleated skirts, white blouses, and a ribbon in their hair, as they hop through the mud. Older boys wear ties. They learn about Musset and recite Lamartine's poem *Le Lac*.

We made a stop at Kyona Plage for a swim and coffee. Today we went to Pétionville, the affluent suburb above Port-au-Prince: A sumptuous lunch, the luxury of reading *Le Canard Enchaîné* over coffee, bookstores, more reading about voodoo and the Knight Templars' supposed influence on that tradition.

Port-au-Prince. Sunday 28 November 1982.

Today businessman Carl Debrosse took us for a trip aboard the Christina, his twin-engine fishing boat with 70 hours' worth of fuel. It reaches 9 knots in fair weather. Two women and a young Black named Solon came along for the trip. The first turns of the propellers, in the harbor, stirred up the stench we had experienced from land, but the sea was beautiful once we cleared the channel. We caught a fine barracuda, then found a quiet beach, where we had lunch and a swim, diving from the boat into perfect waters, only to be dried by the sun in minutes once we were back on deck. We sailed close to Gonave on the way back to Port-au-Prince, and docked at sunset.

Yesterday we paid a visit to Joe Namphy's family. He showed us his new Caribbean Christian Center, built with money from American evangelists. We went to a reception at his mother's house. It was attended by General Henry Namphy, the no. 2 man in Haïti, and several businessmen who drove down from *Habitation Leclerc*, loudly deploring the poor service in typical Ugly American fashion.

We have collected recent stories about the local voodoo. Some *houngans* have been arrested recently, carrying a bottle filled with a suspicious liquid. They called its contents "Patenté" which meant "Pas attendre le thé", in other words "No use to wait for the tea." It was a deadly poison, its main ingredient said to be the saliva of the dead. Maria claims to know a *woman who was abducted by beings who live at the bottom of the sea*. She assured us that the animals we might meet at certain crossroads were not really animals, and that she had seen many unexplained lights in the sky.

Hyde Street. Thursday 2 December 1982.

We are back home. The transition has been brutal, from the "phosphorescent azure of tropical seas" to coral islands to the abrupt luxury of a restaurant in Miami, and a few hours later the rain washing the shaky boards of our Victorian staircase, the glistening cable car rails. From Alcatraz to the Golden Gate the Bay is like a gray cloth, a silver veil that fails to stop the icy wind.

We found San Francisco drowning in a storm that had ravaged Hawaii and was proceeding east. Our street was deserted, blocked to traffic: work has begun on the cable car tracks. Our daughter had kept the house cozy and clean. Now I only go to the office to pick up the mail, use the phone, and clean up a few deals. With each trip I bring back an armful of books; they find their place on my downstairs shelves, in the basement office, my headquarters from which I plan to launch a new phase of our life.

My job hunt takes me to SRI and Churchill Capital, where I bump against a discouraging banker's mentality. On Sunday I will fly to Chicago to speak at a session of the AAAS on science and computers. Unfortunately I will miss Allen who leaves for Montevideo but I will visit Fred and Cufos.

Chicago. Monday 6 December 1982.

The Conrad-Hilton. Chicago still fascinates me, even when it is deserted, dark and rainy as it was last night. Fred and his wife have separated, so he is suddenly lonely and short of cash. He plans to give up his condo in Hyde Park and move to California. To cheer him up I invited him to dinner *Chez Yoshi*, a great Japanese cook who serves French cuisine. Fred told me Allen had come back from Korea and quickly left again for South America. He doesn't bring much information from these trips, only spicy stories he shares with Fred. Their friendship is precious. With his fine intelligence and his sense of humor Fred throws new light on everything he touches.

Fred has never felt any urgency in attacking the UFO problem. His excuse is that we are far from being able to solve it. Is that any reason to remain firmly in his chair, eating duck pâté and drinking *Montrachet* while others busy themselves trying to clear the underbrush? Fred was a pioneer who treated epileptics with biofeedback as early as 1951. He wonders why he hasn't gained fuller recognition. We agree that Allen is a historic figure, more worthy to be remembered than Sagan or Menzel.

Simonne Servais has forwarded a contract with *Le Rocher* for the French edition of *Messengers of Deception*. I plan a new novel, *La Mémoire de Markov*, while I listen to the industrial sounds that rise from the city, the trucks and the construction. Our son was born here nineteen years ago, I recall with emotion. Janine, how sweet your name has remained on my lips...

Chicago. Wednesday 8 December 1982.

The AAAS conference has begun—their very first session on science and computers. The sad thing is that I know everyone here, and I also know what they are going to say. Today I woke up too late to hear Ed Feigenbaum's talk. Because of the current recession attendance is sparse, no more than 200 people, mostly men, bland academics. Yesterday I went to hear Bob Metcalfe and had a pleasant lunch with him, comparing notes about investors. The area was richly attired for Christmas, with bright shops and cold wind, sidewalks filled with solid Midwesterners. Yet Chicago depresses me after the first contact. Night is a desert; the days are slow and opaque. This city has missed a turn, far from the creative waves. I am anxious to return to California.

In the flight to San Francisco. Thursday 9 December 1982.

The conference was a surprisingly stale affair. In my mind a parade of professors fades away in the dullness of hollow words. Only Bob Johansen was well informed and bright. I gave a single, straightforward talk, with the feeling I had reached the end of my interest in computer science; it was time to move on.

Hyde Street. Saturday 11 December 1982.

For more than a year, my ARPA friend Connie McLindon has urged me to meet with Bill Macklin of IRT (Instrumentation Research and Technology, of San Diego and Washington) where he is a vice-president. So we had dinner last night. Connie's idea of the two of us launching a new company is not realistic, but Bill thinks I could be useful as a consultant, given the experience I have gained in crisis management over networks.

IRT specializes in explosive detection, anti-terrorism and quality measurements for uranium mines. The more he spoke about crises the less his image as a harmless college professor (tweed jacket, pipe smoking, glasses) fit the words he used. He finally revealed he was working on a project to build computers and communications networks for use during World War III and beyond. The nodes would be disguised as transformers; they would hang from power poles on high-tension lines: one node every ten miles. The circuits would be immersed in heavy oil, and would have two weeks autonomy on batteries.

Over dinner at *La Baie* he described to me the government's emergency headquarters, a structure installed in Virginia by FEMA. Dug out of the rock, it contains 21 underground buildings and a crisis center, a dozen telephones on green desks.

"Let's hope the Soviets have the same problems," I said.

"Don't expect that," he replied. "They are burying all their industry, including entire railroad yards!"

The big problem in a nuclear war, he said, the problem nobody wants to talk about, is the dust cloud it will release, weighing one third of the bomb's TNT-equivalent tonnage. A 12-megaton device would release 4 million tons of extraordinarily fine radioactive dust.

During the volcanic eruption at Mt. St. Helens the local Air Force base evacuated most of its planes before the ash cloud arrived. But once engulfed in it, it took a thousand men an entire day before one plane could take off, and another six hours to start the second one. When they hosed down the dust with water it turned to cement. Aircraft engines inside hangars were rendered useless. And the dust was even found in the sealed anti-nuclear shelters.

We went on to discuss other terrorist scenarios, like anthrax: he assured me one man had been caught six months ago, equipped with such a container. I drove Bill to his hotel after dinner. He reiterated his offer for me to join his company, but what could I contribute? I know nothing about World War III, when cities wouldn't be able to pump water anymore, crude oil would congeal inside the pipelines of Louisiana, and the Utilities would grind to a halt...

Hyde Street. Saturday 18 December 1982.

My life seems slack and frail. I haven't gone to InfoMedia in four days. The staff sent me a nice card and a little gift, sensing I could use some cheering up. Now I try to take each torn strand in turn, and see where it leads. Yesterday I saw venture capitalists Jean Deléage and Peter Wolken. Kindly, both took time to encourage me. Deléage offered lunch and asked me the usual questions: "Do you want to work in venture capital? If you were to start another company, what would it do?" To that second question I answered that one should keep track of telecom development in France and bring some products or services back to the U.S., an idea that had also occurred to him. He suggested I join him as a consultant for six months, which could lead to a permanent position at Sofinnova. After lunch he asked me to stay to hear a presentation by the president of a graphics terminal firm who wanted to start a new company. For the first time I found myself on the investor's side of the table, along with Jean-Bernard Schmidt, the president of Sofinnova Inc.

Peter Wolken, who looks like a diminutive version of Luciano Pavarotti, hard-working, bearded and paunchy, also suggested I would make an effective consultant. He asked me to visit a company where he is considering an investment. On Saturday I'll meet the Thomson people and publicity genius Regis McKenna.

French researcher Jean-Francois Boëdec writes me a friendly note with sad news about Gepan: "The Toulouse offices are half empty now. At the instigation of Monsieur Pellat (**31**), science adviser to Cnes, the project is going through a phase of "decompression"... In a few months rumor has it that it will be disbanded. It isn't even certain that a data-gathering function will remain."

He goes on to describe a visit by Jean-Pierre Rospars, a member of Gepan since inception: "He came back from Toulouse somewhat dispirited, because he had done everything in his power to move things along. Now Claude Poher's secretary in Paris has told me that Alain Esterle had asked to be relocated from Toulouse to Paris."

Hyde Street. Tuesday 21 December 1982.

Cheryl Weiner tells me that a contract is on the way from McGraw-Hill for *Computer Message Systems*, and Bill Macklin has sent me a proposed contract from IRT, together with a book on Soviet nuclear strategy. Reading it, I find that the world has reached a level of murderous potential that transcends anything in history. The vast majority of us (even among scientists and the educated citizenry) only have a vague idea of the limits of the unthinkable. As a peace-loving man, I have difficulty stepping over that threshold of the absurd; as a scientist, I do not even believe that a survival scenario exists, beyond nuclear horror of a full-scale exchange with the Soviet Union; as a science-fiction writer, I know that civilizations do need planetary disasters to test the limits of their stupidity; so I regard IRT's offer with a mixture of fascination and disgust, like an invitation to a sadistic orgy. I plan to decline their proposal, and look towards venture capital as my next challenge.

Fortunately Olivier has arrived for the holidays, filling the house with jokes and laughter, pictures of San Diego, and enough electronic components to start a museum of the computing arts.

Hyde Street. Thursday 10 February 1983.

On Monday I flew to San Diego. Olivier was at the airport. "You look like a spy," he said, "with your raincoat." I brought him technical magazines and a case for his camera. We drove to La Jolla, had dinner at *Carlos Murphy's* (Irish-Mexican cuisine!) laughing at a thousand memories, trading jokes. The next day after my meetings he took me to the company where he works: evidently everyone likes him there. On Tuesday I reached Los Angeles where I was a guest on the Merv Griffin Show and had a long private discussion with one of the UFO witnesses I had invited. The mystery goes on.

5

New York. Hotel St. Moritz. Friday 18 February 1983.

The mounds of snow that threatened to block Manhattan have been hauled away and dumped into the Hudson. Now the streets are black, they glisten like leather jackets on the back of young toughs. My energy returns: venture capital opens doors I never suspected when I was the manager of a software company.

The dangerous subculture of UFO contact I described in *Messengers of Deception* expands with its own style, a novel way to explore deviance with individuals who avertise their alienation and paranoia, but also their ability to create alternative artistic realities: A recovering New Age friend tells me about her days in Berkeley with

Allen Michael the Messiah, the "Comforter": he believed that God spoke through him as he ran for President, advocating a bizarre form of communism based on celestial messages and saucer visions.

In the evening I had a long discussion with a New York executive who was starting a satellite communications business. The next day I went to the Village for lunch with Ingo, who had brought out his best Limoge plates. He served a soup that was divine, followed by fresh salmon and Italian wine. Sitting across the table from him in his vast artist's studio I understood why he never felt at home in California: his whole world is lower Manhattan, where he can walk around in an old sweater over a blue T-shirt, galoshes and faded blue jeans. A spotlight enlivened his large triptych called *Millennium*. The room, he said, contained nothing made after 1925. Through narrow windows I could see pickup trucks, cabs and the shops of Greenwich Village near the intersection of Bowery and Fourth. On the sidewalks were piles of black garbage bags and banks of snow.

Ingo spoke of Wilhelm Reich, who complained about mankind's "emotional leprosy," an illness that prevents society from overcoming its prejudices. "Why was Mesmer forgotten?" he asked, "Why was psychic research of the turn of the century swept under the rug? Why is science refusing to acknowledge that the UFO phenomenon is real and that psyche transcends matter?"

He told me of his meeting with Eva Reich, of her attempts to make contact with her dead father: Reich's ghost once appeared to her, with instructions to burn all his papers.

Last night I went back to the Village to meet with Cheryl Weiner, my editor at McGraw-Hill (**32**).

Aboard the flight to Paris. Saturday 19 February 1983.

New York was sunny when I left after lunch with Jean-Paul Emard of the Online organization. He doubts that I can find receptive managers in France willing to come and start companies in the States: "French communications experts are chauvinists" he said, "narrow-minded folks who won't bother learning the American market. They have cozy relationships with government officials, sleazy distributors and corrupt salesmen, that's how they run their business."

I spent the afternoon at the NYU Center for Alternative Media. I interviewed professor Red Burns and her staff about the status of Videotext (**33**). I got the same answer everywhere: it's a disgusting mess; only AT&T may be able to profit from it some day.

Paris. Sunday 20 February 1983.

A little hotel in Les Halles. A twisted iron bed, anonymity out of time, alone, cutoff from the world. There are new coins in France (two francs) and Pacman electronic games in every bistrot. The Paris sky is speckled with silvery gray, filled with gasoline smells. I went to *Capitole* for coffee and *tartines*, holding imaginary conversations with Janine.

Two years of French-style "socialism" have not changed Paris. Crowds seem carefree, dressed in fifties retro-style, ignoring the black buses full of riot police posted at every street corner. One such vehicle was parked in *Rue de la Grande Truanderie*, its motor idling, belching thick blue smoke over the little shops. No one dares complain. The riot police of socialism has the same ugly face as that of the right. It is the same buses with grillwork over the windows, the same clubs ready to crack the skulls of the populace.

Janine, I think of you in the detachment of dawn. I hear the little lift across the hallway, its iron door closing. It must be the waiter who brings me breakfast. Out there Paris is chilled with frost; it will take a few hours for the city to shake up its Sunday morning gloom. In this void I'm an unknown man with a light suitcase, holding this one precious thing, your trust, your tenderness, rare treasures.

Rue de la Clef. Saturday 26 February 1983.

The sounds are a concerto for singing sparrows and speeding cars over wet asphalt. I run from ruffled coffeehouses to wandering cabs: all week I have walked, loitered around from Sofinnova headquarters to a meeting with master engineer Gérard Théry who ran the French phone system for seven years. Over breakfast at *Le Crillon* he told me how Mitterrand had abruptly sacked him. His view of French communications is bleak, the system economically gripped, waiting in vain for political and bureaucratic decisions.

Bernard Lefort, number two man at IBM France, met me at *Les Deux Magots* with similar gloom: French financiers, he said, were not much better than socialist bureaucrats. But I got a different response from Matra's Henri Sulzer, director of the communications branch, who is interested in pursuing contact with us. His office windows open on the Arc de Triomphe. Yet all these men are too entrenched in their obsolete system of privileges to think of startups, innovation, and risk-taking ventures: why should they bother?

In a dusty old building of the ninth *arrondissement* I had an interesting discussion with a young sociologist, Serge Gauthronet, who assesses new interactive communications schemes. He has written an interesting book entitled *La Télématique des Autres*, reviewing electronic community experiments outside France.

Simonne Servais has arranged a series of meetings with publishers as well: *Messengers* will finally appear in French in June and I'm trying to get *Network Revolution* translated (**34**). Simonne invited me to dinner with Rémy Chauvin at her apartment. He came over after three lectures at the Sorbonne and was visibly tired. He has recently remarried with one of his students, a 30-year old woman, and has two little kids. A warmly passionate man, he writes novels and pursues experiments with bees, ants and psychics. He has isolated a substance that enhances longevity in bees and has shown that mice were able to have a PK effect on random experiments. Thus parapsychology goes on in France, although psychic Jean-Pierre Girard has reportedly been discredited. Rocard continues to experiment with dowsing at *Ecole Normale Supérieure* in spite of the sarcasms of his peers. "We looked like two idiots," Chauvin told me, "walking down these august corridors with forked branches in hand!"

Yesterday Claude Poher and I ate a couscous *Chez Bébert*, at Montparnasse. I came away convinced there was no Poher mystery. Always solid and lucid, he showed me the Cnes circular that breaks up Gepan, leaving him with only a secretary and a part-time engineer. Claude has remarried with his new lady-love, who came along on his journey at sea, during which his only involvement with ufology was a stop in Indonesia. He had planned a visit to Grenada through his contact with Eric Gairy's mistress, but when he sailed into the Caribbean Sea "Sir Eric" had already been thrown out by his political opponents. Financially wiped out by his journey (he sold his house in Toulouse to buy his boat), Claude works hard to rebuild his life but he has no illusions about long-range planning at Cnes.

I dream of starting our own quiet experiments at Spring Hill. We have rented out the ranch to a school for troubled kids, but we have told them we planned to take over the property again some day.

Rue de la Clef. Tuesday 1 March 1983.

Further evidence of an undercurrent: Jean-Francois Boëdec tells me that Rosicrucian groups are increasingly leaning to an extreme right ideology. Simonne agreed with his concern: she played for me a hymn heard on a New Age station with proclamations from some "Knights of Light" (*Chevaliers de la Lumière*) that would have been appropriate for a Nuremberg nazi rally. The ufological creed is becoming weird and conspiratorial.

Rémy Chauvin has built a tapping table full of detection instruments, in disagreement with Ambroise Roux, an influential executive and parapsychologist from CGE (**35**) who told him, "Spirit tables only work with women!"

Rue de la Clef. Wednesday 2 March 1983.

A well-filled day: breakfast at *Deux Magots* with a colleague from Infomedia-France, then a nostalgic walk around *Les Halles* in the morning light, smells of wet cobblestones, a visit to France-Culture where Simonne and I met with radio producer Cazenave, followed by a pointless visit to Matra and a good meeting with Jean-Pierre Pineau, the No. 2 executive at *Air Liquide*.

Simonne says that if Giscard had won over Mitterrand there would have been strikes, social strife. She told me I was a source of positive thoughts in her life. She plans to put me in touch with Patrick Aimedieu and Denis Renaudin, two French parapsychologists doing interesting research.

The businessmen I meet in socialist France easily fall into neat classes. A few are serious, eager to learn about venture capital and the financing of innovation, while most of their peers remain securely encrusted in the system, whether their political heart leans to the left or the right. They just wait for government subsidies, or a promotion to a top post in the bureaucracy.

Rue de la Clef. Thursday 3 March 1983.

I am anxious to fly back to California now, to be with Janine again. Her image, light or pensive, follows me everywhere. On Rue Monge, I saw two small Fragonards in a gallery, two lovely *amours* that will put a fanciful and gracious note on our bedroom walls. In a Champs-Elysées library yesterday Simonne thumbed through *Holy Blood, Holy Grail* where a passage mentions General De Gaulle and a man named Plantard, presented as a key man for the right-wing *Comités de Salut Public* that brought him back to power. She had never heard of this Plantard (**36**), evidently another product of New Age hype.

This brought back an episode from 1958 that is not in the history books: "The *Comités* had issued an order for a massive demonstration at the Arc de Triomphe," Simonne told me. "I knew that if they were allowed to go forward with their plan bloodshed would be unavoidable, with riots and an intervention by the paratroopers. Time was short, and De Gaulle was unreachable, so I took it upon myself to issue a communiqué on the General's behalf, telling everybody to stay home. I made 300 copies and rushed them out to all the papers. We wanted De Gaulle to return to power in a peaceful manner, not in the smoke and blood of Paris riots."

Now I am reading *Marry Me* by John Updike, a story of two couples intertwined in such complicated intrigue that I quickly lost interest. (Will Ruth get mad at Sally because the maid told her that her husband had called to meet her at the beach?) How can Updike be considered one of the leading literary figures in America when his subjects are so pointless? When I think of the complexities of love I strive to envision a lifestyle based on irreversible commitment of the soul, combined with freedom, the adventure of being, the energy of mystical sex, and the immense happiness of the heart.

On the return flight to the East Coast. Friday 4 March 1983.

Last evening was spent at my brother's new apartment near *Porte Dorée*, an area in the eastern part of Paris for which I don't have much feeling. It is a well-lit, well-ordered place with few personal touches, nothing that gives hold to emotion, a true scientist's home, rational and dry. Yet Gabriel is warm, relaxed, more of a diplomat than he used to be, avoiding those controversies of French intellectuals that so easily degenerate into screaming matches.

Our mother and Gabriel's three children were there, Eric back from Kenya where he shot *L'Africain* with Catherine Deneuve, Denis who just completed his doctorate in psychiatry and Florence, a systems manager with Bull. My brother and his wife are comfortable in a country drifting around like an old ship whose breakdowns have become predictable. Simonne feels that the French are losing the last of their civic sense. The franc has been devalued three times since Mitterrand came to power. Every layer in French society finds something to complain about.

On the long plane journey I study the Pontoise abduction file entrusted to me by Boëdec, who has done fine investigation work, but I do not understand the secret services role in the affair (**37**).

Reading Bergier's book on occult wars *La Guerre Secrète de l'Occulte* (**38**), I see he was already aware of Ingo's role in locating ships, notably the disabled sub picked up by Hughes' Glomar Explorer (**39**). He repeatedly mentions that a breakthrough could take place if Ingo were to train some students.

Bergier also mentions the strange death of Adrian Dobbs in 1970. Dobbs was a Cambridge mathematician who worked for the British military on applications of parapsychology. In spite of the efforts of knowledgeable thinkers like Jacques Bergier or Aimé Michel, France continues to ignore this area of research under the absurd argument that psychic functioning would violate "rational" science.

Hyde Street. Sunday 27 March 1983.

Back on the West coast, where Mamie has joined us from Normandy for a few weeks. It rains; we feel weak from colds that squeeze the head and pressure the chest. I keep working on this house, nailing tongue-and-groove pine boards over the old walls, upgrading my study and my son's room in the back. Such luxury: taking an old structure, molding it to our taste, saving it from decay, restoring the old house to the stunning fantasy of its youth!

Tonight I spoke to a somber Hynek, tired of traveling, depressed at his colleagues' indifference to the UFO problem and at Cufos' failure to make an impact. Allen is disappointed in Spielberg who gives a pittance to Cufos while he finances Sagan's expensive toys for Seti.

Now the carpet in my new office disappears under piles of paper, the notes from the nine chapters of my future computer textbook for McGraw-Hill. Most of the data comes from my days at Infomedia, giving a nostalgic perspective on the last few years. What great work my little team did! I am proud of them, Rich Miller keeping the system running so well, the women in sales and support... We were too early. Now I must step out of my own shadow into a new world, a society transformed by communications. Those are big words for a field that attracts superlatives, and where trends are blurry.

Hyde Street. Sunday 10 April 1983.

Janine and her mother have gone off to see Olivier in San Diego. I went to SRI on Friday to work with Ingo. Tom and Debbie (a disciple of Howell McConnell at NSA) were there, too. Ingo told me my psychic "signal line" was excellent, and I am now comfortable in the second stage. At noon I picked up my daughter, back from holiday, burnt with the sun and the snow. We had lunch together at Hippopotamus on Van Ness Avenue, as two great friends.

On the way to Germany. Sunday 1 May 1983.

Lufthansa flight to Munich after a couple of days in Connecticut for an investigation into the most recent sightings along the Hudson Valley. This morning was wonderful, all flowers and rainbows. I went to the little town of Ossining to see Andrija's old place. It has a hawk over the door, a porch with windows. Legend has it that Geller was teleported through the screen door of that porch. A stupid cult tried to burn down the house because of the paranormal experiments inside, surely the work of the Devil... Puharich has been in hiding ever since.

Night has fallen now, with the suddenness of our fast eastern route over the North Atlantic: *Gegen den Wind und nuit Wellen*, "breasting the wind and the waves." I'm on my way to Munich and Paris in a plane full of German engineers. Our first stop is in Düsseldorf.

I renewed some useful contacts in New York: Shel Gordon in his glass office controlling the trading floor at Lehman Brothers, Bill Whitehead at Dutton on Park avenue, Peter Guzzardi at Bantam, at the "Top of the Six's", the enormous building at 666 Fifth Avenue.

Bill Whitehead had two interesting remarks. The first one was about Ira Einhorn, now considered as a dangerous fugitive from the FBI. Something doesn't seem right: "Why didn't they contact us, his former associates?" He wondered. "It's as if they were relieved that he had agreed to just go away and disappear." I have heard that remark before.

Bill's second observation was about Uri Geller. "When I think back over that period we both lived, I remember that I saw Uri bend metal with the power of his mind and I still do believe he did it. Yet that did not change my life. Why not? It should have changed your life, and mine, everything!" Yes indeed: why didn't it change our lives?

When I travel I build dream houses in my head, I draw them on paper. Castles are great for the soul, they embrace and protect. They define a territory. They have permanence. So I drew a castle for Spring Hill that could be a meditation site and psychic escape, like Carl Jung's stone tower in Switzerland. Beyond this, Spring Hill is my private experiment with the control system hypothesis: Is it possible to trigger paranormal effects through the systematic creation of an information singularity?

My first technical career is coming to an end as new opportunities open in high-tech finance. I recently spear-headed an investment in Rugged, a company making computers for industrial and harsh environments (**40**). Another deal or two and I may be ready to earn my wings as a venture capitalist.

Paris. Sunday 8 May 1983.

From this Brasserie I can see all the way to the Boulevard, where lines of umbrellas blossom. I met with Boëdec again today. He was precise in his documentation about Cergy-Pontoise. As I have dinner alone, eating frankfurters and fries and drinking *café-crèmes* I dream of the time when Janine and I lived half a block away.

Blood was spilled on Thursday night in the streets of Paris. The Socialists are making big mistakes, angering both the students and the middle class as they earlier angered the bourgeoisie. There were barricades and burning piles of rubble in the middle of the street, and repeated charges by riot police. At 6 pm helicopters were flying over the Latin Quarter, convoys of police buses were screaming through the streets. At 7 pm near Alma the bridge was blocked by cops, generating huge traffic jams.

Jean Deléage, Simonne Servais, Jean Pineau and I had dinner *Chez Francis*. I was surprised by Simonne's negative reaction to Deléage. She thought he was reactionary and ill-tempered as an old bear. We discussed Aimé Limoge and his proposed startup company using currents for brain stimulation. At midnight young artists were singing Jacques Brel songs in the street: "*Sur le port d'Amsterdam, Y'a des marins qui dansent...*"

At *Le Châtelet* the area was vibrant, filled with people who had no intention of going to bed. The French are having a good time even as they despair of their political future. What a difference with 1968! I remember Hynek's visit. Paris was gray then, with gloom everywhere. Madame De Gaulle had institutionalized her crazy notions of morality. Today the mood is a drunken carnival.

When I got home Maman happily told me a courrier had brought her *La Grande Manipulation* and she had started to read it. The credit for publication of this book in France (four years after *Messengers* in the U.S) goes to Simonne and Professor Chauvin.

On Monday night we had dinner with Patrick Aimedieu and Denys Renaudin, pillars of French psi research. Aimedieu is a director for the High Atmosphere department at CNRS. Renaudin, an older white-haired man, is an engineer who once designed nuclear plants. Using electronic instrumentation, he has determined that the table movement in séances was produced by the unconscious moves of the participants falling into phase. He has never observed levitation of a table, but he thinks very much along the lines of the Toronto group that invented the ghost named "Philip" (**41**) and manifested it.

I have stumbled on a second-hand copy of the French edition of Cliff Linedecker's book *Un Médium Agent Secret* (**42**). The dedication reads: "*Pour Junko—mon passé, mon présent, mon avenir.*" We knew them both in Chicago days, and again in New Jersey. I wondered how they had separated, and how this particular copy of Cliff's book is ending up in my hands.

I took Maman to lunch on *Quai Saint Michel* across from Notre-Dame. She ordered some Beaujolais and told me she feels most happy in that section of Paris, so after lunch we walked from bookstore to bookstore. In spite of its carefree appearance, France is in trouble. Mitterrand borrows money from other countries as he once did to delay the devaluation of the currency, to no avail.

The top executives to whom I speak tell me that creativity is dead here; the nationalizations have been a disaster. Companies now just wait for subsidies. And the last few months have shown that the Left didn't hold a monopoly on riots.

TWA Flight to San Francisco. Thursday 12 May 1983.

Denis Renaudin and Patrick Aimedieu have told me some interesting things about Jean-Pierre Girard: they are still convinced of his talents. The proof exists in the form of cylinders of metal that were partially sawed off every centimeter or so, then coated with plastic and painted in a uniform metallic color without his knowledge. The cylinders bent, but not at the natural breaks.

My last day in Paris was filled with interesting discussions with Professor Aimé Limoge. I was impressed with this jovial white-haired man. We discussed his portable generator for "Limoge currents" already in use in the Soviet Union to control pain. We speculated about possible applications in parapsychology.

Hyde Street. Sunday 15 May 1983.

Janine and I quarrelled as soon as I got home. When I picked up Catherine at the French Consulate where she was a guest at a party I told her we'd had a fight. She wisely said, "People can't love each other for 23 years without some rough time. You and Janine are like two equal, powerful magnets. You do everything well." She asked if she could help. I felt like crying but the tears didn't come, I was too scared and hurt. There's a shadow over our life.

San Diego. Sunday 5 June 1983.

Reconciled, Janine and I spend the weekend in San Diego. Olivier was in the hospital for an allergic reaction so we went to see him, then drove around the harbor after our visit had reassured us. This morning he was better so we took him home. He seemed confused by the medication, but his good smile was back.

Hyde Street. Sunday 12 June 1983.

My daughter flew away yesterday for two months of travel through Europe with her friend Rhea. They have arrived in Paris happy and tired, reports my mother. Janine and I are alone again, our life a long pleasurable conversation, with interruptions for *café-au-lait* and writing: I have started a new novel, entitled *FastWalker*.

Ingo is at work on a proposal for the next five years of research into parapsychology. I wrote the section on databases for him, and a paper summarizing Soviet methods of data collection.

Hyde Street. Sunday 24 July 1983.

Curious news from France: shortly after *Messengers of Deception* appeared in the stores, with its exposé of the Cergy-Pontoise abduction as a psychological warfare experiment, one of the three contactees named Prévost "confessed" to hoaxing the case. His confession seems to disprove my hypothesis and put the matter to rest for everyone --except for those who know that he was not in a position to do what he claims. He could not have driven Franck Fontaine to his apartment eight days after his disappearance: I have reliable information that Prévost was with a journalist who witnessed the reuniting of the two fellows. Therefore the new "confession" itself is a hoax.

Simonne sends me comments on the book from Madame Mitterrand, Jacques Chirac, the director of Cnes, and François de Grossouvres. After my interview in *Figaro Magazine* and the broadcast at France Culture, my warning, this time, had a real impact. One mystery remains: is Gepan really being disbanded? Poher and Boëdec say so, but Jean-Claude Bourret states that the project is still going on covertly.

We've spent a delightful week with our son. He showed us pictures of his recent American tour: Niagara Falls at night, Boston harbor, Texas, storms in Wyoming. Catherine has sent us a touching letter, too delicate to be quoted, except this: "*dans mon coeur, je sens votre présence irremplaçable, ce qui me donne le pouvoir de conquérir n'importe quoi.*" Such a beautiful mature feeling in a 15-year old, a much older soul...

The other morning I woke up in a glow of happiness, dreaming that we were back in Belmont, the four of us, in the soft light.

Hyde Street. Saturday 27 August 1983.

Producer Robert K. Weiss of *Blues Brothers* fame (**43**) has contacted me about *FastWalker*. He is coming here in a week with a contract to buy the rights for a movie. He called me at Infomedia as I was attending my last board meeting there. At my new office on a high floor of Embarcadero Center, would-be tycoons bicker about various deals; I work hard to learn the venture business with them.

In the evening, a hot and muggy time in San Francisco, we met with Luisah Teish. I encouraged her to write a book about the voodoo traditions she knows so well, giving her a personal introduction to Clay Carlson at Harper & Row. Afterwards we went to see an avant-garde theater play, *Mindfreight*, that enchanted us. The whole day has been like a great psychic feast. I don't even regret putting so much work and money into InfoMedia. What I've learned is priceless—about business, about myself, about what it means to create new technologies, and to live in the new network society.

Hyde Street. Monday 5 September 1983.

I finished writing *Computer Message Systems* today. Bob Weiss has read *FastWalker* and says he loves it. He came over for dinner, with a gift of UFO stamps issued by the island state of Grenada, commemorating our UN session.

At Sofinnova, Jean Deléage proposes to launch a new venture fund and giving me responsibility for it.

Hyde Street. Tuesday 6 September 1983.

The house is caught in a web of scaffoldings and a swarm of masons, carpenters, electricians, plumbers. The pipes that insulted the Victorian elegance of the old structure have been rerouted; removal of a layer of shingles in the front of the house has exposed original scrollwork, fish scales and other ornaments we will restore, "a Gift to the Street" in the San Francisco tradition. Downstairs a full apartment has taken shape, including a well-lit workshop and a dining nook, "Twilight Bar," where I can retire to write in peace.

The SRI team, with whom I work often, is split by various quarrels. Ingo has packed up his office and mailed it back to Greenwich Village. The third floor where classified paranormal research was concentrated is a gloomy place, under a black cloud.

Hyde Street. Sunday 18 September 1983.

Approaching the ripe age of 44, I see man as a mere particle of a greater intelligence, seeking his way through tunnels of reality. That cosmic intelligence is not the God of bureaucratic churches. Nature must have provided higher references for our thoughts. My own modest temple is just a starting point into the underground passages, catacombs loaded with symbols of lives where time is suspended, peopled by creatures of infinity.

The vitality of consciousness that was California seems in peril today, all around us. Not only is the dreadful plague of AIDS decimating the community, but there is a new sense of greed and egotism in the air. Polk Gulch, a street of antique stores and quaint restaurants has become quiet. Even the Trattoria at the corner of California Street, with its sidewalk terrace where I often read my mail and the paper over lunch, seems forlorn.

Our children cheer us on. Olivier came over last week with his friend Laura, a funny girl with frizzy hair and a pleasant voice that seemed to come through a sackful of gravel.

Wahweap, Arizona. Sunday 9 October 1983.

Journalist Renwick Breck and his father, a retired banker, are buying the InfoMedia assets, including our software technology. A big weight is lifted from my shoulders. To mark the transition, Janine and I rented a car in Las Vegas this weekend. We drove through fantastic Zion and reached Lake Powell, retracing the steps of my solitary trip last year with the lake squeezed between its canyons all the way to the rainbow arch framing the view of Mount Navajo, sheer walls of red rock. I was eager to show her these marvels.

It is hard not to feel on a pilgrimage here, with an impression of subtle contact with another plane, with the deeper intelligence of nature more palpable, intimate and genuine than anything science provides. "What wisdom have we lost when we found knowledge! What knowledge have we lost when we found information!" wrote a poet half a century ago. His remark haunts me as I look at the sandstone cliffs. Here you can stop at any moment and commune with other worlds, or your own deities, without once looking back.

On Sunday, I had lunch with Dick Haines and Bruce Maccabee who represent a newer phase of ufology. Dr. Richard Haines is a Nasa specialist with a Ph.D. in perception psychology. He is intense, honest, friendly. Bruce Maccabee has a doctorate in optics, and is a co-founder of the Fund for UFO research. Yet I was disappointed in our conversation, which revolved around some blurry pictures.

In contrast, many of our friends are unimpressed with technology and seek flimsy comfort in fantasy. Sandra, who feels disoriented after the death of her father and an aunt, is acting in increasingly bizarre ways. We visited her at an institution in Belmont where we found her singing mechanically, her eyes unfocused, full of phony drug-induced enthusiasm. Janine cried when she saw her: "What a horrible fate, to lose one's mind... we'll never know our Sandra again. If I go crazy some day, never put me in a place like that!"

Moab, Utah. Monday 10 October 1983.

We drove through Page today and reached Navajo territory, red lands covered with stones and scraggy brushes. We turned north into Monument Valley, with its towers of red sandstone, purple streaks, the October sky with a few grey-white clouds. We stopped in towns called Gouldings, Blanding, Monticello, the landscape a fracas of hell-red stone, satanic delirium, seemingly scattered over tormented Earth by Beelzebub himself on a drunken spree. As we approach Vernal, I pull out my maps, books and research papers. I plan to spend the evening reviewing Dr. Frank Salisbury's book *The Utah UFO Display*. Frank is one of the few genuine scientists in the field.

Vernal, Utah. Tuesday 11 October 1983.

We have settled at the first large motel as you drive into town. Between Page and Vernal we've seen three dead cows by the side of the road, but no mutilation. Obviously the locals don't care enough to bury carcasses. On Navajo land we saw a dead horse, a dog pulling at the flesh. Just beyond Price there was another dead cow, her legs up in the air, stinking up the landscape for miles around.

The countryside is biblical in its savage nature. It doesn't get softer when you reach Vernal. Canyons and rockslides give way to softer shapes but you see the same weeds and low brushes. Janine is the only beauty around, in her jeans and striped blue and white top. Wherever she goes conversation stops, cowboys put down their beer, people stare. We take our time on this trip, following our fantasy. The summer tourists are gone. The air has the freshness of approaching winter. North of here, the mountaintops of Utah are resplendent with early snow.

Vernal, Utah. Wednesday 12 October 1983.

Breakfast by the window. Between our hotel and the highway lies a wide green lawn under blue sky, a simple picture, deceptively obvious. The curtains are white with early sunshine. Trucks drive toward Roosevelt and Duchesne, or the Colorado border. I am blissfully free of asthma. For several weeks now I have slept normally. I don't even wake up at three o'clock in the morning, as I did for years.

Vernal, Utah. Thursday 13 October 1983.

Dinosaur National Park occupies the sheer side of a hill with a lazy river at the bottom and thousands of bones stuck in the mud since Jurassic times. This is a work of genius, an enormous glass museum right on top of the hill, its roof integrated with the cliffs. I detest most museums with their obscure little fragments locked up in boxes and cages. None of that here: As soon as you go in, you step back millions of years, you witness a dead world re-emerging full scale, ugly bones spreading, empty eyes staring.

On the way back we went to see local researcher Junior Hicks at the high school in Roosevelt, where he teaches science. A bit reserved at first, he soon got caught up in the discussion. He showed us his UFO models, based on the dozens of cases he has investigated.

One of them is a huge V-shaped craft with lights along two sides, the same configuration I found in the Hudson Valley.

Junior Hicks receives about one new report per month. He once observed a multi-colored, illuminated object himself, following a phone call from a local Indian family. He has several mutilation cases in his files and even one instance when an object levitated a horse and took it away. As we sat in the teachers' room one of his colleagues volunteered that he had seen a craft with a transparent tube "sucking up" rocks and bushes. The man realized this was absurd, but felt he had to tell us about it.

We drove on to the Flaming Gorge reservoir in a landscape with astonishing geology, all red and yellow and white and purple, splendid amidst the gold of the aspens. We took the winding mountain road that goes down north of the gorge and runs into a flat region that is part of Wyoming. On the way back, caught behind a herd of cows we had ample time to admire the snow over the Uintah Mountains, the only American chain that runs East-West.

Spring Hill Ranch. Sunday 30 October 1983.

We have spent a quiet Halloween weekend, the ranch nestled in Autumn-golden foliage. I measured, surveyed and mapped in anticipation of great projects in my head. All week I have worked with a colleague newly recruited by Sofinnova in France. My own full time work starts in January. We had dinner at the home of Jean-Bernard Schmidt in Berkeley, an opulent sliver of French life with framed engravings showing Louis XV visiting Strasbourg. The discussion around the table centered on the ills of socialism. I became aware of my own profound indifference to such arguments.

Hyde Street. Thursday 24 November 1983.

Thanksgiving. The house restoration is almost complete, except for the painters who cannot work under this rain.

I was in Washington again last week, testifying before Al Gore's Congressional Hearings on the role of information systems in emergency management (**22**). This was an opportunity to meet with Tom Belden again, and Dave McManis, the National Intelligence officer for Warning (**44**) who led the committee for which I served as rapporteur. On Saturday Bill Best introduced me to Craig Fuller, President Reagan's Cabinet secretary.

I spent the evening at Kit's house with his four wonderful kids. Remote viewing is finally recognized at high levels: Kit has attended a briefing by Hal and Jack Vorona for CIA director Bill Casey, who canceled other afternoon appointments to hear them fully. There is a second group of military trainees now, equal to our own SRI team.

In addition to directing the SRI program, Hal now consults with a group financed by entrepreneur Bill Church, pushing the limit of physics. They have a device that focuses an energy blast to punch holes in steel walls.

Hyde Street. Sunday 11 December 1983.

Scattered notes: on Monday I had lunch with Hal, Ed May, and Beverly. They seem in awe of computer technology, a fixation I find ill-placed and expensive. Dave Saunders was with us, conducting a psychological assessment of our psychic subjects. He administered the Wechsler-Bellevue test to me, an amusing situation (**45**). The project has been expanded: Ingo now has his own classified students away from SRI, causing no end of bureaucratic turmoil. Russell Targ and Keith Harary have traveled to Russia together at the invitation of the Soviet government, visiting several centers, presumably not the most advanced ones, held secret.

Political ambitions converge with the investment world as Silicon Valley flexes its new muscles. On Tuesday Mitterrand's economic adviser Henri Sulsman attended our monthly meeting of the Western Association of Venture Capitalists. The next day I had lunch at Ming's with the former Governor of California, Jerry Brown, amidst a small group launching a commission for industrial creativity.

Now Janine and I have cleaned up the house; the workers are gone. The books are in place. It rains. We are so close to the Bay that the ocean wind shakes everything with angry blasts of ocean spray.

Part Ten

VENTURE CAPITAL

6

Hyde Street. Sunday 1 January 1984.

New plans for a new year: In two weeks I'll be in France again for Sofinnova, looking for an investment formula that could bring European entrepreneurs to America through high-tech companies we could finance on both sides. It all moves too slowly for me, but I enjoy a happy interlude at home. Once again the holidays have brought the family together. My son, unshaven like an old sailor after a long journey, crashed and slept, cleaned himself up. Now he goes around San Francisco taking pictures. Waitresses at the corner pizzeria hover around him. Janine's brother Alain is here too, debating whether to re-open the "Little Store" in Woodside.

Phone calls to friends: Sandra is improving; Colorado researcher Richard Sigismond is in town again, presenting his psychic theories.

Paris. Sunday 29 January 1984.

Vignettes of a trip to France: I left California under cold rain and landed in Boston after a snowstorm, finding the city frozen, its sidewalks slippery. We are helping a French businessman start a company with Apollo Computers as an industrial partner. The next day I boarded the New York Shuttle with a long line of businessmen in winter coats. Ingo was waiting for me to have lunch with his friends. He threatens to break up from Hal Puthoff's project. He has draped large charts all over his flat, seeking various correlations.

Paris is gray, socialist and moody. My partners greeted me warmly, however, and I found my mother in better shape than I had feared, after a fall on the steps of the Sorbonne. She gets up slowly from her chair but she still goes shopping on rue Mouffetard and argues about the price of food with the produce men. On Monday our business meetings started at Sofinnova on Rue Saint Georges, the theater and

Vaudeville area of Paris perched on the way to Montmartre. We run from one little software company to another; we look at computer prototypes. We even went to Blois to follow the tests of the French Smartcard, which left me unconvinced (**1**).

We hear absurd complaints about the economy. France remains chronically unable to harness its potential for innovation, and Mitterrand's nationalization program is simply embalming the cadaver of industrial creativity. The meeting of Sofinnova investors was a high point of the trip, however. All the large French banks were represented, as well as several insurance companies.

Thérèse de Saint Phalle spent an evening with Simonne and me. Later she asked me to come to her apartment for dinner "with a few friends," artists and theatre stars: Guy Béart, Nicole Avril, Françoise Dorin (*L'Etiquette* had just completed its 300th show) and George Harper, a cousin of Thérèse, producer in Hollywood, who came with a French girl named Danielle who amused herself by making passes at me all evening. It was a fun and brillant time in the French style of 18th century salons, an atmosphere of elegant superficiality of which America is incapable—even California, although San Francisco knows something about superficiality. French culture knows how to create an environment where minds can be exposed to new ideas, where diverse personalities can meet around polite or naughty rites of the dinner table and the salon.

Jean-François Boëdec told me a dozen rumors of ufology. We spent the evening reviewing details of recent sightings in Brittany.

The French press speaks of the farmers' discontent, of the "sniffer planes" hoax (**2**), of gangsters and hold-ups, of the high value of the dollar: it has doubled in the last four years. Things that are rarely discussed include technology, where France keeps falling behind, and the sale of armaments to third world countries, which pays for much of France's wellbeing and supports her elegant lifestyle. In financial circles the old misunderstandings go on: government subsidies get labelled as "investments" and the line between control and servitude remains unclear. French institutions have no concept of a true "partnership" and remain obsessed with owning their employees, even if that means stifling their creative energy.

Hyde Street. Sunday 19 February 1984.

Back home: quiet day, sunny. Olivier is back in San Diego, where he now works for Teradyne. We spent last weekend in Yosemite, where I gave a lecture before the Danforth Foundation. The snow had created a paradise, the Ahwahnee lodge a marvel.

San Luis Obispo. Thursday 1 March 1984.

Anton and Diane came to see us on Tuesday. He had called me for advice: Diane is looking for a computer she could use for word processing. They had dinner at our house, where my daughter demonstrated her Atari. She also instructed Anton in the use of videogames, so we enjoyed seeing the Black Pope playing Donkey Kong. They seemed happy and relaxed, speaking eloquently of little-known films and favorite cars, talking about their early years.

Diane was a wild teenager in Pacifica when she fell in love with Anton. She started a torrid affair with him, accompanying him to his organ concerts. One day Anton had to drop off his wife Carol and daughter Karla at his mother-in-law's house, so he was forced to exfiltrate Diane, hiding her in the trunk of his Renault ("quite comfy, actually," she recalled) as the family drove away. "Yes, it was a difficult time," joked Anton, who added in his inimitable tone, "we all have our crosses to bear."

Hyde Street. Sunday 11 March 1984.

Russell Targ and Keith Harary (who has dropped "Blue" as his nickname) have just published *Mind Race*, another layer in a series of parapsychology works that include *Psychic Warfare* by Martin Ebon and *Mind Wars* by Norman McRae. This week Keith and Russell gave a party in the apartment of a friend of theirs, Pat Walker. On Friday business took me to the Peninsula, so I had lunch with Hal and we discussed the book. He said he didn't like *Mind Race*, first because Russell discloses that the Pentagon paid SRI for ten years (a fact that was technically classified, although everyone knew it) and also because in the future SRI is less likely to be trusted by funding sources. Skeptics like Marcello Truzzi have lost no time in attacking the book: Keith and Russell are not able to defend themselves because the real data is still hushed up. Besides, some of their claims are overblown: they give the impression that remote viewing works every time, which is obviously untrue.

Hal and I conducted a dowsing experiment today with scientist Marshall Pease. The two of us left the Institute and walked off, discussing favorite topics. When we came back Pease showed us the place on the map where he thought we had been, but he was far off.

Ren Breck has just shown me imagery of Mars that displays what some people consider a giant sculpture representing a "Face", near a series of pyramids they are already calling "the City", which left me unconvinced. When the photograph was passed around the table at SRI, with only the information that it showed a face, six people found it at six different spots!

The dark "undercurrent" of American ufology continues to confuse the research picture. Recently Bruce Maccabee attended a meeting at Dick Haines' house where Hal, Peter Sturrock, and Jim McCampbell heard him talk about a certain *Project Aquarius* document given to him by "a highly placed source." It was supposed to point to a military research site on UFOs. Again, it was heavy on rumors and light on specifics, but many people eagerly swallow the bait.

Another anonymous source, allegedly a Sandia engineer, has hinted at two other codenames: *Blue Paper* and *Old New Moon*, which talk about crashed saucers, captured humanoids and lights flying over nuclear facilities.

All that stinks to high heaven. Why are people so eager to disseminate this garbage before checking it? I am reminded that Kit once interviewed a soldier of fortune, specialized in nuclear security testing, whose group used helicopters designed to appear as flying saucers. American researchers spend a lot of their time chasing false stories planted in their midst, just like Spanish UFO research was discredited by wild tales of Ummo. Maccabee acknowledges that his group may be used as a channel for fake information.

Later the same day.

Hal and I discussed again the topic of sites designated by Pat Price as potential UFO bases. In every case, according to him, subjects reacted by describing “space technology” and “objects I don't understand.”

In one case the remote viewer reported a psychic contact with two entities that captured him, held him in a white room, and gave him a vision of his deceased father. Hal speculates that the whole thing is a psychic mousetrap designed by someone who is waiting to see who will track the information, armed with which clearances.

This discussion brought us back ten years in the past, when Hoova was supposed to fly above SRI while Geller was bending our spoons. Hal also told me one of his remote viewers had been given a sealed envelope as an “inductor.” It contained photographs from a soviet film of a rocket being fired, and a white UFO officially explained as a weather balloon. The film later vanished, allegedly destroyed by the agency that owned it. If the object was a weather balloon it was travelling at 17,000 miles an hour...

Hyde Street. Saturday 17 March 1984.

McGraw-Hill has just published my *Computer Message Systems*, in their Data Communication collection, the first textbook on messaging, collaboration and conferencing. Teish is having some literary successes, too: she has obtained a promise of advance payment from Harper & Row.

Olivier has written to us from San Diego:

> If you don't believe in bad luck then read this: there's a little breakfast fish-n-chips shop on the docks over on Shelter Island where sometimes I do homework on the outdoor tables. A couple of days ago I sat down and found out I had accidentally thrown out all but one important page of my previous work, and instead I had kept the scrap paper... As

I'm feeling real bad about this, the wind picks up the one remaining page and throws it in the water.

"I went down to the piers to try to reach it and... believe it or not, as I am reaching it, stretching as far as I can bend over the water, a seal pops out of the water between me and the paper! He pushed the paper out of reach and then turned to me. I don't think he had any idea I was right over him—and screeched and headed for cover. I don't know who was more surprised...

Hyde Street. Tuesday 20 March 1984.

Hal and Bruce Maccabee continue to research the crash rumors: is someone in government guarding a captured UFO? Or, as Hal put it in an electronic mail message today, "what would be the signs that whoever is in charge might have a hardware problem they hadn't been able to solve?" One such sign would be an effort to tap the best minds in physics, so Hal resurrected an old contact at Edwards AFB.

A couple of years ago the Air Force Rocket Propulsion laboratory set up an Advanced Concepts group, with a task to produce "breakthroughs in energy and propulsion," starting with a survey of concepts that might explore loopholes in presently known laws of physics. The contract was let to Dr. Robert L. ("Lull") Forward, on a leave of absence from Hughes Research Labs in Malibu. Forward, a respected expert in general relativity, focused on antigravity and wrote a report that was straight engineering physics, even when it mentioned the energy from zero-point vacuum fluctuations and the Casimir force. He did a separate study on an antiproton annihilation propulsion scheme, which seems prosaic in the context of UFO behavior. (**3**)

Does that mean that the Air Force is stuck in classical concepts, and does that confirm that there are no crashed saucers? Always the optimist, Hal is encouraged by the fact that his own contractor was told by his superiors to go as far as he could "to uncover any kind of new concept, no matter how unconventional." But if they did have Alien hardware they wouldn't need to go fishing, would they?

Hyde Street. Wednesday 4 April 1984.

The downstairs kitchen is finished, and I put the final touch on the little nook I call *Twilight Bar* as homage to Arthur Koestler. Fred Beckman came to see us. We took him to Maxwell's Plum for dinner. He was full of superior airs and utterly lacking in kindness.

I miss our days of breathless research. Tonight I picked up some of my best files and was seized again with dizzy awareness of the problem's complexity. It's not surprising that McDonald and Jessup committed suicide, and that the governmemt got so confused about what it should tell the public. Janine and I are reading *Mind Wars* by Ron McRae. Not much is remaining secret: even the Scanate project is exposed and taken apart, and I'm the only team member who hasn't leaked data or published a book about it!

We shook President Mitterrand's hand today, at the Palace of the Legion of Honor, along with the folks from the Consulate. The occasion was his visit to Silicon Valley, his alleged interest in high tech frontiers. Yet French science still refuses to delve into the dangerous waters of parapsychology.

Los Angeles. Friday 13 April 1984.

On a visit to Bob Emenegger I found he had become involved again in "the whole business," as he calls it. Two men from the public relations side of the DoD have been talking to him, namely Dr. Robert Miller who is a "special assistant" and his boss General Robert Scott, who reports to Defense Secretary Caspar Weinberger. Both men are political appointees of Ronald Reagan. Bob approached them with the idea of doing a documentary on terrorism; the UFO subject came up: Miller and Scott hinted that the goverment had "lots of information" but the time for release hadn't come in this election year... Always the same hall of mirrors, dangled revelations.

Bob has a lifelong friend whose father worked at General Atomic. One day his friend was inebriated, bothered by a talk with his dad:

"Who got the Nobel Prize for transistors?"

"Shockley"

"Who got the Nobel Prize for integrated circuits?" No answer.

"See, nobody got it. You know why? We got the idea from a crashed saucer. The electronics were in the form of ICs. They were taken to RCA."

The whole thing is absurd, I told Emenegger, since every step in the development of integrated circuits is well documented in laboratory notebooks, in patents and in the minds of people still alive today.(**4**) Besides, the IC is a technology development, not a breakthrough in physics, and does not qualify for a Nobel Prize. So where does this absurd story come from?

I spoke to Hal, and gave him five new sets of sighting coordinates from my files for the remote viewers. The numbers I gave him were for Green Ice, Sugar Hill, Italian Hexagon, Copper Medic and Timber Douglas (**5**). We discussed the developing story around Bob Emenegger. Bob Miller, who has degrees both in science and technology, was in the Army under Patton and claims to have attended Patton's meeting with Rommel (at which Patton suggested to Rommel that they join forces and clean up Europe... "You sonovabitch, I've read your book! Why are we killing each other in this stinking desert? Put your tanks in formation with mine and let's drive together to Moscow!" Patton is supposed to have said).

Researchers are being approached with bizarre stories they are encouraged to spread: Ufologist Bill Moore was visited by an agent who talked to him about Christ, and journalist Linda Howe is being fed dubious documents by a man from Kirtland AFB who pretends to act on behalf of a secret (and probably fictitious) MJ-12 group.

Paris, rue de la Clef. Sunday 22 April 1984.

Easter. We're back in Paris, planning a short vacation trip to Normandy and Brittany. For now we rest after two intense days in New York where we landed on Wednesday, took a room at the Waldorf-Astoria and went out again for dinner with Cheryl Weiner, discussing education software. Janine and I had lunch the next day with literary agent Ned Leavitt. He gave me wise advice: "Write your novels in French," he said. "In English, your characters just don't come to life. Writing fiction is like playing music, if you're meant to play the violin you shouldn't try to play the flute."

On Thursday we had dinner at Ingo's place with his friend Stuart. I was happy that Janine finally saw Ingo's apartment. He told us that a certain "private" group of government researchers had hired him to remote-view a set of coordinates where a UFO base was supposed to exist. Pat Price has done similar experiments, as Hal has told me.

The next day we had lunch with Marie-Monique Steckel, an executive of France Telecom, in the Rainbow Room at Rockefeller Center. She spoke effusively of future technologies, of her company's ambitions in venture capital. Yet we find France in a real crisis this time, struggling with the economic problems of the steel industry, two years of industrial stagnation, and deep financial worries precipitated by Mitterrand's disastrous policies.

Binic, Brittany. Monday 30 April 1984.

This is a tiny harbor near St. Brieuc in Britanny. We took the road from Bayeux to Saint-Lo with a feeling of blessed detachment from the world. We passed Villedieu-les-Poëlles, Avranches, and visited Janine's sister Annick and her husband Michel in Brunville, reviving our memories of the eventful UFO conference we organized 13 years ago when Aimé Michel, Guérin, Charles Bowen, and our friends from LDLN all joined us at the farmhouse. The mystery is still here.

France is troubled by real crises and false problems, yet there was a joyous fair in Bayeux, colorful crowds, flowers; every trouble seemed set aside the time of a few songs. Janine and I spoke about our life, happy that both of our children are reaching independence.

We had trouble finding a room in Brittany. The weather is glorious, more summer than spring, yet most of the hotels are still closed up, like the stubborn *Bretons*.

Later the same day. Le Conquet.

We spent the morning exploring the countryside around Guingamp, hoping to discover prehistoric raised stones (*menhirs*) with the help of the Michelin map and local guidebooks. Many of the megaliths are secluded away from prying eyes.

We found our first stone in a wheat field under the morning sun, having driven for an hour between tall hedges that hid the landscape. The next one, further south, only revealed itself after we trekked for a kilometer or so along a muddy path. As for the third one, we would have missed it if we had not left the car by the side of the road and asked a local farmer for directions. We plodded along the edge of the swamp, climbed a raised bump topped by a hedge, half-crawled through bushes and finally discovered it. It was a marvel, a giant stone that lorded over a circular prairie by the side of a brook. We jumped over and walked through the wet grass.

At the foot of the huge stone one felt cutoff from the world, lifted beyond time. The monument seemed both a vestige of an eternal past when men had the taste and luxury of symbolic thought, and a witness to the present with its massive reality, its almost-luminous mass of granite in the bright green forest.

It was a scene worthy of *Brocéliande*, a magical site hidden and alive; in the mud at the foot of the stone were fresh footprints left by people who had evidently walked around it several times, counter-clockwise. Are the ancient rites still active? Janine wore a blue velvet dress in the clearing in the morning sun, and we felt privileged to be there, in love, in the perfection of that vision.

Later we reached Brest, in all the agitation of an industrial city; trawlers were sailing beyond *Pointe Saint Mathieu*, the sun set over the Atlantic. Some bigots have desecrated the landscape, carving Christian symbols in raised stones or topping them with ugly cement crosses, revealing their shortcomings in a land where ancient wisdom refuses to die. Tonight is the Night of Walpurgis.

Le Conquet. Tuesday 1 May 1984.

France is becoming a country of friendly pensioners and career bureaucrats. These idle folks have all the time they could wish to create, to learn, to start new things. They could write books, compose music or paint, but they do none of that.

Yesterday was a Monday but no one worked because it was the day after Easter. Next weekend is also a "bridge holiday," for some obscure reason. Companies no longer fire or lay off anyone: security in stability is the new worker's slogan, amidst intellectual indifference, a gray ocean of the spirit that washes over everything.

I used to see Michel Rocard as an exception, a socialist with novel ideas, capable of lifting this régime out of its morass, but he has become just a wrinkled Minister of Agriculture who lives among the same lost illusions as everyone else. There is much softness in the air along with indifference and laziness; the industrial crises are real, but people are still feeling wealthier. The countryside is dotted with new homes, two-storey houses with wide garages and American-style comfort. We went to bed, leaving the open window to see the ocean, waves reflecting the flashes from the lighthouse called *Phare de la Jument*, and Ouessant Island on the horizon.

Auray. Hotel du Marin. Wednesday 2 May 1984.

We drove across Brittany after admiring the carved Calvary of Plougastel-Daoulas where the mouth of Hell devours a pretty woman who must have committed some carnal sin. The obsessions of the priesthood and the brooding nightmares of bigoted peasants are spelled out in stone for the convenience of passing psychoanalysts.

Quimper was pretty but deserted: Mayday, no one works, shops are closed. We had difficulty finding a restaurant where we could eat pancakes and drink some good cider. We drove to Eliant to track down the elusive Jean-Pierre Prévost, one of the Pontoise contactees. He'd tried to start his own sect, living in an old farmhouse on the road to Rosporden. A young woman told us Prévost was gone until evening. I left a message for him and drove off.

It rained in Lorient. All the young people had left the beach for the cafés. The big submarine base looked dreary. Auray is a small medieval harbor miraculously spared by the warlike insanity of the 20th century. The steep streets paved with big stones lead down to quiet piers where sailboats rest. I was surprised to learn that Benjamin Franklin had first landed here when he came to France.

Did he visit, as we did, the megaliths of Carnac, an enigma open to the sky like a screaming challenge? Carnac is one Pagan monument the Church will have trouble hiding or disguising.

Brunville. Thursday 3 May 1984.

We drove back through Rennes, Mortain, and Vire. The rain had stopped, the Norman landscape defined by light fog in multiple planes. Near Mortain a kind of higher consciousness seized me, with blissful detachment of the whole body, a state I have learned to recognize in the paranormal training at SRI. Was it the landscape itself, or some ancestral memory? Was it only the beneficial effect of a few days of freedom away from work worries?

Finally it was time to drive home. We were alarmed by the eerie silence we found in Brunville. Mamie told us Annick's husband Michel had suffered an accident, a high-speed car crash. He survived, thanks to the solid Mercedes, but was deeply shaken.

Hyde Street. Sunday 6 May 1984.

Back in California, I just had an important conversation with Kit, who requested my help in urging Hal Puthoff to leave SRI. "We're Hal's closest friends, we care for him," he told me. "His project has a good record at SRI but he would have a better future accepting the position Bill Church has offered him, starting a physics institute in Texas. Perhaps if we both urge him to move on he'll step away from a project that will soon reach a dead end."

I promised to talk to Hal. Kit is working hard on a new medical device company called Hemokinetics, developing an inexpensive system to monitor blood pressure and heart arrythmia.

Hyde Street. Monday 28 May 1984.

The renovation of this house continues. Plaster gargoyles I brought over from France stare at me as I work. We just celebrated Catherine's 16th birthday with a dinner at a Morroccan restaurant, eating with our fingers under a tent. My daughter is a smart fine young woman now, and a trusted critic of my books.

I am reading Alan Turing's life while Janine reads *Brave New World*. We get along so well...everything is an occasion for pleasure, whether we are rebuilding this house, or shopping for a new car to replace our old white Ford.

The Wye Plantation. Sunday 10 June 1984.

The Aspen Institute has convened a conference on "future social structures" at the edge of Chesapeake Bay. After my presentation someone offered me a Faculty position at UC Berkeley, but I feel my true path remains in high tech. On Friday I was in New York with Rothschild Ventures, who urged me to co-invest in *Digital Productions* (**6**). While in Manhattan I also met with Astrid Merlo of Olivetti and with Ingo Swann whose major interest at the moment is a study of religious apparitions.

Hyde Street. Tuesday 26 June 1984.

In a few days I will join Sofinnova as a Partner; there will be more continuity in my life, and a better view of innovation in the U.S. and France.

Where does Janine find her reserve of patience and wisdom? I know that some day I will miss this time on Hyde Street, even if I bring home occasional frustrations from my work and the slow progress of my books. The Spring Hill ranch remains my long-term dream: I draw up new plans to build a tower on the property as a library and research center, and as an experimental site to study psychic information structures and the role of entropy.

Hyde street. Saturday 30 June 1984.

Boëdec has received a terse note from Aimé Michel in response to some UFO data:

> Thanks for the documents, but as I thought I'd told you, I am no longer interested in this problem because the only methods that could bring progress require large resources. I made a mistake in 1952 when I thought I could make a contribution. You are an active person. You should look for a science that actually works.

Does he believe this? Is this the same man who was telling me in 1958, to shake all the pear trees? Perhaps he just wants to distance himself from dogmatic ufologists and hysterical skeptics. If so, I don't blame him.

Hyde Street. Tuesday 24 July 1984.

Business is picking up: the Sears venture fund, at my urging, will invest in Rugged Digital, where I am a member of the Board. This decision, supported by Sofinnova and our colleagues at Walden, insures that the company will be able to go on with new products.

Teish came to see us on Sunday, wearing a beige turban and a blue dress over brown pants. She was dragging two heavy bags with fragments of her *Jambalaya* manuscript for me to review. We spoke of her trip to New Orleans; we tried to cheer her up: She was afraid of losing her ability to look into the future, to see the world to come. We walked and talked, Catherine joining into the debate, until I was so tired I said, "I don't have enough training in gumbo ya-ya," and drove her back, laughing, to Hayes Street.

Now I've read her book, strikingly vibrant, funny, and infused with her formidable persona. I feel privileged to be able to guide her in small ways through practical details of dealing with publishers.

Life goes on at Hyde Street: Janine works in her sunlit office, cable cars clang and ring their jolly way up the hill again, Catherine plays Frisbee with Olivier's dog Señorita who returns exhausted, drinks a full bowl of water and stares at us with her big soft eyes. On Friday Fred Beckman took us to a fancy restaurant in Berkeley, the kind of trendy place we detest, where snobbish customers slavishly wait an hour and a half for a table. We spoke of music and his Chinese gongs, a welcome contrast to my current work among the perverse universe of venture capital. Many of these financiers are narrow, bland, humanly uninteresting, even as they deal with new companies that will change the world.

Hyde Street. Sunday 29 July 1984.

The twin fields of ufology and parapsychology are pulsing with crazy notions. Uri Geller and Jeff Mishlove have a proposal to develop business applications of psi, an unrealistic idea at a time when psychic functioning is still largely undocumented. In spite of the good work at SRI, the field lacks a fundamental underpinning, let alone a framework for applications. Ufology is not in much better shape: ufologist Todd Zechel promises that he will "soon" reveal to the world the ultimate truth about crashed saucers. That would be very nice indeed. I could move on to other subjects.

Hyde Street. Monday 30 July 1984.

There was a terrible accident on our street today. The shock was so great it made the house shake like an earthquake. I heard the crunch of cars and people screaming in terror. Opening the door I found a scene of panic: a black Camaro barrelling down Russian Hill had slammed at full speed against a cable car full of tourists that was slowly climbing the steep slope. The collision sent the cable car and its passengers down our block towards the pier, out of control.

What a stupid way to commit suicide! The crumpled Camaro was smoking, all tires blown, the hood and front of the car squeezing the dead driver. Firemen began cutting the metal to free the corpse. The gripman of the cable car had managed to stop it before it ran off the track or hit more cars down the hill, but there were wounded victims everywhere. Olivier, just back from France, watched all this with his sister and me: Another bloody day in San Francisco.

A week ago I was having lunch with professor John Newkirk, the founder and CEO of Silicon Solutions (7) when a woman came over to our table and spoke to me in French. She was an abductee whose story I had researched. We spoke of her memories of her childhood abduction. She told me more details had come back to her.

Allen Hynek has a new project. Mimi told me today he was in Scottsdale talking to a British millionnaire who proposes to finance his research, to establish a full facility and to help in further fund raising, "but there is nothing in writing," she hastens to add. The man is a Monte-Carlo resident with a home in London, who "winters" in Arizona.

Hyde Street. Wednesday 22 August 1984.

Hal sends me coordinates for the four mountains that Pat Price, in an extensive remote viewing survey, suggested as possible UFO bases on Earth. Kit spent the night here: we were able to talk about many things, especially the Cash-Landrum case, with its medical aspects.

Hyde Street. Sunday 23 September 1984.

Driving up to Spring Hill, our retreat from the world, we found the ranch in full construction, with four workers around a cement mixer, heaps of dirt all over the place and our contractor friend Earl Bates building a new, crenellated retaining wall.

Behind the house the forest rises all the way to Willits. The workers have seen two bucks with tall horns: They would have gladly put down their shovels and gone hunting. Our tenants have already found another place for their school; they will leave in a few days, then the ranch will be ours. Olivier has sent me his drawings for a computer-controlled equatorial mount.

Hyde Street. Sunday 30 September 1984.

It rained last night, lifting the leaded heat that stifled the Bay Area. The Silicon Valley culture is changing. We witness a realignment of the electronics industry with the collapse of overblown claims for microcomputers, while the industry is being revolutionized by the move away from mainframes, towards a "client-server" model that separates processing from the programs with which users interact locally, at great expense in new coding. Too many deals are concluded in haste and confusion. Companies large and small are swept in the current, and a feeling of gloom hangs over venture firms. Even the Rothschild funds, which I visited last month in New York, have felt the impact. I have just spoken to Astrid Merlo (still with Olivetti in Paris) who expects further shocks. This is a rough awakening after the euphoria of the success of Apple and other firms. Many a young manager may have to sell his Ferrari and re-learn programming. I see this financial debacle as a return to sanity, because company valuations were clearly overinflated.

Another sign of changing times is the strange wind that destabilizes the denizens of New Age research. Janine is sad to witness the desertion of many friends as fine people with good minds spin away from reality. It's a general phenomenon, a society crashing headlong into the scary unknown, technologies out of control, everything seemingly possible yet nothing recognizable. Should we see this as a healthy transition away from the easy rationalizations and phony reality of Reagan's America, of Mitterrand's France where Fabius is the new prime minister, where "centrist socialism" is painting everything gray, with the same dull brush?

On a flight to Paris. Thursday 11 October 1984.

A French television station has invited me to *Droit de Réponse* for a lengthy live debate about UFOs. Thus the subject is forcing its way back into my life. At InfoMedia the new Board has elected Phil and Ren Breck as directors. They still believe they can turn the business around, but InfoMedia came too early into an immature market at a time of absurdly high interest rates.

This white Air France airliner flies south over Glasgow. Back in California Janine must be on her way to Ukiah. She meets every success at the Bank of America, adored by her colleagues and praised for her work at the Technology Center.

Reading Koestler's *Case of the Midwife Toad*, I am struck by his remarks about seriality and Kammerer's studies. He has written a lucid analysis on synchronicity and takes pleasure in pointing out that Carl Jung read Kammerer but refused to use his terminology.

Koestler's book encourages me to pursue an old research of mine, first articulated in a short story entitled *Le Fabricant d'Evénements Inéluctables*. I now see that *Invisible College* and *Messengers* were developments of the same concept. Through such a study the whole body of occultism could be placed into question. The issue of structure arises immediately; the issue of secrecy too, since this research is still too shocking or convoluted for the general public.

Rue de la Clef. Friday 12 October 1984.

Paris drowns in silvery dust, in icy fogs, her sky brushed with aluminum. This light would be appropriate for a religious scene or one of those cards evoking Christian miracles kept in the Missals of our boyhood. The light comes from everywhere at once to put a shine on the old stones, bringing an overwordly glow to the whole city. I took my mother to a restaurant near Square Viviani, and then we went over to the library of Shakespeare and Company and came back through *Rue de la Huchette*. She delights in watching people: the faces from every country, every race.

Rue de la Clef. Saturday 13 October 1984.

Simonne Servais invited me for lunch at her apartment today. She was relaxed. "I have found my path," she told me, "I have made my psychic transformation." She does seem to have recovered her sense of humor and her remarkable energy. She has changed her style and let her hair flow freely. We ate lightly: *pâté de grives* from Valensole, as a culinary homage to *le Père Masse*. Later she drove me to the office of Stock (in a building where Molière once lived) where Thérèse de Saint Phalle gave us some comments about *Alintel* and promised an editorial decision in November.

Another drive to *Ile de la Jatte* where television producer Michel Polac, wearing a thick scarf, was getting ready for his show. A short impulsive man with a scattered approach to his work, he told us he suffered from back pains. I had brought my best slides but he said "UFO cases prove nothing." He'd toyed with the idea of bringing Geller into the show. Geller once twisted a fork for him, and Polac has the tape, which the French science establishement proudly refuses to watch.

Patrick Aimedieu met us over dinner. He is a solid, rectangular fellow, glasses firmly set on his nose. He heads up a research laboratory specialized in the high atmosphere. He exemplifies the best French scientists who would like to spend time studying the paranormal but are forced to do it on the sly, in their spare time, with no resources. We discussed the Valensole case, trying to come up with new hypotheses. We spoke of the painful jealousies that divide French researchers, making them so ineffective.

Aimedieu told me that a friend of his had done a series of psychic studies for the French secret services. This man's wife is a medium who witnessed poltergeist phenomena inside his own home. Gaullist minister Michel Poniatowski took an interest in the project. Yet the report ended up in a drawer, like so many studies, and nothing more was attempted.

He mentioned a recent list of serious Soviet ufologists that includes Vladimir Azhazha (named by Andropov in 1981), astronomer Dr. Nikita Schnee, cosmonauts E. V. Krunov and Y. G. Nazarov, Vice-Admiral M. N. Krylov, physicist Mikhail Dmitriev (a ball lighting expert) and astronomer Lev Guindilis.

The conversation returned to the French situation. Simonne describes it as the decline of an old culture. "In your own books, you talk about the end of Greece... in such periods those who remain attached to the past are doomed," she said, adding: "The legacy of the General is in the hands of people incapable of carrying it forward. Those I served, De Gaulle and Pompidou, transcended both the right and the left."

When I urge her to write her Memoirs she answers: "I don't have anything to do with politics any more, or history. I will never again belong to any group where you lose your freedom of judgment, and where others (socialists, for instance) have to be labelled as your enemies." What a remarkable woman.

Paris. Saturday 20 October 1984.

Paris-Match publishes an interview of physicist Jean-Pierre Petit by Marie-Thérèse de Brosses, which brings me back to our television show (*Droit de Réponse*) where Petit almost came to blows with television journalist Jean-Claude Bourret. Bourret was exasperated by Petit who kept needling him, accusing him of exploiting the UFO subject and making money from lectures. Bourret produced old letters where Petit thanked him for giving him funds for his research.... The whole argument became sordid.

At the studio I had a chance to see "Dr. X," the witness in a celebrated case with medical sequelae. He told me there was trouble in his marriage.

Hyde Street. Sunday 28 October 1984.

François Truffaut died last week. Every man is an equation where the term on the left side may be more or less complicated, but the term on the right side is always zero: equality in the face of death.

Yesterday Janine and I loaded the truck with two beds and various items of furniture, and we headed up to Spring Hill. Life was slow and nice in Ukiah. In every shop people warmed up, welcoming us when we said we were moving to the area.

A young buck with fine horns was eating tender grass along our creek. We spoke to contractor Earl Bates about the tower plans; we ordered a flagpole from Sears. The store manager told us, "I live on Tomki Road, a bit further than you, just let me know if you need anything." I've started reading *Harlequin*, by Morris West. The weather is cold and gray.

7

Spring Hill. Thursday 1 November 1984.

When we stopped at the Denny's coffee shop on the way north, the waitresses were dressed up as witches, colombines and pumpkins. Little kids had turned into rabbits. At the ranch we found the workers fixing windows, removing trash, and the school managers loading the last batch of their equipment. The director came for a last friendly visit while the hammers pounded nails throughout the house. The sky was clear; the smell of wet leaves was pungent in the air along with rotten apples, wet dirt. We started cleaning the bedrooms.

It feels as if we are settling down at Spring Hill forever, an impression that reminds me of our arrival in Texas, the beautiful newness of that American country so few Europeans have taken the trouble to really understand, perhaps because one must stop and settle down to fully understand it.

Spring Hill has a sinister side, too. Some windows are broken; the big house is dark amidst 143 acres of silent pines and somber redwoods. The night swirls, heavy on the heart. I struggle with incoherent dreams. When daylight came Janine drew improvised drapes over the frosted windows. As I write the sky is blue again, birds start singing. a black cat is staring at us. And then, barely audible so far from San Francisco, a radio bulletin reports the assassination of Indira Gandhi.

Later the same day.

I spent the morning fixing the water lines in the creek bed and organizing the tool room. Janine made a fire in the old fireplace. Every chore once accomplished and struck from the list, suggests two more. No stars tonight: the sky is overcast. In the beam of my flashlight a big toad hops away through the grass. Janine is reading

Wired, the life of John Belushi. I have made no progress in my writing but I'm a rancher now. I can show you the mud on my shoes.

Spring Hill. Friday 2 November 1984.

In addition to the black cat we now see a gray one and a white and black specimen who meows all day long, begging for food. We slept deeply. The rain woke us up, a downpour that made a raging noise like a river. We started painting the cottage, chasing spiders. On radio we only get one faraway station that brings us confusing news of Reagan and Mondale. All evening the moon has tried to break out among dark clouds. In India the Hindus are carrying out a massacre of the Sikhs along the railroads. So much for Eastern wisdom.

Spring Hill. Saturday 3 November 1984.

The weather is divine today. When old countryfolks in France speak longingly of magnificent seasons and glorious mornings of yesteryear they recall days like this. Yet nobody ever drives up to Ukiah. Tourists gravitate to show off in Napa or jet ski at Clear Lake. Senior citizens aboard their Winnebagos drive north to Shasta Lake. Ukiah is a small town of bureaucrats, Vietnam vets, aging hippies, welfare recipients and shop owners. Many dangers lurk behind the beauty: the essential element of the local economy is marijuana, and many crimes are committed over dope. The Daytons tell us that the harvest season, just coming to an end, has left four people dead in this county.

We had a champagne dinner tonight, first celebration at Spring Hill.

Spring Hill. Sunday 4 November 1984.

Allen Hynek called this afternoon. He'll come over to San Francisco on Wednesday, so we plan a reunion with Fred. Allen was happy at the idea of spending two days with us. “Let's agree on protocol,” he said, “Fred has to pick the restaurant.”

Allen will bring a copy of the paper he intends to deliver at the Csicop meeting (which we call the psy-cop meeting") when the arch-skeptics gather at Stanford.

Spring Hill. Saturday 10 November 1984.

Allen spent two nights at our house on Hyde Street, where Fred joined us. They are both taking vitamins that are supposed to keep them young and handsome. We spoke joyfully of our Chicago days, over a good dinner at Maxwell's Plum. Allen told us his new Center was now duly established in Scottsdale with the backing of wealthy Englishman Jeffery Kaye, a pro-Israeli businessman who maintains homes in three countries. "I now realize I was blind for much of my life," Allen said, "dedicating myself to academia; all those professorial games seem so pointless now..."

Allen seems to have discovered a world of business contacts and big projects. Jeffery Kaye doesn't really intend to fund the Center, however. He is only providing an initial framework and startup funds. His idea is to launch a series of publications and film projects whose proceeds would support the organization, starting with a movie about Allen's life. John Fuller has been contacted to write it.

In the midst of all that Allen is as gentle and friendly as ever, a very sweet man indeed, but he seems a bit lost and disoriented. He is touched by all the attention. He saw that I had a portrait of him on my wall, a framed photograph from our writing session when we compiled *Edge of Reality*, and this moved him.

We spoke about the rumors of dead humanoids, which have evaporated. Leonard Stringfield, who claimed first-hand witnesses of UFO crashes, is unable to produce anybody. Fred and I keep coming back to the idea of a conditioning of humanity. But for what purpose? And done by whom?

"We need a real research effort," Allen says, "with real investigations, and translation of foreign cases." He speaks of spending two million dollars a year on such a project, but Mr. Kaye will not provide that kind of cash.

Hyde Street. Sunday 11 November 1984.

Allen rested well here. He found our bedroom wonderful. The Stanford meeting went fine, he said, but the press only mentions Philip Klass and James Randi, the debunkers: Allen's rebuttals are not covered. Philip Klass even stated that his Pentagon contacts denied that the DoD had ever sponsored psychic research. This is an obvious lie, and Klass must know it; the SRI project is only partially classified, and anyone well connected in Washington can find it.

Fred called me tonight with concerns about Allen's health. Three blood tests have confirmed an abnormal condition usually linked to a cancerous tumor. Allen is getting worried, and so are we.

Hyde Street. Sunday 18 November 1984.

An associate of Jeffery Kaye named Dr. Glazer called me last week on Allen's behalf. He confirmed they were starting a publishing company and wanted to raise money for a docudrama on Hynek's life. He wants to enlist my help, because "your name would help attract funding." He pressured me to drop everything I was doing and fly to Phoenix to see the project. Allen tells me that Glazer is a psychologist who sells his house to him in connection with a divorce.

Spring Hill. Friday 23 November 1984.

We've made a lot of repairs; the place is coming alive. In the evening I play chess with my daughter by the fireplace. Janine tells me she has never been so happy, "because I am nice to her."

"I've always been nice to you," I say.

"True, but you don't always pay attention to how I feel; how anyone feels."

Spring Hill. Sunday 25 November 1984.

My good friend Bill Murphy is selling his house in Mount Shasta.

"I've finally discovered the secret of the spiritual community..."

"Will you reveal it to me?" I asked in the tone of a dutiful disciple.

"Gladly. You just have to give expensive lectures and ignore anyone who asks serious questions. Yet this town includes many sincere seekers. They just get caught up in a meaningless game."

Spring Hill. Friday 14 December 1984.

Morning: Janine pulls the drapes out over the beige and grey hillside. We're alone at the ranch: both of our children are in San Diego; they'll come back together for Christmas.

Last week, on a rapid visit to Paris, I saw several publishers with Simonne Servais. Our best meeting was at *Mercure de France* where Madame Gallimard received us in a wonderful old house on *Rue Furstenberg*, above Delacroix's workshop that has been turned into a museum. Her assistant Nicole Boyer was with her. They told me they had enjoyed *Alintel* and wanted to publish it, so we spoke of a contract. It was a good surprise after the rejection by Albin Michel, where Henri Bonnier told me he thought the book was "narrow."

Hyde Street. Sunday 16 December 1984.

We drove back under the rain, in the belly of a mean black cloud dragging along the pine trees. Our new tenant in the cottage told us it was snowing up in Willits.

I haven't had time to write down my impressions of France, but I now realize they wouldn't shed much new light: I found the country lost in false problems. Mitterrand's government is losing credibility and scaring the French, who stand at the mercy of the tax collector, abusive Labor Unions, and the overwhelming bureaucracy. People are increasingly worried about the petty thiefs and small-time gangsters who take over the suburbs.

I've seen those suburbs, their flimsy pretense at "quality of life," an ugly excuse for a semblance of progress. How could the local kids avoid growing up into delinquency? In the course of my visits to startup companies I went to the *Zone de Courtaboeuf* that brags about becoming another French Silicon Valley. But cabbies won't take you there after dark, and firemen don't drive into the zone to put out fires unless accompanied by heavily armed police.

Simonne Gallimard complimented me on my writing style. She said I knew the lost art of using semicolons, and I didn't load my sentences with adjectives.

Air Force Colonel Bill Coleman, now retired in Florida where he tends his orange trees, has advised Bob Emenegger to talk to Hynek; Bob didn't follow up, but a few days later Hynek's new staff called him saying somebody wanted to shoot a documentary about Allen and the Hudson Valley sightings. Bob setup a meeting with Allen and contacted again "his sources within DoD."

"My contacts thought it was a great idea," Emenegger told me. "It would enable them to leak out some pieces of information they wanted to declassify."

"What games they play!" I laughed. "We've heard all that before, haven't we?"

"It's only the game that fascinates me," confessed Emenegger. "I really don't care one bit about the so-called phenomenon."

Spring Hill. Sunday 30 December 1984.

Olivier spent Christmas with us. We watched old movies and played with Señorita. Now we are alone at the ranch, Janine and I, rummaging through our research files. Lots of projects: a new satellite imagery company called EarthData started with Professor Peter Banks and other Stanford scientists, and a possible film project with Bob Weiss to be based on *Alintel*. Night comes early. Now the fire crackles and sings in the fireplace.

Hyde Street. Tuesday 1 January 1985.

We enjoy luxurious sleep, a long night after the tiredness of Spring Hill. We felt an odd depression as we drove between Healdsburg and Cloverdale. In that part of the Russian River valley landscape it was like passing through a black fog. We celebrated the New Year at the ranch, drinking champagne offered by our tenant who was already rather tipsy in mid-afternoon. Janine wore her blue and purple long dress, the one I like best.

Now we rest, and will miss Luisah Teish's ritual in honor of Legba, Guardian of the Threshold. She says I am one of his children. Janine tells me it is time to turn the pages of old concerns and obsolete friendships, to look forward, to build anew.

Spring Hill. Saturday 5 January 1985.

Last night I had dinner with Bill Murphy's friend Gretchen at Harry Drake's. She was as "chicana" as ever, searching for English words. She lives in Cuernavaca now, in a castle built by an eccentric woman. Gretchen gives lectures on art and dance, works with local groups, helps villagers set up medical clinics. Immersed in a world of mysticism and esoteric pursuits, she feels on the edge of a great contact. One evening the chatelaine confessed to her she had experienced a unique event following a channeling. She had demanded proof: "I'll only believe when I've met flesh and bone ETs," she said. A few days later, on board a bus, a man approached her: "You wanted to meet us," he said, calling her by name. She made the acquaintance of two of his companions. They were humans, of various height and hair color. They said they came from Orion and had normal jobs on Earth. She had intimate relations with one of them, and remembers it as an extraordinary experience.

Hyde Street. Sunday 13 January 1985.

Allen called yesterday, urging me to visit him in Scottsdale, perhaps in mid-February after my trip to New York. He warned me that I would get a formal letter from Dr. Glazer, as Jeffery Kaye's business manager: "Don't let the formalities scare you."

Hyde Street. Monday 21 January 1985.

This time we drove north into rain, found the ranch cold, hills covered with frost, and we felt an oddly secret joy at being so far from the world. *Omni* has just interviewed Allen. He repeated old theories and didn't give anyone credit for having oriented his research, which I find disappointing. Yet Janine insists I must go and see him in Arizona, if only to give him some pleasure at this stage of life, as he tries to rebuild his network.

I am losing interest in reading fiction. Instead I have begun collecting biographies, memoirs and journals. Yet when I read Ned Rorem I find his alcoholic dilemmas even more meaningless than his adventures with men. I agree with Janine when she says a diary should serve as a tool to explore the world and the people around us rather than a narcissistic pursuit of your own mood.

On Thursday Simonne called to say that *Mercure de France* had agreed to publish *Alintel.*

Hyde Street. Sunday 10 February 1985.

Two days ago I had a curious call from Paris: a man named Jacques Sapir, who got my name from Magnaval at the French Consulate, is coming to the US for a study of cross-border data flows and the vulnerability of databases. He works with an organization I've never heard of, the Center for Advanced Strategic Studies, on Boulevard Raspail.

Michel Rocard, the French minister for Agriculture, was here a week ago. He shook hands with our small cohort of French expatriates and gave us a very relaxed, short speech, with a bit of self-deprecating humor, making fun of socialist pretensions.

New York. Friday 15 February 1985.

My daughter speaks of her plans for the future. She is ready to spread her wings. I am at the end of a business trip to the frozen East Coast: first to Atlanta, where snow covered everything and where I attended a reception organized by Apollo Computers. The company was celebrating its fifth anniversary and a meteoric rise in business, having just delivered its 10,000th computer. Bill Poduska, the CEO, made a typical "American Dream" speech. Later, in the elevator, a visiting businessman remarked to me: “I don't think I'd enjoy working in an industry where surviving five years is regarded as such a great achievement...”

Flying on to New York for lunch with Cheryl Weiner of McGraw-Hill, then a meeting with communications tycoon Archie McGill at Rothschild. The landscape was frozen, the suburbs dead. This morning I had a few hours of leisure to roam through Soho, the holography museum and the bookstores of Greenwich Village. Real Estate prices are rising to absurd levels in Manhattan; fortunes made and lost. Now I wait for the flight to Phoenix, where I expect to see Allen Hynek in his new surroundings, and to make plans with him.

8

Scottsdale. Saturday 16 February 1985.

Allen and Mimi were waiting for me at the airport, driving a small yellow truck, an International Scout. The house they just bought from Jules Glazer is located on Vista Road in Scottsdale. It is a fine white ranch-style, two-bedroom two-bath home with a large den that Allen uses as an office. It comes with a pleasantly shaded patio and a diamond-shaped pool. The living room, quite large, could accomodate a reception with twenty couples. Windows are decorated with colored glass that enhances the place's Western style. An elaborate security system protects the property and there are bars on all windows because Glazer used to maintain an expensive collection of ancient stock certificates.

Around a pot of coffee we discussed Allen and Mimi’s move, and their feelings about Arizona. Allen is thrilled to have such a spacious office and a personal computer. He loaded Astrocalc and demonstrated it to me proudly as we reminisced about the Bright Stars database I once implemented for him at Dearborn Observatory. This led us to pleasant recollections of Chicago. "Tomorrow you'll meet our new friends, Tina Choate and Brian Myers, and Jules Glazer. We'll talk seriously," said Allen.

I will also meet Jeffery Kaye, his elusive English backer.

Allen and Mimi haven't quite settled here yet. They plan another trip to Evanston in a few days. The Ridge Avenue house has just been sold, and they need to bring back more furniture.

"There's been some politicking when I left Cufos, of course," confessed Allen. Sherman Larsen still insists he is the president. John Timmerman, who has invested some $300,000 of his own money into the Center, wants to keep a measure of control over the publications. Allen is fed up with what he calls "all the bickering." To make a clean break he has incorporated a new organization called Icufor (International Center for UFO Research) with its address at Brian and Tina's apartment. Mimi reminded Allen of a remark by their Chicago attorney, who felt he had moved a little too fast, without signed commitments from their new backer.

Scottsdale. Sunday 17 February 1985.

It was under pleasant sunshine that I met Allen on the patio this morning. I felt well rested, happy to be with my old mentor again. Allen led me to his orchard where we picked a dozen oranges. He was proud of his trees and clearly enjoyed his new surroundings. We sat down at an outdoor table and began talking seriously.

Emenegger's bizarre revelations were our first topic of conversation. Allen spoke very tentatively, on the defensive, seemingly fearing my criticisms: "Maybe I made a mistake, Jacques," he began, "but I did go to their meeting and I spoke to General Miller. All the audiovisual archives of the Air Force are at Norton AFB, about 75 miles outside Los Angeles. Miller's in charge. He's a former aide of Patton, you know."

I had heard all that from my own conversation with Emenegger. What I didn't know was that General Miller had told Allen that he had actually been inside a flying saucer. Yet Allen didn't ask him for any details! Characteristically, he felt oddly embarrassed by that revelation, and didn't probe. When I asked him about it he shuffled in his seat and said, "Well, I felt as I often do with contactees and visionaries, that I am before a deluded person; there's something almost obscene about it; I'd rather change the subject."

Later, however, he did call Miller to say he had "gotten the message." They will meet again on Tuesday, "in private," yet he is taking the whole team, including Brian and Tina. Allen is nearly convinced that the Pentagon is ready to reveal some secrets and will use him as a channel. I cautioned him: "It could also be the opposite. The Pentagon might want to lead the public to believe they know the secret of UFOs; they might use you as a channel, all right, but for disinformation. Remember, you don't have any facts."

It is a credit to Allen's almost childlike innocence that he couldn't grasp my argument, so we dropped the subject. Either way, we will know more on Tuesday.

Next, Allen asked my advice about the documents he'd brought back from Hessdalen in Norway. They reminded me of the Concorde photo of a high-altitude meteor. Allen did go and spend a week in Norway, including three days and nights in a tent in the middle of winter at 65 degree latitude. He is justly proud of that expedition but it could have ended badly: the car in which he was riding gave up along the way, frozen while in motion. He would have died of cold if they hadn't been fortunate enough to be within walking distance of a farmhouse.

The Hessdalen lights are indeed unexplained. The data is impeccable. But perhaps the high latitudes should lead us to consider geophysical phenomena rather than "true" UFOs? Allen didn't see anything significant himself during his week in Norway, so he has to reserve judgement, as I do.

Our third topic of morning discussion was his move to Phoenix. Allen told me it all came from a meeting he had with Tina, who in turn put him in touch with Jeffery Kaye, an English millionaire she had known for several years. Tina and Brian, who are involved in gold mining, knew Mr. Kaye as a potential investor. Tina and Brian are New-Age devotees committed to a spiritual quest: Brian has even gone off to talk to the Hopi, when the tribe was looking for ways to send a message of peace to the United Nations. We spoke of all this over a leisurely breakfast, in several stretches with many interruptions, pleasant side conversations with Mimi, and the unavoidable silences while Allen perused the Sunday paper, absorbed in the comics pages of the *Arizona Republic*.

Mid-morning. Tina arrives, a striking blonde in a light grey pantsuit, bursting on the scene like a flash of the full Arizona sunshine. The energy level in the house rises by several degrees as she takes a lounge chair and tells me her life story: journalism school, a job in Chicago with an agricultural firm, first inkling of the world's intrigues. One of her clients turned out to be a PLO agent who wanted to control grain distribution in the Middle East. She moved to the oil business, commodities, precious metals. Tempted by adventure, she tried to salvage sunken treasures in the Caribbean and to exploit mines in New Mexico. That's where she saw "her" flying saucer. Her life changed. When she met Mr. Kaye and his manager Jules Glazer, she put them in touch with Allen Hynek.

Allen listened to this with high interest. Evidently he had never asked about her full background. Easily dazzled by vibrant ladies, he had joined in her breathless vision of exploration.

Mimi had prepared a simple but tasty salad for lunch, after which Tina drove us to the apartment she shares with Brian: The "Center" consists of two neat rooms, well lit, with a small library and a conference room. A distinguished lady named Ann Eller, a volunteer, serves as a research assistant. I began to see a real working operation shaping up. Ann had class, poise, and experience. Combined with Tina's unsinkable energy and Allen's scientific depth, the potential does exist for genuine work in a way that was never possible in Chicago. Heaven knows the material is not lacking: there are researchable issues all around.

Jules Glazer joined us, a tall, serious fellow. I liked him more than I expected, after some guarded comments I'd heard from Mimi. A practical businessman, he attacked the questions that Allen had avoided: would I lend my name to their center? Would I write books, give conferences for them? Would I help in fund-raising? I had anticipated some renewed form of association with Allen, of course, and told them so: under any structure they choose I'll always be ready to work with him. But I want to devote my time to solving the problem, not to promoting it or marketing yet another UFO group. Besides, I thought, Allen had clearly indicated that the Center was solidly financed. What about the backing by Mr. Kaye, the English millionnaire? Had Allen moved to Arizona only to find himself having to beg for support again?

Glazer had anticipated my reluctance: "What if we created a private company?" he asked, offering a share in the ownership and thus long-term profits from the books, videotapes and other publications we would create.

I have worked in venture capital too long to fall for that concept.

"Such a company couldn't represent to its investors that they would ever get their money back," I said, "let alone make a profit. There is no business model in ufology today. Shareholders would have to understand that this is exploratory research. The plan would be flawed. I've always written my books out of a sense of duty to the data and the research, never to make money."

Glazer didn't argue the point, to his credit. We went on to discuss other forms of collaboration, if they made a movie for instance. He asked if I knew people who might invest in such a movie... some people from Hollywood have already been approached... vague projects... more golden expectations... nothing concrete. Glazer left for a dancing class, western swing, his way of working out the stress of a messy divorce. His ex-wife attacks him physically in public whenever she sees him, and Scottsdale is not a big town.

Once he was gone I asked about Mr. Kaye, whom I had yet to meet. I was beginning to form certain ideas about him, however. Mr. Kaye's fortune was inherited from his father, the founder of a supermarket chain. Glazer spent six years with Jeffery in Monaco, helping manage the business. He now advises him in U.S. investments: real estate, stocks, and private companies.

"Glazer jumped on the idea of ufology as a money-making operation when he saw the Meier photographs from Switzerland," said Tina. I winced. Allen said nothing.

"I miss something," I told them. "Wasn't Mr. Kaye going to finance the center so you could do real research?"

"He does—in a way. He gives a thousand dollars a month to the center."

"How long does this deal last?"

"Until March."

"What happens after March?"

"He didn't commit to anything."

Tina broke in: "the idea is that Mr. Kaye is providing us with start-up money and that we will use his contacts with wealthy families to raise more substantial funds. He keeps bringing his friends in here; he likes to take a hand in the research. Especially since the day he happened to be in the office while a television crew was filming Allen, and he ended up on the screen," she added with a wink.

Before I left, Tina and Ann bombarded me with questions about my field research: how I screened cases, how I conducted investigations. They asked about specific events. They also asked me about Allen, who was out of the room: why does he shy away from close encounters and abductions? Why is he both attracted to and fearful of paranormal incidents?

I was Allen and Mimi's first guest in Scottsdale. "I think that was very appropriate," Allen told me warmly when I took leave of them.

Hyde Street. Monday 18 February 1985.

Some items I forgot to note in Arizona come back to mind: taking advantage of a moment when we were alone, Glazer brought up "a topic he didn't like to mention in Hynek's presence," namely the continued existence of the Center after Allen. I answered evasively. Allen, at 75, appears to be in fair health (**8**). He has become more sedentary and walks with a slight swing from one foot to the other, in a sort of shuffling dance, but his energy level seems as high as ever. The projects we'd discussed during his visit to San Francisco have made little progress, however. There is still talk about a biographical movie, but he doesn't take it seriously. As for the documentary about Hudson Valley sightings, John Fuller's involvement in it is doubtful.

The most interesting recent happenings center on Norton AFB and General Miller. I recommended that Allen check his career, but he said he didn't know how to do it, so I advised confiding in Colonel Friend, former head of Blue Book, a man he can probably trust.

What bothers me with the dangling of "hard evidence" by General Miller is that the connection comes through Pentagon PR man Colonel Coleman and Bob Emenegger, two accomplices in blatant manipulations of public opinion. The story also involves Colonel Weinbrenner, former head of the Foreign Technology Division. Allen mentioned to Miller that he wished he could ask Reagan to give blanket immunity from prosecution to any member of the military who had seen a UFO (suspending the JANAP rules). General Miller replied: "I'll mention this to Nancy." Allen is going from one amazement to another among these people.

Hyde Street. Sunday 3 March 1985.

Hal Puthoff called me on Thursday, in search of advice. He was indeed thinking of changing jobs and needed to talk to a friend. On short notice, Janine came up with a superb dinner, which gave us a chance for a long evening in our Victorian library, while cable cars clanked and whined on their way up the hill.

Hal summarized the history of the SRI secret project—as much for himself as for me. He recalled how following his master's degree in Florida he'd joined the Navy and NSA, finished his PhD and left the agency, where he had risen to GS13. He decided not to pursue a promising career in laser physics (his book was already a standard text) and joined SRI under circumstances with which I was familiar.

The first project was a test of the existence of tachyons involving hypothetical plant-to-plant communication. In connection with this experiment he contacted Ingo, who reoriented the project from plant telepathy to remote viewing. Sponsorship of the work moved under the CIA, who requested a development plan. This led to a proposal for a five-year, $15 million project, along with provisions for partial publication of the scientific results. The rest is well known, with all the ups-and-downs of funding, budget schedules, inter-agency infighting, down to the current project, which has a good chance of entering a new phase of expansion.

In the meantime, as I know from Kit, Hal has a new opportunity that would imply leaving behind the work he has built over the last 12 years. His old friend Bill Church, founder of the *Church's Fried Chicken* franchise, has just created an R&D company called Jupiter whose model embodies Hal's ideas in physics involving relativity and MHD theory. Bill Church has already hired a genius instrumentalist named Ken Shoulders. They have demonstrated the ability to punch holes into titanium plates with the energy of a flashlight. Hal, who consults with Jupiter, found the idea of such energy conversion in mainstream physical literature. So Bill Church proposes that Hal move to Austin with an endowment. Together with his salary, this will enable him to catch up financially after all those starving years on slim SRI budgets. Hal is tempted, but he worries about leaving the destiny of the parapsychology work in the hands of untested managers. In particular he is worried that Ingo's connection with the Institute may be cut off, because he was the only one able to handle his complex personality.

I gave Hal a standard dissertation on S-Shaped development curves and discontinuities, enthusiastically endorsing a change in careers that might help him jump into a new phase of intellectual achievement, even if it appeared initially as a step backwards into the conventional life of a physicist. His ideas are anything but conventional. They involve local manipulation of spacetime. Hal is boldly investigating paranormal reports in the widest sense, including the more bizarre effects.

"Have you noticed how levitation affects not only the body of the saints but their clothing as well?" he asked me. "When praying nuns get levitated their robes continue to cover their legs in whatever position they find themselves. That's not what would happen if they were lifted by some action of the flesh itself. It implies that gravitation is locally reoriented around their bodies. And it's the same thing in your UFO cases."

He believes that extensions of relativity can explain all that.

"What about the light effects?" I asked. "Most UFOs are seen as luminous objects, not as the metallic craft of science-fiction."

"Under my hypothesis the light witnesses see is actually heat energy that is radically blue-shifted into the visible spectrum. It doesn't come from a normal light source."

Spring Hill. Friday 15 March 1985.

Business life is moving on, with a proxy battle at Rugged Digital Systems (a former employee wants to take control) and a lively financial conference in Monterey where I met venture capitalist Pierre Lamond of Sequoia Ventures, and investors from Bechtel. At a reception in Pebble Beach under the rain I had a chance to speak with some old acquaintances like Mel Schwartz of Digital Pathways (most people there didn't know he had a Nobel Prize in Physics) and General "Johnny" Johnson of Telebit.

The best thing about this AEA conference was the return drive along magnificent Highway One through Santa Cruz and Half Moon Bay. I stopped for breakfast near the ocean and took time to read the paper. The world seemed far away beyond the cliffs, pine trees, battering waves.

Spring Hill. Saturday 16 March 1985.

Everything is wet here at the ranch and the rooms don't have any doors yet. Earl Bates, our contractor, has promised to put up the new ones this week. But it feels good to be here with Janine, and so much in love! All the bushes are already in bloom, red and gold; the place feels wonderful.

I reorganize an office, hanging my mother's paintings on the walls. Ned Rorem writes in his journals that we're not aware of happiness at the time: he is wrong.

Hyde Street. Sunday 24 March 1985.

For several months I'd been free of asthma but it is coming back now, preventing sleep, forcing me to get up every night and waking up Janine as I cough and fight in search of air. Then I get sleepy during the day, lowering my energy level when I most need it. At least there are some helpful medications now. I pity those who suffered from this in earlier times, like Marcel Proust.

At Spring Hill our developer neighbor to the north came over for a beer and offered us his land for $100,000. He has given up, temporarily at least, on the idea of logging it. It is a fine piece of California hills, covered with redwoods, full of springs and wild life. Yet Janine thinks we have enough space as it is, and besides, where would we find the money? Although my current salary gives us some independence we are far from wealthy, and cannot live the life of the gentleman farmer.

When I leave this world I will take with me a great puzzlement about humanity, specifically its inability to experience happiness and fulfilment. I will also take with me profound contempt for what people call their moral laws and their embodiment in religion.

So much for the negative side. Two major feelings will stay with me till the very end: deep gratitude for the privilege of having known my children, whom I adore and respect, each in his or her own way; and as Jacques Brel sings, "*un prénom de femme...*"

Hyde Street. Saturday 30 March 1985.

I have been flying around for most of the week, from Boston to Los Angeles, where I went to Norton AFB on Wednesday, visited the Defense Audiovisual Agency and met at length with Generals Miller and Bob Scott. I came back with a curious mixture of amazement and skepticism.

Norton is located north of the little town of Redlands, near San Bernardino. The huge DAVA building is clearly visible from outside the base. It is reached through Gate 5. I gave my name to the guard and was immediately escorted into Dr. Miller's office, a windowless, paneled room with a portrait of General Patton and various impressive testimonials on the walls.

Dr. Miller wore a black suit, a shiny white shirt, a bright red tie, a bright red handkerchief sticking out of his breast pocket, and bright red socks. He closed the door to his office, sat in an armchair in front of me and smiled.

"How can I help you?" he asked. This astonished me since he knew perfectly well that our meeting had been arranged as a follow-up to his discussion with Hynek. All right, I thought, so we are here to play games. I told him that I was an associate of Allen, that I had a longstanding interest in UFOs going back to the 1954 wave of sightings in France, and that I understood he had had a personal experience with unidentified objects. He told me he was perfectly familiar with my books and background. He himself held two doctoral degrees, one in political science from Heidelberg University in Germany, the other, interestingly enough, in theology. He had indeed experienced several sightings over the years.

The first one took place at White Sands in 1956. While filming a rocket launch he was suddenly aware of something above him to the left. He looked up and saw a large circular object hovering over the base. A Jeep arrived at high speed. An officer came out, confiscated the film, and told all personnel present that what they had seen must not be discussed.

"They (the UFOs) must have been observing our technology," General Miller said to me.

The second sighting took place about 1980, in the desert 80 miles away from Mojave. He had driven there alone to hunt and to take some pictures when he suddenly heard a whirring sound and saw an object, which, however, was not located in the same place as the sound. "It was as if it was able to project the sound to a different place," he said in answer to my questions. The craft was curved and landed on four pods, about six feet in length and six inches wide. A ramp was lowered. A man approached the opening. He wore a small mask over his nose and a pointed helmet. Miller could not tell if he had any hair. He was a normal human being, with smooth skin and intensely blue eyes with the oval shape of an Oriental.

"Would you like to come inside?" the man asked. Miller accepted the invitation and was escorted into the craft. He was struck by the stark simplicity of everything he saw there. The atmosphere was very pure and gave him a sense of elation. There were three other beings aboard, all of whom breathed normally. General Miller's escort also removed his mask. The controls consisted of touch panels and sound-activated devices, exactly the kind of technology that was beginning to appear in laboratories across the U.S. at that time. The seats were molded to fit the men, who appeared to be about 40 or 45 years of age, except for one who seemed younger, in his twenties.

"I spent about fifteen minutes inside," Miller told me.

"Did you notice anything unusual when you left?"

"It was dark when I came out," he replied.

"Did you feel your sense of time was altered?"

He hesitated, finally looked at me and said:

"Something did happen to time."

"Were there any traces?" I asked, looking for some physical confirmation.

"No, there was nothing in the desert. The craft flew away, with the lights at the periphery glowing with all the colors of the rainbow."

"Any sounds?"

"No sound at all."

Miller added that he had trouble sleeping for six weeks after the event. He felt that he had had further communication with the entity from the craft, but he did not elaborate.

His last sighting took place near Vandenberg AFB last year. He was with a group of people who stopped at dusk to observe a large oval object in the sky. He showed me a snapshot. It looked plainly like an ordinary lenticular cloud. If I had not been speaking to a former member of Patton's personal staff, and if the picture of the General himself had not been staring at me from the back wall, I probably would have gotten up and left at that point. The story I had just heard was a contactee tale of the type made notorious by George Adamski in the early Fifties. **(9)** Miller even stated he thought the beings were from Mars or Venus.

I had to remind myself I was not hearing this from some pseudo mystic in the back room of a New Age bookstore, but from the deputy director of a Pentagon agency. I have always had a huge amount of respect for anyone who fought under Patton, so I swallowed hard and waited for Miller's next move.

He called one of his assistants, a Mr. Atkins, into the office and instructed him to give me a tour of the facility, which included the audio-visual archives on film, tape, and slides for all four services, representing 400 million feet of film, or eight years of continuous viewing. Naturally, some of the footage at DAVA is classified. After the tour we came back to Miller's office and I turned the discussion to the specific topic of the now notorious UFO footage and its possible release. He felt very strongly that such data existed, he said, and that it should be freely discussed with the public and with the scientific community. But he did not indicate that he knew what that alleged evidence was, or where it was located.

Next Dr. Miller introduced me to his boss, General Robert Scott. I asked him about DAVA and its relationship to other agencies. I learned that the Defense Audiovisual Agency had been established by Department of Defense Directive 5040.1 dated June 12, 1979, a text that states that it is "under the direction, authority, and control of the Assistant Secretary of Defense for Public Affairs," the Pentagon P.R. organization that employs Colonel Coleman.

General Scott said he had seen a UFO in 1959 while visiting some land 70 miles north of Phoenix in the company of a psychologist and a photographer. They saw the object for about one minute. Unfortunately, the photographer did not have his camera with him!

Echoing the speculation of many ufologists, Scott believed several classes of beings visited us. "There aren't only good guys in the cosmos," he said. He told me flatly that several human civilizations, notably Atlantis and Lemuria, had destroyed themselves, and that the UFO beings were trying to warn us not to repeat such mistakes. Government secrecy, unfortunately, was preventing the message from being heard.

"It should be fairly simple for the UFOs to circumvent such petty human secrecy," I pointed out, "all they have to do is show themselves." Scott replied without a moment of hesitation: "They are probably bound by ethical principles not to interfere with our free will. They are waiting to be invited by us."

This argument made no sense, of course. The mere fact of causing thousands of UFO sightings to happen—if such beings are in fact responsible for it—already creates a major interference in our culture. Witness the hundreds of books, films, magazines, and television shows that have been inspired by this intrusion.

Scott said he believed strongly in the survival of the soul, thus the destruction of an entire continent might not be regarded as an irreparable disaster by a higher race. Such an argument is dangerous since it could easily be twisted to justify genocide.

I came away from Norton Air Force Base unimpressed with what I had seen and heard. I found no high technology at DAVA. The building appeared as a backwater government service facility filled with old film machines that had been phased out of Hollywood editing rooms many years before. Scott and Miller were two friendly contactees who were trying to validate their own beliefs, I later told Hynek. But there was no indication that they actually knew of any unreleased evidence, or that they would have the clout to get it released if it did exist.

Both men were political appointees: Miller said he once served as the first Hollywood agent of a promising actor named Ronald Reagan.

What happened at DAVA? Was there a genuine attempt to leak secret UFO data to us out of government archives? Or, more likely, was someone simply dangling false information in front of our faces, playing childish New Age charades? We have not been given anything concrete. Were we pawns in a bizarre little game?

Perhaps the whole affair grew out of crosstalk among UFO enthusiasts, some of whom were on the government payroll, hoping to push their own beliefs.

Yet one of the assistants named Paul Shartle assured us he had seen a movie that was more than a training film. Who made it, and why, remains a mystery.

Hyde Street. Sunday 31 March 1985.

We're staying in the City this weekend. Olivier came over to see us with his Swedish friend Karlin. San Francisco is paradise in any season but it feels especially luscious in the spring. My passing thoughts of accepting a job with Rothschild in Manhattan are fading away. When I see the ships passing by Alcatraz, or when I look at the three-masted *Balclutha* anchored at the pier two blocks down, I feel a sense of belonging, stronger than in any other place in the world. I enjoy walking up Polk Street, rummaging through antique shops with their overpriced trinkets, browsing the used bookstores, gossiping with a friend at some little café. But my greatest pleasure is the intimacy of home. Our bedroom has a fireplace; we take our afternoon coffee there and speak softly about life.

Hyde Street. Monday 8 April 1985.

We had our first guest at Spring Hill this week-end when Bill Murphy came over from Mount Shasta to spend two days with us. A keen observer of nature, he spoke about the wildlife that surrounds us, the hawks and the buzzards, the moles and the toads, and the deer that come down from the high hills. Since our last visit the colors have exploded. Lilacs are blooming among yellow bushes.

Bill shared with me his puzzlement about a recent visitor to Mount Shasta, a middle-aged woman dressed as a New Age devotee, wearing beads and crystals. He offered her the hospitality of his home for a couple of days while she attended every mystical group meeting in town. She abused his friendship by charging numerous long distance calls to his phone.

I asked to see the bill from the phone company and was intrigued by all the communications with Washington, so I dialed the number: it rang at the Intelligence desk of the Secret Service! I will never look at a gathering of tea-drinking New Age little old ladies in quite the same patronizing way.

On Thursday we had Stanford aerospace Professor Peter Banks and his wife Paulette as our dinner guests here. I brought up the topic of

UFOs. He does not reject their possible reality out of hand, but, like Ed Condon, he places them among unresearchable topics: "Science deals with repeatable, verifiable facts," he says.

I disagree with that definition. The Big Bang is not a repeatable fact, yet astronomers study it. I prefer Bill Murphy's simple but open approach: he strives to remain available to new experiences.

Paris. Rue de la Clef. Sunday 21 April 1985.

My Sofinnova partners and I have travelled all over France from Vernon to Grenoble, from the European Propulsion Company pursuing remarkable work on magnetic suspension to dreary French hackers who dress up like Steve Jobs, and devious schemers who try to use us to sell obsolete gadgets like their Minitel in America.

Paris was as sensual and unpredictable as ever. On the first night of my stay I was shaken out of bed by two loud explosions: opponents to Mitterrand's regime had blown up some offices of the immigration department. The next day the girls of the red light district demonstrated in the streets, wearing masks and little else. They protested a stupid edict by the mayor who wants to board up the studios from which they ply their trade. If he drove the women away, not only would he gain the support of the bigots and prudish, but—more to the point—he would make room for juicy contracts with developers who dream of getting their hands on that part of Paris.

Nostalgia: Maman has given me two paintings she made of Spring Hill, based on my photographs. Seeing them makes me wish I were already back in California. I spent the afternoon with Elizabeth Antébi, remarkably well informed on the early years of French venture capital. We also spoke of literature, of Marie-Thérèse de Brosses and her novel *Astaroth*.

Paris. Rue de la Clef. Monday 22 April 1985.

My colleague Astrid Merlo, with whom I spent Saturday evening (we went to see Pirandello's *Henri IV* after which we had dinner at the *Taverne de Maître Kanter*) has just left Olivetti to become president of Asystel, a computer distributor. She brought me up to date about the problems at Rothschild Ventures in New York. Archie McGill, who had offered me a job, has now left the firm. Astrid told me I wasn't demanding a salary commensurate with my experience. "Your reputation is that of a nice guy, smart and even brilliant, but that's not a compliment, to be too sensitive in a tough business," she said, adding with a sad smile, "I am telling you this all the more freely that I have the same problem."

Yesterday I saw Simonne Servais. She was amused by what she had heard about me from French parapsychologists: "People know you're in Paris but they can't find you, so they build all kinds of theories. You remember Schneyder, the ufologist? He is fascinated with the story you've published, of a near-landing of a UFO in the property of a European head of state; he is convinced that it was in France, so he has been tracking down General De Gaulle's chauffeur, a man I know very well... Of course he didn't get anywhere." We spent the afternoon going over the contract for *Alintel* that we will negotiate tomorrow with Madame Gallimard.

Paris. Rue de la Clef. Tuesday 23 April 1985.

The weather was windy and cold over Saint Germain des Prés today when Simonne and I walked over to the exquisite little *Place de Furstenberg* where Madame Gallimard has her private apartment, a few blocks away from her office at *Mercure de France*. Simonne had sent ahead a magnificent bouquet of white and purple lilacs with green leaves and a few yellow flowers. Madame Gallimard had invited a young journalist named Jacques Pradel, who has co-authored a book called *Parole d'Espion* with François Gardes. Pradel left after coffee. Then our hostess straightened herself up and told us:

"You and I have been talking about a contract for a long time. Things have been dragging out. In the meantime my company has expanded greatly. Therefore I have thought about it, I am not going to sign the contract the way it is."

Now I am furious, and Simonne is speechless.

Madame Gallimard wears a dark green skirt and a black sweater. As she speaks she is nervously fingering a wide necklace of large pale grey pearls. We stare at each other for a long time, neither one of us averting the eyes. And suddenly, as we keep staring, her necklace breaks, an explosion! All her fine pearls pour through her helpless hands, overflowing, rolling over the sofa, bouncing on the floor, under our chairs. It's a cascade, a cataract of pearls.

We get down on our knees to help her gather the precious objects; we put them unceremoniously into a dish. She sits down again, catches her breath, resuming the argument.

"It's a great honor for a writer to be published by us," she says proudly. "Romain Gary sends me his manuscripts without bothering with a contract. Besides, I demand all foreign rights, except for English. And without any time limit."

I reply (calm now, contained anger) that a contract is an agreement between two parties: you can't write it with yourself.

"Take a month or two," she says, "talk to other publishers. You know my terms."

"How do I know they won't change again?"

"I am ready to sign today," she said.

Her assistant, Nicole Boyer seemed stupefied. Once we were alone she assured us she hadn't known we would be walking into a trap. We made a few concessions, insisted on keeping the main terms. Nicole agreed to present the amended contract. Madame Gallimard, *sans* pearl necklace, came back from the kitchen. She looked over the changes we'd made, signed on the spot, and stormed out.

A few minutes later we left with Nicole Boyer, who took us to the quaint, elegant old building occupied by the Mercure on *Rue de Condé*. The authors' waiting room is the small red office where Beaumarchais wrote *Le Mariage de Figaro*.

Later, over coffee at *Le Drugstore*, Simonne Servais said: "What you just saw was a typical feminine reaction. Don't forget she is the *first* Madame Gallimard. There's a new one, a younger woman, the daughter of a *Ministre*. Losing her necklace at that precise moment, in front of you… What a psychological disaster for her!"

Simonne suspects me of having used some secret SRI-style psychokinesis training to blow up the necklace, and perhaps I did, out of sheer frustration.

Near Place Maubert I saw a golden angel in an antique shop, a wooden statuette from Goa. She dances naked, her wings spread wide behind her. I fell in love with her, thinking of Lilith, and bought her on the spot.

Hyde Street. Monday 29 April 1985.

Allen called with two pieces of news: one, we have been invited to go to France along with Richard Niemtzow to visit Gepan, following similar contacts the French plan to have with the Russians to discuss UFO research. Two, there have been some abrupt changes at DAVA. Scott and Miller have just been sacked in a sudden “reorganization” of the agency.

Luisah Teish came over for lunch with us, a yellow flower in her hair and the cover of her *Jambalaya* in her hands. She is buying a pretty house in Oakland, as Janine had predicted to her. Now she suspects we are a couple of sorcerers.

The fog screens the sunshine over the Bay, creating those light displays that are unique to San Francisco. Ship sirens call to one another and respond. Our life is strongly affected by our teenage daughter. Her mood jumps wildly from laughter and hearty comradery with us to brooding silence. But we love her so much...

Spring Hill. Sunday 5 May 1985.

Every weekend here, away from the city, I find Ned Rorem's journals again, filled with anguish, sometimes pathetic and occasionally laughable, like life itself. What strikes me is the artist's vulnerability to the publication of his intimate thoughts, those guiding fantasies that form the essence of any being. Isn't it essential to reach that murky root of potential, that intimate *subspace* in order to find our true identity? Here at Spring Hill, as I build a personal sanctuary, I think about my own explorations.

The subject is Contact: access to the Invisibles. It is the *only* subject. I do not care for disciples or ideologues. Professionally, I only want to make money to the extent it guarantees free exercise of my spirit. Spiritually, I only want liturgy to the extent it provides a framework for the rise of consciousness, like the glow of sunset informed through stained glass, illuminating the intimacy of love.

We are here for one week, a vacation, a Paradise. The new gray carpet erases all memory of that rough, drafty place we found when we moved in. Irises and roses grow freely here, not as garden ornaments but as wild beings.

Spring Hill. Monday 6 May 1985.

Speaking to Richard Niemtzow I've learned something new about Gepan. The changes relayed by Allen's call to me have their origin in a decision by Prime Minister Laurent Fabius who gave orders to increase Gepan's budget. Velasco is now looking for better international contacts, including the USSR.

In this country Bruce Maccabee is now claiming that Reagan's Star Wars initiative is nothing but a cover for a secret conflict with extraterrestrials. Many ufologists believe it, while the field continues to lose credibility in Washington.

Spring Hill. Wednesday 8 May 1985.

This isn't laziness: I listen to the crickets, watch the lizards who sun themselves on the retaining wall, the salamanders, the birds building their nest under the eaves of the roof, and the hummingbirds who always startle me. I rest from clearing a site for the observatory, drawing up plans, and listening to the news of a faraway world: Reagan at the Bonn Summit, Gorbachev's quandary, the future of Mitterrand's government. Olivier has a new job, a great position with the Western Behavioral Sciences Institute in La Jolla: "Congratulations!" we told him, sitting by the fire, drinking champagne, singing the *Marseillaise* like happy fools.

Spring Hill. Thursday 9 May 1985.

Here I experience the same country landscapes of my childhood in the Oise valley. There is a whole region of visual treasures to be discovered, yet I hope tourists will never overwhelm it. Poor Impressionists, if they returned to the *Vallée des Peintres* I once knew, (it was still the landscape of Van Gogh, Pissaro, Cézanne when I grew up, playing near *The Mill at Pontoise*) they would be shocked to see what horrors have been erected in their golden fields.

On my latest trip I drove to Vernon and felt sick: the same people who brazenly destroy the beauty of France are proclaiming "national values" with good conscience. We have a similar problem here. Our neighbor has changed his mind, he now wants to log his 100 acres of redwoods; we don't know how to stop this massacre.

Every day I read a little more of Ned Rorem's journal, wondering why he appears so pure, when everything is said and done: perhaps because musicians are expected to lead lives of debauchery on the way to greatness? Rorem is vulnerable and the final judgement is ours; we have the power to forgive him because he creates. A New York model who once posed for Dali, had been warned that the Master was wont to masturbate at his easel while painting. Is that shocking? Or does it simply mean that a certain form of genius can only be brought to the light of normal reality by wrenching it away from the depth of the flesh through passion or terror?

Spring Hill. Friday 10 May 1985.

Early this morning we took delivery of six yards of red rocks. A "yard" covers 150 square feet, two inches thick. We hired local helpers to clean up the place and pull the weeds. I have drawn up the final plan for the tower. Janine asks why we need it. For the books, I reply, and as a temple for spiritual study, as a retreat, a chapel... It is a launching pad for the psyche, for hard to define experiments with information singularities. I cannot convince her and feel dejected: what good is it for me to fulfill psychic needs she doesn't share?

Spring Hill. Saturday 11 May 1985.

Bill Murphy tells me about a woman who lives near Mount Shasta. She saw the Lemurians, just like that, in her own kitchen, on January 1st, 1978, at dusk. They arrived as a sheer vapor that slipped under the door and took the shape of five beings eight feet tall. There were three witnesses: "They were not cloudy or nebulous at all," they reported. "They were material, opaque. You couldn't see through them." Unfortunately they didn't explain to her how to reconcile relativity with quantum mechanics, or how to cure cancer. They only uttered the usual platitudes.

Hyde Street. Sunday 19 May 1985.

Richard Niemtzow finally called: we do have a formal invitation from Gepan for Allen and me to travel to Toulouse and also to meet with members of the science board in Paris. This is Gepan's last hope: the managers need to hear face-to-face confirmation that real American scientists like us are interested in the phenomenon. So I'll be there in late June. Simonne Servais has promised to help me sort out various political currents. Richard made it clear that the higher levels of Cnes were thinking of disbanding Gepan. If our trip fails to convince them that the subject has real scientific potential they will probably stop all funding.

Allen is delighted at the prospect of us travelling to France together. We touched briefly on the Norton AFB mystery, which puzzles him intensely. Bob Emenegger tells me there is a movement within the Pentagon trying to purge the military of Reagan's political appointees like Scott and Miller: "Those two guys were cutoff from reality," he said, "They've antagonized their own staff." He hints that their efforts to declassify (or leak?) the alleged UFO film led to their demise. More games, but Allen and I now get the joke.

Bob's contact at Norton is a staff member who was ordered by Miller to retrieve the film (presumably showing an Alien landing at Holloman). He told the general that his request was inappropiate and that he should know it. The same staffer told Emenegger that Tina and Brian hadn't impressed him when they came over with Hynek: "too pushy." But perhaps I wasn't pushy enough?

Last week we had a visit by all our French investors including an older man named Boissonnat, former head of Schlumberger R&D. We had a long conversation during our dinner cruise around the Bay. He knows Yves Rocard and is open to the reality of dowsing. I also spent time with Gilbert Grenouille of France-Telecom, a network pioneer with excellent knowledge of communications and a good sense of humor. There are many smart researchers in France. Unfortunately, nobody supports them.

Spring Hill. Saturday 25 May 1985.

Why do I need to build this observatory tower? In my city work, in my office or travels, I am always looking towards the future: investing, reviewing plans, projecting strategies. Here I can reach a solid place, an anchor. I can touch eternity, or at least that subtle kind of permanence that is associated with the Earth. Janine pulls me against her and asks: "Isn't it like this, already? Doesn't Spring Hill mean silence, the luxury of living away, far from towns?"

Yes, it is all that, but I need to structure it myself. We won't bring many people here, only Annick and my mother, and special friends like Bill Murphy or Luisa Teish. We would like to have Allen come over, if only he was able to rest in one place for two days, which I doubt. Janine gets up to draw the drapes, her graceful body catching the morning light. She laughs at my crazy dreams.

Country life: painting the long wall, scraping the moss that smells of varech. When we go into the pool we swim in luxury among rose petals and the flowers of the apple tree. Our friend Hans Rasmussen has offered us a subscription to the *New York Review of Books*, which we save to read here but I find it hard to get into the mood of such intellectualized magazines. I have the same difficulty with *Scientific American*. That kind of writing suggests arbitrary structures defining knowlege and culture, handing down genius awards. It all looks so fake! The topics that interest me are orthogonal to the preoccupation of that self-defined elite.

Hyde Street. Sunday 9 June 1985.

I spent three days in New York this week, staying first at the Chelsea Hotel, notorious refuge of poets, dancers, and musicians from Arthur Miller to Sid Vicious, moving the next day to the Algonquin to facilitate various meetings, notably a Manhattan-style "power breakfast" with a partner of financier Alan Patricof. It was one of those glorious spring days that New York is capable of displaying. People were actually smiling. I won a verbal fight with a cab driver who was reluctant to take me across the Brooklyn Bridge. He assured me he "didn't know where it was," so I guided him there, laughing at his greed. I had time to visit the Metropolitan Museum to see the Tiffany stained glass and the impressionists, with their paintings of Pontoise that gave me a shock of recognition.

Back in San Francisco my daughter picked me up at the airport. She said Niemtzow had called, anxious to plan our French trip.

Spring Hill. Friday 14 June 1985.

The weather is hot. We feel sleepy and lazy; we lounge around or talk to friends. Teish is flying from success to success, having edited the proofs of her *Jambalaya*. Now Harper & Row want her to write another book. Yet the atmosphere of San Francisco is far from reflecting our happy mood. A series of murders fills the papers again with horrible visions of torture and paranoia.

It started with a banal incident, someone trying to steal a tool from a hardware store. The police checked a car driven by a man named Leonard Lake. The tool had been stolen by a friend of his, Charles Ng. Lake's former wife helped Ng get away.

What sounded like a simple theft soon took horrible proportions: intercepted by police, Leonard Lake promptly swallowed a cyanide capsule and died. This led to a hellish trail of murders and torture. Lake and Ng owned a property near Stockton where police found videotapes of sadistic pornography, a hidden torture chamber and Lake's diary, detailing his life in Calpella, a few miles from here.

Lake thought a nuclear war was imminent, so he conceived a crazy personal survival plan based on fortified shelters where slave women would be serving him. This delusion was shared by Ng, convinced he was a reincarnated Japanese warrior. Both were former Marines who served in Vietnam. In the Kelseyville property police found several cadavers, eventually extracting no less than 50 bags of human debris, calcinated bones and broken limbs. So Northern California distinguishes itself again in horror, a perversion of that freedom that should flourish here as it does nowhere else.

I see this tragedy as another pathological deviation of the mystical impulse that called itself the New Age. Authorities simply label Lake and Ng as "crazy." Looking for a way out of the world's nuclear absurdity is not crazy. Nor is it crazy to build shelters for survival: The Federal Emergency Management Agency has a billion-dollar budget to do just that. In a crisis it would not hesitate to eliminate anyone who didn't follow its rules. The survivalist movement borrows the same fantasy, the mistaken concept that one could survive nuclear war. Once they are driven to such extreme speculations, psychological aberrations replace the earlier dreams.

Five years ago Leonard Lake and his wife were peace-loving hippies, keepers of a unicorn named Lancelot created by a sweet, cheerful commune, the Church of All Worlds (**10**).

9

Paris. Rue de la Clef. Friday 21 June 1985.

We landed in Paris under a gray sky, filtered sun. Catherine travelled with me, which gave me great pleasure. She is a good explorer. She says that after the travails of her trip to Greece with Aunt Helen two years ago, she is capable of surviving anywhere. Allen is in Paris too, staying at the modest Hotel Violet, near the Chatelet, close to Cnes headquarters in *Les Halles*. Back in San Francisco Janine is down with the flu. My mother is sad, mourning the recent death of her sister Mimi. A few days ago Janine's uncle, Robert Simonneau, a musician and distinguished chorist at the Paris Opera, also passed away. So this is a sober time, to observe the great human parade.

At noon today I went to pick up Allen and brought him here for lunch with my mother, after which I took him to see the Arènes and Notre-Dame. He was obsessed with the idea of buying a *béret*, but we could not find a single shop that had one in stock. Contrary to Allen's preconceived image of the French, nobody in Paris goes around wearing a *béret* any more, so it was a ludicrous expedition.

We did talk on the way and I learned all about his recent trip to Denver. He spoke at length to Linda Howe, who half convinced him that "the Governments of the world" were in contact with flesh and bone Aliens, and that these ETs were giving the U.S. the technology for Star Wars.

This absurd notion set me to think about the ironies of human history. In medieval times people had monarchs of divine rights, which had at least a certain class. Today we believe our democratically elected presidents are blessed by extraterrestrials. Human nature has not changed very much. It still craves supernatural guidance.

Allen told me that his financial backer, Mr. Kaye, had come to Paris on the occasion of the Gepan meeting. He is staying at the expensive *Prince de Galles* hotel, where he is inviting us for lunch tomorrow. It appears he is a strong backer of Israel, having helped finance Menachem Begin, among others, so there is an unexpected political angle to all this. Allen himself now feels he may have rushed a bit too fast to set up his new center in Arizona under pressure from the fair Tina. She had met Jeffery Kaye in Las Vegas, inspired his interest in ufology and suggested inviting Allen to Scottsdale. Once she had his approval she went to see Allen and sold him on the concept: "A multimillionaire from Monaco begs you to join him in solving the UFO problem; he pledges his support..."

All this was true, but only temporarily. Allen jumped without nailing down the long-term details. Can I blame him? It was good for him to move away from festering Cufos and gloomy Evanston, and retire to the sunshine. The purchase of Glazer's house was a fair deal, even if Kaye did little more than arranging a few parties and offering the use of the duplex he owns in Phoenix to house the new center. Allen has wisely kept his personal files at home. While we discussed all that Allen and I stopped at a sidewalk shop to buy a postcard for Fred Beckman, of a pink elephant flying upside down.

Allen and my mother spoke of Halley's Comet, which she remembers well. She was 10 at the time, while Allen was only a few days old: his father carried him to the rooftop so he could see it.

Paris. Rue de la Clef. Sunday 23 June 1985.

Jean-Jacques Velasco, current head of Gepan, was supposed to meet us at Hotel Violet at 9:30 am but he was two hours late, having boarded the wrong flight in Toulouse. This gave me time to talk at length with Niemtzow and Allen. Dr. Richard Niemtzov, a close friend of John Schuessler and Kit who has a long term interest in physiological effects of UFOs, is an intense-looking man with a high bald forehead, mid-forties, eyes alive, a curious mind. A major in the Air Force, he heads up a trial project for cancer treatment. He hopes to get invited by the French military to study UFOs in France.

"Do you think I should ask Velasco to help me?" he asked.

"He doesn't have that kind of access," I said. "You'd do better with Mr. Gruau. I understand he is the interface with the puppetmasters."

The three of us next went over what we knew of the Cash-Landrum case. Niemtzow and his friends have managed to track down the helicopters involved. They belong to the Army, but it declines responsibility because the machines had been borrowed by "another agency" to carry out that project. Niemtzow thinks NSA is the party involved, but a general has pointed out to him that "if they liked their jobs they should both keep quiet about it."

Since Velasco was still missing Richard went on to tell me about his adventures with John Schuessler in Houston in the days when Valerie Ransone was stirring up ufology:

"When we entered the office of the organization where she worked all phone conversations stopped; no documents were visible on the desks. We were asked about our research, and left with no new information, convinced the group worked for a clandestine outfit."

Niemtzow is certain that the extraterrestrial evidence goes very far. His ambition is to be the first physician to uncover the existence of Aliens, and he dreams of the day when the first alien autopsy report can appear in a medical journal. He is in touch with Leonard Stringfield who promised to introduce him to a doctor who had done such an autopsy, so he mentioned the conversation to Kit, who got angry at what he saw as his naïve acceptance of the claims: "Tell Stringfield to drop the whole thing!" Kit told Richard. When Stringfield lost his job shortly afterwards, Richard's curiosity was further excited.

Velasco arrived and we caught a cab to the hotel *Prince de Galles*.

Later the same day.

Claude Poher was waiting for us in the hotel lobby. He was heavier than I remembered him but friendly and cheerful. I noticed that he now wears a hearing aid.

Jeffery Kaye, whom I was meeting for the first time, appeared typically British, but without the easy, classy style of English aristocrats. He gave us a business card that introduced him as the proprietor of a Monaco-based travel agency. I found this curious since he was supposed to have made his fortune with shopping centers. I instinctively mistrusted him. He also passed around pictures of his boat, registered on tax-free Guernsey island.

The lunch started on a funny note, with Kaye requesting some *rosé* wine from the sommelier of the *Prince de Galles*, who must be used to such gaffes: Jeffery did not want to have to choose between red and white. Claude Poher, a great *connoisseur*, winced but said nothing. To his right was Allen, dishevelled and tired, wearing a remarkable tie adorned with portraits of young women, reproductions of Renoir's *grisettes*. "Allen, you are the last person on Earth wearing ties like that!" remarked Jeffery.

Allen spent much of his time trying to explain to his backer why contactee and abductee stories should be taken with skepticism. Yet Kaye is ready to invest in Meier's stories in Switzerland. With suitable solemnity, he even pulled out of his pocket a purple rectangle "anodized with aluminum" that he handed around the table, claiming that this Alien-inspired artefact had medical benefits. It is even helping his old mother, who can barely walk. Embarrassed by the scene, Allen looked like someone who would love to dive under the table and disappear.

Kaye did confess he was having trouble raising money in Arizona, even in a circle of wealthy people who help each other finance their favorite charities. When he assembled his friends to hear Allen, he collected a measly $250 check after the lecture. In contrast, when an ordinary concert was organized in Scottsdale, all these people sent money. One man, who could not attend, mailed a $1,000 check to Jeffery with his apologies for missing the musical event. Allen is beginning to measure the distance between his dreams and reality. His age is a factor: At 75 he no longer projects the old charisma. His arguments are dated and he often gets his facts confused.

When Jeffery turned to Poher and asked him what he thought of Roswell and saucer crashes, Claude answered that he did not believe a word of the stories, which made me happy. His argument was that the rate of failure in contemporary terrestrial technology was improving rapidly, and that an advanced civilization would have achieved zero defects long before crossing the galaxy.

After lunch Allen, Niemtzow, and I met with Velasco again. He introduced us to Dr. Bréhamet and François Louange, both members of the Gepan team. We went over to Louange's place, a fine apartment on the top floor of a house in the Marais, "older than the United States of America," he said. We reviewed the cast of characters at Cnes and their personal ambitions.

The same evening I had dinner with Simonne Servais at the Invalides. As soon as I mentioned Jeffery Kaye, "Isn't he tied up with Israel?" she asked. I was surprised at such a fast connection. She added wistfully: "I sniff around, you know; like a hunting dog."

Simonne is convinced there is a secondary project: "It's really very simple," she said. "French academics, as rationalistic as ever, want to kill Gepan. It's that attitude that disgusted Poher and drove him away. Now they stress the fact that Cnes has the mission to supply data, but not to process them. Gepan can go on, with Velasco as the head, a mere technician with a tiny budget. But to whom is he supplying the data? Obviously, it is going elsewhere."

She reminded me that an attempt had been made to setup a research project within the European Space Agency, an organization for which Louange long served in Madrid. The idea got nowhere. Other people tried to establish a team under SGDN, the General Secretariat for National Defense. Hubert Curien, minister of Industry, wrote to Hernu (at Defense) but the message went astray, going up the line of command instead of direct cabinet-level, and the project was aborted along the way. The Soviet connection seems genuine, however. The Russians have requested that the UFO topic be placed on the agenda of an upcoming joint meeting with France.

I have given a new research proposal to Allen, Velasco, Niemtzow, and Poher. It concerns the implementation of an expert system for rapid computer screening of UFO reports. I deliberately picked information processing as my topic in forthcoming presentations to raise the technical level of the debate and keep it non-controversial.

Paris. Monday 24 June 1985.

Half-success: We met with Professor Lions today, a mathematician who serves as the current head of Cnes. We assured him there was great interest in UFO research among many American scientists: it would be a shame for France to disband Gepan, we said, adding our strong recommendations for an international extension of its work.

Later, at *Hotel Violet* with Niemtzow, Allen, and Kaye, conversation turned to the status of the new Center in Arizona. When Allen left the room, Kaye expressed his concerns: first because he realizes that Allen, like me, has carefully (and, in my opinion, wisely) kept essential findings to himself; second because it is clear that Allen's health is deteriorating. I was shocked to hear him state that Allen had cancer. Niemtzow did not confirm it. He did state that Allen had consulted him as a friend, but wanted nothing to do with doctors and wouldn't hear of an operation.

When we sat down in a conference room in the modern building of Cnes headquarters I counted 25 people, including Alain Esterle who ran Gepan after Poher. I was disappointed that Claude had not been invited. The other participants were: Perrin de Brichambaut, a meteorologist; Lionel Bréhamet, a physicist from CEA; Jean-Pierre Rospars, a neuroscientist; Françoise Askevis, a psycho-sociologist; Jean-Claude Lorin, a physicist; Pellat, a meteoritics expert from Cnes; Michel Bounias, a biochemist from Inra; Le Gall from Dieli; Manuel Jimenez, a psychologist; Jean-Claude Caroff, head of the ESO-Science department at Cnes; Daniel Mavrakis, a psychopathologist; and Pierre Teyssandier, a relativist with Henri Poincaré institute who did some early research with Poher at GEPA.

Allen's presentation was eagerly expected. He had prepared a statistical review based on 400 cases, coded in rough categories that tabulated their major characteristcs. For the first time in his life he had the opportunity to impress a group of foreign scientists with a professional interest in the UFO phenomenon, who were asking for his guidance. What followed was near-disaster.

Allen stumbled. He read his paper badly, with many false starts and hesitations. He must have written up his text in a hurry. He got mixed up in his own statistics: “You can see that 30 percent of all cases mention the object departed at high speed...” but the slide showed nothing of the kind. People looked at each other, too embarrassed to request a correction. Fortunately Richard Niemtzow saved the day with an impeccable presentation on medical effects. He mentioned Cash-Landrum, Bentwaters (**11**) and six cases in Texas, including the diamond-shaped skin discoloration noted in Tyler on 24 January 1979.

I witnessed a sharp exchange between Perrin de Brichambaut and project administrator Gruau, discussing a commitment that Gepan's current budget would be maintained or increased.

"We cannot increase this budget," asserted the bureaucrat, very much in his role as Chief Marvel Extinguisher, as the press calls him, an *Etouffeur de Merveilles*.

"It's ridiculous, Gepan can barely run two investigations a year!"

"We cannot increase the financial level," said Gruau again.

"That means putting this research in idle mode, then"

"No, more like a rotating beacon. We keep Gepan alive, but only with current resources."

In other words, some data collection and nothing more.

I am especially impressed by Louange, head of a sophisticated photo-interpretation consulting company. In Madrid he was in charge of an ultraviolet satellite for ESA-Nasa. He seems familiar with the military world. Le Gall, too, impressed me. He is supposed to write a report for Prime Minister Fabius. He listens to everyone without taking notes, and keeps a friendly attitude.

We had lunch with the whole group at *Les Bouchons* in Les Halles, after which Jeffery Kaye went away, to everyone's relief. Allen didn't appreciate the fact that Kaye had invited himself to the morning session, even proclaiming insolently, "Well, I want to know who all these people are..."

Before he left, Jeffery took me aside to tell me that a woman contactee had received a message that "the Frenchman and the Englishman must meet." He concluded the future of this research rested on the two of us, since Allen would soon pass from the scene, which left me very sad. I have no intention to work with Jeffery.

Toulouse. Tuesday 25 June 1985.

Last night the Cnes people had foolishly planned to take us to Orly by metro and train for the flight to Toulouse. When I saw poor Allen dragging his heavy suitcase I rebelled and ordered cabs. Allen stumbled as he came out of the hotel and stepped fully into dog crap, to Niemtzow's laughter. I assured him it was a portent of good luck, but Allen was disgusted. Not only was he unable to buy a *béret*, but Paris is making no progress in cleaning its sidewalks.

Here Cnes has made reservations for us at *Hotel Ariane*, an ill-equipped monstrosity in the middle of a dismal lot no one has bothered to landscape. Across the street are the buildings of Matra, similarly rising among weeds and debris. One can only be amazed at modern French architects as they erect these ugly suburbs without a plan or a design for those who will work and live there.

Our little group dined together in a much more relaxed atmosphere than in Paris, gently mocking the officials ("Gruau is even fatter than before," someone remarked). In the plane to Toulouse I was seated between Allen and Velasco, which gave me a chance to probe his reaction to Jean-Pierre Petit's ugly campaign against him. I urged him not to let such hatred influence him. "Much progress in science has come from people with no academic title," I pointed out.

"Don't worry," Jean-Jacques replied warmly, "I let this kind of attack roll over me. I'm solid enough to take it. I'm the mayor of my village; I understand human nature, and my own limits."

Before retiring for the night Allen, Richard, and I went for a walk in the dark countryside of Toulouse, under a bright starry sky. Allen spoke of his new Center. Obviously it is both a new identity and a burden for him. Niemtzow and I made the same recommendation to him: establish a real Board, a working science group to which we both pledged to belong, suggesting that aerospace engineer John Schuessler should be brought in as well.

A small bus came to pick us up this morning. It took us to the gate of the Space Center, where we faced a problem: Allen had no identification with him! In his absent-minded way, he had left his passport at the hotel, so Velasco had to come and collect us. We drove past some old rockets: Diamant, Véronique, which brought back dusty memories of my unhappy days at Meudon Observatory.

Gepan occupies several large rooms and a small lab where the files of the Gendarmerie are piled up. The turnover in management has resulted in disorganized analysis methods: This is not an active operational center. The office reminds me of a scaled-down version of Blue Book, with its file cabinets and metal closets, and a very incomplete library. We met in a conference room where Mr. Bescombs, Velasco's direct boss, made a brief appearance. Esterle has come over from Paris. Caroff was there too but he remained silent throughout the proceedings. I found out he worked on a Franco-Soviet space project.

We discussed data handling and catalogues. I went over historical details and tried to explain again how an expert system to screen data from the public would save time and money and benefit their operations. They were interested but clearly did not know much about artificial intelligence, how it worked or what it could do.

Once again I had the feeling we were in front of people who were curious and well trained, but who had not been brought together by a common passion. They study the phenomenon as a side issue; they are paid to do it. Tomorrow they could be reassigned to propulsion studies or telemetry. Their questions are those of good engineers, not intensely engaged researchers.

We went on speaking of databases. They demonstrated their system, several features of which have already been lost because the programmers are gone. Young Dr. Mavrakis made an interesting presentation about contactees. He argued they presented typical cases of paraphrenia, characterized by: (1) overvalue of the self; megalomania, inflated pride but also veiled forms of it, as in false modesty; (2) flawed judgement, with no possibility of self-criticism, and zero tolerance for debate; (3) juxtaposition of fantasy and reality; (4) inconsistent social status with an awareness of inferiority, but no persecution complex.

Mavrakis finds that these people have usually experienced a frustrating episode in their lives. Their delusions are consistent, logical, and relatively plausible. They attract disciples easily and are not dangerous. Their fantasy is a source of balance in their lives so the prognosis is often good. They experience remissions following happier events. Occasionally they have hallucinations that respond well to treatment. The approach he recommends is a neutral one, with no argumentation that might increase tension with them.

We had reached the last phase, practical recommendations to Cnes. Allen lost the thread again. He kept insisting there should be official ties between Gepan and his Arizona Center, which is impossible since Gepan can only have "official" ties with national bodies, not private groups.

I suggested that data exchange between us be facilitated (they agreed, since that costs nothing), that they implement an expert system, and that we remain available to them on an individual basis. This was followed by a small press conference, during which we had to tell Allen what to say. He seemed tired, lost, and overly defensive. Niemtzow and I looked at each other with helpless resignation.

Paris. Le Capitole. Friday 28 June 1985.

Yesterday, at *Mercure de France* offices on *rue de Condé* I finally signed the first two contracts for my novels, *Alintel* and *Mémoire de Markov*. Later Simonne and I discussed publication plans and schedules with the editors.

I am thirsty for random walks that this city affords. The substance of a hundred novels lingers in these noble streets. The secret that so many people have been striving for is simple: a secret like ours, Janine, so deep even our closest friends hardly suspect its intensity, uncompromising even under the trappings of an official marriage with its rules and conventions. So I wake up before dawn and think of you with all the sharpness of our separation. I feel a flood of truths washing over me, the truths I don't know how to express in words.

Spring Hill. Saturday 6 July 1985.

We came back in time to enjoy the warm pool, Independence Day, long swims under the galactic display. I am redrawing the plans for the observatory tower. This old ranch is turning into a castle, or an Abbey. Janine has varnished the bookcases I made for the biographies and memoirs we collect. From Paris I brought plaster gargoyles and the lovely statuette from Goa.

In the last few days of my stay in France I had dinner with Claude Poher. He kindly drove to Paris to pick me up along with Maman, and took us to his house in *Saint Quentin des Yvelines* near Montigny. He told us of his utter disgust with French academic science. His skeptical colleagues have always declined to investigate in the field with him, even refusing to meet the witnesses in the best cases. For a whole year he corresponded with cosmologist Evry Schatzman, who conceded that several UFO cases escaped analysis in conventional terms, but simply stopped corresponding when he ran out of arguments.

Claude is remarried with a woman doctor, a blonde pediatrician named Danielle. They live in a modern home in the heart of a new town. He drove us around to show us the wasteful displays erected by the new architects. Claude is as busy as ever, building an airplane in his garage and an electronic organ upstairs. Overall he seems satisfied. But the great potential of this man has been negated by the stupidity of false scientists.

Over dinner at *Le Mors aux Dents* Simonne recalled for me her memories of the Gaullist era. She explained to me how the General had restructured French institutions in six short months when he came back to power. She also told me what it was like during "*la Déchirure*," the break between De Gaulle and Pompidou. She will never publish her experiences of that time, unfortunately.

She put the discussion on the topic of SRI research: "I've heard that the project has changed form," she said, "it has gone operational." I told her I knew nothing about that.

I have drawn two conclusions from the Toulouse meeting: first, Richard Niemtzow has convinced me that there was a secret project within the U.S. government. In the Cash-Landrum case there were 23 helicopters around a flying object that melted the asphalt in the road and injured three people.

These helicopters had been borrowed from an Army base by a group with extensive powers. The road was repaired the next day, the median strip repainted, all traces erased...

Second conclusion: if the government were to decide to launch a campaign for the "revelation" of fake UFOs (possibly in support of a political plan relying on strategic surprise) such manipulation could succeed. Even scientifically trained people would embrace such revelations because they are eager to be vindicated in their belief in extraterrestrials.

Hyde Street. Sunday 7 July 1985.

I have reconstructed Gepan's organization chart, starting with Prime Minister Fabius and Hubert Curien as minister of research and industry. Two agencies are involved: Dieli (with Lefevre and Le Gall) and Cnes, headed up by 50-year-old mathematician Lions. They maintain contact with the Soviets through Migouline.

Within Cnes the power gets divided between Colonel Gruau, who is inspector general, and general manager Dellest, former President of Arianespace. The head of the Toulouse facility is Bescombs, who supervises Gepan. Jean-Jacques Velasco is at the end of this long line. On the science board are Pellat, who wants the work to stop, and Perrin de Brichambaut, who thinks it should continue.

San Diego. Sunday 14 July 1985.

Allen Hynek has sent me his draft of a letter to Senator Goldwater to report on our French trip, suggesting a private meeting. The text surprised and saddened me: Allen's sentences are half-formed, with grossly misshaped syntax.

Now Olivier invites me to La Jolla to lecture about computer networking at the Western Behavioral Sciences Institute.

I resigned from the Board of InfoMedia today. This marks the end of a long road, nearly ten years. We are still guarantors of the company's line of credit ($105,000), however. Ren's father, a banker, will run the business, but he is no software entrepreneur.

Hyde Street. Sunday 21 July 1985.

Alain Esterle came over for dinner on Thursday. He wanted to talk about business, his plan to spend a year at Stanford and perhaps develop microgravity technology. When we spoke of Gepan, his attitude convinced me he had never had any passion for the job. We spoke of Allen, whom he had found in bad shape. He was shocked by the mispellings in his proposals to Cnes, where Allen wrote "acceive" instead of "achieve" and "Vellasa" instead of "Velasco." I am afraid Jeffery and Fred are right about his declining health.

Yesterday Teish came over. We drove to Spring Hill, regaled along the way by colorful tales of her life as a priestess of Erzulie-Oshun. We went swimming, took walks in the sumptuous woods.

Hyde Street. Wednesday 24 July 1985.

On the way to lunch with Hal yesterday I drove by Menlo College. A wave of memories flooded me, from the days when my little son went there; my eyes filled with tears. I was not sad: it was a quiet, sweet emotion of the passage of time. I saw Olivier in San Diego recently. He now teaches computer networking to a group that includes Michael Crichton and Marlon Brando. My son has become a valued colleague.

Hal and I had a lot to talk about. He is leaving the area, a fact the "client" in Washington doesn't know yet. Neither Ed May nor Jim Salyer or even Ingo are aware of it: there will be an abrupt transition.

There was a meeting on frontier subjects in Washington recently. When Hal arrived he discovered the topic was UFOs, and the overall project was structured in multiple layers, like an onion. The meeting was classified above top secret, under a codeword. Fifteen attendees reviewed cases like Kirtland AFB, Cash-Landrum and Tehran. They included Howell McConnell and John Tyler. Kit had been invited but couldn't attend.

Two aspects of the meeting were ironic, Hal said. First, attendees were there because they ran programs that were impacted by unidentified signals but they were not necessarily interested in the UFO phenomenon itself.

Second irony: they came to the conclusion there must be a secret UFO project, *somewhere else*! Does the government have in its custody some saucer fragments? Perhaps it does not know what to do with them, someone suggested. Perhaps American industry should be given access to the supposed hoard of alien treasures? Perhaps it already has? In the absence of any hard fact this remains wild speculation, even at such high levels of the government.

Hyde Street. Saturday 27 July 1985.

Janine flew off to France on an unplanned trip this morning. Her mother is in the hospital for a kidney operation. Catherine has risen to the occasion, taking charge of our house.

Hal has put his California house on the market. He has an office waiting for him in Austin. I spent one last evening with him, before he left for Texas, to show him the extent of my files. He seemed fairly astounded when he saw how much ground I'd covered without funding and without fanfare. He left with a proposal from me that he will take to the Washington group (which I now nickname the "Secret Onion") on August sixth.

Hyde Street. Tuesday 30 July 1985.

Bill Calvert, one of my most trusted sources, called me on Friday with some urgency. "I've heard about a new group in Washington," he began, "a high-level project headed up by John Alexander, an Army expert. They study UFOs. Fifteen participants are positive; five are negative about UFO reality. One of them is John Gardner, who controls billions of dollars, probably for Star Wars. Creation of the group seems to have been precipitated by rumors started by the Soviets. They have hinted to their friends in Washington that they had pieces of a saucer and didn't know what to do with them."

"How did you learn all this?" I asked, astonished that the supposedly classified group ("above top secret" Hal had told me, swearing me to silence) was already compromised.

"I heard it from Jack Houck, an engineer at McDonnell in Huntington Beach. He is a student of a woman friend of mine, a medium in L.A. He keeps bringing her some CIA types who give her coordinates and ask her what she sees. The sites they give her are always in the Soviet Union. Everybody knows that Puthoff and Swann are doing this at SRI and that the government has gone operational with it. You know how it is. Jack Houck also believes there's a giant UFO base in Brazilian jungles."

So I called Hal, suggesting lunch, and I confronted him with the leak of his "supersecret" information. Hal was shocked when he heard it: "After all the care we took to define the secret according to different layers of the Onion," he said, "we've already failed! The idea was to dangle our collective skills before whoever is running the Big Project. Now that will never happen; we blew it again!"

I reminded him that anything known to more than five people couldn't be kept secret. The French *Résistance* relied on groups of three. I also pointed out the Soviet game was far from clear in all this. Perhaps they dangled their supposed "saucer hardware" to see what reaction they would get in Washington: who would rise to the bait; a cheap way to flush out the experts. "At least you've got to admit my own information is pretty good," I pointed out as he left.

Hyde Street. Wednesday 31 July 1985.

Bad news from France. Janine just called to say that surgery had disclosed her mother had cancer, and it had spread. The doctors removed a kidney but entertained little hope for the long-term success of radiation treatment—a few years' remission at most.

Hyde Street. Sunday 4 August 1985.

Olivier is here in San Francisco, visiting old friends. Catherine is cooking steaks for our dinner. I savor every day with my children: soon they will be gone, leading independent lives. We talk and argue, we go out to the Hippo for lunch. But Janine called again this morning with sad news, complications from the surgery, which I didn't have the heart to mention to my children. I only asked them to call the hospital with me. Their grandmother's voice was weak but she was conscious, and happy to hear them.

Now I learn that Allen will be operated for prostate cancer. Niemtzow had suggested radiation but Allen followed other counsel. His Scottsdale secretary told me he was in Canada. He will be operated on in St. Louis and will return to Arizona to recover.

UFOs continue to be reported. I feel flush with project ideas, with the love of my kids, with a sense of mysterious emotion. Yet I also feel that I am missing something, some signal, a force trying to call my attention, a subtle presence off-stage.

Hyde Street. Monday 5 August 1985.

The Board of EarthData, Peter Banks' fledgling remote sensing company, met this morning to discuss satellite strategy with John Egan, from the same branch of Coopers & Lybrand where Rod Frederickson went to work. Casually, I asked how he was.

"Rod Frederickson is dead," said Egan drily.

The news left me stupefied. Rod brought me to California, hired me at Stanford. "He was only 43. Massive coronary, while rowing on Chesapeake Bay. We were stunned," John added.

Shit, I thought. I felt such admiration and loyalty for him. Rod was always searching, never content with what he knew.

Hyde Street. Friday 9 August 1985.

Janine comes back from France tonight. Her mother is about to be operated on for the third time. I told the children the doctors were worried, to prepare them for the worst. The world is cold and tragically foggy. I think of your pain, far away over there. I am not hungry, and don't feel like writing.

Clouds are dragging low over the Bay. The *New Jersey* and the *Enterprise* are steaming by, crushing the grayness: forty years ago the United States won the ugly war in the Pacific.

Hyde Street. Monday 26 August 1985.

Yesterday Janine and I attended Bob Weiss' wedding in Hollywood. Our film project is making progress; the contract has been signed for *FastWalker*, but we have yet to develop a good script.

We went to Spring Hill with Olivier on Saturday and played in the pool for hours. The night was magnificent: the moon in crescent, warm air scented with apple smells. But when I called Arizona and spoke to Tina and Brian they gave me worrying news about Allen: he was scheduled to give a lecture in Boston, but as he stepped to the podium he was unable to go on. Paramedics were called as he fainted. A few days later however, the devil of a man was in Florida visiting his friend Willy Smith and working on his case catalogue. He is scheduled to enter the hospital on September 4 and to undergo a prostate operation the next day.

Allen occasionally has trouble breathing and shows confused thinking, as we saw in Paris. When he presented the Center before the wealthy folks of Scottsdale the confusion was so obvious that Jeffery Kaye had to deliver the conclusion himself. This is the reason for Kaye's continued pressure on me to take over from Allen. But I have no inclination to run such a group, no matter how well intentioned.

Hal sends me a note from Texas, where his own institute is now established. He tells me that my proposal is included in what we still jokingly call the *Secret Onion*, because of the layers of increasing secrecy around the core people. Leaks have been stopped. John Alexander's horse had already fled the barn, however.

Once again I have tried to read the book by Stuart Holroyd, *Prelude to the Landing on Planet Earth*, relating the adventures of Dr. Puharich, Phyllis Schlemmer and Sir John Whitmore with Hoova (**12**). Again I had to stop before page 50, lost amidst silly proclamations by supposed extraterrestrials. I may see Puharich again at a conference in Costa Rica in October. I'll be curious to hear if he is still getting messages from the sky.

My geologist friend Gerald Askevold has called from Montana. He asked me to come give a lecture for a state education conference in April. He told me the sad news of the death of Elizabeth Michaels, our colleague from Stanford days, in a car accident last month.

Hyde Street. Sunday 8 September 1985.

Allen was operated on in St. Louis three days ago. He tells me the surgeons removed the whole prostate tumor. He should be back in

Scottsdale in two weeks. I agreed to work with him as he organizes the new center, and this cheered him up.

Journalist Jack Anderson has exposed (**13**) our SRI team's work with Pat Price and Project *Grill Flame*, blowing the cover: "One of the institute's top psychics, given only the geographic coordinates, described the Semipalatinsk nuclear facility in Soviet central Asia in detail only confirmed afterward by spy satellite photos."

Driving through San Francisco at one o'clock in the damp morning, I can hear the waves across the dunes along the Pacific Coast Highway. A piano piece plays on the radio to the beat of the windshield wipers. Tires squeal at the turn of the Cliff House. The traffic lights on Geary Street stretch out in the steady rain like a tunnel. My tired body seems to hold all the answers of life; all the answers, but few of the questions. Above Ghirardelli Square the view reveals the diamond necklace of the Bay, from Tiburon to Berkeley. The water is an abyss of blackness. Janine's body is warm as I slip into bed next to her.

Hyde Street. Sunday 15 September 1985.

We worked hard at the ranch: gutters to clean, fences to mend, bushes to trim. Long talks with my daughter about cars, life, and jobs. She detests business life, especially computers.

Tina called with more bad news. While Allen was in Saint Louis for the prostate operation the doctors did a brain scan and found a large tumor, as we should have known from the signs of mental confusion. He will be operated in San Francisco in two weeks. We have offered to Mimi to stay with us during his hospitalization.

Spring Hill. Saturday 21 September 1985.

What are Allen's chances of survival? Fred tells me the tumor is a glioma, a tumor of nerve cells, located in the left posterior temporal lobe, 5 cm in diameter. "They can probably remove most of it," he said, "but the edges of such tumors remain active, and they are ill-defined. That's why he comes to UCSF neurology department, a top institution. Dr. Charles Wilson will supervise the operation."

"What do you expect as a prognosis?" I asked.

"Allen may be all right for six months; then his quality of life will deteriorate inexorably. He doesn't seem to realize what is going on."

Hyde Street. Sunday 22 September 1985.

Allen called this morning: He flies in tomorrow morning. Fred will meet me at the airport and I will drive them to UCSF. The old positive energy does remain in Allen's voice. After thanking us for putting our house at Mimi's disposal he even told me: "If all goes well, we'll have to go out on the town and celebrate!" Yet all of us (Tina, Fred, and Niemtzow) now feel guilty for not having alerted Allen to the problem much sooner. Tina had noticed his confusion as soon as he came back from Norway. But as Fred remarked ironically, Allen's lectures were never models of order and clarity; he was easily led onto tangential improvisations, one of his charms.

On Thursday I attended a meeting at Apple with Steward Brand, John Markoff and half a dozen developers of computer message systems. The consensus was that the technology was still ahead of the market. Steve Jobs had just resigned from Apple, so the company was in disarray. We saw an unconvincing demo of Apple-link.

A new scandal is shaking the French government: their goons have blown up a Greenpeace ship in a New Zealand harbor, killing an innocent photographer.

Somebody had to take the blame, so the Defense minister, an old friend of Mitterrand named Hernu, has resigned. Greenpeace was trying to expose the stupidity of France's continued atomic tests in the South Pacific. Now the entire world is scandalized by the killing.

Boston. Wednesday 25 September 1985.

Staying at Stouffer's Inn in Bedford. I feel tired, sad about Allen's illness, confused about my own direction. "It's the weight of the years," jokes Janine: I turned 46 yesterday. Back in Bayeux Janine's mother is home, at the farmhouse in Brunville again, among the things she loves, and in Annick's gentle care.

Allen landed in San Francisco on Monday with Mimi. He looked frail, walked slowly. Fred urged me to put up a good front, to cheer up our old friend. As we walked over to the baggage claim Allen took me aside: "You'll be glad to know that I've cut off relations with Jeffery Kaye," he said. "He doesn't understand science."

I drove them to the University of California medical center on Parnassus. The long painful wait for registration began: papers, blood tests, room assignment. They put Allen in a wheelchair and took him away. The rest of us drove to our house so Mimi could settle down. We went out to dinner together, and then Mimi took my car to return to the hospital.

Allen was operated on yesterday at noon, for over five hours. Surgeons removed most of the tumor but they had to leave one section that touches a vein. Richard Sigismond, who jumped on a plane from Denver as soon as he heard Allen was hospitalized, was with Mimi when Allen woke up. He recognized them, said a few words. Here in Massachusetts I can only recall the years of our friendship, and cry about the inevitable.

Spring Hill. Sunday 29 September 1985.

Allen is recovering but he is naturally worried. He searches for words and occasionally loses coordination. Mimi spends every day at the hospital. Sigismond told me of a remark by Allen, when it became clear he would undergo the operation in San Francisco: "At least I'll have the pleasure to see Jacques."

During my stay in Manhattan I visited the offices of Alan Patricof on Madison, but had to shorten my meetings when the building was evacuated because of a hurricane. I walked back to the Algonquin; no cabs anywhere, the sidewalks littered with umbrellas bent by the wind. Airline flights were cancelled, store windows taped. With a free evening ahead, I called Ingo who agreed joyously to have dinner with me at a Chinese place near Bowery Street. The disintegrating project at SRI, in the wake of Hal's departure, has left him in uncertain circumstances. There is talk about his continuing to work with Ed May, but Ingo doesn't trust Jim Salyer, the federal monitor, who tried to get him fired last year.

"So Jacques, since you are psychic, how do you see my future?" he asked in his calm and smooth way. I nearly chocked on my beef *à l'orange* and laughed.

"Ingo, you've only taught me the first three levels!"

"To Hell with the levels, use your abilities."

"I see you writing, studying things that were blocked when you were heavily involved in the project."

We walked back to his apartment and watched the new *Twilight Zone*. I expressed my dismay at the Jack Anderson article that exposed *Grill Flame*. Ingo told me the leak came from a member of the National Security Council. The man finds the research interesting but he doesn't take the operational aspects seriously. He spilled the beans before a colleague of Anderson in trade for information on other topics: a lesson for the future, you cannot trust the government.

A cab drove me back to the Algonquin and as we turned into 44th Street a police car rammed us. The cops took it all as a joke, saying they just hadn't paid attention to where they were going. My poor driver had borrowed a friend's cab to make a few dollars, so he was in an irregular situation. The NYPD laughed in his face when he tried to complain. Just another day in the big city.

Hollywood. Friday 4 October 1985.

Staying at the Franklin Plaza suites. I have failed to find a French publisher for *Computer Message Systems*: Masson, an academic house, turned it down. They believe they know everything about networking because the French built the Minitel! They told me the Internet would never amount to anything.

In San Francisco we now sleep downstairs while Mimi uses the master bedroom. She spends every day with Allen, who is getting a bit better but is still unable to walk unaided. I spoke to him yesterday for the first time since the operation. He understood everything I said but had trouble forming words and got tired quickly.

I also spoke to Hal and Adrienne: both thanked me for the advice I had given Hal, to regard a proposed career move positively. "Hal has always had a negative perception of change," Adrienne said. "The first upheaval in his life was his father's death when he was 13. But Hal was struck by your argument about intersecting exponentials, the fact that every technology that becomes mature is overtaken by a newer one that comes from below."

Spring Hill. Sunday 6 October 1985.

It rains here. We listen to Luisa Teish's lecture tapes. Allen is stable but he went through deep depression yesterday and gave Mimi his last wishes. Yet when I spoke to him on Saturday, and stupidly told him, "We will do all we can to make your stay more..." it was Allen who completed my awkward sentence: "Under other circumstances one would say *pleasant*, right?" Therefore he has retained his understanding of nuances and access to language. Catherine has given him her radio, his only distraction at the moment.

Hyde Street. Monday 7 October 1985.

We spent the night at the Silverado Country Club where I gave a lecture on the management impact of computer networks before the Young Presidents organization. Neither Janine nor I can get comfortable with the display of wealth in Napa Valley, all those clean tennis courts and impeccably maintained golf courses for the so-called elite. In a few days I leave for the Costa Rica conference on paranormal research.

El Salvador. Friday 11 October 1985.

The plane gains altitude through woolly clouds. When they part one can see wide green swamps, cultivated fields, rows of palm trees and some thatch-roofed structures crushed by all the greenery. Janine drove me to the airport with Mimi, whom we had picked up at the hospital. She said Allen was stable but terribly depressed, to the point where he wanted no visitors and requested that she let him take an overdose of sleeping pills. Yet he doesn't suffer physically. He asked her to read passages of Rudolf Steiner. He struggles hard to preserve his lucidity, his ability to think.

Now I am flying above the beaches of South America to a meeting of researchers who will debate the higher functions of consciousness. Back in San Francisco, Allen is struggling to stay conscious and there is nothing I can do to help him.

San Jose, Costa Rica. Saturday 12 October 1985.

The sky is black, pregnant with rain. I saw some of the city, the library and a public park with a statue of some statesman. The conference has begun with the lack of focus that gives Latin America its charm. It does represent an opportunity to renew contacts with friends and fellows in research. My California friend Gretchen is on the organizing staff along with Carlos Ortiz and a government official who speeded up custom formalities when I landed.

Salvador Freixedo arrived in the afternoon with a young blonde woman, his new wife. We had dinner together. A former Puerto Rico Jesuit, Salvador bitterly laments wasting 30 years of his life in the service of the Order. He takes revenge in thunderous blasphemy against all gods, including extraterrestrial powers. He says they do exist, but their only goal is to exploit mankind's psychic energies. As for the Alien visitors of which abductees speak so fondly, he thinks they are diabolical impostors who can teach us nothing.

One of my correspondents, Monica Williams has come here from Ecuador, where she works in a bank and spends her free time foraging in search of esoteric books. She is very smart, with a kind, incisive turn of mind.

I woke up happy, at ease in the Latin atmosphere, a welcome escape from anglosaxon stuffiness. Freixedo tells me, “What is important is to be fully human.” John Keel is supposed to come tomorrow in the same plane as Puharich and Berlitz. Monica tells me he lives in New York in poor circumstances, sick from hypoglycemia and a lithium deficiency that forces him to lie down every few hours. I spoke to Janine, on the phone in the sunshine of Spring Hill. She said Allen was stationary. His son Joel will come to see him tomorrow and spend the night at our house. His visit will surely cheer up our old friend.

San Jose, Costa Rica. Sunday 13 October 1985.

A local researcher named Rafael came over at breakfast with his 14-year old son Gustavo who passionately wants to be an astronaut. The shy enthusiasm of the boy and the obvious pride and love of his father moved me deeply. We spoke for a long time, and I tried to give Gustavo some heartfelt advice.

Professor Aguilar, an archeologist, offered to drive us to a site he is exploring in the mountains, so we climbed up in a jeep with Javier Cabrera, the Peruvian physician who claims to have assembled a collection of carved stones dating from prehistory. The stones are controversial but Cabrera strongly believes in their ancient origin.

The jeep dashed along an impossible road climbing the flanks of the Irazù volcano, deep into a gorgeous jungle site where blue butterflies the size of birds played among the flowers. Aguilar showed us a series of constructions with large flat stones, carved by whom? And for what purpose?

On the way back we stopped to admire some granite spheres that baffle local specialists. One hypothesis states they are magical tools, amplifiers of spiritual powers. Remote viewing them only led me to general impressions: altitude, a wooden platform, large leaves with scalloped edges, red color, a broad expense of red; but nothing specific regarding location or purpose, and I could not "view" the workers at the site.

San Jose, Costa Rica. Tuesday 15 October 1985.

Yesterday I gave my lecture in Spanish. The questions lasted for an hour. Interestingly, I was later told that the Soviet ambassador to Costa Rica had attended my presentation.

Flying back over Guatemala. Friday 18 October 1985.

The sun goes down over the Pacific, throwing strange blue and red splashes into the clouds. I am bringing back many addresses of people who want to stay in contact, as well as some books, golden earrings Rafael's sons have given me for Catherine, and an alleged metal piece from a flying saucer.

The conference had started well. John Keel, whom I have grown to appreciate, spoke intensely of his research, his worries, and his "larvae." All of us found ourselves on another excursion at the very top of Irazù where contactee Enrique Castillo told us his story of involvement with U.S. interrogators who flew him to a place near Washington to probe his story at great length. The Irazù site is magnificent, with dark precipices over sulphurous ponds, black powder under foot, red stones, a true landscape of Hell. Puharich walked along the lip of the crater. John Lilly was with us too, as well as Freixedo and Ortiz.

Puharich, who now cultivates a resemblance with Einstein, lectured the assembly about his latest unified theory of psychic effects. He explains everything with low frequency radiation (ELF), applying it even to psychokinetics and levitation without the slightest proof for what he says. He claims ELF even explains weather changes and the AIDS epidemic: those wily Russians, based in Cuba, have been beaming forbidden frequencies over us, triggering deadly properties in the otherwise benign HIV virus, he said... His lecture began as a bizarre rambling and ended in irresponsible fantasy. The audience seemed to swallow these absurd statements as if they were witnessing a major event in modern physics. They lined up to buy metal bracelets from him at $36 each. They are supposed to immunize them against the ill effects of ELF waves and AIDS.

I left in disgust. The next day Father Freixedo gave a grand speech against all deities, preaching with that wonderful thunder that Catholic orators can throw around with such flair. Salvador is permanently locked in magnificent combat with the Angel. He will die with his sword in hand. In contrast Andrija Puharich still staggers in response to what he believes to be guiding instructions from unknown superiors on Hoova, psychic emanations of his own mind.

Now we fly somewhere over Guatemala. The pilot is trying to go around a big thunderstorm.

I remember a few vignettes from the conference: Gretchen telling me about her distress during the deadly earthquake in Mexico City, the deserted streets among tall buildings where all the glass panes had fallen from the windows, and all those useless curtains blowing in the air over a landscape of debris.

John Keel at 55 looked sick, but underneath his rough New York persona is a warm, intelligent man who genuinely seeks understanding and friendship. I liked it when he told Puharich, "If you stopped talking to Hoova you would fall into some other entity's orbit, you'd start believing in Ashtar, or Clarion..."

The most puzzling conversation I had was with Enrique Castillo. After his observation (**14**) he was "invited" by some mysterious American who flew him to Washington. He gave me a detailed description of his interrogations, of the house where he was given extensive tests and injections.

Enrique also told me about the Bogota specimen, a fragment of light silvery metal gathered after an incident in which a flying disk appeared about to crash, ejected some molten material and stabilized. He gave me the specimen, which I sealed into an envelope, asking them to sign it to start a chain of evidence. I promised to do a new analysis of its composition (**15**).

Hyde Street. Sunday 20 October 1985.

With only a few hours to pack another suitcase on my way to Boston, I think back over the Costa Rica conference. Puharich remains a mystery. He told me some things in private, claiming that Geller's lectures and all the media excitement around him were just a cover for something else that I had to promise not to reveal. Uri is selling his houses in France and Mexico, as well as his mansionette in Connecticut, to make his home in London.

Spring Hill. Saturday 26 October 1985.

On the phone, Simonne tells me that *Alintel* will be out early in February. As for French venture capital, it leaves me cold. This community revolves around narrow interests and bourgeois values that turn me off: "Is the *Polo de Bagatelle* a better club that the *Racing*? Should one play tennis in Enghien, ride in Rambouillet?" I find it hard to conform to this model. It reflects both the arrogance and the insecurities of the French upper class, *les notables*.

We managed to run away to the ranch today. The weather is beautiful all over Mendocino County. The trees are yellow, brown, red, and purple. My daughter paints the fences while the flag of Spring Hill flies over our little retreat from the world. Janine takes me in her arms, cuddles me, and reassures me: "I am only a traveller on this Earth, I will go anywhere with you."

Last Sunday I saw Allen at UCSF, where he has stayed over a month now. He had requested my visit. I was touched that I was the only person he had wanted to see, other than Mimi and their son Joel. I found my old mentor sitting in a chair, his hair starting to grow back, the scar barely visible on his scalp. His eyes were clear, and quite aware. He spoke without difficulty but his frailty was obvious. He was so emaciated that he looked like Gandhi.

I spoke to him of Costa Rica. "I would have liked to be there," he said when I showed him my pictures of John Keel and Puharich. He was interested in Castillo's story, saying he was envious of the shadowy government folks who evidently follow these cases from the depth of their agencies. He reminded me of his discussion on the subject with Linda Howe. Mimi was surprised and happy as she followed our conversation; she had feared these memories were lost.

As I related Puharich's statements about AIDS Allen remarked with sad tiredness, "People like him can afford to be completely irresponsible. I almost envy their freedom from any standards. You and I are scientists first, we could never launch into such wild speculation."

He wanted me to see what he had to go through. He still needs help for every move, because he has not regained use of his legs, one of the disappointments following the operation. He told me the nights were horrible: Nobody to talk to. One evening he tried to read but a nurse came in and forced him to turn off the light. We spoke of Rudolf Steiner. Mimi has never taken much interest in his works, which admittedly are rather obscure. I will give her Steiner's biography, which is a little more accessible.

On Monday Allen left the hospital. Mimi took him back to Arizona. They arrived safely but Allen needed oxygen during the flight. He gets tired quickly, can only read in short stretches, but he is strongly motivated to walk again. Sunshine will be good for him.

10

Spring Hill. Sunday 10 November 1985.

Time passes differently here, Janine observes with pleasure. In the city one is always pulled aside by obligations and opportunities, or lost in meaningless haze. But here every minute takes a special place; every hour has its proper light, a savor, a texture.

It rained when we arrived yesterday with Sandra, so we spent the evening by the fire in conversation, the light from the flames dancing on the open beams in the big room. She gave us an eloquent lecture about Hindu philosophies and the San Francisco underground she knows well.

Hyde Street. Sunday 17 November 1985.

We flew to Texas on Wednesday. Janine had not come back to Austin since 1963, and I had only returned once, so we looked at the city with new eyes when Hal picked us up at the airport and drove us around. Austin is now nestled in the wide loops of several freeways that did not exist when we lived there. Hal and Adrienne are at ease in a magnificent house that is an ideal environment for their kids. They have embraced a macrobiotic diet and an outdoor lifestyle.

The next day we went to the Institute for Advanced Studies at Austin, where we met Bill Church and his brother, as well as Ken Shoulders, laboratory genius, former electrical engineer at SRI and NSA consultant. I had brought the Bogota metal sample, which we extracted from the signed envelope. We took photographs and recorded the operation to authenticate the analysis, which Ken began by sawing off a corner of the specimen. Later we took it to the University for analysis. We found mostly aluminum with phosphorus, nitrogen and oxygen. The structure validates the story I was told during my trip, of a molten mass falling into a pool of rainwater on the road, but of course it doesn't prove conclusively that any Alien craft was involved.

On Thursday we had lunch with Bill Church at the Austin Country Club where women wore shorts and high hairdos as they did 20 years ago. The small town atmosphere is in contrast with Hal's revolutionary physical concepts. Bill Church is a bright fellow, somewhat taciturn. He was a typical math student, rather bohemian, until his father died and he found himself trying to run *Church's Fried Chicken* with his brothers. They floundered for a while, finally deciding to turn all management over to him. He gave up his academic studies and in a few years built a great company.

When *Church's Fried Chicken* went public he folded a 28 million dollar check into his favorite philosophy book, went to the bank with it, and his next visit was to Cleve Backster, expert practitioner of the lie detector, offering to support his paranormal research on plants. Backster told him he didn't need any money but he had just received a worthwhile paper from Hal about a possible experiment to verify the existence of the elusive tachyon particles (**16**). Bill Church met Hal and Adrienne and began a long association with them. Ken's discoveries and Hal's theories have resulted in 18 patents, but the government might pre-empt any practical use of these inventions in the name of national security. Among other devices they have a technique using super-electrons (charged clusters of 10^{23} electrons)

Fig. 9. In Costa Rica with Enrique Castillo, John Keel, Salvatore Freixedo, Charles Berlitz, October 1985.

Fig. 10. Last meeting with Allen Hynek, Scottsdale, November 1985.

capable of punching holes in titanium plates with the energy of an ordinary flashlight.

Hal's work on theoretical extensions of general relativity leads to techniques for the manipulation of the vacuum index of refraction and to prediction of many phenomena reported in UFO cases: objects vanishing on the spot, and apparent fast departure with the object's dimensions decreasing while time expands. He thinks it might also explain those elusive craft with diminutive occupants.

On Friday we left Austin for Phoenix, where Mimi awaited us. Paul Hynek, now a tall and serious young man, met us at the house on Vista Drive. Allen was sitting proudly in front of his new IBM PC where he had typed a welcoming message. He got up with the help of his walker and came to the living room with us.

Richard Sigismond, who had flown in from Denver, regaled us with his latest stories. Allen has just undergone his first radiation session. He spoke more fluently and coherently, although he still sought some elusive words. Mimi deployed enormous energy and strong optimism.

Allen told me that Cufos, from Chicago, had sent a sternly worded letter to Tina and Brian, forbidding them from using Hynek's name in connection with their work. This saddened Allen, who gave Tina credit for bringing him to the freedom of Arizona, although he no longer wants to be associated with Jeffery Kaye. Mimi told me that Allen came alive when he was with me, noting the bright exchange of energy and stimulation between us. I found him wounded but not destroyed, and his sense of humor has returned.

Spring Hill. Saturday 23 November 1985.

Storm over the ranch. The night is cold. White fog and dark flashes of rain soak the hills, as in Chinese watercolors. Hal's new physical considerations center on the dielectric constant of space (designated as "K") that expresses the relationship between gravitation and other physical properties of space. A Princeton physicist named Dicke has published several relevant articles along these lines in *Physical*

Review. Hal cites an equation giving the speed of light in a polarized vacuum as the ratio of "c" to K.

Another relevant relationship is that of the frequency of the light emitted by an atom to the gravitational potential produced by a polarized vacuum. Steve Weinberg's difficult book *Gravitation and Cosmology* **(17)** gives the details. Einstein's relativity states that space is curved in the vicinity of mass but it does not explain it. Dicke's theory would transform space into a gravitational lens in the vicinity of mass. All this is standard physics, but Hal extends the formulation, showing that many of the reported characteristics of UFOs, including the more bizarre ones, remain consistent with general relativity.

"Using the proper wave equation for the space dielectric constant, one might be able to lower the mass of an object to zero and to raise the speed of light (divided by K) in that region," said Hal, scribbling equations on a piece of paper. "The process would also shift black body radiation so that the object would emit large amounts of light; albeit useless light, mind you, merely an exhaust, as well as UVs and X-rays." Is this why UFOs are so luminous and cause physiological damage? Hal speculates that the visible light they emit is infrared radiation shifted into the visible range.

News about Jack Houck: he will not be involved in UFO research with the government group after all, restricting his activity to PK. Hal tells me this results from official reactions when it became obvious that news of the Secret Onion's existence had somehow leaked to his New Age friends. The group has now given a briefing on UFOs to the Under Secretary for Defense. They requested copies of my biography and my proposal.

"If they give us a green light, I'll have to get organized," I told Hal.

"You won't be the only one," he replied. "If they give us a green light, about 20 people will have to get organized."

As a first step, Hal's institute is paying Jim McCampbell to fly to New Mexico, where he will visit a witness who claims there is a UFO base near Albuquerque. The man's name is Paul Bennewitz. I have little confidence in Jim for this kind of research and the move raises questions for me about the seriousness of the proposed group.

As in the case of *Grill Flame*, a super-secret project that was exposed to the press by a member of NSC, the Committee may prove unable to conduct the discreet work I consider essential. My own reaction is to keep the key data to myself and lower my profile.

Hyde Street. Monday 2 December 1985.

Olivier came over for Thanksgiving, a happy interlude amidst our sadness at news from France. Janine's mother has undergone another operation and her deteriorating health concerns us. Life is dragging on. My great joy is Janine, her head on my shoulder in the morning when we make quiet plans for the day; and the great beauty of Spring Hill, even when the rain keeps falling over the dark trees.

The phenomenon is getting closer: there was a UFO sighting in Redwood Valley, near our ranch. Three children camping in their backyard heard a strong "whoosh" about one o'clock. They saw an object that flew from south to north, turned and went southwest. They described it as red on the outside and blue-green inside, "the size of a beach ball." It appeared to halt briefly "over the neighbor's tree." The central part stopped spinning. At that moment the children had a curious sensation. One nearly fainted; another started crying without any reason. I won't have an opportunity to investigate the case, however: in a few days I must be in Europe again.

Paris. Rue de la Clef. Saturday 7 December 1985.

Bombs have gone off in two department stores: the *Printemps* and *Galeries Lafayette*, wounding 30 people. Paris is scared. People look pale, with drawn faces from the cold and the bad news; even the punks at *Les Halles* who try so hard to look mean.

At the giant "Fnac" bookstore young readers sit on the floor and devour the latest cartoons. It amuses me to see that *Dark Satellite* is still on the shelf after more than 20 years. Yet I don't feel I belong in this Paris of concrete and plastic, with its hellish subterranean corridors and escalators to nausea.

Recalling old times with her family, my mother tells me stories of her father, who owned a fur and leather workshop on *Rue du Chemin Vert*. She used to go there as a little girl; he put her to work chopping off the animals' legs.

In 1910 there was a disastrous flood in Paris, everything got spoiled, the family ruined. Monsieur Passavant, in haughty protestant contempt, refused any financial compensation.

Overnight the family had to survive on a meager budget. As the elder sister, my mother had to quit school and take care of a dozen siblings.

Paris. Rue de la Clef. Saturday 14 December 1985.

I had dinner with Jean Pineau (the no. 2 man at *Air Liquide*) to discuss venture capital. At the next table were three tall Black men who spoke of nothing but extraterrestrials! Pineau, who has read my books, was struck by this coincidence: an *intersign*?

There were other strange episodes during the trip, and an especially curious one when I finally met occult expert Roland Villeneuve in his apartment on Rue Monge, near my mother's place. His bookcases were filled with ancient volumes. I saw a framed Baphomet by Giger and some fantastic paintings on the walls. He was skeptical of contact stories: "Don't you think many of these people are inventing their experiences?" he asked.

He was right about many of them, I said, but missed the deeper phenomenon in spite of his wide scholarship on sorcery and occult traditions. We came to talk about Anton LaVey, whom he characterizes as naïve:

"He speaks of Satan as if the Devil never asked for anything in return for his services," he said. "But he always wants something: a life, a soul, or at least some blood, a sacrifice..."

I left Villeneuve, walked a short way down Rue Monge, and found the sidewalk blocked by emergency teams around firetrucks and ambulances at the Censier Métro station, whose gates were closed. Someone had just committed suicide by jumping on the tracks.

Spring Hill. Saturday 21 December 1985.

Returning to Paris to find the cold again, I saw my brother, and Astrid Merlo who rents a luxurious apartment on *Ile Saint Louis*.

Simonne organized another simple dinner for me with Patrick Aimedieu, one of the few French scientists engaged in serious parapsychology research. I found him somber; he said that the field was dying under the absurd attacks of self-styled rationalists: "We only have 50 members in the *Institut Métapsychique*, and they have to pass the hat among themselves to pay the rent."

The trip was a success with several investment projects, notably a deal with a computer company called LineData and a venture seminar at Sophia Antipolis, spurring new contacts. A magazine has just published an article that highlights my argument that any French technology company that starts without a global strategy is doomed to failure. **(18)**

Spring Hill. Sunday 22 December 1985.

This is our first Christmas at the ranch. Our daughter is helping me fight the weeds and Janine now encourages me to build the observatory tower. She has just received a well-deserved promotion at Bank of America for her work at the technology center. Our love is deep, tender, peaceful, enhanced by the quiet surroundings. The sky is absurdly blue, the bushes insolently red: already, an exciting feeling of the nearness of spring.

Spring Hill. Wednesday 25 December 1985.

A French sociologist named Bertrand Méheust has just published a significant book on *Folklore and Flying Saucers*. It reinforces an important notion: one cannot "study" this phenomenon without becoming involved with it, entering into the difficult and dangerous dialogue with the unknown. **(19)**

Christmas: we opened up our presents around the big tree in the living room. The weather was mild. Tonight the full moon was rising; we took pictures of it with Maurice's telescope. This fine instrument has followed us everywhere, since Pontoise; it is something of a symbol for my wanderings. As the four of us sat in front of the fire, the dog Señorita falling asleep at our feet, we knew how close we had come to true happiness.

Hyde Street. Wednesday 1 January 1986.

Olivier has driven off again with his dog and his guitar, two blankets, boxes of books and a new computer printer for Marlon Brando who attends his networking seminar. I feel forlorn, at the edge of tears, as I do whenever he goes away.

I reconnected with several friends on the phone today. When I called my mother I found her happy and optimistic. Hal told me the Secret Onion project was delayed again. Allen feels better but has trouble reading.

Spring Hill. Saturday 4 January 1986.

Silence; gray sky. Catherine is still asleep. I am happy that she can enjoy the ranch before going off to college. She has a set pattern here: she wraps herself in a blanket in front of the fire to read comic books, and then she does her homework at the rickety old table. This house is filled with memories, artefacts from another time and continent. Nothing is really valuable, but everything is priceless.

Hyde Street. Sunday 12 January 1986.

Enjoying solitude against a background of quiet sadness I don't quite understand. I am a bit sick with a cold; I shuffle papers and I ruminate against various intrigues back in France. Advanced computer technology increases chaos, instead of resolving it.

Kit, a great admirer of John Fowles, brought an extraordinary book to my attention, a novel entitled *A Maggott*. Back in Scottsdale Allen's health keeps deteriorating. He did well with radiation and physical therapy but he is falling into a pattern of slumber and word confusion. Mimi is deeply affected and tired, according to Tina.

Spring Hill. Friday 24 January 1986.

My daughter and I drove up to the ranch, again talking all the way like old friends; when we got there we called Janine in Bayeux, where she visits her mother. Now that my children are reaching adulthood one of my principles is to keep their lives separate from my own notes, to respect their privacy. I should keep silent about the pleasure of being with them, of talking to them along our long drives. I do cherish my conversations with Olivier on the way to Mount Shasta. Now I enjoy Catherine's ideas and her sense of humor, a very precious gift.

Hyde Street. Sunday 26 January 1986.

Last week I went to see Bob Weiss in Hollywood to discuss *Messengers of Deception*, which he still hopes to turn into a movie. We had lunch with Joe Dante at Musso & Frank and later he introduced me to John Landis (**20**). We have yet to find a director. While in Los Angeles I also met with the executives of Retix and Symbolics, two high-tech companies looking for funds.

Janine has called from Bayeux, the sparkle back in her voice, and it lit up my world again: my mood always responds closely to hers. I watched the Superbowl (Chicago beat New England), then I packed my suitcase for Washington and France.

Washington. Wednesday 29 January 1986.

Yesterday I went to Radford in Virginia to visit a factory that makes magnetic bearings. The temperature had fallen below freezing. Blowing snow made white streaks on the pavement. Even the car keyhole was caught in ice.

In the middle of our meeting someone burst into the room to say the Shuttle Challenger had blown up and the crew was lost.

Stunned, I didn't feel the full impact right away. We got up and joined the assembled workers in the cafeteria. The TV channel was playing the tape of the launch and the accident, again and again. I just felt numb. It is in the afternoon, while driving alone towards Roanoke, that I looked up at the sky, a cold sky so pale and blue and empty that I began crying. The crew had been carrying something of us in that spacecraft, something precious and irreplaceable.

Paris. Rue de la Clef. Wednesday 5 February 1986.

Awake in the middle of the night, I listen to the thin traffic on *Rue Monge* and feel dejected. Janine is distant and moody, and business depresses me: the notion of venture capital as a promoter of innovation makes no progress in France, rendering our efforts pointless.

French bureaucrats have seized upon the silly notion that startup companies that survive here on government subsidies should establish U.S. offices in order to seek more subsidies… from the American government! This is an absurd attempt to do venture capital with no risk and no imagination. Back in Silicon Valley such a notion of bureaucratic subsidy as an engine of creativity is anathema and the Department of Commerce is viewed as an obsolete dinosaur, but socialist Paris cannot grasp the clear message of innovation and risk-taking that comes from California entrepreneurs.

In the dark living room where I write these notes, I feel like giving up on everything French. But Janine quietly walks into the room, and tells me to forget that riot inside my head.

Hyde Street. Monday 10 February 1986.

Confusion: after every journey, images of California overlap those of Europe. We brought back a small rifle that belonged to Janine's father. He mostly used it to kill sparrows, being a very good shot, and roasted them for breakfast. He had bought it in Morocco and brought it to France at the end of World War Two.

We also brought back the first copies of *Alintel.* I recall with amusement the typical Parisian chaos of the book signing at *Mercure de France*: Simonne Servais speaking non-stop, nervously shuffling papers; Marie-Thérèse de Brosses telling everybody about the beings from Ummo and complaining loudly that she wasn't given enough time for an in-depth interview.

Yves Kasgha was there, and Antoine Dulaure from *L'Autre Journal*, asking penetrating questions. Yrmeli Jung took pictures; she's a woman from Finland, her eyes intelligent and wide: true eyes of a great photographer. Not everything is bad in French finance: A Sofinnova colleague who is fond of Parisian luxury invited Janine and me to the Polo Club in Bagatelle: *Oeufs au coulis de crevette* and *Médaillon de chevreuil avec purée de marrons et céleri.* We were very far from the sandwich lunches of Silicon Valley.

In the meantime bombings continue in Paris, for obcure reasons the government does not feel obligated to disclose, which only adds to the general sense of panic. Even the Gibert bookstore, so popular with students, was blown up the evening of our dinner with Simonne. Then a cleaning lady found a suspicious package at the top of the Eiffel Tower. At least that particular bomb could have had a beneficient effect, depriving Paris of its insipid TV programs for a few blissful weeks.

Spring Hill. Saturday 15 February 1986.

General Namphy has seized power in Haïti following the departure of Baby Doc. We had met him over dinner in Port-au-Prince.

We drove up to the ranch this morning after an impressive storm that closed up several roads and filled the Russian River with muddy turmoil. Irresistible waterfalls crash over the slopes along the way. Catherine joined us in our private celebration: Janine just got a raise at work, my role has expanded at Sofinnova, and *Alintel* is published.

On Thursday an anthropologist named Randy Polos invited me to Palo Alto to join Ren Breck, his father, blonde Tina and a group of New Age researchers to discuss planet Mars, and more significantly the face-like mountain they speculate must have been sculpted by an

Alien race (**21**). They asked me if I agreed with their assessment, so I assured them not only that it was a face, but I even knew who it was: none other than Cyrano de Bergerac, whose pointed nose can clearly be seen by the long shadow it throws over the plains of Cydonia. I tried to convince them it was a Martian *hommage* to the 17th century Frenchman who designed fancy moon balloons and wrote about life on other worlds. Unfortunately New Agers take themselves too seriously to see the humorous side of their craziness.

Hyde Street. Saturday 8 March 1986.

We have hired a contractor who will dig up a pond at Spring Hill and pile up the dirt where I plan to build the observatory, whose blueprints are now clear in my mind. We spent a delightful evening with Sandra: dinner at the Cliff House, and a stroll along the Pacific shore under the stars as the woods loomed menacingly over the highway, the magic of the place oozing from the hanging rocks.

Sunshine over the Mendocino woods has awakened life in every bush. It is an irresistible force, green shoots at the tip of branches, with the added touch of a diamond-like drop of dew. Young grass grows out of the gutters, the roof, even the plastic welcome mat. Nothing can stop that energy; it brings a sense of exhilaration.

Simonne forwards letters from Guérin and Aimé Michel following publication of *Alintel*. Hal urges me to pursue my UFO work. I have developed a screening process for reports, based on my expert system, and wrote an article about it (**22**). Hal promises funding from the Secret Onion, but I am not holding my breath.

Spring Hill. Saturday 15 March 1986.

Aimé Michel believes there is an overall system guiding humanity; its agents know who they are and why they act as they do, driven by their destiny. Sometimes they act openly, yet their actions are only detected centuries later: "I have identified four cases that leave no doubt," he writes. "These agents hide behind the obscure laws of history, which look unpredictable."

All that remains vague: where are the names, the facts, and the patterns? In his current persona as the Old Man of the Mountain, Aimé himself is too obscure.

The first person who reacted to *Alintel* was none other than François de Grossouvre, Mitterrand's *Eminence grise*. He sent me a note suggesting a meeting. He is in charge of liaison between the Elysée and French secret services.

Guérin read the novel "with immense interest," he writes. He questions the notion that UFOs could be detected by spy satellites "since they seem to manifest and operate in the lower layers of the atmosphere."

He concludes his warm letter with the remark that "we will die, you and I, without having the final word in this affair. That's the only certain fact about these objects that have mobilized our thoughts for a great part of our lives."

Other letters arrive in prestigious envelopes: from Jacques Attali, and the chief of staff of the Interior Ministry who writes: "I admire that you had the idea and took the time to write it."

Hyde Street. Sunday 16 March 1986.

American life is becoming narrow, reduced to an obsession with money. The same is happening in Europe. Where did the great movements of the mind and heart go? This decade has produced no genius, not even an evil genius. In art, we have Cristo wrapping up the bridges of Paris in plastic sheets to the amazement of crowds: hardly a statement for the Ages. In science, the Challenger disaster is an illustration of the current malaise, our inability to acknowledge the extent of our ignorance. Americans are fascinated by Carl Sagan regaling television audiences with speculations about Halley's Comet, but nobody is checking the O rings in the Shuttle rockets. Real problems get swept under the rug. In France Mitterrand's rotten tacticians are locked in obscure maneuvers with the despicable Right. Even the creative signals that used to be inspired by the student movement of May 68 have been dulled by bureaucratic complacency.

On Friday Kit was in San Francisco, wearing the presidential Medal of Intelligence at his buttonhole. He received it from Reagan for his work on "Yellow Rain" in Indochina. I had lunch with him in the financial district. We spoke of his friend Seagrave (**23**), of John Fowles' novels, and his old boss Ed Gregor.

Hyde Street. Sunday 23 March 1986.

Janine is spending the weekend in San Diego with our son. Catherine is doing the cooking and running this house. In today's paper is an alarming study of the use of electronic bulletin boards by extremists, notably racists and neo-nazi. The basic power and subtlety of electronic message systems is still misunderstood, and the press is only now discovering Doug Englebart's work, 20 years later, but it is already clear that the technology has a dark side.

Over dinner with Hal on Friday I learned that the Secret Onion wasn't quite dead: a briefing was recently given to McMann, number two man at CIA, who seemed to favor releasing some funds. He was asked two questions: (1) Would a study of UFOs be useful to the Agency? and (2) Are other groups already doing it?

McMann answered yes to the first question and no to the second. This surprised us: there must be an investigation somewhere and if McMann doesn't know about it, who does? We also discussed the ongoing SRI work, which has moved behind locked doors in the secure section of the Institute. The work now centers on psychokinetics. Ingo is no longer financed by the project: He made the tactical mistake of taking sides by supporting the Army project against Jim Salyer and the DIA just as the vagaries of the bureaucracy shifted that group under DIA control.

Hal is afraid that Pentagon bureaucrats might try to block industrial applications of his discoveries. Unfortunately other countries are worse: in France, petty politics stifle creativity at every level. I told Hal he would be better off seeking counsel from an eminent businessman with a technology background, a David Packard or a Robert Noyce.

Spring Hill. Sunday 30 March 1986 (Easter).

The irises are open along the white fence; hawks are building a nest, bees have begun their work; Our daughter catches frogs, and we even saw a rabbit yesterday. "Did he carry a little basket with chocolate eggs?" asked Janine when I told her.

Richard Niemtzow came over for dinner on Thursday. We spent the evening in conversation, starting with the whole array of medical effects of UFOs such as the Dr. X skin coloration (I had brought back a series of new photographs from France) and ending with speculation about the structure of the problem as a whole.

"Aren't we faced with a phenomenon that demands that we leave behind our classical methods? Doesn't it mock our attempts to measure it?" he asked.

"Of course," I said, "but that's only one more reason to drive all the measurements to their fullest extent, so we have calibration."

I don't believe in John Lilly's approach, exploring the paranormal with drugs: he goes somewhere but he doesn't know where, so he can never go there again! All he demonstrates is that the universe is a mysterious place, something we already knew.

Richard has noticed the same thing I did, about the phenomenon acting as a concentrator for coincidences. Peculiar events coalesce around special people, sites, or circumstances: In my case, the Melchizedek episodes, or the Gryphons at Stanford, two blatant examples of *intersigns*. If this is part of an informational (as opposed to physical) reality in some way, it should be possible to focus such events. The key question is, would that necessarily force a transition to a state where the subject would lose the ability to distinguish right from wrong, truth from falsity, the real from the virtual?

Philip Dick explored all this. So did Geller and General Uchoa, and they lost all credibility in the process.

New York City. Wednesday 9 April 1986.

I stopped in New York for dinner with industrialist Pierre Simon, a friend of Fred Adler and the Dassault family. His apartment is across the street from the Metropolitan Museum and gives a splendid view of Fifth Avenue. There are original Matisse drawings on the walls.

Paris. Thursday 10 April 1986.

Responding to the invitation from Mr. de Grossouvre I went over to the Elysée palace today. In the stately courtyard three rows of Republican Guards in parade dress were awaiting some high dignitary.

François de Grossouvre wears his 60 years with refined elegance. Amusingly, his mustache and white goatee give him a striking ressemblance with a character in Tintin, the man who steals wallets in *The Secret of the Unicorn*. His office is from another age, with green velvet armchairs for visitors. Two curtains on my left hide something: Closets? Tape recorders? To the right is a door to the secretaries' office. Before me stand his desk (two telephones) and a window giving onto Avenue Marigny. Trumpets sound in the courtyard, the tune greeting a high-level military official ("*Vlà l'général qui passe...*")

"You wished to see me, Monsieur Vallée?" he asked. As if he hadn't just read *Alintel* and requested me to contact him. I feel oddly at ease. I remind him of the book. He says he enjoyed it. Getting up, he comes and sits down next to me; he looks for his glasses.

"Where are you working now? I believe you live in the States?"

I tell him about Sofinnova, the leading French venture company.

"And you have an interest in these subjects?"

I summarize my background, the research on Blue Book files, which led me to the conclusion that the phenomenon was real.

"Well, you see, I went through medical school, although I never practiced. My mentor was one of the early people who became interested in this topic, so he influenced several of his students." A pause, then: "This is a very indiscreet question, but do you have a religious belief, a personal faith?"

"I was raised here, in the Catholic church," I said. "But it's hard to reconcile catechism with science when you study astronomy, so I stopped going to Mass. I never fell into the other extreme, total 'rationalism,' denying everything. I have developed a personal notion of... mysticism is a big word; let's just say spirituality. I have always felt there was a higher level and we had access to it."

"You've read Teilhard?"

"I tried. I found him difficult. I do agree with him about consciousness throughout the universe; in fact our newest computer networks represent a form of spiritual evolution, extending the range of consciousness."

"You work with a group, a team?"

"Not really. An isolated researcher can cover a lot of ground."

"But you know people who do this work in France?"

"Of course: I'm in touch with the Gepan team within Cnes."

The phone rings:

"I'll be home by 7:30. I see the President in half an hour."

He turns back to me: "In any case, your book is excellent. Tell your publisher to call me; perhaps I can help promote it. Is there anything else I can do for you?"

"If there are new cases in France, I'd like to be involved in the official investigations." He shuffles in his seat. "Look, I can only help you with the government side, either the researchers or the military. The researchers, you know them already."

So he is tacitly offering to put me in touch with the Defense establishment. He gets up to see Mitterrand. "Keep me posted. The Defense people have their own archives."

I picked up my passport at the guardhouse on my way out. Paris was cold and wet. Simonne warned me: "Don't wait two years to follow up. De Grossouvre is not going to stay in that position."

She was amused by the reference to Teilhard: "Of course you can't agree with Teilhard! You're like me: you believe in the Sacred, not in the Divine. To follow Teilhard you need Faith, with a capital F."

Stockholm. Grand Hotel. Sunday 13 April 1986.

A professional meeting on computer networks brings me to Sweden for a few days. The snow falls on the royal palace, on the black street, on the building of the *Svenska Handelsbanken.* My friend

Rune Sodestrom, as pale as someone who hasn't seen the sun in six months, was kindly waiting for me at the airport. On the way to the hotel he showed me the place where Prime Minister Olaf Palme was assassinated a few years ago. The luxury of Grand Hotel dissipates the heaviness of my latest stay in France.

The atmosphere was decidedly sick in Paris; Simonne told me that all her former political colleagues had gone back to high responsibilities, even Jacques Chaban-Delmas, and Foccart. The latter called her before she could learn of his new appointment from the newspapers: "At my age, it is a very great burden," he said.

"I know" she replied, "you are among those who are rejuvenated by intense work; you draw your substance from feverish activity." **(24)**

She says I am made of the same metal.

Stockholm. Monday 14 April 1986.

The snow gets thicker over the piers. It underlines the cornices of the Opera House and turns every garden into a Christmas postcard. The Swedes are calm and courteous. So is their State television: For the last hour I have been watching an elderly librarian who reads aloud from a book. She wears round glasses, her sparse hair in a bun. She sits on a wooden chair. This is live, on Channel Two! After a long walk in old Stockholm I came back to Grand Hotel, frozen but happy.

On the SAS flight to Heathrow. Wednesday 16 April 1986.

Stockholm is magnificent with its bridges over torrents, its steeples, its medieval streets, and hundreds of seagulls crying overhead. Last night I dined alone at *Angelen*, a restaurant frequented by a young and vibrant crowd. I drew up an alchemical alphabet.

The flight plan today takes me from Stockholm to London to L.A. to San Francisco. Yesterday our computer seminar came to an end, so we had a great dinner of smoked salmon and reindeer with arctic berries in cream.

The computer business is alive in Sweden, but it is the exclusive world of men, preoccupied with machines. There is no woman in any of these meetings, no softness, and little humor.

I am reminded of *Montenegro*, the delightful movie by Makarejev where a beautiful American woman living in Sweden goes into terminal frustration and madness when she tries to adapt to the local culture. I did see Thomas Ohlin with the folks from COM, the group that bought our Forum code ten years ago. They have developed it into a piece of software that is now used by the European *Esprit* project.

Sweden was sunny this morning, and blessed with a delay in world news. It took me a while to get reliable information when I heard that the U.S. Air Force had bombed Tripoli. People hardly commented about the air strikes. Frantically, I turned on the TV to find out if travel was disrupted by the latest outbreaks. On Channel Two I found the same old librarian still reading her book, while Channel One was broadcasting a documentary on the life of bears. Channel Three showed industrial films, barely disguised commercials about Burroughs and Greyhound.

I did meet several interesting people, including Paul Galli of Datateknik who had studied Bob Monroe's work, and Davis Bohm who knew about Bob Beck, having built one of his black boxes. He seemed familiar with computer cryptography. He confirmed what another seminar participant had told me, namely that Swedish mathematicians had broken the much-advertised public key cryptosystem.

As for the DES standard proposed by the American government for use in banking, the Swedish experts said it could be compromised in about four hours with current technology.

A final look at Stockholm, a restored Drakkar in the harbor, sunshine over the domes of palaces, rich windows of fur shops.

Later the same day. TWA flight to L.A.

As soon as we landed in London we stepped into a whirlwind of news: details of yesterday's massive air raid that sent a squadron of

F-111s against Khaddafi amidst criticisms of the cowardly Europeans, accused by the U.S. of capitulating before bloodthirsty dictators. Security is extreme throughout Heathrow. Most people cancelled their international flights, especially on American carriers. In this TWA plane there are only five of us in business class.

France is rumored to have made a deal with Arab terrorists. Mitterrand refused to allow the American planes to fly over French territory, so they had to go around the Pyrenées from their bases in England. By coincidence an Americam bomb has reduced to rubble the French embassy in Tripoli…

Now I think about François de Grossouvre as I listen to Vivaldi, played by Menuhin. The plane flies over Greenland. I expect nothing from my recent visit to the Elysée, as I expect nothing from Hal's project with John Alexander and the Secret Onion.

Hal has become fascinated with Sitchin's theories of ancient astronauts (**25**). Sitchin thinks everything began with the Sumerians. On the contrary it seems to me that Sumer was only the end of something, a culmination. The Gilgamesh Epic tells about a contact with space-born intelligences in a distant past. It became banal under the pen of religious chroniclers of various stripes who betrayed the facts in the name of their belief, as scholars and monks always do.

All they say is that there were a Flood, celestial signs and powerful angels who were horny in more ways than one. Their erotic energy was so vibrant that Catholic ladies are still bound to wear a hat or scarf at Mass, so as not to excite angelic concupiscence...

A team of Berkeley biologists recently had the bright idea of searching for the first woman, whom they appropriently call "Mom." They began with an analysis of the placenta of 112 women of various races who had given birth in San Francisco hospitals, and they searched for a common origin by studying mitochondria, a structure that passes from one generation to another through women.

These mitochondria come from the ovum. They produce all the energy in the body using oxygen to burn nutrients and feed the cells. Their DNA only changes slowly, about 2% in a million years. The team's conclusion is that the common source must have existed about 250,000 years ago, so Mom must have been a Neanderthal woman, or even a female of Homo Erectus, the first hominid race thought to have come out of Africa. Homo Erectus discovered fire, built shelters, used clothing, and cooked meals. The Berkeley biologists concede that the theory is fragile, the African origin uncertain.

What is sure is that an enormous gap exists between the first human female 250,000 years ago and Sumer, barely 3,000 years before Christ. It is within this chasm that all religions take their root, and that the megalithic civilization mysteriously thrived. If one takes an occult viewpoint, all sacred texts from the Pyramids to the Bible simply boil down to this: There was an extraordinary event in the distant past. It has to do with the betrayal of the plans made by a divine dictator. Rebel angels decided to bring their seed to the Earth, as well as fragments of their science. If the biologists are right it isn't Lucifer who matters in all this, even if he seduced Eve, but Lilith, because she seduced Adam. Now I read in a book by André Nataf about alchemy and eroticism (*La Maîtrise du Souffle Sexuel*): "It isn't surprising that we should find in the whole of alchemy some traces of distant origins, older than Sumer, where sexual rites and natural religion were synonymous." Such are the words that resonate on this spring afternoon, ten kilometers above the icebergs sliding away to the horizon, as the world expects Khaddafi to seek revenge.

Spring Hill. Sunday 20 April 1986.

The drapes filter the sunshine that flows into our bed in great flowery swaths. After Stockholm I went to Los Angeles for an AIAA panel that included Dick Haines and Jean-Jacques Velasco: I presented my expert system as a filter for UFO reports. Jean-Jacques will take it back to Cnes. Bill Moore brought me up to date on his investigations at Roswell.

While in the L.A. area I had dinner in Hollywood with Bob Weiss. One of his assistants came to pick me up: "Little Dipper sent me!" he said, alluding to one of my more charming characters in *Alintel*.

Catherine is in Colorado, visiting the campus where she plans to study. Richard Sigismond will show her the highlights of Boulder. Richard also gave us sad news about Allen: He has trouble standing up now, does not follow conversations, and stops in mid-sentence when he speaks. "We must all come to grips with the fact that he will soon disappear from our lives," Richard said sadly.

Hyde Street. Friday 25 April 1986.

Peter Sturrock had invited two physics colleagues, a psychologist, Jim Harder, Jim McCampbell and Paul Cerny for a meeting at Stanford yesterday, at the aerospace science building. All listened to Velasco who presented the case of Trans-en-Provence with my help, because his English is so poor nobody understands him. Jim, Harder and Cerny have not aged gracefully. I have known them eager, dynamic. The creative streak has turned to bitterness.

In contrast I admire Velasco, the son of a simple worker, well aware of the inequities in the French system.

He told me of his recent visit to Alain Esterle, whom he describes as entirely focused on his career goals. They went to see Gilbert Payan, an industrialist from *Compagnie Générale des Eaux* who secretly serves as the Gray Eminence of French ufology: his factory makes the diffraction gratings for Gepan, which they hand out to the gendarmes in hopes of getting a UFO spectrum, to no avail so far **(26)**. Payan is from *Ecole Polytechnique*, so he immediately addressed Esterle: "which promotion are you from?" Then he turned to Velasco, asking him the same question. But Jean-Jacques didn't graduate from Polytechnique; he is a simple technician who studied within Cnes to become an engineer. After that all conversation was between Esterle and Payan.

Jean-Jacques eagerly observes everything in California. He has an open mind, capable of admiration, but he also notes the dark facts: the poor homeless huddled in doorways, the drunk along Market Street, the wealthy insolence of Palo Alto.

We also spoke about Gepan. He told me that contacts with the Soviets had come to a halt when their Russian colleagues were thrown out of France for espionage, notably a scientist who had befriended François Louange. It turned out they were not interested in UFOs at all, but in some novel optical technology Cnes was using.

This weekend I fly to Montana for the education conference: my old Stanford friend Gerald Askevold, who now lives on a ranch there, has initiated the idea of a special conference for gifted kids, 100 bright youngsters aged 12 to 16 from all over Montana.

Kalispell, Montana. Monday 28 April 1986.

I called Phoenix tonight. Mimi told me Allen died yesterday.

He had declined steadily over the last two weeks but was only in pain for the 20 minutes that preceded the end. So I went out in the Kalispell night, looking up at Allen's starry sky through my tears. I told Janine, and Fred too, because I couldn't let him learn of it through someone else. From my room at the Outlaw Inn I can see Flathead Lake, which looks grandiose and cruel.

Kalispell. Tuesday 29 April 1986.

I gave two lectures today in front of an enthusiastic public that would have delighted Allen. Some of the kids were four or five years ahead of normal schooling, and were not intimidated by concepts such as higher dimensions. I could touch a wider public, as popularizers of science such as Carl Sagan have done. Yet it is this research I treasure, even if it is lonely and remains confidential. I enjoy knowing that I am simply planting a few ideas in the darkness.

Kalispell seems like a void, especially in the evening. The nostalgia of the old West lingers, a proud memory of great herds and flourishing mines, and those easy women with fleshy thighs whose portraits adorn the walls of the Outlaw Inn, but today's reality is a prudish community without texture or savor.

Kalispell. Wednesday 30 April 1986.

The news media are mobilized by the Chernobyl nuclear accident. The Soviets are frantically trying to get safety advice and information from the West. They have asked the U.S. nuclear safety community for help and someone from their embassy is reportedly trying to find me. InfoMedia still has our extensive database representing two years of daily exchanges on the topic among 72 nuclear plants in the Western world, but the experts from the Institute for Nuclear Power Operations stopped using Notepad four years ago, claiming they could develop a better system on their own. They never did, of course; it's always the same story.

Montana is quiet, fresh, and too clean: something is missing in this majestic landscape. People have lost the secret of passionate conquest. So they drink, they turn clay into ceramic art, they watch insipid television, they go to church for endless banalities about an unreachable divinity that mirrors the immensity of their boredom and their enormous mountains.

Last night I picked up the Bible, the only book I could find, and read the *Revelation of St. John.* The text struck me again, not as a grandiose mystical vista, but as a venomous statement that is simply insulting to humanity, trembling and miserable before its Eternal God, submissive to His terrible angels bent on genocide. Western civilization has never shaken off the psychic slavery of human masses in the form of religion, man's exploitation by false Gods.

This brings my thoughts to the wonderful kids I have met here over the last couple of days. The only message they need from our generation is, “You are free to think and create.”

It is a fact that mankind is limited and often mean, and that meanness translates into evil. It is a fact that the only economic system that actually works today is capitalism, based on individual achievement and thus prone to crush the poor and the weak. But these are real problems, tangible problems we can fix with hard work and patience. Let us at least eliminate the false problems, the insolvable conflicts of fanaticism.

What happened here is sadly typical of the American education system: the Association for the Education of Gifted Children has brought 600 members for a conference in Kalispell, but they hadn't planned anything for the kids!

Fortunately Gerald stepped in, to give them the opportunity to attend a few lectures that would expand their minds.

Phoenix. Thursday May 1st, 1986.

As soon as I arrived I drove restlessly all over the area, from Mesa to Tempe where I lost my way before heading back to Scottsdale. The sun went down behind Camelback Mountain, turning purple, then a menacing dark mauve, a grandiose display of dark power, Arizona sunset. The Clarion Inn is an opulent oasis at the edge of the desert, with a fake lake and a green lawn imported, no doubt, from a wetter clime. Every few minutes the air conditioner rumbles on, turning the room's environment from oven to sticky greenhouse. An employee fires up a lawn mower and thunders away under my windows. In America it seems there is never enough noise to drown out dangerous thoughts. Mimi has invited me to lunch with her children. The *New York Times* will print Allen's obituary.

Later the same day.

Today would have been Allen's 76th birthday. He was born May 1st, 1910 and was five days old when his parents took him up to the rooftop, in Chicago, to watch Halley's Comet. He flew off with it again, as he had predicted. When I went to the house on Vista Drive Scott opened the door for me. I had never met him, or his sister Roxanne. Paul was there too. Mimi told me about Allen's last days as we sat in the living room. He had gotten to a point where he could not speak. One of the last things this brave man told his family, characteristically, was: “I wish I could do something for you, too.”

On Sunday he felt pain whenever he was moved around. He stayed in bed all day, Mimi holding his hand. He seemed conscious; she thought he still recognized her through his eyes. He started having trouble breathing. Mimi called the paramedics, who gave him an injection and took him to the hospital, trying to save him. Everything became confused in intensive care, where he died alone, drugged up, among the nursing staff and the electronic monitors.

I sat down for lunch with Allen's family but barely touched the salad Mimi had prepared. I tried to talk of other things, of events in the world, which they seemed to welcome, to forget the grief if only for a moment. I told them Allen was a greater scientist than he knew himself. After lunch Scott resumed packing, Roxanne went out to buy something. Mimi told me I could take whatever I wanted of Allen's personal objects. I didn't know what to tell her. Paul brought me the slides from Allen's last trip to France, his pictures of Toulouse and Paris. There was just one photograph I had taken with Allen's own camera at the *Arènes*, and I requested it. I asked for Allen's copy of Manly Hall's masterpiece, *Secret Teachings of All Ages*, perhaps the book that meant the most to Allen. The date he inscribed on the first page was May 1st, 1931, exactly 55 years ago. He was 21. He annotated many passages in pencil, underlined others.

Phoenix. Friday 2 May 1986.

Spielberg's people called from Hollywood yesterday. They wanted to know if money contributions were appropriate. "Allen would have found this interesting," Mimi said, adding: "They never gave money to support Allen's work during his life, while they contributed lavishly to Sagan's promotion for Seti."

I rediscovered Tina and Brian last night, and the friendship between us. They have distanced themselves from Jeffery and the English community in Scottsdale, an enclave of utter snobbishness. Jeffery's wife Susan has arrived from London on the wings of a powerful personal psychic tornado that sweeps everything around her, including Jeffery: now she plans a conference in London. Allen never understood why Jeffery didn't simply sign a check, and Jeffery never understood why Allen didn't come up with an action plan to solve the UFO problem in a few years. Research in the field will again fall back to the responsibility of our Invisible College, as Allen and I had realized in Toulouse while walking under the starry sky.

Part Eleven

DARK SCIENCE

11

Spring Hill. Saturday 3 May 1986.

We sit by the fireplace after a long day of work building a small wooden tower on top of the studio. Our daughter sleeps on the sofa; Janine reads a novel. The San Francisco *Chronicle* has published a ludicrous orbituary, hardly mentioning Allen's astronomical work. It stressed that he came up with the term "Close Encounters," including those of the second kind where UFOs "have left tire tracks!" Fortunately the *New York Times* did a better job.

Mimi promises to locate the framed reproduction of the *Lady and the Unicorn* I had given Allen; presumably it still holds the text of the secret Battelle document I saved from his files. She said it hangs on the wall of Allen's office at Corralitos Observatory (**1**).

Spring Hill. Sunday 11 May 1986.

The warm, windy days of spring have taken over Mendocino County. Catherine is here with a friend, an Italian girl named Carla. They took the truck and went off to visit the area, from the People's Temple site to the local eatery that serves juicy "corral burgers."

I worked hard on the small tower while making plans for a trip to Detroit to see Kit, to Boston for Optima, and to New York for a meeting with Fred Adler that could be an opportunity to start a new fund with an American team. To Kit I intend to present strong comments about the Secret Onion project: I have no intention of becoming part of the outer skin of some shadowy organization whose chiefs I don't trust and who seem to know less than I do about the problem. (**2**)

Hyde Street. Sunday 18 May 1986.

Kit and I only had two hours together at Detroit airport. He shares my concerns about the Secret Onion: some of the participants seem increasingly willing to believe any wild rumor they pick up from ufologists, without checking their reliability. He refused to take part in the meetings as long as no budget had been allocated to give it an official status. He recommended that I stay on the sidelines.

"There are two communities involved," he said. "On one hand are the scientists, together with the paranormal researchers like you and me, Hal and Dick Haines, Sturrock, Niemtzow, Schuessler; we represent a small community, 20 at most; on the other side are the analysts, who come from Intelligence. So the idea would be to take some members of both groups, as in the Manhattan project, the intersection of these two sets. The challenge is to pick people carefully, so they can attack the problem in some concrete fashion."

"So what's the hang-up?" I asked.

"Simple. The folks from the government side come from Star Wars; they are used to enormous budgets, so they have escalated their ambitions. What they have in mind is none other than your *Alintel*. By the way, in the process they've become convinced that there was no other project."

"So what's the structure?" I asked.

"At the core is a group of bureaucrats from DoD running the proposed budget. The next layer would include scientists like you and Hal. You'd know everything except where the funds come from. The next layer would be composed of mission specialists with particular assignments. The outer layer of the Onion will be made up of consultants."

There were many problems with this concept when I reviewed it in my mind. For one thing, the core members include high-level analysts who have a religious agenda. The subject attracts fundamentalists of every stripe, from those who believe they are in contact with Aliens, to men who want to save America for Christ. Kit has observed the same thing: "What intrigues me isn't the fact that so many ufologists have paranoid schizophrenic tendencies, but it's the unfolding of their behavior. It seems that the more paranoid they become, the better they are, as you once pointed out to me. It's the opposite from what I'd have expected in dementia."

He gave a little laugh: "When I talk to them I wonder if the crazy ones are not you and me, and the rest of society!"

Another problem I have with the Onion has to do with its supposed secrecy. These people are giving briefings left and right throughout Washington, looking for money. So isn't the confidential nature of the project already compromised? This would explain the recent attentions directed at me: François de Grossouvre has asked for my personal address, and other folks in France have asked precise questions about my background and career. It seems many people are compiling *dossiers*.

My professional plans have made progress. I met a colleague in Boston to arrange the second round financing of Optima, and then we flew to New York for a meeting with a young attorney named Paul Jacobs. Dressed in flashy shirt and splendid yellow suspenders, he is the son-in-law of industrialist Pierre Simon. The latter wore a black tie in deference to the recent death of his friend Marcel Dassault. The meeting must have gone well, because Fred Adler soon joined us. A wiry man of small stature, about 65, he strode into the room like a litigator stepping into a court of law, looking at us with piercing eyes showing no trace of common human warmth: the eyes of a lucid paragnost, or an eagle that has seen a prey.

Adler shook hands with us and launched into a brillant discourse about venture capital, his long experience with the field, his recollections of the stormy early days of Data General, and even hotter days at Intersil, a Silicon Valley company he turned around.

I still had a little time in Manhattan, so I spent it at the fine hologram museum in the Village. I arrived at Kennedy in time to meet my mother who was stepping out of the Customs area, walking as straight as a naval officer, dressed in a white suit and fashionable purple scarf. The flight to San Francisco was full, so I gave her my business class seat. She slept on the plane and for the last two days she has astonished us with her vitality and her optimism, in a tired world worried about its failures, from Challenger to Chernobyl.

Spring Hill. Saturday 24 May 1986.

Short holidays at the ranch. Catherine and her Filipino friend John met us there, driving the truck. Maman is enjoying the ranch, even if she walks a bit hesitantly, leaning on my arm. Young does are coming down from the forest to taste the tender shoots on the bushes around the house. UFOs are back in the news. It began with a series of pilot sightings in Brazil, including military planes.

At dawn on Thursday there were some twenty observations south of here, between Rohnert Park and Petaluma: People saw a large X-shaped object with orange, green, and white lights.

Spring Hill. Sunday 25 May 1986.

Happy days, lazy reading in bed (Janine reads *Easy Travels to Other Planets*, I read Tennessee William's biography). My mother swam in the pool, with my assistance, for the first time in ten years. She emerged feeling younger and happy. She even noted that she didn't miss the news reports she always followed so intensely in Paris, of Chirac and Mitterrand and the thousand follies of the world. Spring Hill is like a mountain monastery, where politics and the vagaries of humanity only manifest as a distant echo. We drank Champagne by the pool and only went inside when we saw the first stars.

Hyde Street. Sunday 1 June 1986.

Olivier has come up from San Diego with a portable computer and Jill, his new girlfriend. I reorganize my work in the expectation that we will start a new investment company with Fred Adler and that I may have to work alone on the West coast for a while, only equipped with a phone, computer, and a fax line, writing at this small desk. All the true venture capitalist pioneers I admire, men like Arthur Rock and Wally Davis, started out this way.

Allen's death continues to make ripples in intellectual and journalistic circles. *Time Magazine* published an ironic chronicle of his life, saying that Hynek had made the study of flying saucers "semi-respectable," having been asked by the Air Force to investigate them as possible spaceships. Not only is that statement false, but it makes it obvious that *Time* is incapable of grasping the notion that this phenomenon could represent something far more fundamental than spaceships, just as Allen Hynek was far more than a ufologist, or an Air Force consultant.

According to Richard Sigismond, Allen's move to Arizona caused deep trauma in the amateur community. One side of the dispute is Chicago-based Cufos, as conventional in its beliefs as the late Nicap; on the other side, the Scottsdale group that now organizes conferences in Phoenix and a series of lectures in London. I am not aligned with either chapel. My own research at the moment centers on the analysis of the Costa Rica photograph (**3**).

Spring Hill. Sunday 15 June 1986.

The weather is fresh, mornings and evenings, with the warm caress of the sun at midday, an ideal setting to work on the small tower or watch the stock car races in Ukiah with family and friends. I have brought my files here to work on the new venture fund.

Luisa Teish came to see us on Wednesday, flushed with her literary success, television appearances and the sales of her work, but she is wise enough not to take any of it too seriously. It is a pleasure to help her whenever I can, with some point she wants to discuss or some passage she is editing, while I learn from her own perspective.

Hyde Street. Sunday 22 June 1986.

We stayed in the City this weekend to attend the annual conference of the Society for Scientific Exploration founded five years ago by Peter Sturrock. Although I was responsible for his interest in the phenomenon, and influenced his decision to start SSE, I am discouraged by the narrow academic orientation the Society has taken. Again, I gave a talk on the use of expert systems to screen out identifiable objects among incoming aerial anomalies, but I don't expect the idea will be picked up.

The conference did offer an opportunity to see our very dear friend Michel Gauquelin, who came to our house for dinner. He told us his hopes and disappointments: At 57 he finds himself separated from his wife Françoise, who goes on publishing her own astrology work. He believes she took umbrage at having to publish jointly with him.

Michel is humble and smart. He deplores the narrow nature of French society. He recalls that I once found him a job in California. He never pursued the opportunity, and regrets it. His "Mars effect" keeps being verified, to the consternation of the skeptics. (**4**)

At the SSE banquet we saw Fred Beckman again. He launched into a bitter tirade about brain research, citing his own investigations of consciousness and intelligence tests. Afterwards he asked me for $20 to pay for his parking. Many other friends were there: Ed May invited me to visit him at SRI, where he now runs the psychic project. Marcello Truzzi had gone off to visit Anton LaVey. Keith Harary, Stanley Krippner, Dick Haines and Marsha Adams were also in attendance. Hal whispered to me that on July 2nd the briefing for the Secret Onion would be submitted to Lieutenant General Abrahamson, head of the Star Wars project.

Later the same day.

Janine and I spent the afternoon with Hal, Adrienne, and three of their children (Brendan, Gavin, and Devin). We took them to Pier 39 for lunch. Hal beat me 90 to 50 in a game of Whack-a-Mole, after which we came back here to talk seriously. We spoke of Ingo, who believes he acquired his talents after a close encounter: "I hope he'll tell you about it some day," Hal said. "He keeps it very private."

"So what's new with the Secret Onion?" I asked. "Is it just another club, people who want to talk about flying saucers?"

"No, they're completely serious. The committee now includes the president of an aerospace company. He is willing to analyze any hard samples. The project comes before Lieutenant General Abrahamson on July 2nd; he is supposed to give us a charter, as I told you."

"What if he doesn't?"

"Then it's a major setback, but we're working on other leads."

Hal also brought me up to date on his own project. Ken Shoulders has been brutally beaten up by the Austin police, under the pretext that they suspected him of having burglarized someone's office. Ken had driven to work, parked next to a police car without paying attention to it, went into his office and began eating a snack when five cops burst in, beat him up, pushed him to the ground and sat on his body for 20 minutes, yelling at him to stop resisting arrest for the benefit of their tape recorder. While he was down they went through the office. Now Ken is suing the city, and Hal wonders if the attack was a cover to look at their proprietary technology.

Jim McCampbell has made an interesting contact with some military pilots from the Wild Weasels. According to Jim, these are expert pilots who use F-4 planes equipped for electromagnetic detection, designed to identify ground radars, and first deployed during the Vietnam War. The story goes that they have detected many UFOs and have continued in this role in the United States.

We also discussed paranormal talents. I don't feel I am a good PK subject. I understand remote viewing but I cannot control it and make it useful: my successes remain anecdotal. If I have any real talents they express themselves in precognition through my writing: the Spirogyres of *Sub-Espace*; the Blue Mosquitoes of *Dark Satellite* that were 20 years ahead of technology, as was the reality-shifting radiation, and shielding against brainwaves. But these notions have culminated in *Alintel*, to such a degree that I had to cut out some parts of the fictional story when it was overtaken by actual events.

This led us to discuss means of identifying the metasystem, along the lines of my experiments at the ranch, or to force it to react. I hypothesize there is a higher level of reality and it interpenetrates our everyday life, creating coincidences and apparitions. A pre-condition to observe it in its pure form is to reject or ignore all phenomena of the lower level. For a scientist, of course, that is the hardest part of the assigment.

On Tuesday I leave for France, with a stop in Washington. I will see Simonne Servais and also Mr. de Grossouvre at the Elysée for the second time. He requested that I contact Pierre d'Alançon, of the President's staff, to get through to him.

François Durand de Grossouvre, who lists his profession as *exploitant agricole*—a mere gentleman farmer!—is the effective boss of French intelligence. He was born in Vienne on 29 March 1918. Married in 1943 to a Miss Berger, they have six children. Studies in Grenoble, then Lyon school of medicine. President of *Le Bon Sucre* (1944-63) and *Société Berger* (49-63). A member of the socialist party, he has served on Mitterrand's staff since the latter became president in 1981.

From Paris I will fly to England where Tina and Susan Kaye have scheduled their conference, which should be an opportunity to meet researchers Jenny Randles and Andrew Collins.

London. Tuesday 1 July 1986. Marble Arch Holiday Inn.

In an hour I leave for Glastonbury with Brian and Tina and Susan Kaye, a welcome change of pace after the excitement of the lectures and meetings of the last few days, when I did see Jenny Randles, Sir John Whitmore, and my old friend Gordon Creighton. Uri Geller is in London, too. Puharich and Whitmore had a meeeting with him three weeks ago to revive their "quest," filled with all the previous delusions: they are now convinced that Uri's adventures in America in the 70s had to do with an imminent nuclear war, fortunately averted. Therefore the Aliens did not need to intervene! Puharich, who had worked so hard with John Whitmore's money, was discredited when the landing did not take place, but he believes it's only because he played his role so well. Today the world enters a dangerous phase again, they claim, because of Chernobyl.

John Whitmore invited me to come to Austria for a dialogue with Aliens who now speak through a medium named Phyllis Schlemmer. Politely, I begged to be excused: any Alien who needed to speak to me would presumably know how to find me wherever I am.

More interesting was the private talk I had with Gordon as we took a long walk around Connaught Square. He remains lucid, critical, well informed, in contrast to our poor friend Charles Bowen who has had several strokes and heart problems. I also spoke with Jenny Randles. When I sat down with her and a Bufora investigator in the hotel coffee shop I found Jenny smart and gifted, with a good sense of humor. I was dismayed by some details in her behavior, however. She wore many layers of clothing, too warm for the season. She recorded our entire conversation and never looked me in the eye.

Wednesday 2 July 1986. On the flight back to California.

Early this morning I walked up to Glastonbury Tor alone, having discovered a small dirt path between two private gardens. The landscape was very soft, bathed in whitish haze. Brian and Tina joined me at the top, with George Dewberry, a Chicago attorney who is Tina's financial advisor, and some local friends.

Tina is an interesting woman, a former Chicago deputy sheriff who became involved in turn in the commodities market, in the search for sunken treasures, in gold mines, and in psychic research. It is during a stay in Las Vegas that she became interested in UFOs, when she met a man named Ed Slade. He took her to a secret room in his basement where he kept a collection of weapons and some jewels and icons from Russia.

Slade told her that he was a "former agent" who could fly to Russia whenever he wanted and bring back anything he liked. He assured Tina that the saucers existed, that the U.S. government had captured some craft and their occupants; one of them was at Nellis Air Force Base (**5**). A collector of old share certificates, Slade shared this passion with Jules Glazer, who already served as Jeffery's financial manager. However Kaye long refused to meet with Slade. When he finally agreed he was fascinated by the man's brilliant conversation and the fact that he did have access to Nellis; however Jeffery never obtained access to the project that Slade had described to Tina.

Tina is intrigued by the fact that Slade doesn't seem to have a stable job: he would go to a table at a Las Vegas casino and quickly win a thousand dollars, which he said was his way of drawing down a salary when he needed money. Slade has led Tina to believe he was a contactee, showing her a scar on his neck to "prove" it. He also showed her supposedly classified documents about the government's

UFO secrets. Tina also mentioned to me that Glazer had written a dissertation on necrophilia.

I have understood certain things about Jeffery Kaye during this trip. I now believe he was sincere in his misguided efforts to help Allen. Jeffery simply doesn't know how to establish a relationship with people except though money, which gives him control. This became obvious during a conversation with Timothy Good at the conference, before my lecture at Covent Garden. Jeffery explained to Good his interest in the subject. He said he had approached Hynek as the one man he regarded as the primary authority but, he said, "no sooner was he under my... I mean no sooner was he in Arizona, that we discovered he had an advanced form of cancer."

An interesting slip of the tongue. "Under my..." what? My control? My influence?

Susan Kaye left Jeffery after 10 years of marriage, taking her two daughters with her. She is intelligent and vivacious, and seems lost in a personal spiritual upheaval.

Tina and I had a long private talk in Connaught Square. I hadn't realized the Square was a private garden, for which residents each had a key. So she took a cup of coffee in one hand and the key in the other, we sat on a bench and spoke of Allen.

"You represented everything he would have liked to be," she said to my surprise. As for herself, she has visions of a future filled with great adventures, cosmic achievements. We also spoke of Apro. To my question about the status of the group Tina answered that the Lorenzens were ill: Jim has cancer and Coral is not much better. They have given up their research and live in a trailer in Tucson. Tina had dinner with them recently and tried to cheer them up, but she expects the group to disappear soon.

In Glastonbury the team meditated and looked for Templar signs. I found no such connection but felt oddly at ease, in familiar surroundings, as I once did at Gisors castle. A local scholar told me that the way I spontaneously climbed up this morning was not the normal route but the path used in the 14th century to reach the main portal, which no longer exists. The road taken by tourists today is a newly built path. Indeed it is hard to climb up that hill without feeling a strong link with an intensely passionate age in history.

We drove on to Warminster, at my request. We stopped at the crossroads in the fields and looked at the sky. We saw five artificial satellites and several shooting stars, but the horizon was empty of paranormal presences.

Spring Hill. Friday 4 July 1986.

Janine was waiting for me at SFO airport, so we drove north after only a brief stop at the house. Once at the ranch I thought about my three intense days in Paris, where I had met Pierre d'Alançon, the assistant to M. de Grossouvre. This young man works at CGE, a large French company whose close connections to the corridors of power are notorious. He serves there in "international public relations," hence his assignment to the subject.

As I tried to describe to de Grossouvre what the witnesses reported he broke in: "All these people who see saucers that leave traces on the ground, don't you think they ought to consult a shrink?"

The discussion went nowhere. The next day, at the invitation of Simonne Servais, I had lunch *Chez Marius* with general Henri de Bordas, former president of the Foundation for National Defense Studies (the current president is Admiral Lacoste, who headed up French secret services until he lost his job after the Greenpeace scandal). There was a political demonstration in the area, and the streets were blocked.

Henri de Bordas is a much-decorated aviator, *Compagnon de la Libération* and a man of the Right. He has read *Alintel* and said he wished I had further developed the last 10 pages, because he is fascinated by the manipulation angle. At the end of the meal he made some suggestions: I should see M. de Saint Germain, the chief of staff of the Defense Minister, or M. Perget, the Controller of the Armed Forces. All that revolves around the DRET agency that oversees military research.

He walked with us to the end of the street, now empty of demonstrators: "Your book has scared me," he said as we parted.

"Well," I told Simonne once we were alone, "now I have scared a French General!"

"Other reviewers have written that your book was disturbing, that its author was running certain risks..."

"Perhaps it is my role to be disturbing," I agreed.

Later, as we had a drink near Palais Royal, she launched into a long historical dissertation. Behind her I could see an aquarium where a large lobster had died, and two other ugly beasts were fighting. It was a hideous fight, and I had trouble concentrating on Simonne 's Gaullist memories. Through the open door I could see the busy life of Paris, buses and cops, ambulances screaming, people rushing home.

I paid a visit to *Mercure de France*. They will publish *La Mémoire de Markov* in late October. I hope reviewers will find it less "disturbing" than my Alintel. In truth my conversations in England and France have left me feeling confused and a bit dirty. It was good to come back home to the Mendocino woods, and swim naked under the stars, letting the grime of Europe slip away from my skin.

Hyde Street. Tuesday 8 July 1986.

Is it the result of all those recent trips, or the uninspiring atmosphere at work? I feel heavy, unfocused, a bit depressed, although I enjoyed having lunch with Ed May and Beverly Humphrey at SRI yesterday. Jim Salyer was there; they asked me to come back to work for the project. Oddly enough, they have a lot of money now, while Hal's departure and Ingo's separation from the project left them in a state of technical stagnation. The project has gleaming new offices and state-of-the-art computers, but it lacks the spark of genius it enjoyed when it was the poor child of old SRI.

Spring Hill. Saturday 12 July 1986.

On Thursday Ren Breck and Ed Zebroski of EPRI (Electric Power Research Institute) asked me to lunch in order to discuss the Chernobyl nuclear accident and the possible role of Notepad in

Europe. Ren confirmed that after the accident the Soviets tried to reach me in an effort to revive our *Nuclear Notepad* program, to be installed in Geneva on an OECD computer, so their safety experts could communicate with the West in an online conference. Unfortunately we never established contact, and no conference has been organized with the folks in Geneva. (*)

After lunch, Ren and I loaded what was left of InfoMedia in our vehicles: two desks, the computer console, three modems, and our old bookcases. We left the empty computer room, the massive safe. I saw our old offices for the last time and was surprised not to feel much emotion. What I left behind represented a great burden over the last few years of my life, and Janine's life. We drove all that equipment to Berkeley where Ren's old father ruled, tycoon like, over a few rented rooms. He assured everybody that he would turn the company around in no time, having drastically reduced the costs of operation.

Janine got up gaily this morning, "I'm off to see my lilac tree!" she stated brightly. But she came back white and trembling: As she opened the front door she came face to face with an adult buck, standing on our porch: an awesome, dangerous presence.

Spring Hill. Sunday 20 July 1986.

Paradise. The air is sweet liquor. Deer are everywhere, munching on mint and weeds along the slope; birds are courting or fighting in every bush. I work on the small tower (I have yet to nail down the roof) and I read John Keel's latest book. Setting aside his speculations about a supposed "super-spectrum," parallels between the development of his views and mine are striking. Keel, Freixedo and I have reached the same point in our challenge of metaphysical

---

*Mohamed El Baradei, director general of the International Atomic Energy Agency, would later say: "The first lesson that emerged from Chernobyl was the direct relevance of international cooperation to nuclear safety." See *New Scientist*, 14 July 2007. By then, unfortunately, Notepad was no longer available to support such cooperation.

phenomena and of that peculiar control system people call God, or "The Gods."

Hal told me yesterday that the Secret Onion briefing to Abrahamson had been postponed until August 7th. Janine has a new position at Bank of America, right in San Francisco, saving her the former long commute.

Spring Hill. Sunday 27 July 1986.

Reading *The Life of Tesla* by Margaret Cheney. Last week I spent two very pleasant days with Olivier in San Diego. Now there are changes in the SRI parapsychology project: Ed May, who came over for dinner on Monday, asked again that I return to the Institute as a consultant. Russell Targ now works as a research engineer with Lockheed, applying lasers to the detection of aircraft wind shears.

Hyde Street. Thursday 7 August 1986.

Sick with intestinal flu, unable to work. We are setting up a schedule to reimburse the InfoMedia debt that Ren Breck and his father are proving unable to cover. Now I read *Acid Dreams* (**6**), the definitive history of psychedelic manipulation during the 60s, and of the touching but naïve wave of pseudo-mysticism that swept America. The same models that propelled the psychedelic movement apply to the New Age and the current notions of Alien contact.

Catherine will go away to College in two weeks. I bought her Manly Hall's *Secret Teachings* as a gift. She is ready to live her life, to leave us. I think of Allen often. I am angry with him for dying.

Hyde Street. Friday 8 August 1986.

Still sick, so I stay home, making plans for my next trip to New York, another meeting with Fred Adler and an agreement with Siparex in Lyon. For our scheme to work we need support in Europe. Siparex is a small but stable investment organization with support from *Caisse des Dépots*, the largest financial institution in France.

Acid Dreams provides a powerful lesson in contemporary history. It also reinforces the notions I posited in *Messengers,* about disinformation in ufology: the same mechanism that was used for the manipulation of the psychedelic movement in the 60s can exploit the public's interest in extraterrestrial contact. We must remain very critical in what we believe. Yet when skeptics Truzzi, Klass, and Oberg state their positions in the name of "rationalism" I have to bite my tongue. The disinformation is blatant, coming from these well-informed men who must have the same data I do about *Grill Flame*.

Spring Hill. Sunday 10 August 1986.

A tepid wind lifts the drapes gently; all is quiet. Last evening our neighbor told us the wild stories of this region, in the days when the outlaw Black Bart had his lair near Willits. He used to attack coaches on what is now Highway 20 and would go up our road to go hide in the redwoods. At night we see bats chasing insects. When we light up the pool they dive close to the water to catch them. In the fault zone there are many caves full of bats.

Pope John-Paul II has just issued new pronouncements about the nature of angels: he says they have intellect and free will "to a higher degree than humans." Angels are personal beings and compose nine classes or "choirs." How does he know all that?

Hyde Street. Sunday 17 August 1986.

Philadelphia, New York, a quick trip and another cold that makes me cough miserably. In Philly I attended an artificial intelligence conference where Neuron Data made a presentation (7). Then Manhattan, where a corporate lawyer and I set out to define the legal structure of our new Euro-America venture fund.

Returning home, Janine handed me the galleys of *La Mémoire de Markov* and we started planning for our daughter's departure. She will drive away in my Cheyenne truck. Olivier comes over on Tuesday to see her off, and afterwards there will be great emptiness, but I am proud of my darling daughter, and proud of us for having raised our two childen well. I cannot think of any more important achievement. Books or business don't matter very much compared to a smile, a kiss from them, a quiet talk in the evening, a book shared.

Later the same day.

I had a long conversation with Hal: Abrahamson heard the Secret Onion briefing, reacted in an encouraging way, and appointed a scientific committee to make a recommendation, in true bureaucratic fashion. It is headed up by a man Hal describes as a friend, who financed part of the SRI work over the years (**8**).

Hal told me many stories he brought back from a visit to Colonel Stevens, now languishing in jail for some incident in Arizona. Ron Blackburn, a retired Air Force colonel, was along for the trip. Stevens told them about an alleged hybrid Alien child with big ears in Mirasol in Brazil; about the Ummo saga in Puerto Rico; and about his own claims that he was framed after the FBI warned him not to look for proofs that Eisenhower had classified the UFO matter above top secret.

The problem is not Stevens, but people's willingness to believe him. The obvious fakery of the Meier photographs that Stevens takes for granted, and the many contradictions of his extraterrestrial zoo should put them on guard.

Hyde Street. Thursday 21 August 1986.

Yesterday as I climbed the stairs of our Victorian I saw all the boxes on the landing and realized this was Catherine's last day in San Francisco. My daughter who laughed with us, who put so much life and light in every room, joked on the phone with her friends and discussed philosophy or politics with us over dinner, is now far away. At this moment, she is driving with Olivier over the Sierra Nevada. On Saturday she will reach Colorado. I am happy for her, for this transition. Yet last night I had to leave the house and walk along the ocean shore so she would not see the tears I couldn't stop. The grey clouds hung over low, the Alcatraz light tower was a sad reminder of passing time; the waves in the Bay struck the dirty sand with odd sounds I'd never heard before.

This morning the four of us had breakfast together. I left early, went to work. On the way to the Bay Bridge they stopped along the Embarcadero to call me and say goodbye. I went home and couldn't stop crying over a memory of a little girl I have known so well and will never see again; crying even though I know she will be replaced by a young woman of whom I will be even more proud.

Now we are alone, as in the beginning. We have lost Allen to death and Catherine to life. Janine and I have not been alone since Texas, 24 years ago. How fine is the light over the bay, my love, and the flash of your eyes! And how heavy my heart, how heavy.

12

Spring Hill. Sunday 24 August 1986.

The paranormal research project at SRI has entered a new phase. I went there on Friday to plan for the application of expert systems to the remote viewing data, in an effort to better describe the mechanisms of perception that seem to be involved. Ed May led the discussion, with Gary Langford and Beverly Humphrey. I attended a remote viewing session where Gary was the subject. One important question is whether or not the cognitive "signal" can be detected in the form of photons, as some Chinese researchers claim. This seems improbable to me, but Ed May is testing the hypothesis with target slides in darkness, before a high power photomultiplier.

Hyde Street. Tuesday 26 August 1986.

Metaphysics is becoming popular again in Reagan's America. Not only has the Pope affirmed the reality of the Angels, but a new film with David Bowie (*Labyrinth)* features goblins and magic. Some occult manifestations are more sinister: a few idiotic self-described "satanists" have defaced a cemetery in Stanislaus County; then a Muslim couple killed a girl they suspected of sorcery.

Spring Hill. Saturday 30 August 1986.

Our daughter says she's happy on campus in Boulder; Olivier is leaving for France with Jill, and we are on vacation at long last. So after one final review of the investment portfolio with my colleagues I put down the mental burdens, slept a while, and we drove off under the stars, so tired with the world that we spent the day in bed and only got up at sunset, relishing the view of the golden hills across the canyon.

Spring Hill. Sunday 31 August 1986.

Over dinner on Thursday Bill Calvert told us about recent events in Brazil, cases of injuries attributed to those flying objects local people call "chupas." During his most recent trip he interviewed a man named Cosmo who was fishing in the Parnarama River and was chased by a ray from such an object, which hit him repeatedly. He managed to hide among the low branches of a tree on shore. The ray does not seem to kill directly but it paralyzes people.

The Brazilian witnesses claim that the chupas are attracted by the slightest light (a cigarette, a watch with a luminous dial). Most curious is the irrational feeling of terror that the chupas seem to project, out of proportion to their actual behavior. Bill has spoken to a woman doctor in Belém who treated 35 victims of the chupas in the late seventies. Most of her patients had a double puncture mark above the left breast. One of them, an older woman, died a few hours after exposure to the beam from the chupas.

Spring Hill. Sunday 7 September 1986.

Alone at the ranch. On Monday in San Francisco, we had coffee with Paul Hynek who told us that our visit to Phoenix with Richard Sigismond had been Allen's last happy memory, because he could still speak coherently, and walk around. Paul has brought me the copy of the *Lady and the Unicorn* tapestry I had given Allen in 1967. I opened it up, pulling the backboard away to extract the letter from Howard Cross we used to call the *Pentacle Memorandum*, the secret document from Battelle I had found in Allen's files. Now I need to decide whether to publish it, and how.

Friday was a wonderful day. The night sky was pure magic. We feel happy, the great current of our love so full, so certain. Janine's wisdom is like a vast underground river. I will remember this trip through Mendocino, our symbolic purchases (a weather vane) and the feelings that engulfed us.

The deer come very close to the house now. There is a young mother with her two fawns who delight in eating the ripe figs. Janine has found a magnificent dragonfly in the pool. Now she has driven back to the City, taking with her the grapes I gathered for her behind the house. I remain alone at Spring Hill.

Spring Hill. Monday 8 September 1986.

Mars is very bright. Jupiter is already high in the east. I am relearning amusing constellations like "Job's coffin," a small lozenge in the Dolphin, close to the zenith. Janine called, regretting not to have taken more time off: "What difference will that make, in ten years, that I worked five more days for the Bank?" All I could answer was that I loved her, that nothing else really mattered: not my books, not my business, not even research, certainly not money. We have learned a lot this year, and cried a lot, with Mamie's illness, the death of Allen, our daughter's departure: such fragile happiness.

There is freshness in the wind tonight, a precursor of autumn. A worker is here with his bulldozer, enlarging a site to make a pond. We make improvements to the ranch, in anticipation of building the observatory. Rotten boards fall away under my hammer along the fences, cracked by the sun and the rain.

As I set to work on a new manuscript I stumble on a question that has puzzled greater minds: are we a simple product of nature? But then, where does our ability to innovate come from? Or are we a form of life subjected to the influence of more subtle intelligences? But then, for what purpose? If we are but pawns on the board of destiny, what is the point of the game? And who are the players?

Spring Hill. Wednesday 10 September 1986.

The bulldozer has completed its excavations, redrawn the contour of the hill and erected a platform where I will build the larger tower once the dirt settles. The last few passes of the blade revealed watery mud at the bottom of the future pond. I pulled a hose all the way from the spring and a clean, limpid flow began. The workers believe the strong clay will keep the water for us year round. As they were noisily working this morning, two tall bucks strolled by, indifferent to the machine. There are few opportunities to observe such majesty.

Spring Hill. Friday 12 September 1986.

The rain has come, a fine soft rain under a gray sky that lifted in the afternoon. Janine is back with me, so my energy has returned and I am busy with walls and roofs, fences and trenches. We have to sow some wild grass on the naked lands before the big rains come. Autumn is here; it puts a trembling in the trees and wide scars of white in the blue sky.

Spring Hill. Sunday 14 September 1986.

The holidays are almost over. Plans are made for a new meeting in Paris with Siparex and Adler. In the meantime I rebuild my strength here, and I read aloud to Janine from the *Defense Diaries of W. Morgan Petty*, a comical English story that highlights the folly of our nuclear age better than any great discourse by historians or philosophers. I feel an affinity for poor Mr. Petty, a retired glove salesman, as he alerts Soviet authorities to the fact that he has declared his house and yard a nuclear-free zone, begging them in his pathetic letters to refrain from nuking his part of Kent.

What makes me sad is the observation that humans can be made to believe anything, to follow any idiotic instruction. Tonight there is a religious fundamentalist rally downtown; we saw a man walking along Main Street in Ukiah with a large wooden cross covered in stickers that proclaimed pseudo-mystical truths. As a realistic American, he had installed little wheels at the base of the cross to pull it along more easily. Will the next version be motorized?

Hyde Street. Monday 15 September 1986.

In the offices of Sofinnova, high above San Francisco harbor, the atmosphere is heavy. Hervé Hamon, the distinguished boss of Sofinnova France, is moving on to another job, which opens the way for me to run the U.S. side of the organization. But I am tired of their bureaucracy, dominated and constrained by *Crédit National*, a huge French administration. I only have three weeks to decide if I launch a new organization with Fred Adler. From our conference room on the 25th floor of the Embarcadero Center I can see Alcatraz, Telegraph Hill, the Port of San Francisco, and the phallic-looking tower erected by the Coit sisters as a Freudian *hommage* to San Francisco firemen.

Spring Hill. Saturday 20 September 1986.

Quiet rain, sunshine over glistening tree leaves. The new pond is filling up nicely. A buck munches on the willow by the barn. I feel the anxious anticipation of changing jobs. In two weeks the whole team of our proposed organization will meet for dinner at *Taillevent* and the next day we're scheduled to sign a memorandum of understanding. Sofinnova would like me to stay and manage the affairs of their U.S. group but I feel a need for change.

Hal Puthoff tells me that the big Secret Onion briefing of September 5th has been sidetracked: a highly placed official decided the Abrahamson committee was the wrong venue. Unfortunately he never said what the "right" venue would be. The UFO phenomenon is in a quiet phase anyway. There are few reports, and the specialized magazines that survive publish more obituaries of ufologists than sighting analysis or field research. I had lunch with Steve Millard, president of Metricom and friend of my mentor Paul Baran. A business graduate from Northwestern, he once attended one of Allen's lectures and became fascinated by the phenomenon. He suggested starting a small UFO working group in Silicon Valley.

Rue de la Clef. Wednesday 1 October 1986.

Now I feel unsure of my new partners; anguish before one leaps into the future. Paris is anguished, too. The Métro becomes an avant-garde theater with guaranteed audience participation. Yesterday a drug addict gesticulated among passengers, yelling he was about to kill us, and then kill himself. At the next stop most of us left the car with a cowardly sense of relief. The streets are deserted at nightfall; Parisians tacitly observe a self-imposed curfew. Taxis finish their work early and drive home. The city holds its breath, expecting more bombs. Doors are closed, windows shuttered, shops are barred along *Rue des Ecoles*; the night is lugubrious.

Rue de la Clef. Friday 3 October 1986.

My darling, your voice on the phone put order in my mind. Things are going better here. Simone Gallimard invited me for lunch, along with Maryse Condé who has written a book on sorcery in the Antilles, and with the director of *Parisien Libéré*. The sorceress came but the journalist "forgot." We ate the Gallimard *soufflé* without him.

Yesterday evening I met my future associate, the founder of Siparex: competent, professional, in control. We reviewed my proposal for the Euro-America fund and spoke about Fred Adler. Everyone awaits him like the proverbial dragon, who comes out of his lair once a year to devour all the innocents in the countryside.

Can we raise a significant fund in Europe with the Adler connection and our good contacts in Lyon?

Jean-François Boëdec, with whom I had dinner near Cnes headquarters in *Les Halles*, suffered a bad car accident recently but he is resuming his activities, trying to get his influential friends from Brittany to reawaken Poher's interest in UFO research, but Claude is too tired, or too wise.

Pontoise. Hotel du Coq Hardi. Saturday 4 October 1986.

Tonight I took the train alone to the place of my birth, the town of the childhood I spent waiting for Janine. This is an appropriate time to return. Our kids have grown up, beyond their own childhood. Next week I will resign my job and launch a new firm that will invest in high technology on both sides of the Atlantic. We have to dare, to embrace the future.

So I walked over to the cemetery and found my father's grave. On Monday I will be at Mercure de France for the launching of *Mémoire de Markov*. I will sign cards for the press on the august wooden table where Paul Léautaud used to fuck his secretary, as he proudly reports in his many books.

I just had to come back to Pontoise, see the old house, the steeple of St. Maclou. Pontoise is the ideal home of the provincial bourgeois with easy blinders, but for me, a reservoir of nostalgia and unshed tears I must release.

Over the North Atlantic. Sunday 12 October 1986.

To my surprise, I wrote some 50 pages in Pontoise, evoking the flavor and the pangs of growing up in the France of 40 years ago. I also bring back with me from Paris the taste of *Taillevent*'s hazelnut ice cream and our weird negotiations with Fred Adler.

Mercure de France had assembled the literary press: Hélène Renard who works with Louis Pauwels, Marie-Thérèse de Brosses, Jean Cau, Jean-Yves Casgha, photographer Irmeli Jung, a reporter named Muriel Greta, and a dozen others.

Sofinnova still wants to keep me. There was a clash between them and my new partners at a meeting of the French Society for *capital-risque*.

This little village of Paris finance is amused by our trepidations. Adler has signed nothing yet, so everything is up in the air. My mother saw his photograph on the cover of a financial magazine and declared: “This man, he seems like a *sacré filou*, a sly rogue, a pitiless henchman.” Indeed Fred has few friends, suspects everyone, demands perfection, only has respect for those who stand up to him, and has no qualms about chopping heads. But he is one of the finest brains in the business.

Marie-Thérèse de Brosses interviewed me and charmingly invited me for dinner at the *Pré Carré*. She regaled me with a string of incredible stories about parapsychology, Ummo, Ambroise Roux, and poltergeist phenomena.

She recently went to see psychic researcher Hans Bender in Germany, and sadly found him senile.

Spring Hill. Saturday 18 October 1986.

Full moon over the little studio, which we have been painting and fixing all day. There is often reason for aggravation here: careless workers blocking drains, dumping cement in gutters, drunken tenants backing their truck into a wall, neighbors erecting barbed wire lines across our road. Janine is ill with cramps and nausea, which increases my anguish.

As we finish painting the studio the weather turns to soft autumn warmth that troubles my soul, announcing Halloween, pumpkin lanterns, the coming of magic. In Northern California autumn is not the prelude to winter but a season of fresh rains that turn everything green again, a mirror image of spring. Already the edges of the pond are covered with tender grass, bright with the jewels of morning dew.

Our contractor says he can build the observatory tower for a fair price. My plans include a full library.

Hyde Street. Tuesday 21 October 1986.

New York attorney Paul Jacobs just called to tell me that Fred Adler had signed the letter of intent setting up the Euro-America fund and the management company for which I will be president in San Francisco. So the page has been turned.

Fog drifting over the hills: the big trees are draped with mist, dead leaves glued on the path. Yesterday I relocated my operations to Adler's office in Sunnyvale, in the heart of Silicon Valley.

Gretchen called from New Mexico. She works there in a literacy program under Indian Affairs. She has just received a shipment of library books, including *Challenge to Science*. "It gave me a strange feeling," she said, "taking your book to the Navajos!"

Hyde Street. Sunday 26 October 1986.

It would have felt comfortable to run Sofinnova Inc, with a position in the French community, invitations to dinner at the Chamber of Commerce, handshakes from visiting ministers from Paris... But I am not tempted to become a "notable."

"You are jumping from the frying pan into the fire, by joining Fred Adler!" warns my clever friend Barbara Lunberg who just left the Patricof Ventures group for Kidder Peabody in New York. She may be right. But I will be able to work with real Silicon Valley startups, rather than marginal French spinoffs caught up in a maze of disguised government subsidies.

Spring Hill. Sunday 2 November 1986.

We drove through San Francisco's Halloween celebrations this weekend in the convertible, an easy target for creatures that fired confettis and sprayed purple glitter over us. Sandra joined us, dressed up as a nun. Later we drove up to Spring Hill for the weekend. Friday's paper contained an article about Anton LaVey, "recently divorced." So Diane must have left him, as he sinks deeper into the complacency of his own myth.

Spring Hill. Saturday 8 November 1986.

A thick carpet of yellow and red leaves, the glories of autumn, has spread itself under the fig tree. We setup the old stereo in the house and moved our records there for quiet evenings by the fire. Janine reads a biography of Coroner Noguchi; I listen to *Boris Godounov*, the only opera that touches me deeply. This afternoon we went to the waterfalls to reconnect the water system, and then we climbed up the rocky slope of the canyon to the East. At the top we found a small patch of dirt carved out by the rains, a delightful shelter from which we could see the whole valley.

Peter Sturrock is back from a trip to China. He found it tasteless and full of lies.

Hyde Street. Monday 10 November 1986.

Yesterday Janine and I attended a meeting of an exclusive UFO study group assembled in Silicon Valley by Steve Millard. It was an opportunity to present a series of well-researched cases and get their advice. The group included John Hanes, former undersecretary of State under John Foster Dulles; Charlie Rosen, the founder of Machine Intelligence and a luminary of American robotic science; Attorney Bruce Garrett; and a group of high-tech engineers and entrepreneurs.

Charlie Rosen gave an enlightened critique of my work. He forcefully encouraged me to continue this research. He also made the interesting observation that the humanoid form of the ufonauts was the strongest argument against their extraterrestrial origin: not only would the biology of another planet be unlikely to produce beings adapted to our atmosphere and gravity, but an advanced civilization would have used genetic manipulation to engage in space travel.

Spring Hill. Friday 28 November 1986.

Our Silicon Valley UFO group met again on Monday. This time the audience included General "Johnny" Johnson, former head of communications for the White House, and rear admiral Bill Houser, former deputy chief of naval operations. The group wants to do something concrete, so Houser will ask the Navy to analyze the photographs I brought back from Costa Rica.

We have put the Euro-America partnership into motion, in a flurry of phone calls and meetings with the lawfirm I selected. Zycad is buying Silicon Solutions, one of my investments at Sofinnova, at a good rate of return for the portfolio. It is nice to leave on friendly terms, and a financial success.

Hal tells me that the Secret Onion project is dead. After all those high level meetings, someone who was even higher threw a monkey wrench into the gears. I believe they became visible prematurely. The ludicrous episode with Jack Houck has demonstrated that they were incapable of maintaining confidentiality.

Rue de la Clef. Friday 5 December 1986.

We continue to build the Euro-America fund, between Paris and Lyon, returning late in the TGV. Last night I had dinner with Simone Gallimard and Hélène Renard from *Le Figaro*, Jean-Yves Casgha and his wife, and folks from *Antenne Deux*. At one in the morning I walked home. The area was effervescent, after a monster demonstration that turned into a riot before the Invalides. There were groups involved in intense arguments in every café, in an atmosphere of eager expectation. Will anything good come of it?

Today, at *Ecole Polytechnique* I gave a lecture about computer message systems, sponsored by the Telecom ministry. The market is finally emerging, too late for my poor InfoMedia. I learn that my book on the subject has become a reference for software developers.

Rue de la Clef. Saturday 6 December 1986.

My mother brings me the morning coffee and some bad news: during the night the cops cornered and struck a 22-year-old student, killing him. Today, at the exclusive restaurant of the *Polo de Bagatelle* where I had lunch with my new colleagues among the horse set of

Paris, there was no awareness of the "incident." Some elegant damsels from high society were trotting in a circle.

In the afternoon I went back to the Latin Quarter to meet with professor Lorin, a humble, self-effacing man who teaches physics at Orsay University. Peter Sturrock had asked me to contact him to retrieve a sample of the Ubatuba magnesium Lorin had been analyzing at his request. So we sat at a table at the *Rostand*, he opened an envelope and extracted a tiny round box full of resin where the miniscule shard of magnesium was embedded.

Outside a new student demonstration had assembled, yelling slogans, complaining against police brutality.

Lorin went on calmly, explaining to me how he was measuring the presence of various isotopes of oxygen in the sample to determine if it might be of extraterrestrial origin. Now the demonstration had grown so loud that I could barely hear him. Without raising his voice, he went on to tell me it was a shame that the Nobel prize had been denied to Fred Hoyle, who deserved it for explaining the formation of Carbon 12 in stars; but Hoyle had dared to speculate that some spectral anomalies might be explained by the presence of complex organic molecules in space, which of course was anathema for his conservative colleagues.

Guarding the precious sample, I went through the ranks of the angry students: *Malik est mort—assassiné,* they screamed in anguish. Police brutality is bad enough thing, murder is quite another.

I had dinner again with Astrid Merlo, who had invited some friends from Brazil. We could see the flashing lights of police cruisers in front of City Hall; we could hear the rioters who ran from one street to the next. Later I saw the shattered phone booths, the grillwork torn off and some fledgling barricades. Riot police was lined up along the shores of the Seine in full battle gear, gleaming helmets.

In a disgusting editorial author Louis Pauwels said the demonstrators suffered from "intellectual AIDS." Poor Malik Oussekine, at 22, didn't die of that: He was just a bystander but he looked Arabic so the thugs of rightist minister Charles Pasqua shattered his skull. An entire generation finds itself confronted with rotten prospects, a skewed value system and a corrupt elite.

Flight returning from France. Wednesday 10 December 1986.

As we took off we left behind the unhealthy fog of Roissy and images of a country torn by doubt. In the Latin Quarter, Saturday evening, I saw students setting cars on fire on Boulevard St. Germain in the name of democracy and peace. Two days later I was on a stage at the Palace of Congresses with a panel of entrepreneurs and Alain Madelin, minister of industry. Before 4,000 young businessmen he said that Liberty and Equality were sometimes incompatible, that the young might have to choose between them. He said nothing about Fraternity.

Returning from Phoenix. Monday 15 December 1986.

Jeffery Kaye's team, headed up by Tina, has succeeded in pulling off their conference in Scottsdale, quite an event. I was impressed by abductee Travis Walton, who spoke after me. I don't think this man is lying when he describes his five-day ordeal: His crew chief was there too, confirming the sighting. After 11 years of self-imposed silence they have gathered up enough courage to face journalists and skeptics and talk about it again.

The conference took place at the Scottsdale Center for the Arts, attended by fashionably-dressed men and women, adorned by large blow-ups of Billy Meier's fake saucers (**9**) and punctuated by media types and the occasional Navajo artist. Jeffery's newest girlfriend came over in a pastel dress, offered me her hand and said in French, "Je suis Kiki." Susan has flown in from London; all the talk is about the silly Face on Mars, which they continue to take seriously.

I spent the night at the Hyneks where I had a long conversation with Paul. This morning I spent an hour alone in Allen's office. Mimi is sending his files to Cufos in Chicago but he had requested that she entrust me with his private Rosicrucian archives. She also gave me the Steiners, the Heindels, written in the pompous language of occultism of the thirties. Some of those volumes were studiously annotated by the young astronomer: Allen's marginal notes interest me more than the books themselves.

I always think of Allen when I fly over the magnificent landscapes of the American West, with its impression of infinite freedom, of timeless beauty beyond the wanderings of our lives. When I read his annotations in Rudolf Steiner's *Knowledge of the Higher Worlds*, his favorite bedside book (he owned two copies, heavily marked up in color pen) I feel that some of our dialogue continues.

That side of Allen was always accessible to me, even when his mind was distracted by external events, a passing damsel, a funny cartoon, or a television camera.

In Steiner's book there is a passage that Allen underlined most heavily. It reads:

"*Provide for yourself moments of inner tranquillity, and learn in these moments to distinguish the essential from the non-essential... it is just these moments of seclusion, when used in the right way, which imbue one with strength to perform his daily tasks... Our aim in these moments must be to contemplate and judge our experiences and actions as if they were those of others.*"

On that level he was wise, sharp, and critical: he was a soul on the very edge of initiation.

Hyde Street. Saturday 27 December 1986.

This year is ending softly, although Olivier always gets bored after two days at Spring Hill, so we drove back to the city, where he could find electronic stores, chips, motors, and software.

Aimé Michel has read *Markov's Memory* and wrote me a long letter. I had assumed there was nothing more to say between us, because he kept repeating the same old tune: "France is the last refuge of Culture!"

Such a joke. But Janine thinks I am unfair.

I am writing in bed. My children are having breakfast, arguing and laughing. I keep trying to reach people in Lyon to setup our management company.

Janine brings me a second cup of coffee, she kisses me: the world becomes a happy, simple place.

Hyde Street. Saturday 10 January 1987.

The holidays are over; our daughter leaves again tomorrow for Boulder, and the Euro-America fund has the rudiments of a structure. I just spent two days in New York with Fred Adler and his own mentor, industrialist Pierre Simon. I admire the New York feeling of unlimited intellectual and financial potential, even if it hides the difficulties of an unpredictable business.

Arriving from Boston (where I made a stop to help Optima, on behalf of Sofinnova) I spent the first evening in Manhattan with a journalist from the *Wall Street Journal.* She gave me a tour of their offices on a high floor of the World Trade Center. Dinner afterwards at the River Café, a barge anchored under the Brooklyn Bridge.

Adler's office: no desk; an oval-shaped table, two telephones, and family scenes in numerous frames. Reigning over all this is the sharp eye and cutting tone of the old financier. I gave him a quick report on the state of our documents and contacts with European investors. He approved a text, changed the date of our next trip.

In the morning a pink sun lit up Seventh Avenue, the air was cold and clean. I went over to see Pierre Simon at Multiparts. We had lunch in his office: "I prefer to call out for lousy sandwiches and eat them here, rather than going down to an expensive restaurant on Wall Street and eating lousy sandwiches there," he said.

In quiet moments I read Aldous Huxley's *Perennial Philosophy*, pondering again the passages Allen has underlined. Huxley chastized "ordinary people" and their boring universe, "so dull that they have to distract their minds from being aware of it by all sorts of artificial amusements." I find sadness and irony in that quote. One of Allen's most exaperating traits was the fickleness of his attention, constantly distracted. The most serious debate, at the point of crucial insight, could be derailed by a joke, a cartoon or the sight of some new toy in a drugstore window. Our last really serious discussion had taken place at Corralitos Observatory, where he was isolated from most "artificial amusements." Yet it is through that weakness that Hynek was most human, close to things mundane, to these "ordinary people" Huxley despises so arrogantly.

Hyde Street. Wednesday 28 January 1987.

In 1921 Sigmund Freud wrote this remarkable statement: "I am not among those who are set against what people call occult psychological phenomena and who regard them as unscientific, worthless or even dangerous. If I was at the beginning of a scientific career rather than at the end as I currently am, I might choose no other domain of study, in spite of its difficulties." (Freud's *Letter to Hereward Carrington*).

Hyde Street. Sunday 1 February 1987.

Last Wednesday, over dinner with Keith Harary and Darlene we discussed the People's Temple debacle. And this afternoon we drove over to see Jim Jones' building in Redwood Valley, newly repainted in blue and gray by the County of Mendocino.

A Russian book accuses the CIA of killing Jim Jones and his followers to prevent them from emigrating to the East, a grossly flawed theory that misrepresents the facts. That does not exculpate the CIA, however. It is likely that the People's Temple was closely watched, if only because agents interested in mind control had every reason to investigate how such a group could be influenced. This docs not imply they were responsible for the suicides. The internal dynamics of the cult led to that tragedy, inexorably.

The real mystery that lingers concerns the murder of Al and Jeannie Mills. Did their son actually kill them? If so, where is the murder weapon? Why did the media drop this unsolved case so quickly?

Hyde Street. Friday 6 February 1987.

We are staying in the City this weekend, planning repairs to this grand old Victorian and checking our offering memorandum for the Euro-America Fund. On Tuesday I fly to France to contact investors.

This afternoon I met with Ed May, Beverly Humphrey, Gary Langford, their team of analysts and remote viewers. My SCI clearance (for "Sensitive Compartmented Information") has been reactivated in the context of our project to investigate the potential use of artificial intelligence and expert systems in parapsychology.

Rue de la Clef. Sunday 15 February 1987.

A little rain, cold and dirty, falls over France and plugs up my lungs. My partners and I are paying a visit to every institution of French finance, from the *Bourse* to Air Liquide, Saint Gobain, and the larger banks. We will go on to Geneva and Lyon in the next few days.

Yesterday I visited Roland Villeneuve again in his apartment on Rue Monge. He was so happy with my gift of *Man into Wolf* that he gave me three of his books. Villeneuve, who had a long career as a banker with Crédit Lyonnais, is a great scholar of witchcraft and the occult, with a predilection for the artistic manifestations of the grotesque and *outré*. He urged me to compile an iconography of Magonia, a wonderful project if only I had a year I could spend roaming through great museums and visiting every church in France in search of snarling devils and gnomes abducting maidens.

Villeneuve told me a nice story about the Devil who, strolling along with a companion, saw an excited crowd arguing in a village square. The young man went ahead to get some information and came back alarmed: "Master," he said, "the news is bad: these folks have found part of the answer." "Don't worry," answered the Devil with laughter, "I will make them believe that it is the *whole* answer."

Rue de la Clef. Friday 20 February 1987.

Snow is falling over *rue Monge* and eerily, over the nearby Paris Mosque. The temperature has dropped below freezing; the city has withdrawn into its shell. The police expect trouble during the trial of Arab terrorist Abdallah, so the atmosphere is tense. When we flew back from Geneva this afternoon our plane was detained on the runway while the authorities evacuated one of the terminals at Roissy and blew up an abandoned package.

I wish Janine were with me. I miss her, when I sit down in a warm coffeehouse, when I watch the snow putting a softer touch on the rough edges of the world, and when I roam through the bookstores.

Hyde Street. Sunday 1 March 1987.

In Simone Gallimard's office, whose windows open on *rue Condé*, I had to listen to her speech as she played the unlikely role of the impoverished publisher: "Business is bad, people don't read anymore, bookstores are closing, television has killed publishing, we can't survive, we have to pay our authors too much..."

I wondered if I had not strayed into the nearby *Comédie Française* theater by mistake. I could have come up with some excuse and walked out, but I fell under the charm of these old walls dripping with French literary tradition. Besides, her *Mercure* has published two of my novels in one year.

The person who stands out from the memories of this trip is Jean-François Deluol, an artist who told me he had been inspired by my books: he dedicated one of his shows to Carl Jung and me. He runs a house for children with special needs in Paris. His paintings show green phosphorescent skies, red fabrics, and beings from another reality handling objects that remain closed, their contents hidden from us. The eyes are empty. Something is missing from these disquieting scenes, and it is precisely that omission that makes them interesting. It parallels the anguish I recognize in the phenomena.

Spring Hill. Saturday 7 March 1987.

Colin Wilson is the contemporary writer with the deepest insights into the gears of consciousness, because he does not shy away from probing its sensual nature:

"I have always been fascinated by the problem of sex," he writes, "because it seems to hold the key to the secret of intenser consciousness. I have been obsessed by the way sexual experience seems to slip through the fingers like fairy gold."

In *The Hedonists,* one of his key novels, he dwells on an erotic scene, of a man caressed by two girls, and observes: "The man who can spend two hours upon such a sweet pinnacle of ecstasy has experienced something of the state of the gods, and must become larger of soul thereby."

The book I hope to write some day on the theme of Lilith would try to extend Wilson's insight.

I continue to be interested in Vintras' cult and the strange border zone between the mystical and the grotesque, so well illustrated by Roland Villeneuve.

Separately, Kit and Hal have assured me that plans for the Secret Onion were being revived in Washington. A budget "niche" has been found, but someone has requested that the group brief the Air Force on their plans. The Space Command gave an enthusiastic green light. Already, arrangements are made for investigators to dig into some cases, but the first targets would be dead horses like the Bentwaters incident, Ummo, or the *Prieuré de Sion*, all that conspiratorial stuff that obscures the genuine mystery. I have no doubt they can easily spend millions of dollars on such wild goose chases and come up with nothing. All this reinforces my suspicion that nobody in or out of government has taken the measure of the real problem. If there is a real research group it is very well hidden, away from normal structures.

At a recent conference of forensic pathologists Kit heard disquieting reports about a sharp increase in human cases of ritual mutilations. In two years the number of such crimes has gone from two or three to over 200.

A feeble sun is shining over the ranch while I try to dismiss these horrible thoughts. A moment ago I found the unmistakeable claw marks of a bear in the mud around the pond.

Hyde Street. Sunday 15 March 1987.

I spent Wednesday in San Diego, working with Olivier and his colleagues on a model of computer conferencing they are developing for Digital Equipment.

Colin Wilson writes:

> All my life I have obscurely felt in the grip of powers beyond myself... If I am tired, and my brain feels dull, I am easily discouraged; I become a bad instrument of these powers. On the other hand, if I keep faith and drive myself hard, and keep up a high level of optimism by sheer will and imagination, I have a sense of being used for a purpose that goes beyond my own, and seems to endow me with new powers. There is a sense of inevitability and ease, and I feel surprised, like a sparrow that suddenly finds itself flying at the speed of a jet.

That is how I feel now as I restructure my life and work. I am getting a new computer to run tests of my model for the SRI paranormal research project. At a recent meeting of our discussion circle in Silicon Valley Charlie Rosen told me, "I admire your patience." Indeed I will never give up my efforts to understand what lies behind the UFO phenomenon because it offers an access path, an avenue of discovery to the nature of those "powers" mentioned by Colin Wilson. But there is a rational restraint in me, and the wisdom of Janine, preventing me from rushing into the "Sciences of the Night."

13

Paris. Saturday 18 April 1987.

Sounds of France: police cars rush by, sirens blaring, while the bells of Saint Médard ring in anticipation of Easter. Another fine evening, another nice walk along the Seine after dinner with Astrid Merlo. She says it would be a mistake for my new fund to invest in Europe.

She thinks a financial mess is coming with unstable prices, France especially vulnerable. What politicians say about entreprise creation and innovation here is a sad joke, mere window dressing.

Paris. Sunday 19 April 1987 (Easter).

At the corner bistrot on *Rue des Abbesses*, women speak with the gravelly accent of Edith Piaf; men wear caps, they order ham and cheese sandwiches with dill pickles and beer with soda. I enjoy the detachment of a place where nothing was calling me. The cat of the establishment jumps on my knees with a contented whir before extending an eager paw toward my *croque-monsieur*. At the bar, a group of men are reminiscing about World War Two, the invasion of Germany, Baden-Baden... The *Sacré Coeur* basilica inspires no fervor even when the organ plays at full strength for a tidal wave of young tourists from every country. It is undistinguished and dirty.

So I go out again, losing my way in the little streets of Montmartre. Janine must be back at Spring Hill today with a family friend, visiting California again after all these years. I read Jules Verne and George Sand. I find marvels in bookstores, like Maurice Magre's poems entitled: *La Montée aux Enfers*, the ascension to Hell.

Numerous meetings at the big French banks with Adler and my French colleagues are teaching me how venture capital funds get raised, the negotiations involved. Fred takes the high road, talking in sweeping terms about the American economy; he boasts of his financial exploits. French bankers listen skeptically. We have only circled about two thirds of the commitments we were seeking.

"Why is the well-known Fred Adler wasting time to help manage a modest European fund?" asked a BNP manager.

"I'm interested in Europe," answered Adler with his acid voice, running his hand through his hair, which he dyes blond. "I've been coming here for over 25 years. I've seen more changes in France in the last 5 years than in the previous 20. I believe it's time to move assets here. I hope I'll live long enough to enjoy the proceeds!"

"But you already know that you won't enjoy them" said the banker wistfully. "You'll always be attracted by some new projects."

"Well, you are right," Adler agreed, leaning back in his chair. "Frankly I could have stopped a long time ago. If I listened to my kids, I'd put everything in municipal bonds right now. But it's the future that fascinates me. The past is dead; the only important things in it are the mistakes it contains, the mistakes I made, because they teach me real lessons I can apply today."

There was an amusing scene on *Place de la Bourse*, as we came out of another meeting with bankers. Adler wanted to sit down with Paul Jacobs and me to discuss plans, so I took him to a local café. He ordered cappuccinos. The waiter had never heard of it, they don't serve cappuccinos in Paris. So Fred asked for three *cafés crèmes* and one hot chocolate and he proceeded to explain to us the economic destiny of Europe while distributing equally the chocolate into our cups, one spoonful for Paul, one spoonful for Jacques, one spoonful for Fred, and another dissertation about trends in interest rates.

We took the high-speed train to Lyon to meet with former Prime Minister Raymond Barre. This led to an interesting exchange on the topic of power. Adler said that power should be delegated: "It's only effective when you give it to someone else." That is the venture capitalist's view, the perspective of a kingmaker. Barre disagreed. He said power was only effective when it was exercised. He believes in the mounting economic strength of Southern France: a triangular alliance of Barcelona, Marseilles, and Genoa could be the new power once the Middle East settles its quarrels in ten years or so. It is a professor's hopeful vision. Barre also said: "People will have to lose their jobs before they grasp the notion of competition." That statement is light years ahead of French political reality. On the contrary the fabulous sums the State is earning from denationalization of major firms like Paribas and Saint Gobain (which they call "privatization") are being used to prop up dinosaurs like the steel industry.

There is sunshine over Montmartre. Near the *Moulin Rouge* the old coffee shop where we had our late snacks still stands, Frankfurt sausages and French fries on the menu. Police patrols keep the area in check. I saw them arresting an African in a blue robe and tiger hat who was selling fake jewels on the sidewalk while stout German couples walked by, eager for spicy thrills.

Paris. Monday 20 April 1987.

Still in Montmartre, hidden in a cheap hotel, the better to work on my manuscript. When thinking about the future of artificial intelligence and venture capital it is crucial to take a long-term view, but I cannot find it in Paris. My romantic attachment to old stones is itself a search for stability. I seek a balance between the pregnant future of technical revolutions and a rich past that contains far more than our mistakes. Fred is full of contradictions; he owns a house in Jamaica and a Mercedes, and works 80 hours a week. My French partners all dream of a Mercedes and a million dollars. They would retire in Neuilly where they would never see an Arab or a Black and devote their lives to collecting pastels. These people amuse me; they already think of golden retirement, running their lives on obsolete criteria.

Rue de la Clef. Sunday 26 April 1987.

At Shakespeare & Co. I rummaged along the shelves and found a copy of John Fowles' *Ebony Tower*, a first edition, marked at only 44 francs. The shop owner was astonished. "I must have priced it a long time ago," he said as he reluctantly took my money. I am also reading Charles-Louis Royer's *Le Sérail*. Curiously, both books are about a man who lives with several women. In both stories he is an artist, a painter. Artists can be excused for leading dissolute lives and experimenting with love. Engineers and businessmen cannot, except in Truffaut movies. *L'Homme qui Aimait les Femmes* speaks of that great despair, breathless search of things that slip beyond our grasp, marvels that seem possible one moment and are withdrawn the next, new realities that come to the surface only to be denied and ridiculed, like the Loch Ness monster.

I had dinner with Simonne Servais who confessed her metaphysical anguish. I spoke of the bigger questions: magic, the higher levels. "It's too easy," she complained, "just another escape." She drove me back to *Saint-Germain des Prés*. Every terrace was full; every café was overflowing with revellers, the Seine passing by like a voluptuous lady dressed in black velvet.

Rue de la Clef. Tuesday 28 April 1987.

Jean-Jacques Velasco generously brought me two files regarding Gepan cases, sightings near Arcachon and Grenoble. We had dinner at the *Pot-au-Feu*. He was discouraged once again, because the management of Cnes had turned down his request to publish a notice about Gepan's tenth anniversary: it might detract from the 25th anniversary of Cnes itself... By the same token he was not invited at the celebration, reserved for the bureaucratic elite, the media, the *Polytechniciens* who run French science.

TWA Flight to NewYork. Wednesday 29 April 1987.

We have only raised 10 million dollars for Euro-America so far: too little to launch the project, too much to give it up. Siparex has promised to raise another five million in Lyon. I hadn't spent an entire month in France since 1968. I have the impression of being stuck in a tunnel.

In the woods around Paris chestnut trees are loaded with heavy flowers bending their branches over ponds and lakes. Maman is happy, alert and active. She enjoys our evenings in restaurants near Notre-Dame. Yet she has occasional episodes of anguish and panic tears. She has kept my letters from my teen-age years, when I wrote with silly adolescent advice, railing against the French *bourgeoisie*. The style makes my grinding teeth hurt but my anger hasn't changed.

Spring Hill. Sunday 3 May 1987.

Spring Hill means Janine in my arms again, blue sky, purple irises. A deer runs along the window at full gallop; he wheels around effortlessly, clears the white fence.

Paranormal research is getting obscured by petty schemes and sensational trivia. Uri has just published *The Geller Effect*, a series of unsubstantiated claims that leaves me cold; and an artist named Budd Hopkins has become fascinated with the lurid sexual context of abduction stories, now spreading all over the media.

Nearly two decades ago, I pointed out the parallels between alien reports and medieval stories of witchcraft, incubi and succubae, demons and ghouls. The public is now ready to embrace the idea in a new fashion. After John Fowles' admirable story entitled *A Maggot*, Whitley Strieber's *Communion*, a novel cleverly reframed as personal reality, has become a best-seller.

The two books by Hopkins and Strieber mark a major change in the public perception of the phenomenon. Gone are the speculations about advanced physics and rational statistics. The field has been ratcheted into a higher level of paranoia and absurdity, on the basis of poorly-documented but lurid tales of rape and anal probing aboard interplanetary spacecraft piloted by emotionless "Grays."

The fact that many of the details used to assemble this picture have been obtained under hypnosis at the hand of amateurs has passed unchallenged: the public swallows it all as gospel. Spurred on by the promotional campaigns behind these two books, abductees are coming out by the hundreds in America, eager to get hypnotized.

Alien scientists wouldn't need to exert terror and torture on hapless victims in order to collect human seed or make hybrid babies. They wouldn't need to traumatize an entire generation to influence human evolution.

Once again, the only constant in this equation is absurdity.

Hyde Street. Thursday 7 May 1987.

Heat wave over San Francisco. The air is brown, stagnant. On Polk Street crowds go almost naked, the occasion of scenes that range from the titillating to the ugly. Beer bellies roll down the sidewalks amidst miniskirted girls and hairy musclemen in leather briefs. They jostle each other on buses, line up in coffee shops and bars, or just ignore one another. Life goes on unperturbed.

I continue my work on the expert system I am building for Ed May's new remote viewing project at SRI but I am tired of the heat and of the uncertainty in our lives.

Janine now works across the Bay in Concord, at the technology development center of the Bank of America. She was always an outstanding business programmer, but she has now demonstrated a keen ability to manage very large systems, repeatedly receiving the President's award. Among other big projects, she served as the manager for the reliability assurance project for the massive network of ATMs deployed by the Bank, 1,500 machines from Oregon to the Mexican border.

Hyde Street. Saturday 9 May 1987.

In a world where professional work conditions most of our lives, why is it so hard to combine it with realization of the self, of our mind? Perhaps I am only good at ruminating among old books.

Janine and I went out to run some errands. Catherine has written from Colorado, a long letter filled with confettis for Mother's Day. Olivier calls often; we delight in these conversations but we miss our friends. I especially miss Allen Hynek. I seldom talk to Hal Puthoff, who has become secretive about his own work. At SRI the psychic project has acquired a "scientific" veneer that is superficially more rigorous, but the broad inspiration of the early years is gone.

Hyde Street. Wednesday 13 May 1987.

Reading Stendahl's *Journal* in publisher Tchou's pretty collection of bedside books, a nice editorial idea. It contains the feelings and analyses of a young man from a bygone era. People were telling him, "You have too much soul!"

Ed May came over last night for a demonstration of my expert system characterizing remote viewing sites. It is one thing to get gifted subjects to describe a place, and quite another to judge whether or nor their statement matches the target. The problem is to classify the sites in systematic fashion.

Spring Hill. Sunday 17 May 1987.

Recovering at the ranch, playing tennis with my daughter, inventing new games. Sheer physical activity feels good, even if my tennis balls get lost in the bushes. We play at counting frogs and the bear's footprints.

Hyde Street. Monday 25 May 1987.

Memorial Day, filled with color, noise, work and laughter. We made a big fire at the ranch to get rid of dead branches, bushes, and weeds. Catherine found a snake as fat as a water hose.

Alien abductions remain the fashionable novel topic. On the phone, Paul Hynek described an amusing scene in a Scottsdale restaurant when two members of Cufos came over to tell Mimi about Budd Hopkin's latest ideas. Outraged, she screamed: "Do you mean to tell me the Aliens are spying on Earth women and fly down to abduct them just at the time of ovulation?" All conversations stopped at nearby tables while forks fell on the plates of astonished diners.

Behind the scene are ugly stories of bitter competition for media attention between Budd Hopkins and Whitley Strieber, each trying to delay or out-market the other's book amidst ugly acrimony and mutual accusations, creating an even angrier atmosphere in a field already characterized by distrust and paranoia.

Budd Hopkins' sensational claim about the reality of abductions rests on the transcripts of his hypnosis sessions with a woman he calls "Kathie Davis." She wrote to him in September 1983 after a series of incidents at her parents' house that involved strange lights in the yard, ground traces (in the form of strongly-pressed, hydrophobic patches of soil), memories of an early dream about gray-faced creatures showing her a box, and strange phone calls while she was pregnant with her second son.

"Kathie" was invited by Hopkins for a visit to New York City where she spent six days in October 1983, undergoing a series of sessions with a local psychologist in Hopkins' presence. What emerged was a scenario of contact, sightings and multiple abductions, evidence for what Hopkins concludes was "an intense interest in her by a specific group of UFO occupants."

The witness in this case, a 24-year old woman who struggled to raise two boys, gives every indication of being sincere. It seems clear she needs help making sense of the ordeal, which comes on top of a frightening series of medical challenges. Given all this, and the fact that she contacted Hopkins soon after reading his first book on abductions (*Missing Time*), did it make rational and scientific sense to subject her to a series of hypnotic regressions based on strongly-held hypotheses by Hopkins, his pre-established certainty that she was selected by Aliens for medical and sexual procedures?

The manuscript of *Dimensions* is complete, as a compilation and review of my earlier works, updated to serve as introduction to our fieldwork, which will appear under the title *Confrontations*. Bob Weiss, who flew up from Hollywood this week, told us he had finished *Dragnet* and was ready to take *FastWalker* to Joe Dante. He brought us a colorful gift, a ceramic cookie jar shaped like a saucer.

Peter Beren called with bad news about Bill Whitehead, my editor of *Invisible College*. He is ill with AIDS and lives at the Chelsea Hotel, where he awaits a cure—or death. Once again, I experience this vacuum: not knowing what to write, only this sadness.

Rue de la Clef. Monday 29 June 1987.

Midnight. How boring, all this time slipping away without you! The weather is gray, humid. Taking two steps makes me feel sweaty and dull. I thought this would be a short trip but I still have five days here. There are strikes, street demonstrations and arguments with my partners about the direction of the new venture fund.

TWA Flight to Boston. Friday 3 July 1987.

Every plane flight brings a memory of Allen. He was, at heart, an observer, as I am. He always sat by a window, surveying earth and sky, noticing things, some new sights. He dreamed of flying over the moon in a spacecraft, observing its craters and crevices.

Back in Paris I met with Claude Poher again in his office at Cnes headquarters and I gave him a fragment of the Bogota specimen. Spare furniture there: a metal cabinet, a Macintosh computer, some space photographs on the wall. Claude thinks that UFOs paralyze witnesses with gamma rays tuned between 0.5 and 2 Mev at 1,000 pulses per second and a flux of 10^{12} photons. Total exposure would be under 50 rad, the dangerous threshold. He wants to find out if the effect varies with distance. The mechanism could involve muscle membrane depolarization, sodium/potassium exchange.

I bumped into Elizabeth Antébi as I rushed out of the subway: "So you come to France without telling your friends!" she chided me. I had dinner at her house with her friend Anne, a banker and his wife, and another businessman. Conversation came to the subject of corruption, which is on the increase in French business. Anne, a producer in Mike Wallace's *60 Minutes*, has just returned from Russia with stories of a social system rapidly falling apart.

Hyde Street. Sunday 5 July 1987.

Janine picked me up as I landed and we drove straight to Spring Hill, arriving at midnight. I stripped off my travel clothes and swam for a long time, to wash away the tiredness of the flight.

Sleep takes root here, like our massive redwoods, and doesn't let go. Dreams slither away. We wake up heavy with fresh reality and pleasure to be alive. An architect came over yesterday to look at my plans for the tower: Suddenly the observatory project feels real. Financially, however, we cannot afford to relax: we still have to honor the guarantee of our bank loan to InfoMedia. The Brecks are unable to repay it, in spite of their promises.

Spring Hill is comfortably removed from intellectual currents. Here it is the Earth that thinks and dreams aloud, if only one listens. Intelligence is an obstacle rather than a tool in the pursuit of spiritual insight, as every good hermetist knows.

"Consciousness" is the big word these days, a receptacle for anything unknown or bizarre, a potluck cauldron where one can throw psychedelic experiences, parapsychology, and every quantic contradiction left exposed by the messy, incomplete statements of modern physics.

Spring Hill. Sunday 26 July 1987.

Our developer neighbor came over again with an offer to sell us some of his land in exchange for the right to drive his truck across our ranch when he cuts his redwoods. Politely but firmly, we said no.

Jean-Jacques Velasco and his wife Danièle came to San Francisco this week. I gave them a fresh copy of the Ovnibase system and took them to a meeting of our Silicon Valley group, attended by Peter Sturrock, Rear-Admiral Houser and General Johnson. We spoke of Trans-en-Provence at length. Jean-Jacques handed me some of the soil samples.

Another full day at SRI with Ed May's project to discuss site classification, which led to larger questions: is the viewer describing the locale, or the picture that we use as a target? Current protocol assumes it is the photograph that is described, not the site. If so, can we prove that remote viewing is anything other that precognition of the test result, or the feedback itself?

The project staff currently comprises Nevin Lantz, Peter McNellis, Scott Hubbard, Joe McMoneagle, Cathy Flowers, Vicki Walsh, Jessica Utts, Frances Sancado, Gina Trask, Jim Salyer, Thane Frivold, and Beverly Humphrey. Dave Saunders and I are among the consultants. The budget is about $3 million a year.

Hyde Street. Wednesday 29 July 1987.

Curious discussion over the last few days with Sturrock, McCampbell and Dick Haines, all of them suddenly fascinated with conspiracy tales inspired by a memo attributed to President Truman, who supposedly appointed a dozen scientists to study crashed saucers and their occupants. Did a "Majestic Twelve" group actually exist and if so, did it have anything to do with UFOs? Or fake UFO stories created as camouflage for something else?

I cannot help but reflect that Allen left the scene at the right time.

Hyde Street. Thursday 30 July 1987.

Hal, who has news about the Secret Onion project, tells me the latest briefing went to the top of the SDI (Strategic Defense Initiative) staff, who asked for the Air Force's advice. Briefings were set up for the space command.

"There's only one more step, Jacques, for a really massive project to begin," Hal said. "All the cutouts are set up, covers for the funds. We've started a physicist on a study of advanced propulsion."

"Does he know anything about UFOs?" I asked.

"Of course not," Hal answered laughing, "he doesn't even know there's any connection. We're in the middle of your Alintel!"

Back at SRI where I worked with Gina Trask on the classification of remote viewing sites, we spread out some 200 slides over light tables. Ed May confirmed that some of the operational remote viewers have described UFOs and occupants. Satellite imagery used as target showed real objects, but the team was never able to find a trace of them in the official files when they checked with the responsible agencies. Another group, with higher access (all of this is beyond top secret) was told that that "the images had gone back to the place where this kind of thing is centralized."

Today I had lunch with Matt, a young computer programmer who witnessed two UFOs ten years ago in Honolulu. A curious detail came up in our discussion: two weeks after he spoke to the SRI folks (who sent him to me) a woman came to his apartment, claiming she was from DoD and needed information "about his neighbors"...

For a subject that is supposedly of no scientific interest and of no concern to the Air Force, the UFO field mobilizes a remarkable number of shadowy investigators and sundry agents.

Hyde Street. Friday 31 July 1987.

I am surprised to see Peter Sturrock ready to take the MJ-12 papers seriously. He even wonders about the U.S. government seeking an alliance with Aliens. Peter, like McCampbell, doesn't see the contradiction in these scenarios. Here we have rational, open-minded men, scientifically trained, yet unable to critically dissect this situation. Conveniently, they tend to ignore established facts whenever a new spicy rumor springs up.

Olivier arrives this morning with his friend Jeff. Catherine will pick them up at the airport. Alain will join us on Monday: it's a feast!

Spring Hill. Saturday 8 August 1987.

Summertime. A group of our friends has come over: artist Iris Schenke and her husband, their son Matthew, and Astrid Merlo. Catherine is here too, with her friends Carla and John, so the group speaks Swedish, Italian and French. We took little Matthew on a hunt for lizards and frogs. We spoke of the future of information technology with the detachment that comes after a plateful of tortellini and a few glasses of champagne

Our contractor has asked me to mark one side of the tower foundation; so last night Janine and I pulled out our old telescope and aligned two sturdy posts on Polaris. Today we planted steel rods at the four corners, defining a rectangle that follows the Golden Ratio. We have saved enough money to pay for the construction, from my books and my consulting.

On Friday I was finally able to reach Aimé Michel at a clinic in Gap. His voice was weak, but when he recognized me he suddenly sounded stronger: "You know, I've had an operation, they removed a small cancer from my prostate," he said in his singing Provence tones. "So now they're using radiation; I have some chances to remain on this planet a while longer." So that's why I have been unable to reach him since June.

Spring Hill. Saturday 15 August 1987.

Peter Sturrock and I have been close since Velasco's visit and the meetings in Cupertino. He has entrusted me with the combination to his safe that contains his UFO samples.

On Thursday Janine and I had dinner with Keith and Darlene in their San Francisco apartment. The city was overcast and foggy, an evening worthy of the Maltese Falcon with great flows of mystery around the old Victorian mansions. Keith had invited two expert hypnotists as well as Diana Reiss, a specialist in animal communication who works with dolphins and orcas. We spent the evening discussing the use of hypnosis in abduction research. The two hypnotists agreed to help me study Matt's observations.

Now Aimé Michel has written from Gap:

> *Salut Jacques!* What a strange impression, to hear your voice coming down from so far away into the solitude of my hospital. It gave me great pleasure. For me, the UFO affair has been closed since I have uncovered the same stories in ancient historians like Polybe, Tite-Live and others. I know what they are coming to do. We still have to find who "they" are, but Tite-Live already notes that they refuse all contact. Is that the proper word, "refuse?" I think the notion of contact is as meaningless as attempting to find a particle inside a wave. I also think the answer is linked to the discovery, yet to be made, of a different kind of logic.

Diana Reiss has just come back from a conference on Seti in Hungary. She said a debate was going on about extraterrestrial intelligence, at the occasion of research on possible Martian life. Would it necessarily be appropriate to speak of "intelligence?" Isn't communication often based on something else?

I think about what I try to build and realize the immensity of our ignorance. Some answers must be very close: inside us, in our perception of the world. We performed a simple consecration of the tower tonight: to knowledge, love, and the study of mysteries.

Spring Hill. Sunday 23 August 1987.

Going through my archives yesterday I found a beautiful incantation from ancient Greece sent by a friendly reader. It comes from *Papyri Graecae Magicae* edited by K. Preisendanz, Leipzig 1928, translated by E.M. Butler who quotes it in his own book *Ritual Magic* (**10**).

The text, entitled *All Powerful Might of the Great Bear Constellation*, dates from about 200 B.C.

> *I invoke you, Holy ones, mighty and majestic glorious Splendors. You are sacred, powerful earth-born arch-daimons, peers of the great god; denizens of Chaos, Erebus, the unfathomable Abyss. O you Earth-dwellers, haunting the depths of the sky, you nook-infesting guardians of secrets, you scan the mysteries, enwrapped in musk... You are the captains of the hosts of Hell, kings of infinite space, terrestrial overlords, ministers to globe-shaking earthquakes.*
>
> *You are Spirits of the Air who strike with panic, strangle with terror, turn spindles, scattering snows, wafting rains. You are Lords of Fate tossing the tempest with fire tongues of summer sun.*
>
> *You are senders of necessity.*
>
> *You are fire-darters who fan the flames; you are the Spirits of the Air who compell the snow and the dew, raise the gale, plumb the Abyss and bestride the calm.*
>
> *You are heart-crushing despots dauntless in courage, never enslaved, raging wild, the Watchers of Tartaros. You are elusive phantoms of Fate, all-seeing, all-hearing, all-conquering. You are vagrants, wandering through the sky; you are primeval pole-movers who inspire life and destroy it. You are angels, light-hearted dealers of death, revealers of angels, justiciers of mortals, without sum.*
>
> *O you Masters of Daimons, aerial rovers, you holy and omnipotent, by these magic words, perform my behests!*

"To what kinds of beings was this addressed?" asked my correspondent. "Could these watchers be the same as those described in the book of Enoch?" According to Enoch some sons of the sky came down from Heaven and saw that the daughters of men were fair. He is precise in this: two hundred of them landed on top of a specific mountain and set to work. This incantation could also apply to Lilith, goddess of hidden knowledge and forbidden science.

Spring Hill. Saturday 29 August 1987.

Aimé Michel thanks me for some books I sent him. He urges me to read Polybe, the *De Mysteriis* by Jamblicus and Proclus' *Elements of Theology*, edited by Dodds.

Sorting out my old correspondence, I came across an oddly prophetic letter from French composer Raphaël Barret:

> If we want to experience some relative happiness, we must lock ourselves in our tower and live there, with our personal notion of existence. Such is the secret so many human beings look for, and which is within their reach. The number of the Elect is limited because great, repeated efforts are required to reach that special state, that euphoria giving full meaning to individual life.

If my old friend were here he would see such a tower taking shape. I do intend to live there with my "personal notions of existence."

Spring Hill. Friday 4 September 1987.

The moon is red with the ashes from forest fires ravaging Mount Sanhedrin, Northeast of Willits. There are no clouds in the sky but the smoke obscures the stars, which prevents me even from checking the alignment of the observatory's foundations.

Admiral Bill Houser has given us the results of an analysis of the Costa Rica photograph by Naval Intelligence. They took a very cursory look, under the pretext that government resources shouldn't be wasted on such things, and declared that it must be a hoax because the shadows are on the wrong side of the disk. But the shadows are only on the wrong side if one makes the assumption the object is a solid cone. There is no justification for such an assumption.

So once again, researchers' own preconceived idea of the answer gets in the way of genuine analysis. What kind of "intelligence" is this? If the Russians attacked us with upside-down saucers the U.S. Navy would never see them coming.

Spring Hill. Saturday 5 September 1987.

An ashen sun sets behind blurry hills, the valley is full of smoke; fire trucks fill motel parking lots. High columns of gray-white smoke rise and open up like atomic mushrooms. Work on the tower is slowing down, because every bulldozer and backhoe in the county has been moved to the fire lines, where drivers get paid $1,000 a day.

We took the dirt road beyond the ghost hamlet of Hearst, a lost world filled with phantoms. The Eel River was dry. In the fields with the rusty grass there are black goats and horses. Occasionally the road is paved over a few hundred feet in front of an old ranch house.

The whole county has heard the rumor that an observatory was being built. Workers came over yesterday, six men to pour concrete using wheelbarrows and shovels. Local folks make no distinction between astronomy and astrology. When I mention my interest in the planets people listen gravely, nod and tell me, "Yeah, my mother believes in that stuff. She reads her horoscope every morning."

I am still sorting out accumulated documents and letters. Magazines from every country fall out of packages along with letters from readers: "You are on the right track, but you should read the Apocalypse of Saint John," writes a man from New Jersey, while a woman from Colorado assures me, "The key to this mystery is in the Book of Urantia." I have thrown away five large boxes of such stuff that will enrich the garbage dump of Ukiah, along with the old car parts our kids had accumulated in the corners of the garage. The important things, Aimé Michel's correspondence and Hynek's letters, go into new folders in anticipation of finding a home in the tower.

Yesterday afternoon the girlfriend of one of the contractors came to see him on the site, pulled her little dog in her arms and asked, "What is it you're building here?" The fellow, a sun-tanned local athlete, crossed his muscled arms over his naked chest, looked at me with some uncertainty in his eyes and proudly told her: "It's an *observatorium*."

Spring Hill. Sunday 13 September 1987.

The Mount Sanhedrin fire is finally under control. It has devastated the land from Hearst to Lake Pillsbury and it still burns towards Yolla Bolly, in the inaccessible parts of the beautiful and remote national forest. Along the county roads we pass military convoys relieving exhausted firemen. They come in big waves, with communications trucks and military police.

A phone conversation with Hal: he had spoken to the action officer in charge of briefings for the project I still call simply "the Secret Onion." He has been told everything was fine; he should go brief the Air Force, and maybe the Secretary. Finally everybody signed off. The next step is to set up contractual channels. One defense contractor backed out but two others were eager to step in.

"Well, it's a turning point indeed," I said. "Now it is up to us to do something smart."

"I went back and pushed on that point," said Hal, "you're in the right spot; we need you before things get off to a big start. We should avoid past mistakes. We need your international research contacts, and a good expert system."

Something may happen after all, but I still wonder why it should be kept secret, when so much more could be achieved in the open.

Spring Hill. Monday 14 September 1987.

Autumn has come suddenly; leaves turn yellow and orange, drift into the pool. Bees attack the juicy grapes under the arbor.

Peter Sturrock called to tell me that new funds were about to be made available for UFO research, "everything has been signed." An amusing detail: Hal hadn't told Peter I knew about the project. So when I mentioned I would discuss details with Hal, Peter became alarmed, insisting he would have to check with him first.

This is the curse of classified research projects: the secrecy of the plan is already creating complexities and hierarchies even before any work has begun.

Spring Hill. Tuesday 15 September 1987.

Ed May's budget at SRI has been cut in half, by about a million dollars. He will have to let part of the staff go and stop work with outside contractors like me.

I told him I would work for nothing. I believe his project is important. It isn't the first time I see their work torn apart by political vicissitudes.

Spring Hill. Friday 18 September 1987.

I spoke to Aimé Michel this morning. He still has one radiation session before being transferred to a convalescent home near Nancy in Lorraine.

On Wednesday night our neighbor's ranch burned down. Not surprising: his house was surrounded by junk, old cars leaking oil, and he was drinking heavily, a typical scene in this little corner of paradise. Not to mention the ever-present friendly weed.

Hyde Street. Wedneday 23 September 1987.

Larry Collins, co-author of *O Jerusalem!* and *Is Paris Burning?* was in town today, so we had lunch together. He also wrote *The Fifth Horseman,* which was required reading at our recent Congressional Hearings on Emergency Management. Larry is planning a book on mind manipulation. He bombarded me with questions on low frequency waves and remote viewing, knowing of my SRI work.

He told me that the U.S. had recently captured a MIG 23 in Japan that contained a device that seemed to generate extremely low frequency signals. Is there anything to the theory that lower frequencies can induce special physiological or psychological effects?

Could these effects be caused by resonance phenomena corresponding to electrical cycles in the body? The White House is unprotected under 100 Hertz, he told me.

Hyde Street. Monday 28 September 1987.

Our sheet metal contractor came over this afternoon to look at our plans. When he found out we were building an observatory he asked, "You believe there's life up there? I've seen strange things... I've spent several years in the Forest Service. And my dad has seen a saucer that had landed next to a road."

The weather has been delightful; the softness of the morning stayed with us all day, only matched by the sweetness of our long talks, and our swims under the stars.

Tonight I had arranged for Matt to come over to Dr. Van de Carr's house for an experimental hypnosis session intended to set a standard for further abduction research. The two specialists (one of whom teaches hypnosis to clinical psychologists, while the other uses it in medical practice) insisted everything had to be recorded by two cameras at different angles, including the entire induction process—something the ufologists never take the trouble of doing. Blood pressure measuring instruments and stress displays visible to the cameras were used, and the whole session was run according to the standards for admissibility of hypnosis in California Courts, implying the data would be available to dissenting experts, another glaringly missing feature in ufology. Van de Carr pointed out it was the only way statements could be challenged. The evening opened my eyes to the subtle complexities of hypnosis and the evidence of abductees' abuse at the hand of amateurs.

Matt's experience turned out to be much deeper than he had imagined, and the skill of the hypnotists was very much the factor that brought out the real occurrence, masked by the later incident that had caused him to contact me.

Something is real in the abductee's experience, but the methods used in the field are a mockery of psychological practice, an ethical abomination, and an insult to the witnesses. I have now reviewed five videotapes of abductees'interviews by leading luminaries, full of gross errors about the process and plain mis-statements about the results. The next step is up to the skeptics who have a fine opportunity to expose this nonsense; in the process, unfortunately, they will only ridicule and confuse the poor witnesses once again.

When will a real expert come into the field and clean all this up, so these undoubtedly real experiences can be understood?

Spring Hill. Saturday 3 October 1987.

The tower has risen from the earth, a tall black volume against the moon, a ghostly structure with empty windows, the scaffoldings twisting and creaking in the wind. Forest fires are getting closer, threatening the valley. The flames were kicked up again by winds, taking firemen by surprise. One man died on Wednesday.

Hal has received my letter containing some thoughts about the Secret Onion. He will send it on to his liaison officer. I'm reassured to know Kit is in the loop, because he is not naïve about the abduction and hypnosis garbage now oozing out of the UFO groups.

Janine has spent the week in L.A., installing a novel on-line alert system for the network of automated tellers at Bank of America. She was in her hotel room at the Bonaventure when an earthquake hit in the early morning, throwing asthrays and potted plants across the room. Fortunately she was unhurt but the quake, centered in Whittier, caused six deaths.

Boston. Tuesday 6 October 1987.

Boston is a stop for me on the way to Europe but I never did like this city. People are polite enough, some even smile occasionally, but there is a distressing lack of sensual or spiritual feeling. The tall buildings belong to insurance and finance companies, a culture I find uniformly dull and richly aseptic. On the other side of the boulevard you find nothing but brick houses, black with soot, entirely predictable.

Bob Chartrand took me to dinner with his friends from the Smithsonian. He told me he could make arrangements for a meeting with Art Lundahl, one of my heroes, the father of modern photo analysis, and the key expert in the study of UFO photographs for the military and the intelligence community.

Rue de la Clef. Saturday 10 October 1987.

From Paris to Nancy the train follows the rivers; beautiful plains roll by under the sun; the trees turning yellow make a fine backdrop to my sober thoughts. I just came back from Chatel-sur-Moselle, where I visited Aimé at the hospital. The local train to Epinal stops at every whitewashed hamlet with its tiny station. I ate in Nomexy in a sad, deserted hotel, then I walked across the bridge over the Moselle to the medical center.

Aimé was sitting near his bed when I arrived. He had grown a short white beard. He seemed tired but happy to see me. We spoke of our families. His son Vincent is a gifted craftsman now, making and repairing musical instruments in Paris. His younger son, Colin, is out of work. Aimé gave him the big house in the Alps, where he lives on 100 francs a month, growing his own vegetables, heating the house with the wood he gathers himself. Aimé also has a daughter named Camille who lives near Epinal with his estranged wife. We spoke of Antiquity, the Illiad, and Hannibal's conquests.

Three visitors showed up in the afternoon: Bertrand Méheust, Pierre Lagrange, and a young doctor in psychiatry. The conversation turned to the nature of myths, to the relationship between modern phenomena and ancient folklore. I don't always agree with Méheust and Lagrange, but they are asking the right questions.

I went back to Paris on the Mozart train, the Paris-Salzburg, travelling with Lagrange who told me that Jean-Pierre Petit was still antagonizing everybody and that Velasco had taken it upon himself to investigate the Trans-en-Provence case against the advice of his boss Esterle. Lagrange and I disagree about the Cergy-Pontoise case: he still believes it is a simple hoax, which in my view doesn't explain all the facts. I am intrigued by indications the three witnesses were victims of very human manipulation.

Aimé's remark about the scientists who try to study the paranormal: "They would destroy Notre-Dame stone by stone, grind it, reduce the whole thing to a heap of dust, analyze the dust with the utmost care and reach the positive conclusion that it was made of stone." That is exactly what happens now with the SRI psychic project in its declining years.

Lyon. Sunday 11 October 1987.

The city is dark and deserted, shiny with the dark mud that seems to be oozing out of the Rhone River.

In a book by Pierre Gordon **(11)** I find an interesting discussion of Eleusis, "proving the grandiose nature of neolithic notions. Its mysteries truly renewed those who participated in them, changing the level of their souls. It made them realize the existence of the world of light, under the world of senses (…) Sexual union with the divinity must have represented something quite different from what we imagine. We forget that eroticism, even in our own civilization, can flower into a deeper feeling that transcends it."

Lyon. Monday 12 October 1987.

As a child I thought that if confronted with imminent death I would direct my energy to understand who I was and what life meant. If I died tomorrow I would be able to say that I had fulfilled this promise, to attempt understanding—even if I did not attain it: the new tower is there to prove it. I have pursued this knowledge incompletely, with hesitations and mistakes, but I did reach some understanding of the potential reality of other inhabited worlds, and of other levels of consciousness in this one.

We can reach awakening through any activity that breaks the routine of life: traveling to exotic places, carefully observing paranormal phenomena, extraordinary passions; but we can perhaps best reach it through routine things: the routine of deep love, of small gestures, watching the clouds and the stars, and trusting in the naïvety and wisdom of simple folks.

Sunset behind the hills of Fourvière: a fine French sky filled with long dreamy clouds. The *Massif Central* is delineated to the West in vast undulations. The City library is next door, but it is closed on Mondays, so I walk through the old town for hours, exploring the *traboules* (medieval passages under the buildings) and the curving streets bordered by hill, secretive walls.

Rue de la Clef. Wednesday 14 October 1987.

The Lyon library owns two copies of Saint Agobard's *De Grandine et Tonitruis* ("of Hail and Thunder") which allowed me to verify this quote about the belief in the legendary land of Magonia: "We have seen and heard many people foolish enough and blind enough to believe and affirm that a certain region called *Magonia* exists, whence originate ships that sail upon the clouds..."

Some ufologists are mad at me for quoting such old references. Why does it bother them so much? They even accuse me of inventing them, as Cufos once said I had committed fraud when I revealed the Battelle document signed by Howard Cross that became known as the *Pentacle Memorandum*.

Toulouse. Friday 16 October 1987.

Hotel Capoul. The city is pleasant, with tortuous medieval streets and alleys where I feel at home. I had long talks with Jean-Jacques Velasco, about UFOs but also about business and innovation in the area. He is the socialist mayor of Montgiscard, a small town south of Toulouse. We spoke about my Ovnibase while Cnes technicians were setting up a teleconference between Dr. Bruce Murray and a group of Soviet scientists back in Moscow. A big storm came over the city, one of those primeval tempests that would have raised the worst superstitions among Saint Agobard's parishioners.

I am taking back two soil samples taken at Trans-en-Provence and a copy of a tape, allegedly of UFO sounds, recorded by a child near Nantes. Going through the Gepan files I finally read the Gendarmes' official statement about the Valensole case. I was surprised to see that it did not mention any physical evidence. Yet Maurice Masse has told me several agencies took soil samples: where did they go?

I had dinner with Jean-Jacques' family last night: his wife Danièle, his daughter Elise, his sons Matthieu and Nicolas. Tonight we ate in an excellent restaurant called *La Maréchale*, where the trendy ambiance is frankly gay. They have desserts with names like Sodom & Gomorrah, Woman's Caress and Man's Caress, the latter a banana drowning in *crème fraiche*.

The offices of Cnes struck me as sleepy. Many rooms are empty and the computer room seems strangely idle.

Rue de la Clef. Wednesday 21 October 1987.

Fred Adler has postponed his planned trip to France, following the vertiginous drop of the markets on Wall Street (**12**). His venture portfolio is shaky and his enemies suggest he is about to retire.

In a few fateful days there was an earthquake in L.A., a hurricane over England and western France, and this financial crash. Boëdec tells me that the crops are lost in Brittany, with more deaths than media reported. In his village, half the houses have suffered damage to their roofs. In Bayeux, Annick heard slates dropping on the concrete sidewalk all night long. At the tip of Brittany weather instruments ran up a wind speed reading of 220 km/h before being torn away.

Today I had lunch with my brother, after which we went out and bought a phone for our mother's bedroom. She always runs from one end of her apartment to the other with dangerous precipitation whenever a call comes. As I prepare to fly back to San Francisco I will sleep better knowing that her phone is within reach.

Spring Hill. Sunday 25 October 1987.

The rain falls, steadily feeding the red bushes, the yellow trees, and the grass around the pond. Now the sun puts a tiny diamond at the tip of every leaf and a new blade of grass on every inch of dirt. Contractors are up on the crenellated wall, hammering away at the tower roof. Velasco tells me on the phone there is a UFO flap in progress in the North and West of France, and a French ship has been shaken up as an object flew over it near Sicily.

Hyde Street. Thursday 29 October 1987.

Two days ago I collapsed with an asthma attack after running some errands. Horrible feeling: unable to breathe, clutching my chest with both hands. The crisis was aggravated by bronchitis and left me on a gurney in the emergency room in the middle of the night. Now Janine is caring for me at home, and I have learned another lesson.

Spring Hill. Sunday 1 November 1987.

The crash of Wall Street ten days ago has had no impact on us. We are not wealthy enough to dabble in the stock market, but what a debacle around us! The dollar is dropping, investment banks are laying off staff, there is a vacuum in the White House and the economy is shaken. As Maman says enthusiastically when I deplore this catastrophe: "It's so exciting, to live in such times!"

The sky is gray, windy. I installed a big tarp over the tower's unfinished roof. There are new rumors of scandal around Michael Aquino, a San Francisco occultist and former follower of Anton LaVey who has formed his own "Temple of Set." I have never met Aquino, although he lives not far from us on Russian Hill. A three-and-a-half-year-old child is said to have pointed to him as the culprit in a series of molestations at the school of the Presidio. In the current context of satanic hysteria and pseudo-scientific investigations of everything occult, this is a serious accusation. So the police raided Aquino's house, taking away his computer, address book, tapes and such convincing evidence as "29 photographs of costumes, masks, and stars" (!) However he was not arrested. He claims he never even met the prime suspect in the molestations, an employee of the preschool establishment. The press delights in such details, in time for Halloween.

This raises the deeper question of the testimony of children and more generally, of disturbed witnesses. Often the investigation is run by persons driven by their own religious convictions or, in the case of ufologists, by an obsession with their pet agenda about Alien torturers. Whether the imagery is bloody satanic rites or fetuses harvested aboard saucers, the interrogation brings out repressed fantasies in the victim, but especially in the investigator. The process is reminiscent of the trials for sorcery under the Inquisition.

Hyde Street. Sunday 22 November 1987.

Whitley Strieber and I were on the same program this weekend at a seminar on "Aliens, Angels, and Archetypes." Mufon editor Dennis Stacy was there along with Bill Moore and Linda Howe who speaks of contacts with Pentagon officials (or men who present themselves as such) who give her amazing information that never leads anywhere, with stories of Alien underground chambers, short Grays in a hidden city "the size of Manhattan" underneath New Mexico, and reverse engineering of captured saucers.

"Where does the water come from, for a Manhattan-class city under the high desert? Who takes out the garbage?" I asked her, with no answer. Bill Moore insisted to talk to me in private and then tested me, dangling similar tales. I told him I was unimpressed, in the absence of the slimmest element of credibility.

Hyde Street. Monday 23 November 1987.

Whitley Strieber came over for lunch today with his wife Ann and their son Andrew. They were with a young woman from Denver and with Ed Conroy, a journalist from Texas who researches Whitley's childhood.

Spring Hill. Saturday 28 November 1987.

Our faithful old truck brought up two filing cabinets full of papers to be sorted out. I am using the Registry system that the English MI5 had adopted, separating subject files ("Blue files," with a code and a number) from personal and correspondence files.

Last week on the way back from a business meeting in San Diego where I spent time with Olivier, I stopped in Hollywood to see Bob Weiss. We had lunch at the Paramount commissary with the Zucher brothers, influential producers specialized in comedies (*Airplane*, *Naked Gun*), to whom I showed some of my cases in support of the Alintel scenario, but we didn't make any progress.

A group of actors in Star Trek regalia walked in while we were discussing multi-dimensional universes, providing a funny counterpoint. The same evening we had dinner with Joe Dante at Musso & Frank. Joe was already sold on the idea of our film, so Bob's next step is to put it in development at Universal. Unfortunately it won't be his top priority: He is starting work on a comedy with the Zucker brothers.

Hyde Street. Sunday 29 November 1987.

Whitley walks through the woods every night in upstate New York, armed to the teeth. What is he afraid of? If afraid, why is he exposing himself to danger? The emotional level of the field is being raised.

The mysterious Alien that Linda Howe "almost met" through the good offices of Rick Doty, the intelligence officer who had contacted her and "was at the edge of tears," which convinced her he was telling the truth – see Note *) was said to be a reptilian with scales, and deep unfathomable eyes... (**13**)

Note (*): According to researcher Ryan Dube (on the website *Reality Uncovered*, 9 Aug. 2008) Hal Puthoff and Kit Green met at the home of retired Air force Lt-Col. Ernie Kellerstrass with Doty, Dale Graf, Scott Jones, John Alexander and Robert Collins. Dube writes that in 1989 "a follow-up meeting at an Albuquerque hotel included Hal Puthoff, Kit Green, Rick Doty, Bill Moore and Jaime Shandera, and Collins." I only learned of these meetings through the web during 2013. Dr. Puthoff confirmed to me that the meetings occurred: "We were meeting these people with the purpose of hearing firsthand what was being claimed by the likes of Collins, Doty and Kellerstrass but the meetings had nothing to do with Dube's claim of promoting Disclosure. Overall, I was quite skeptical of much of what was being claimed."

At Spring Hill yesterday, going through some twenty years of research I threw away redundant material that had to do with Ira. Reading that mass of documents convinced me, once again, of the remarkable intelligence he had once brought to his network.

"Do you think he will be found some day?" asked Janine.

Who knows? The most probable hypothesis is that his powerful friends have helped him hide some place in Europe. But is he guilty? Ira claims to have been framed, which makes no sense: what he was working on was clever networking, but marginal psi research, and he had no special technical talent of his own.

Whitley gets calls from a man calling himself Enel Crew, implying he is in contact with the Aliens. Whitley hired a detective to find the guy. It turned out his postal service remailed all letters to the name "Goodman" in Houston, where another service sent everything to Denver. When he made a request with the Denver police the detective was harassed by Dallas authorities.

Tracing Mr. Crew's phone leads to the Defense Logistics Agency, then to an empty Boulder address: more indications of the undercurrent, and government meddling, like the woman agent in black garb and purple crystals we exposed in Mount Shasta.

Hyde Street. Saturday 5 December 1987.

Among the tall tales now being spread by Bill Moore is a claim about a revolutionary invention, a time-machine camera that could film the Crucifixion or the execution of Louis XVI. I expect such ludicrous stories are deliberately planted as a test to find out how they get spread, or simply to assess our degree of gullibility.

Over lunch Whitley told us about experiments on rats, creating intolerable stress. Their cages delivered random electric shocks, so their lives turned into an endless anticipation of tortures. According to Whitley the rats displayed a remarkable increase in intelligence evidenced by brain density. He makes the apt observation that the UFO phenomenon has a similar effect on mankind, tantalizing us with fantastic displays just beyond our understanding. Could the eventual goal be to speed up our evolution towards a smarter species? He thinks that would explain why contact is at once close, misunderstood and impossible.

There seems to be deep terror in Whitley's life, a terror whose source is lost in childhood. There was similar terror in the life of Philip Dick, who related his personal experiences with VALIS in a series of letters to Ira Einhorn, of which Ira gave me copies.

On Monday a gifted photographer named Morgane, who attended my lecture on *Aliens and Archetypes*, gave me a marvellous print showing the moon rising over the raised stones of Callanish. Other works by her, from one end of Britain to the other, show megalithic sites in all their glory. She has captured their vibration in a landscape of fog and mystery, and such skies!

Morgane, who studied magic in England with Dion Fortune's group, is a sensitive with a spiritual key to such places. In the sole of her boots she has sewn leaves from plants of her native England so she can “walk on the moors” wherever she happens to be.

Hyde Street. Sunday 6 December 1987.

Strange requests continue around Richard Niemtzow. He received a call from a French lieutenant colonel trained in pharmacology, a Dr. Canonne, who said he was from the French Health Ministry. He was in the U.S. on his way to Russia, had a meeting planned at DIA. Richard was amused to be contacted ostensibly about UFOs. It was like the old French joke, the recipe for lark *pâté*: “one lark, one horse, one lark, one horse…” The man spoke a little about UFOs, a lot about microwaves….

This reminded me of my visit to Poher. He was working on muscle paralysis using electromagnetism. He was talking to the military about this idea, since the process could lead to a non-lethal weapon. Poher is close to Niemtzow who is an expert on membranes' electrical potential and ion transport in muscle cells.

“We like the way you've addresssed the phenomenon,” Canonne told Richard. “We'd like to learn more about the physical effects of microwaves on human tissue.”

“What are you really proposing?” asked Niemtzow.

"We're going to send people from France, we've already written to DoD." Paul Tyler, a retired Navy medical expert, was mentioned.

"This was all very strange," Niemtzow told me. "I assured this Dr. Canonne that I could only help if the request was official. He suggested I serve as liaison to this French group. I'm very suspicious. The man even asked me if I'd be interested in returning to France, and gave me two bottles of wine when he left!"

"What did he say about UFOs?"

"He didn't know Velasco. He said his group wasn't really interested in the phenomenon but all the questions came back to it, which was really strange. He also said his project was classified. He gave an address on Rue St. Charles, as *Pharmacien en Chef, bureau des affaires scientifiques et techniques, Secrétariat Général de la Défense Nationale*." A scientist named Bernard Veyret, a French expert in microwave effects (**14**) was also mentioned. Thus the rejection of UFOs by French "rationalists" continues to serve as a cover for a very serious series of military Intelligence projects, run from Paris, probing into every aspect of the field.

New York. Sunday 13 December 1987.

Omni Park Central. The city is alive with Frank Stella's sculptures at the Modern Art Museum. Happy crowds on Fifth Avenue, millions of lights everywhere, the financial crash nearly forgotten.

At the law firm of Reavis & McGrath young corporate attorneys walk back and forth in shirtsleeves, showing off their green suspenders. In Adler's office plans are being firmed up for our Euro-America venture fund. Since the French are slow in getting under way, Fred has decided to take the lead in the project, to fire one of the French partners, to take me under his wing as a mentor and to rewrite all the poorly drafted documents.

On Friday I had dinner at Whitley's Greenwich Village apartment with his family and Margo Adler, author of *Drawing Down the Moon*, a fine book about modern Pagan movements. Modern art on the walls, a large 3D panel of "the chicken crossing the road" over the main fireplace. No ostentation or ceremony here. Whitley gives the impression of someone swept along by manifestations that constantly reinforce his personal myth.

Little Andrew gave me a present (in return for a cup with a green frog on the bottom that Janine gave him in San Francisco). He gave me a small book he had made, of cartoons about ducks.

Ann Strieber has never seen the Visitors, she told us. But she stressed the role she played in shaping the text of *Communion*: without her advice, Whitley would have tried to use the book to start a new religion. People cannot tolerate a mystery that keeps growing, with no solution in sight. Sooner or later ufologists are going to fall for a new belief system that will fill the void, and absolve them from the need to come to grips with real research.

Hyde Street. Friday 25 December 1987.

Quiet days with our children, a white Christmas tree in the library, the Bay very calm, glacier blue, a single sail in sight. I haven't gone out all day. A friend of ours, supposedly psychic, assures me there is a giant invisible saucer above San Francisco. I declined the invitation to join the group that will "investigate." I prefer to stay here, experimenting with new software Olivier has given me and arguing with Catherine about the decline of Western democracy. We just saw a striking movie, *Man Facing Southeast*. (**15**)

Spring Hill. Thursday 31 December 1987.

On the trip north the truck was filled with boxes of science-fiction books this time, not a vast collection by any means but it does contain a good cross-section of the genre in French, and certainly the largest collection of Jimmy Guieu's cheap train station novels anywhere in America!

I spent the day painting the inside walls of the tower with the contractors. The weather has turned cold. Janine and Catherine are tearing up old bushes. Even in her winter sleep nature is magnificent here, the hills covered in frost.

Hollywood. Friday 8 January 1988.

Bob Weiss and I had dinner last night with Joe Dante once again. We worked on our script and presented the concept to Shawn Daniels, the president of Universal Productions, itself a branch of MCA. The meeting took place in Bob's office among trophies and memorabilia, science-fiction toys and film posters. His latest claim to fame is *Amazon Women on the Moon*, which Janine and I saw on my birthday, quite funny but hardly a masterpiece.

Joe Dante came over, joking, absent-minded, his hair in disarray and his fly open. I told Shawn Daniels that the real mystery behind UFOs has never being shown, not even by Spielberg: "In the first place, if UFOs exist they may not be extraterrestrial in the usual sense. The phenomenon lends itself to every possible manipulation, because it impacts our beliefs in fundamental ways..."

I told him about the time when the CIA planned to simulate the second coming of Christ over Cuba, and reminded him that during the Vietnam war a device called the Mitralux was used to project pictures of local gods onto the clouds. We have the technology to abduct an aborigine in New Guinea, fly him to Hollywood and show him *Star Wars* to confuse his reality. "If you can maintain this tone throughout, you'll have a very important movie," said Daniels. Joe Dante said he'd always wanted to make a UFO film.

Spring Hill. Sunday 17 January 1988.

Our neighbors have seen a black wolf in our pasture. It is a domesticated female who got loose and returned to the wild. She has been attacking dogs. A fat, dirty fellow came to warn us he would fire at her if he saw her. I am more afraid of him than of the wolf.

On Thursday I had lunch with John Alexander, the Army colonel in charge of unspecified research projects who has a long-standing interest in UFOs and parapsychology. We spoke about Cleve Backster's experiments on plants: they still work, said Alexander, but he now uses microorganisms, less sensitive to artefacts. We also spoke of communication with dolphins, experiments in Florida. I found Colonel Alexander lucid, open, and friendly but I wasn't especially impressed with what he told me of the ongoing research in the field. He is one of the military leaders behind the Secret Onion project (*), which is still stumbling along.

14

Spring Hill. Saturday 23 January 1988.

When we step out of the car at night we always feel the same shock: so many stars, so close! Last week as he came home late, our tenant saw the wolf in our backyard. The tower is complete, and so is the structure of Euro-America. The former only lacks a coat of paint on the front door, the latter some signatures, the lawyers' final stamp, and a series of international wire transfers.

Spring Hill. Sunday 24 January 1988.

Laziness. Sunshine everywhere. Still sorting through old papers, finding little treasures and significant bits of information, such as the transcript of Pat Price attempting to track me by remote viewing from SRI when I travelled to join Allen Hynek at Corralitos observatory in the New Mexico desert in May 1974.

The SRI *Star Gate* project has entered a critical phase once again. The DIA now demands results. After many years of research and many millions they want more than statistics. They complain that the

----

Note (*): In his book *UFOs: Myths, conspiracies and realities* (NY: St.Martin's Press, 2012) Colonel Alexander revealed that the real name of the proposal was "Project ATP" for "Advanced Theoretical Physics."

project is not yet able to reliably test subjects to determine whether or not they have genuine abilities.

Spring Hill. Saturday 30 January 1988.

Ballantine Books offer to buy the paperback rights of *Dimensions*. I am happy with the book, but I still have difficulty being heard about networking and artificial intelligence research. Many publishers such as Tarcher have become fascinated with "Consciousness" with a capital "C." They cater to a New Age public that never moved beyond the revelations of the psychedelic era, which I don't see as great liberation but as a wasted historic opportunity. I still mourn the loss of close friends, young people to whom everything was open, but who rushed into a blind alley. Instead of launching a creative revolution against the obsolete structures of the previous generation they fell into the trap of the very drugs like LSD invented by their parents' secret police, symbols of their false emancipation.

Some positive results, 20 years later, have been a healthy change in the arts, notably in music, and a limited overhaul of American images of man and society. But in psychic research and in terms of our understanding of the world, progress has been minuscule. The scientific revolution we are now experiencing owes little to the New Age. It is driven by hard working immigrants: Hungarians like Andy Grove (Intel), Poles (Paul Baran and packet switching), Italians (Federico Faggin and the microcomputer).

Hyde Street. Sunday 31 January 1988.

Calling Ed May at SRI, I proposed a new idea. If we believe that test subjects "remote view" the photograph of the target site rather than the site itself we should be able to obtain the same results with simulated geographic locales. "Synthetic imagery, generated in a computer, should work just as well as our real target set," I told him. This would have the added advantage of eliminating coding, because we could ask the computer to generate a scene with (for instance) 50% mountains, 40% ocean, and a city with tall buildings.

"That's the best idea I've heard in a long time," Ed replied. But it would require some new programming, and resources the project may not have any more.

Hyde Street. Thursday 4 February 1988.

Twenty-nine years together, and I love Janine more than life itself. Last night we went to see *Solaris*, the best Soviet-era sci-fi film. The print was bad, with faded colors and breaks in the emulsion, but the image of the woman reincarnated in the cosmic ocean remains very interesting. The film was broken in several places; it had been repaired with fragments of a dubbed version, and the result was hilarious. When the handsome cosmonaut finally confessed to the girl: *Ia lioublou dva* ("I love you"), she fell into his arms, answering in English: *Oh Chris, I feel so close to you!* The audience had trouble not giggling through such scenes.

Hyde Street. Wednesday 10 February 1988.

Helping Ed May and his team calibrate some new tests of remote viewing ability, I found out they had switched to the use of movie scenes as targets. Honorton at Maimonides hospital seems to have found out these gave better results than photographs. The new tests are to be administered to 15 analysts sent to SRI by the DIA. Ed, Beverly, and Jessica Utts asked me to serve as a subject to test the protocol: two minutes to describe a scene randomly selected by the computer, and inaccesible to the investigators until after the test.

They gave me a piece of paper. I quickly drew two branches of a spiral, wrote "spin," then a series of expanding circles and curves, with the word "disruption."

Ed brought in the disk reader and played the actual target: mushroom cloud seen from above, nested circles, a nuclear explosion. The judges would have had no trouble matching the target to my description, a direct hit. My friends were impressed, yet my mind was far from calm. I slept poorly last night, suffered from allergies that constrained my breathing, and I was under stress from the growth pains of my company, all of which should have inhibited my abilities if we believe in the idea of a meditator calmly using "the Force." Psychic effects seem to be simpler, faster and more robust than generally supposed.

Austin. Sunday 6 March 1988.

On the way to Texas I stopped in Colorado to visit Catherine, who took me on a tour of the Boulder campus, including Woodbury Hall where the Condon Committee held its UFO sessions 21 years ago. I have strong memories of my trips there, in 1962 for the very first Symposium on the Exploration of Mars, and in 1967 with Allen Hynek for that fateful briefing. On the way back Allen agreed with me that the UFO problem was deeper and more significant than the narrow framework where Air Force scientists were trying to force it.

This was a sweet reunion with my daughter. We visited the town and drove up to the snowy Rockies where we had dinner at a mountain lodge. A country music group was playing the banjo, singing old songs. This morning Gold Hill was resplendent in the sun. We spoke of music and prehistory, of politics, and also of Janine's mother who is now very ill, in faraway Normandy.

In Austin I found Hal, Adrienne and their children in their magnificent new home, which includes a large game room, sports grounds and a guesthouse where I will spend the night. Hal has just returned from a series of visits to industrialists in Europe, including Pierre Aigrain who is technical adviser to Alain Gomez at Thomson. Some time ago Aigrain met Ken Shoulders at MIT, where he was running experiments on thermal effects of metal junctions.

We also caught up with news of the Secret Onion. As I had surmised, John Alexander is expected to serve as the operational head and the Army will be in charge, having finally obtained the agreement of its Science Board. Dick Haines was brought in for a briefing about pilot sightings but wasn't told about the full scale of the project. Hal's impression is that the Intelligence agencies do not have a genuine interest in the nature of the UFO phenomenon but only in the peripheral incidence on their own missions.

On a flight to Dallas. Tuesday 8 March 1988.

Jupiter Technologies, the company that Hal and Ken now manage, maintains a lab at Braker and Research Boulevard in Austin, which I visited today. They showed me a source of super-electrons and a micro-camera designed by Ken, and gave me a briefing on the technology. In an Austin supermarket, where we stopped for coffee, we found the latest issue of *Omni* that mentions my Ovnibase software. Bill Church himself works nearly full time with Jupiter, along with several technicians. They develop a research site in Bullhead, 50 miles west of Austin on a 50-acre property. Hal hinted that Jupiter also does research "below the line."

Both of us are increasingly interested in the esoteric aspects of the phenomenon. He told me that the higher grades of Scientology opened up to a world populated by entities that resembled ufonauts, going from humanoid beings to bizarre monsters, a fact that is reminiscent of Morgane's excursions into the "higher planes."

Spring Hill. Friday 11 March 1988.

This morning I drove up along Route 1 and Devil's Slide in the convertible, the Pacific wind sweeping away a few dark thoughts. After this healthy brainwashing, I loaded the truck with Janine to bring up part of the library to the tower. Along the drive that follows the curves of the Russian River Janine reflects that no work of man comes close to the limpid light of the land of Mendocino swept by the heady essence of the forest and the ocean. It takes a meaning that artworks can only reflect or approximate. The sky over Spring Hill tonight is the "obdurate vault" of poetry (James Thomson) overlaid by the majestic trail of Orion.

Spring Hill. Sunday 13 March 1988.

I relearn astronomy here. I only have to climb a staircase in order to touch the sky. So I picked up my notes from my days with Professor Kourganoff and old issues of French astronomy magazines that brought back memories of dusty lecture rooms where bearded professors spoke of spectroscopy. I am building a dome on the roof of the tower. Capella, Sirius, Arcturus, Betelgeuse, Rigel span the night sky. The bookshelves are in place. It hasn't rained for a long time. Drought is a major concern for this region of wineries and ranches. A neighbor tells me the warming is due to the fact that "the earth has left its orbit." There are foxes in the yard.

On Friday I had lunch with Dick Haines. He told me about the invitation he'd received to brief staffers of an Army undersecretary, describing his research on pilot sightings. Hal and John Alexander had suggested this briefing to try to get a final decision. Thus, contrary to what people have been told, the Secret Onion project has not been established yet. Dick was able to attend the presentation that followed his own briefing: An intelligence officer spoke about objects detected by certain satellites. American satellites on low orbits, known as "slow walkers" are often catching luminous objects in groups of two or three that make right-angle turns or even reverse course. These observations, according to Dick, stunned the Army folks, who had been unaware of these "FastWalkers."

In two weeks we will be back in France, for a sad visit to Normandy where Mamie keeps getting worse, and to Paris where Fred Adler is certain to challenge us.

Spring Hill. Saturday 26 March 1988.

The first copies of *Dimensions* have arrived. My friends predict that mainstream ufology will not like the book, because I refuse to embrace the current mythology of abduction, but I don't care: I don't write in hopes people will like me.

Ed May came over for dinner at Hyde street on Thursday, bringing the best remote viewer in the Army, Joe McMoneagle. He is a stout fellow with a relaxed attitude, who gives the false impression of slow, careless motion. As we did honor to Janine's delicious beef Burgundy, Joe told us about his experiences at the threshold of death and beyond. Technically, he died several times during a masive heart attack followed by five days in intensive care. In another episode he was poisoned in a Munich restaurant by KGB operatives. He was there for the Defense Intelligence Agency and his cover was blown.

"I had a drink before dinner, didn't feel good, went out to the night air and just collapsed in the gutter," he told us. "There I saw my own body. I became aware of the fact that I was immaterial. Water was flowing *through* my arm. I saw the rescuers arrive. I followed the ambulance that had my body in it. I was enveloped in a strong white light. Somehow the light told me it wasn't time for me to leave the Earth, and I woke up inside my body on my hospital bed."

Joe added he felt almost sad to be alive again. In the warm intimacy of the light he had known the greatest peace possible; he had been ready to cut the final link. Unafraid of death after that experience, he accepted the most dangerous assignments for the Army where he served for 20 years. His remote viewing talents are exceptional, because he is able to provide both a description and an analysis, with a degree of precision that only Ingo Swann and Pat Price have achieved. His descriptions include three-dimensional drawings of buildings and cross-section views of the inner structure of machinery.

I asked Joe if he felt he was actually transferring his consciousness to the location. Not only does he feel the secondary attributes of the site such as temperature and smells, but in one case when he was given longitude, latitude and time he described an individual at the site. He once went back in time and tracked another person before a car crash, describing his last moments, although he had been told nothing about the case or the individual in question.

We spoke of FastWalkers. Joe once obtained a detailed photograph of a disk. He placed a copy in a locked safe with double combination, a classified safe under his sole control. Yet the photograph vanished.

"There must be a higher level of authority that controls UFO data," he said, "a level beyond the folks who run the satellites."

On Wednesday Janine and I had dinner with Bill Calvert, who offered us a delicious mushroom soup followed by a divinely cooked chicken and Brazilian pastries. We discussed the progress of his contacts with local ufologists in Brazil and made plans for an extensive research trip this summer, from Fortaleza to Belém, where many cases of "chupas" have been reported over the last ten years.

In discussions with Keith Harary, Ed May and others I am moving towards a notion of contact that implies that the experience is mediated by cultural frameworks. Does that mean we have no chance of finding the thread of objective reality in any part of the phenomenon, as Aimé argues?

Spring Hill. Sunday 3 April 1988. Easter Sunday.

The Virgin's apparitions in Medugorje, in Yugoslavia, are fascinating once the theological mumbo-jumbo has been scraped off the reports. What emerges is the simple beauty of contact between the children's pure soul and that infinite source we cannot name, a reality before which witnesses turn into happy slaves. What Catholics call the Holy Spirit is what I call the control system. No wonder those researchers who become embroiled in the phenomenon end up confused and lose their sense of reality.

Now the rain has come, a fine rain falling like a kiss on the multi-colored foliage of Spring Hill. I used to have trouble breathing in wet weather, but my health has improved; now I only need minimal medication, and I look forward to my next trip to France.

Asthma is an interesting condition. According to Professor Michel (*Le Souffle Coupé*) it is also "a way of living, of expressing certains feelings and perhaps avoiding some psychic disorders." Proust, Paul Valéry, André Breton, Queneau, Paul Mérimée were asthmatics. Sufferers are often avant-garde creators, sensitive to subtle influences, he adds.

Paris. Tuesday 12 April 1988.

In France again, with plans for books and new projects. Seeking refuge at *l'Escholier*, a café on the Square before the Sorbonne, I take a break after raiding local bookstores. Polybe is inaccessible, a seven volume translation with a ridiculous price tag.

Pleasures of the promenades with Janine in New York's Central Park under the first of April sunshine, in Paris before the Automaton near Beaubourg, and through our old quarter in *Les Halles*.

Rue de la Clef. Wednesday 13 April 1988.

Lunch with publisher Gérard Klein near Saint Sulpice. Laffont is considering *Dimensions* but Gérard urges me to start writing fiction again. It was raining when I went to see Dr. Hubert Larcher at the *Institut Métapsychique* on Place Wagram. A small contorted staircase leads to the offices that the institute opens to the public on Tuesdays. We spoke of Warcollier and Keith Harary. Larcher inspires trust; he is honest, direct. It feels good to meet a psychic researcher with nothing to hide, after all the secrets of SRI, scientists with clearances sneaking through the muck of statistics.

Dr. Larcher told me that Warcollier's son had taken no interest in his father's research. There must be a large cabinet somewhere filled with valuable files about the earliest scientific experiments on remote viewing. Sitting next to Puthoff at the Cordoba congress, Larcher had pointed out to him that Warcollier had gone further than SRI in several areas, a fact Hal later verified. Unfortunately the Institute has lost some 130 books during a move of its library, including works by Warcollier. The other three founders of French psychic science were Dr. Richet, Eugène Osty and Gustave Geley.

Today I paid a visit to Roland Villeneuve, who presented me with a copy of his *Erotologie de Satan*. He had invited Martine Castello from *Figaro Magazine* and his own niece, also a journalist. They had just spent a week in Spain and they had noted a disquieting parallel between Ummo devotees and followers of Lyndon Larouche in Europe: same methods, same paranoid stories, same overtones of fascist extremism. But for what purpose?

Siparex Offices, Paris. Thursday 14 April 1988.

Between a meeting with the head of research for EDF and lunch with an executive recruiter, I am taking time to write and make a few phone calls. The subdued sound of this affluent section of Paris drifts through the high windows.

Place St. Michel was drowned under steady rain this morning. I sought refuge at the Gibert bookstore where I found a poor translation of John Fowles' *Maggot* under the silly title *La Créature*. Boëdec was on time, as always. There is no echo in France to the feverish excitation about abduction created in America by Strieber and Hopkins. Publisher Gérard Klein hadn't heard about *Communion*, and even a specialist like Boëdec was in the dark. His own attempts to ignite a new round of research about UFOs have gone nowhere: “We've tried everything,” Poher told him, “to no avail.” But Boëdec thinks the answer may lie in an unexplored direction. He suspects the military has kept an active interest in the subject. The amateur groups, however, have all collapsed.

Jean-François Boëdec and I continue to analyze the Pontoise case: why such a manipulation experiment? He thinks a top French technologist named Pierre Aigrain, the same man Hal Puthoff has met, may have been involved. The project deviated from military goals and was aborted, he suspects.

Brunville par Bayeux. Sunday 17 April 1988.

The family is assembled at Mamie's bedside: Alain flew in from Charleston and Eric from Paris. Annick and Michel keep the big house in order, with a beautiful fire in the fireplace.

I drove with Janine to Bricquebec, to take her away from all that sorrow. She spent two years in that region where her grandparents had a jewelry store in the main street that leads to the medieval castle.

Mamie has knitted a magnificent silver sweater for me. She is very tired but she hides her weakness from visitors, reclining in the Norman sun in the yard of the old farmhouse. Will we see her again? Allen Hynek is only a memory now, and Aimé Michel is very ill. The pages of this journal are blackened with the tiny scribblings of our lives; they get turned over and fly away.

I have to be back in Paris tonight: Fred Adler arrives on Wednesday to start the operations of Euro-America. I am beginning to realize how poorly organized most financial enterprises are. Banque Suez is trapped in a bizarre alliance with Carlo de Benedetti (or against him?) in an attempt to take control of *Générale de Belgique*.

At Paribas, which is being reorganized, Robert Lattès is a victim of uncertain destiny. Business deals come and go, flounder on egotism and greed.

Lyon. Tuesday 19 April 1988. Hotel Roosevelt.

Sleep is so deep in these old boring hotels that I feel like staying here a few weeks to write a science-fiction novel, or a new business plan. Breakfast arrives at the exact time, steaming coffee and cream and excellent croissants, improvement over the arrogant palaces of Manhattan where you have to call twice to get an overpriced cup of brew in a plastic cup with stale bread, an hour later from an indifferent waiter.

Professional contacts will take the whole day. Tomorrow, if all goes well, Adler and Siparex will sign the final papers with me for Euro-America.

I called Aimé Michel: "You see, I'm still in the hospital. Two more operations since last time. You ask if you can come and see me. It's not worth it, you know."

Aimé has the soul and the restraint of an old mountain man who doesn't want anyone to see him diminished and sick, yet he became animated again as we spoke.

Chatel-sur-Moselle. Saturday 23 April 1988.

In the train going back to Nancy. We have just spent two hours with Aimé. He seemed happy to have some visitors and especially to see us together, Janine and me. "I have known so many couples where things didn't last," he said.

So we started to talk about Polybe again, his passages about beings who were not human. We spoke of causality in psi research and genetic engineering. Aimé told us a curious anecdote that happened when he was in his mountain house in Saint Vincent, working on a challenging article on some scientific subject. As he wrote, he began humming a tune that became an obsession, and the more he was humming it, the more he realized it was quite interesting, musically elegant. That feeling became so strong he left his work, went downstairs to the piano and played the entire melody. Having done this he walked by the radio set and turned it on: it was playing the opening chords of the very same tune, which turned out to be Beethoven's 109th piano concerto.

"The lesson I draw from this is that conscious precognition is impossible," said Aimé. "If I had realized the tune I was humming was a premonition I could have refrained from turning the radio on... I could have called the station with a bomb threat to prevent playing the concerto..."

Aimé's quick mind is intact but he gets tired after a short time. He has barely survived the two new operations, including the removal of 50 cm of intestines. A nun who was at his bedside told him, "How beautiful that would be, *Monsieur Michel*, if you died today, on Easter Sunday!" He answered, "I am ready, Sister, but perhaps it would be just as beautiful if I died on Easter Sunday... next year?"

"I started hating her, I'm ashamed to say it," he told us, "until I realized she was not mean, but only a very simple, candid woman."

This led us into a discussion of the religious forms of the New Age: "Did I ever tell you about a visit I got from two American women who thought I was the reincarnation of one of the Apostles? A friend of theirs had channeled that information to them from the Dead. They were planning a community in some castle and I was supposed to be their spiritual leader. They did not have any community or any castle; they were as broke as I was. Well, they came back a month later: They had the castle, and money along with it! I told them the world didn't need a new religion. They went away very disappointed."

He sees human stupidity in such enterprises, where I see an immense, misguided new hope, which unfortunately gets caught up in the greed of countless gurus.

I spent Thursday and Friday working with Fred Adler. I saw him in every light: constructive during our presentation at Rhone-Poulenc, stunning in his grasp of genetic engineering research, phenomenal when he calls upon his vast memory. When an associate happened to boast he once dined with Mitterrand's brother, Fred cut in to remind him he was there too, that an eye surgeon was also at their table, and that the doctor's wife had short hair and a gray dress.

On the plane home. Monday 25 April 1988.

Martine Castello is upset with her job at *Figaro Magazine*. I gave her an interview about venture capital and innovation, which they don't want to publish.

"He didn't talk enough about UFOs," her boss told her.

"But he spoke about the financing of high-tech enterprises in France," she argued, "that's the important point."

"Rewrite it with an extraterrestrial slant," he insisted, "we have to make people dream."

"But I made a promise to Vallée, to stay on the technology topic."

"Our business is image and appearance. Your promises mean nothing."

"I gave my word."

"You won't have a long career in journalism."

From this trip I bring one last image from Chatel-sur-Moselle: a river barge was entering the lock in the soft evening. The guard was turning the crank of the water vanes. A young woman jumped out of the boat and ran to the closest bakery. Two dogs were chasing each other in circle. A tall fellow threw a rope to tie the barge and rushed out to help close the heavy doors. They came from Rotterdam and were headed for Arles in the Midi.

The French are nervous. They are afraid of being absorbed in a unified Europe; they are afraid of the big unknown world that doesn't listen to their rationalizations anymore. No less that 15% have just voted for Le Pen, but in the next round of the elections they will surely rejoin the reassuring Mr. Mitterrand who waits for them by the fireplace like an old uncle.

Spring Hill. Sunday 1 May 1988.

In the latest *Flying Saucer Review*, an orbituary of poor Charles Bowen. Now Tracy Tormé calls from Hollywood: Coral Lorenzen died a month ago. With her it is the last remnant of the original generation of ufologists that passes into history with the Apro group, the only U.S. organization that approached the phenomenon with good critical sense and an international scope.

Spring Hill. Sunday 8 May 1988.

Anatole France writes that scientists are among the least curious of men (in *Le Jardin d'Epicure*):

"A few years ago I visited the galleries of natural history with one of the curators, who described zooliths with great application. When we came to the vestiges of man, however, he turned away and answered my questions by saying that wasn't his window. I felt I had been indiscreet. You should never ask a scientist about any secrets of the universe that are not part of his window. He isn't interested."

Spring Hill. Saturday 21 May 1988.

Today was Catherine's 20th birthday, so we had a celebration that also marked the inauguration of the tower. The Daytons were in attendance, along with our tenant and his little dog. Cake, Champagne. Old Ed Dayton is still solid, although a little deaf. His wife Marie is a tough woman, a student of the New Age.

Among the mail was a card from Diane LaVey, looking for books to rebuild her library. She separated from Anton four years ago.

Spring Hill. Sunday 29 May 1988.

This weekend I called Hal to report a close encounter case in Dallas that he may be able to investigate. This led us to discuss the Secret Onion project, ill conceived from the beginning.

"It's unrealistic to believe that the government will finance a large project that can only bring controversy at a time when Reagan is accused of consulting with astrologers," I told him, "while his Star Wars project is being scaled down."

I continue to think the best way to make progress, in a hard science sense, would be a succession of small, discreet, but open independent projects, yet everybody seems to be on a big public crusade. Even with all the precautions they claim to be taking, I don't believe John Alexander's project could be kept quiet for more than a few months.

Visiting Peter Sturrock at Stanford, I was surprised to hear him say he hadn't followed the theoretical debates about superstring theories and higher dimensions in cosmology. If I had his facility with physical concepts it seems to me I would be keenly interested in this question.

Peter is dignified and reserved with a distant British attitude that overlays his basic kindness. There is not a grain of acrimony in him, even if he looks at the world through academic lenses.

We spoke of the nature of time.

"One of the reasons I didn't pursue a doctorate in physics is that I couldn't bring myself to believe in spacetime the way it was taught to us," I said. "I understand the equations, but I can't swallow the notion of time as a dimension that only moves in one direction and accounts so poorly for human experience."

"You should have stayed in physics," Peter said, "and contributed to change all that." But I simply don't have that talent.

Conversation with Morgane about Dion Fortune: I was looking for images of Ezekiel for a stained glass window I am designing. I turned a page in Dion Fortune's book and fell on a card of the Tarot with the four beasts.

Dion Fortune was an interesting magical researcher with a solid critical sense. She rejected theosophy to follow her own initiation. She never fell into the pitfalls where her contemporary Aleister Crowley would wallow, and lose his way.

The weather is unusual for the season, wet, and fresh. The path along our creek is a world of ferns that smell sweetly of rotten wood.

Spring Hill. Saturday 4 June 1988.

It seems I only write on weekends now, because weekdays are so busy. I flew back from Boston last night after an interesting conference and a stop in New York. Fred Adler has suggested that I work directly with him, apart from Euro-America, a flattering suggestion: having Fred as a personal mentor at this point in my life is a great asset and a compliment.

A new biography of L. Ron Hubbard (*Bare-faced Messiah*) gives the gory details of his secret magical operations with Jack Parsons, in the fascinating cauldron of Los Angeles in the forties.

Ren Breck called me from InfoMedia: he is concerned about the Soviets, whom he suspects of trying to steal the source code of our old Notepad software to create strategic collaborative systems for their industrial experts (**16**).

Paris, Rue de la Clef. Saturday 18 June 1988.

Two days in Lyon where I became tired of all our interviews with potential partners. Back in Paris, coffee with Boëdec who has given up his attempts to stimulate a new UFO research project in France: "I do have some friends in politics, especially in Brittany. But as soon as they reach a high level they clam up on this subject."

We reached the conclusion that military intelligence was in control of the issue in France, and would never allow an independent effort. As we finalize our plans to research cases in Brazil with Bill Calvert next month, I hope we will find a more open attitude among military authorities there. Catherine is in France too. We walked through Paris, from Saint Merri to Beaubourg; now she is in Normandy. Aimé Michel is recovering in a small apartment in Epinal, having survived his four operations. We had a long, warm talk.

Later the same day.

Maman is reminiscing, at our request, about her childhood in the days of the *Belle Epoque*. Her parents had settled in Saint-Maur, east of Paris. Early morning she had to get up to fetch the bread and the paper for her father, who was something of a tyrant. She went out at 5 am when everyone was still asleep and came back to savour her own breakfast of buttered bread and coffee before cleaning the dining room quietly, ahead of the other children. Now she is concerned about getting old: what will happen when she is no longer able to climb up her four flights of stairs? We discussed various choices, retirement homes within her beloved Paris. She is reading Strieber's *Transformation*, and clearly sees the novelist's technique: "He never deviates from his topic," she observes, "He manages suspense in every chapter."

It is to her that I owe much of my curiosity towards the world; she is a model of energy, observation, optimism, as my father was a standard of ethical judgment and skeptical inquiry. Both have taught me indignation before fraudulent beliefs and crooked business.

Gerard de Sède has just published another book about Rennes-le-Château and the issues raised in *Holy Blood, Holy Grail*. He presents the interesting speculation that Jesus was indeed married but his wife was Salomé, not Magdalena (according to the Gospel of Saint Thomas, a Greek text of the third century discovered in 1897).

I am struck by the parallel between the hoaxes built on the life of Abbé Saunière and the fancy stories that accumulate around the Ummo myth. Both follow the same mechanism and motivations.

Hoaxes are very important; they can change the world. A well-fashioned fake is always more convincing than messy reality. The world may well be changed some day by such a fabrication. I wouldn't be surprised if someone "discovered" some documents or even some artifacts "demonstrating" extraterrestrial contact with the U.S. government. How would we know what was real?

Hyde Street. Tuesday 28 June 1988.

As soon as I came back from France I flew to Texas to see Hal, Ken Shoulders, and Bill Church. I spoke privately with Hal, who confirmed that the Secret Onion was dead. This didn't happen because higher-ups were not interested but, on the contrary, because there are so many new bits of data, and such concern for military security, that the Pentagon kept the lid on everything. I believe the same thing happens in France, hence the dead-end nature of Gepan.

Hal has seen a 2-inch thick file that details UFO observations by infrared satellites: "The objects arrive 3,000 miles above the Earth," he told me. "The satellites pick them up as they come near the surface and go away the same manner they came in. Their infrared signature shows a level of energy 15 times that of an aircraft carrier. But the data is so tightly classified nobody wants to talk about it." I wonder if those are really "our" UFOs, or natural phenomena of near space, still undiscovered, or even plain energy discharges.

Hal told me that reading *Dimensions* had triggered some new thoughts about Scientology. In the higher grades there is an auditing technique applied to non-human entities: "They go from the larvae well-known to occultists, to a sort of super-Deva including one that claims to be the God of Electrons... There are short beings with big eyes, too, like Streiber's Visitors," he told me.

Spring Hill. Saturday 2 July 1988.

On vacation for a few days, shaking off city dust, old ideas, the weariness of travel. We have poured the concrete of the observatory steps; I continue to put the books on the shelves. I read Meheust's latest work, a mix of folklore and sociology, very scholarly, but the point is elusive. I am also hard at work on *Confrontations*, the report on ten years of our field research. I get up at 8 am and work until noon. We swim, Janine takes an afternoon nap; I join her when she wakes up. Quiet evenings in the setting sun.

Rock music increasingly uses satanic themes Anton has popularized in the last decade, another way for these groups to enhance their scandalous fame. As Diane observes, "Anton is such a fine musician, he must feel terrible when he hears all that noise, and has to bless it!" She says Anton should turn a page, come out of his somber basement where he entertains bitter thoughts. He has played the part of the Black Pope for so long, issuing extreme declarations for the sake of shocking his contemporaries, that he has placed himself in an impossible position. His philosophy never spread in Europe, as he had hoped. Karla's establishment in Amsterdam never became more than an underground club.

"What about Michael Aquino?" I asked, "and the schism?"

"They were both wrong," said Diane. "Anton delegated too much power; he had to follow his own fancy in everything, like a spoiled kid. Aquino had a straight background and was quite naïve."

It was Diane who ran the organization, answered the mail, paid the bills, and wrote much of the literature under various pen names.

Ten years ago I made this observation, that only two of our friends, Aimé Michel and Anton LaVey, had succeeded in structuring their lives in such a way that they had no boss, no assigned job, no predetermined schedule. I admired the fact that they could afford to look at the world with objectivity, untainted by prejudice. Today Aimé is alone, renting a small apartment far from his beloved books, while Anton rots in the darkest recesses of a musty basement, in a house that may be taken from him any day by a court decision.

"He never had to exercize any discipline," observes Diane, "except when doing whatever he wanted." She started again from nothing, in two jobs as secretary. Still a beautiful woman with that luminous skin Anton loved, she has an engineer boyfriend and new acquaintances who do not suspect she was once the High Priestess of the darkest God.

Spring Hill. Sunday 17 July 1988.

We woke up early. We have much to prepare in anticipation of our flight to Brazil on Saturday. We have undergone the required shots, the pills, the immunization for yellow fever, tetanus and diphteria, but who will protect us from the chupas, who are said to hunt their victims with their fantastic beam? Kit speculates their light is a mix of microwaves and particle beams. But how can the marks on the skin be explained? And the other physiological effects?

Far from inaugurating serious research into abductions, the latest UFO books aggravate an atmosphere of venomous hatred.

"Are all these people crazy?" asks Bob Emenegger who calls me to participate in a new documentary. I politely decline. He has interviewed John Lear, Shandera, Bill Moore, Strieber, and Hopkins.

"I don't know what to think, Jacques. They are clutching at straws, at increasingly bizarre theories. The world is going mad."

Bob loves every minute of it. He thrives on frothy enthusiasm. I brought the conversation back to my visit to Norton Air Force Base.

"General Miller died last week," Bob said. "General Scott gave the eulogy. There was a serious project at one time; it went nowhere."

Bob mentioned the Navy holographic projectors, built by Philips and Hughes. He thinks such devices have been used to simulate UFOs in field tests and military psychological experiments.

We have just turned on our well. We won't run out of water this year; the pond is still full. I sort out old tape recordings. It's always entertaining to hear Allen's warm voice, with its tone of astonished optimism when he speaks of the mysteries of the universe.

15

Fortaleza, Brazil. Tuesday 26 July 1988.

The night has been noisy. For the last two hours roosters have been crowing loudly next door. We have yet to learn to find a comfortable position in our hammocks. The wind enters the room from three sides, bringing a little freshness and the savor of the trees, a sugary smell. The rain occasionally drifts inside too. Then the sun rises fast, chasing away any hope of finding sleep again.

Brazil is in winter but here, so close to the Equator, seasons do not mean much. We arrived on Sunday night on a flight from Miami to

Belém, where we slept at the Palace Equatorial under torrents of blissful rain that drowned out the heat. On Monday we flew on to Sao Luiz and Fortaleza over huge expanses of marshland, forests, muddy flats, and occasionally a red dirt road that tried unsuccessfully to reach the horizon. One of these deltas is the mouth of the Parnaiba where the chupas have been reported.

Bill Calvert was waiting for us in Fortaleza along with Agobar Oliveira, a professor at the regional university, from the department of industrial food processing. I was naturally delighted to finally meet someone named Agobar! A well-informed investigator, he covers thousands of miles every year to meet with witnesses.

At the house of Bill and Regina we launched into a sweeping review of the field while their family brought us local fruits: papayas and pineapples, mangoes, heavenly juices with strange heady tastes, and a cream of avocados. The rain threatened again. The wind took us when we went outside, under the arbor. We felt the mean embrace of the heat, ready to crush and dissolve us. Equatorial heat makes us feel like little lumps of sugar dropped into a hot cup of that wonderful Brazilian coffee.

In the evening we spoke with a neighbor whose uncle lives in Santara, three hours away. Nothing is close by here, everything is three hours away, or six, or nine... The uncle has seen the chupas.

We went up to our open room. All night swinging in our hammocks like ships in a storm, we followed the rhythm of the wind that blew the mosquito net around like a sail.

Parnarama. Wednesday 27 July 1988.

We left Fortaleza at 3:30 in the morning, loading our travel bags in Agobar's Fiat. It was a good idea to travel before sunrise. It took us twelve hours to reach Parnarama, our first stop in a series of field investigations. We halted for coffee at a roadside shop and had lunch at Teresina in an air-conditioned room, *Chez Irene*, a restaurant filled with workers of Banco do Brazil who had not been paid for months and were staging a strike.

Beyond Teresina the roads became very interesting. The palm trees that lined up on both sides give way to a series of lakes infested with piranhas. On the warm asphalt an iridescent cobra, some 12 ft long, was sunning itself. It felt our approach and retreated in majesty. We saw large lizards, goats and pigs; a few oxen slowed us down.

The exit to Parnarama is a dirt path, a simple slope that dives from the road into a ravine. At the bottom is a bar where you can buy lemonade in plastic containers. The big river flows beyond. Bands of brown kids wait next to their boats for someone to cross the river. We left the Fiat near the bar and boarded a leaky craft where one scrawny fellow kept scooping out the water from the bottom with an old coffee can. There are piranhas in the river, too.

Smells: wood burning in the evening air; meat drying in the sun (beautiful black vultures with white wings and a red head circle the zenith); a dead carcass rotting somewhere upwind; also flowers, dust, shit, and the charming perfume of heather. The population of Parnarama watched us as we landed on the other shore.

Bill knew what to do: He asked where the mayor's office was. People were sitting on low stools in front of houses covered in straw that were more like open huts, with walls of dried mud. The mayor kindly recommended one of the two hotels in the village and we dutifully followed his advice.

We went out again to the local bar where the first man we met told Agobar he had seen the light of a chupa two years ago while hunting. He had found himself in the center of an illuminated spot. "My first idea was to shoot," he told us, "but I changed my mind; I made a vow to the Lord that I wouldn't hunt again if I came home alive. The light went away and turned itself off."

"So you don't hunt anymore?" asked Bill. "I started again recently," the man confessed, "but only during the day."

Later the same day.

We have just spoken to Cosmo, the fisherman who had to hide on the banks of the Parnaiba to escape from a light beam that made him dizzy. Local people had pointed out where he lived and we found him putting a new roof of mud over his house. His entourage brought out some stools and we sat down with him. Soon there was a circle of a dozen people around us; children sat in the dusty sand.

In the gathering twilight Cosmo told us about his encounter. I asked him the questions I had prepared, trying in particular to determine if he had suffered neurological reactions. We spent a long time with him, until night came and I couldn't write any more.

There are two bathrooms in the hotel, one of which has running water all the time, a great luxury, because the main water supply of the village is turned off at night.

Parnarama. Thursday 28 July 1988.

The local Candomblé "terreno" (spiritual group) gave a ceremony in our honor tonight. Their dances and chants formed one of the most inspiring displays I have seen here. One song in particular (*Maria Douce*) was quite lovely. Bill told us that many of Brazil's popular tunes and celebrated sambas are borrowed from melodies that arise spontaneously from such terrenos, local congregations. The session we attended was a rite of Umbanda, a hybrid of Candomblé and spiritism.

The priest went into a trance. We were told he would try to contact an astral entity to request information for us about the chupas. Afterwards he asked Agobar to come into the crypt. "The entity has told him that the chupas come from Earth; they are not extraterrestrial. But they don't come from one of the major powers," Agobar reported as he emerged from the darkness.

The priest later told us that the larger terrenos, in Recife or Rio, are better equiped for this kind of contact. His own group is too small. A former truck driver, this shaman had an accident that left him blind. Then he discovered the spirit world.

Parnarama. Saturday 30 July 1988.

We have driven deeper into the interior, using a truck we borrowed from a local administrator. Our goal was to track down a man who had witnessed the death of "Ramon" who was said to have been killed by the chupas.

We did find the man, and Ramon did die before his eyes, but the rest of the story is an exaggeration. We elicited a precise description of Ramon's actions before and during his agony. There was no object in the sky at the time, no beam. Someone miles away did see a light that night, but the two events were unrelated. He simply died at sunrise after climbing down from his hammock; what our witness described to us was a classic heart attack.

We spoke at his house among a dozen little black kids who looked at me as if they had never seen a blue-eyed giant like me.

There were kids at the open window and on the dirt floor, watching us take notes. They were fascinated with Janine's pen because it has a series of bands with the colors of the rainbow. She uses it as a primitive device to get the witnesses to describe colors. They have only limited language skills and little sense of technology, so it is often difficult to know precisely what they mean when they speak of a "beam."

Fortaleza. Sunday 31 July 1988.

A red sun was setting over the sand bars of the Parnaiba when we left the country of the chupas, squeezed together in an old boat that listed on starboard, vibrating with all the energy left in its motor and belching blue smoke over the river. By 10 pm last night we had dinner at Hotel San Jose in Teresina; I suggested we spend the night there. Agobar wanted to drive on but my arguments prevailed: everyone was tired; Janine had backpains, I was coming down with a virus; we hadn't slept in a bed or taken a warm shower for a week.

The next day, well rested, we drove back across the Interior, a land of miserable huts and ruined hamlets where we passed large woods with purple trees, tall cliffs with caves in the middle of the forest, and the luxury of the Serra Grande hotel where two blind kids were begging a few cruzeiros. An iguana, beautiful and iridescent, came out of the bushes as we drove by.

Along the way we spoke with Agobar who had many questions about Hynek, alleged astronaut sightings, and cases in Europe. Bill told us about his work in Brazil as an architect, and about his years at Taliesin with Frank Lloyd Wright. Taliesin was first a Gurdjieff center and only secondarily a school for architects, said Bill.

We have brought back details of about twenty cases, two of them involving characteristic chupa injuries. So far there is no proven instance of any death related to the objects.

Fortaleza. Thursday 4 August 1988.

We spent Monday recuperating from the trip. We are both fighting a sinus and throat infection. It left us so weak we could barely get up to eat. When we felt better we went into town with Bill and Regina and found the occult text that had been used by the two men who died on the *Morro do Vintèm.*

Yesterday we left at 5 am for the second phase of our investigations, first to Santana de Acaraù where many sightings have taken place along the river, and on towards the mouth of the Amazon. When people see us they cluster around and volunteer their stories, looking for answers, hoping for explanations. Brazil is a country where witnesses have never been ridiculed by the likes of Carl Sagan or Philip Klass, so people talk freely about what they have seen. It gets so terribly hot inside the huts of dry mud that we are drenched with sweat, often among 15 or 20 people in a small space that feels like an oven. Such extreme heat seems to have killed the virus that bothered me, although I still feel feverish on occasion.

Belém. Saturday 6 August 1988. Hotel Regent.

The Airbus of Cruzeiro Airlines was very late, so we landed here at 2 am. We slept poorly, the loud noise of an air conditioner filling the room. At 8 am we met with a well-informed local ufologist named Daniel who was born in Bolivia. He is a serious fellow, about 30 and

Fig. 11. With Janine during a witness interview: Belèm, Brazil, July 1988.

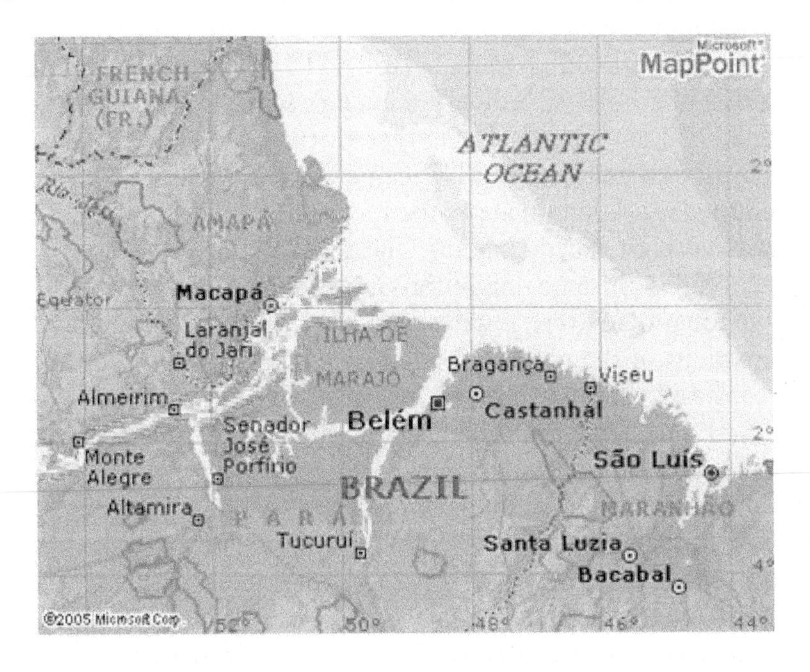

Fig. 12. Site of "Project PRATO" operations by the Brazilian Air Force

well organized. His files are clear, neatly typewritten and illustrated.

Our first meeting of the day was in the office of Colonel Hollanda Lima, on the second floor of the Headquaters of the *Primeiro Comar*, the First Air Force region, which covers most of the Amazon—an area four times the size of France. It is a big rectangular building in the center of the air base.

Colonel Hollanda is a stout man with a round, flat face, inherited from a grandmother who was an Amazonian Indian. He speaks fluent French and English. The colonel has spent most of his career in intelligence, including six years in the jungle among the Indians. He led the team sent to the islands at the mouth of the Amazon during *Project Prato* to observe and photograph the objects that flew over the area for three months from July to September 1977.

We spent two hours in that large office, only occasionally interrupted by a lieutenant who brought papers to be signed, and relighted the colonel's cigar.

At noon Hollanda Lima took us to the officers' mess: tall glasses of beer and Brazilian cuisine. After lunch he left us in his office, saying he had to attend to another matter. Bill and I exchanged cautious glances and spoke only of ordinary subjects. I did express surprise that Hollanda had not mentioned the type of film that they had used: what about infrared emulsions or UV cameras? Half an hour later the colonel returned. I asked him about the recording speed.

"We did have high speed cameras," he said, adding, "by the way, we also recorded in infrared, and ultra-violet."

It was obvious there were microphones in the room, and perhaps our conversations of the morning had been recorded. In any case we must have passed the test, because he was bringing back two big files. The first dossier held all the press cuttings of that period, with pictures taken at night by local journalists.

The second file was the real thing.

It held the military photographs, detailed aerial maps, trajectory analyses by the staff of *Project Prato*. Every page was stamped "Confidential" on top and bottom.

The Brazilian Air force evidently did more UFO research in 1977 than the U.S. Air Force or the Cnes had done in 40 years.

We noted that some of the photographs were only facsimiles.

"Where are the originals?" we asked.

The answer was that Hollanda's superiors had selected the best pictures for another dossier, which was sent to Brazilia.

Colonel Hollanda shook my hand warmly when we left: "I've shown you all this because we know your work," he said. "We've read your books. We know you are not engaged in commercial exploitation."

When we left the base, Daniel told us of his amazement: "No ufologist in Brazil has ever seen these documents," he said. "Or outside the country, either," he added.

Our next visit was to the public health center, where Dr. Wallaide confirmed she had been in charge of the dispensary on the island of Mosqueiro during the UFO wave. She told us about the medical symptoms of patients she saw, including one actual case of death: She had treated an older woman who did not survive the exhaustion that typically followed an encounter with the chupas' beam.

That same evening our Brazilian friends took us to a fine villa in the most exclusive section of town, in a closed community patrolled by security guards. The villa belonged to a colonel, an overweight giant in white shorts and white shirt. "I know you met with Colonel Hollanda Lima," he said once we were comfortably seated in his living room. "There were certain things he couldn't tell you."

He called for his aides to bring coffee. "When Colonel Hollanda and his team installed their cameras on the beach at Bahia do Sul, I was head of security for Primeiro Comar," he went on. "And when our superiors and the damn politicians from Brazilia confiscated out best data, my team got very frustrated because we were not allowed to keep any of it. Politics is a dirty business. So we made our own copies in a hurry, without telling those guys."

He pulled out the real thing, including pictures of objects emerging from the water. We saw a UFO that could clearly be seen against the forest canopy, and another at ground level, with illuminated objects all around. It was an extraordinary evening. We spent hours talking about their conclusions and speculations, and they spoke to us in confidence about the mising pieces of data.

Miami Airport. Sunday 7 August 1988.

At the airport restaurant, my brain sleepy and slow from the heat, filled with images of Manaus: Brazilian confusion, the light along the Amazon as we took off, millions of insects beating the windows of the terminal with their wings, moths the size of saucers...

We travelled with groups of Canadians returning from the jungle, dragging their boots and sleeping bags. There was a fever in the air that I am starting to miss. Manaus smelled of infinity and swampy depths, of heat and unknown landscapes.

Spring Hill. Friday 12 August 1988.

Upon our return we learned that Mamie had been taken to the hospital again. In the last few days, she has gotten worse. Morphine could not stop the pain anymore, and this morning a phone call came from Bayeux to tell us she had died. Catherine and Annick saw her yesterday, and Olivier arrives in Normandy today to join the family. It is the end of a life, the end of a lot of pain she did not deserve.

My library contains every book I could find, in various languages, about life, death, and consciousness: works by scientists and hermetists, mystics and doctors, yet none of them gives an answer or even a reasonable direction of research. It would be comforting to believe in heavenly realms and eternally youthful angels.

Part Twelve

THE OBSERVATORY

16

Spring Hill. Saturday 13 August 1988.

Aimé Michel is back in the Alps, the region so dear to him. He was amused by a paper I wrote about archbishop Agobard, whom I propose to celebrate as patron saint of abductees. He opened his letter to me with a salutation in Latin praising me as a distinguished disciple of Saint Agobard: "*Amatus Michelus Jacobo Valleio Sancti Agobardi disciputo praeclarissimo, Ave!*"

Aimé plans to publish the ancient references he has accumulated, including a passage in the Odyssey, "perhaps the most bizarre text that came to us from Antiquity, along with the story of Achilles' shield," he writes. "What it describes resembles an inside view of a space station, complete with Coriolis' forces in an artificial atmosphere, and all sorts of marvels."

Hyde Street. Sunday 18 September 1988.

This afternoon at the ranch a doe was slowly walking up along the creek, eating tender shoots. The pool was cold; the leaves of the aspen were turning yellow. Autumn brings other changes: Janine has decided to leave her job at the Bank and go into semi-retirement, a decision I welcome. So this is a time for quiet reflexion, retreat and contemplation. Her sister Annick, who's never seen our Mendocino hideaway, will soon visit California. We are very close to her and her husband; the death of Janine's mother last month has made our ties even more precious.

The renovation of the Hyde Street house is complete. We can have our friends around us again, an exciting bunch of travellers and adventurers of the mind. We've enjoyed intimate dinners in Victorian elegance with Bill Calvert who returned from Brazil, Keith Harary and Darlene who came back from diving in the Caribbean where they looked for sunken treasures, and Morgane about to leave for

Iona, where she will celebrate Chtonian rites and enrich her photographic collections.

Last week I flew to New York to see Fred Adler about our investment projects and incidentally to contact publishers about *Confrontations,* the detailed report on my investigations of the last ten years. Much energy has gone into its completion: an obsession, as every book must be. At Ballantine Joe Blades tells me they will reprint *Anatomy* and *Challenge* to accompany *Dimensions* in mass paperback next spring. I am amazed that these old titles are still in demand, more than 20 years later.

The book people I know, like Peter Beren (now at the Sierra Club) and Jeremy Tarcher in Los Angeles, are skeptical when I describe *Confrontations* as a collection of case studies. They want me to emulate the most recent hits: the public, they argue, is looking for intimate, first person, sensational stories like Strieber's. At Contemporary in Chicago, Harvey Plotnick told me the same thing: he'll publish it if I insist, but why don't I write something more personal? I became re-acquainted with his staff and was moved when I met one of the illustrators who was with Regnery 24 years ago: his first assignment had been *Anatomy of a Phenomenon.*

I had dinner with the Cufos team: Mark Rodeghier and George Eberhart, Jerome Clark and his wife-to-be. I was struck by the degree to which they had become obsessed with abduction reports however shaky they might be from a scientific point of view, and impressed by the books of Budd Hopkins and David Jacobs. They've been swept up in the media hype. Allen Hynek would have scoffed at such simplistic fascination with hypnosis.

Hyde Street. Wednesday 21 September 1988.

Today I took part in two shows, the first one a relaxed discussion on radio with Michael and Justine Toms of *New Dimensions*, who now live near Ukiah. The second one was a television discussion on Channel 2 in Oakland with Whitley Strieber. He told me he was re-reading *Messengers* and was beginning to wonder if there wasn't indeed a hidden technology somewhere, controlled by some secret group. In New York I met with Kit, now leaning towards the notion that UFOs do represent a hostile technology.

Hyde Street. Tuesday 27 September 1988.

Annick and Michel have been with us since Thursday. Our talks, our laughter heal the pains and changes of the last few months.

The sad truth is that I am increasingly skeptical of American ufology. The five researchers who are actively investigating abduction reports present a curious spectrum: Jim Harder, a Berkeley engineering professor, tells everybody that we're about to be invaded by gray Aliens and implies that the task of representing Planet Earth will fall on his shoulders.

Budd Hopkins is an artist with no background in science or psychology, whose art has always involved sado-masochistic scenes involving temples with altars and stately non-human "guardians" in enclosed spaces. Now considered as the world expert on Alien abductions, he is convinced of their literal reality: the emotionless Aliens pick up ovulating earth females and forcibly use them as genetic material, placing them on altar-like tables in enclosed spaceships, he claims. After multiple hypnotic regressions, naturally, they do end up telling him the stories he wants.

His disciple David Jacobs is a history professor at Temple University who says he has now dedicated his life to this critical threat, the solution of which is imminent because the invasion is fully upon us.

The fourth "expert," Dr. Leo Sprinkle, is a kind man who does have a formal psychology background. He originated the hypnosis technique in abductions and has put over 300 people into a trance in an attempt to recover their memories. Now he has revealed he had been abducted himself, at a tender age. He has a "mission," he told an American paper: we must seek a pact with the Aliens; television advertising is supposedly hiding subliminal messages designed by Them...

Dr. Richard Haines, the most knowledgeable of the group, left his job at Nasa six months ago. A careful scientist, he is deeply religious and privately suspects (like Gordon Creighton and others) that UFO abductions hide a sinister reality.

That is certainly one of the hypotheses we must consider.

Spring Hill. Saturday 1 October 1988.

Today I drove lazily through Noe Valley and Castro Street, visiting bookstores. There was a marvellous sweetness in the air of San Francisco, bits of idle time and sparkling azure sky dropping around like tinsel. It was an afternoon stolen from the world.

This weekend I enjoyed another rare treat when Olivier flew up from San Diego and we drove up to the ranch where Janine, her sister and Michel were waiting for us.

For old time's sake, my son and I stopped at Denny's in Santa Rosa for eggs and coffee. We miss Catherine, still at the University of Colorado.

There is one aspect of modern ufology I find most disappointing: It is the need that pushes good researchers to embrace simplistic claims. Even Dr. Maccabee, who works on Navy weapon projects, has given a presentation in Washington endorsing a dubious case in Gulf Breeze, in which a local contractor known as “Mr. Ed” says he regularly photographs a bizarre object over his backyard.

Spring Hill. Sunday 2 October 1988.

First light at the new observatory: I setup my old uncle's telescope on its elegant hardwood tripod on top of the tower. We had a moonless sky, millions of lights spread on both sides of the Milky Way. “Shamed into pettiness by the innumerable silences of the stars” (Lawrence) we watched artificial satellites, several meteors, Saturn and Jupiter, the Andromeda nebula, the Pleiades and Mars in its most precious opposition of the century.

My only regret: lacking a more serious instrument. My true pleasure: to have my son with us as we listen to the sounds of the forest and laugh at simple stories.

Hyde Street. Wednesday 5 October 1988.

This morning Janine and her sister flew off with Michel to visit Alain in Charleston, leaving me alone for a week. Without her I feel sad and a bit lost.

The city has moved the three-masted ship *Balclutha* to the foot of Hyde Street. The magnificent vessel, at its new anchorage, swings in thick luminous fog. It reminds me of Jules Verne and of the engravings of Gustave Doré in the musty novels of my childhood. The Alcatraz foghorn howls endlessly. I am alone with my reverie.

Hyde Street. Thursday 6 October 1988.

This morning Ned Leavitt called me to discuss what he called my "literary career." He urged me to write another book, more personal than *Confrontations*. I told him the truth: I don't think the American public of this decade, obsessed as it is with making money and acquiring expensive cars, concerned with superficial television glitter and flashy rock stars, could ever become seriously interested in the contradictions between occultism and science. Even my cautious approach to esoteric matters is radically foreign to the New Age groove. It matches neither the dogmas of religion nor the alternate truths of the crystal meditators and "white light" magicians. I don't use hashish to talk to my Guardian Angel. I don't expect extraterrestrials to come and vindicate me. My motto has become, after Borges: *Hope not even for the savage beast.*

At nightfall, to shake off these reflections, I went to *Les Croissants* on Polk Street for a tall coffee and an amused look at the street scene. There is a big moral scandal in San Francisco: after an investigation of underage prostitution the police have "discovered" a prominent politician among the clients. The bordello in question had existed for many years with full knowledge of authorities, catering as it did to the affluent and powerful.

The sudden awakening of the social conscience, embodied in this new investigation, is prompted by a political vendetta in the best tradition of the Barbary Coast. Teen-age girls were recruited among the lower stretch of Polk Gulch, a sad place where many runaway kids and stray creatures from all over the country end up.

Nobody in the city was very concerned with the welfare of these poor children until they could be used as pawns in this political mess. Little by little a new pretense of morality, spurred on by the AIDS epidemic, tightens its hold on American society. Vice is turning uglier. In those areas where colorful mutants used to roam, the streets turn into a battleground as dangerous and slimy as scenes from *Bladerunner*.

Later the same day.

Midnight. Is it the drizzle, the loneliness, the sadness that comes from my solitary walks among the derelicts of San Francisco? Is it just fatigue? Ideas collide in my head. Vaguely, I imagine a wide theory that could unify parapsychology, UFOs, religion... Yet the crucial elements escape us.

I believe there is an n-dimensional psychic medium embracing the cosmos and us. Is it capable of reflecting our thoughts and visualizations, just as the ionosphere reflects radio frequencies? Suppose it was filled with a proto-consciousness that could emulate human behavior, precipitating the images we create of our gods, our ghosts, our archetypes, our future? What if our own souls were born from that protopsyche? What if we became re-absorbed into it at death?

What if the great movements of human consciousness were nothing but waves in such plastoid material?

What if one could project one's own thoughts into it to implement symbolic commands? What if it was the site of my hypothetical control system, of Philip Dick's VALIS—and all the weirdness of Magonia? **(1)**

This evening I went and saw *Spellbinder* at the urging of Bob Weiss. It was a disappointment. There were only three spectators in the large theater. The plot is a flat, uninteresting story, a caricature of Satanism. On the big screen, even the witches looked bored.

Hyde Street. Sunday 9 October 1988.

While Janine was still in Charleston I watched *Out on a Limb*, Shirley MacLaine's television show. Like her books, the film presents an American concept of a mystical quest, full of cheap miracles and phony "channels" that spin out tale after lamentable tale. After this, I despair of ever seeing the subject of UFOs seriously posed. We seem to have forgotten the spiritual reality of man. Is it so difficult to pose the right questions? Why do sincere people like MacLaine tumble into the first pitfall that opens up under their feet when they decide to move along this courageous path?

Hyde Street. Tuesday 11 October 1988.

When Janine is away I have no taste for reading or writing, no energy for work. I seem to be good only for mechanical things, walking around, buying a few books, having lunch with trusted colleagues like Peter Sturrock and Dick Haines; and dreaming.

Morgane has returned from Iona loaded with photographs, sick with the flu, disoriented. She speaks of her visions, of blue beings from Andromeda and far-away islands in the fog of the North Sea.

Among the pieces of literature I treasure are Philip Dick's insights and the novels by the Strugastsky brothers (**2**). Both have touched the ultimate problem. There is no God and no Devil, but there is indeed a psychic system close to us, a gigantic entity, a Pacific ocean of the spirit of which we are nothing but evaporating droplets. We should explore it, name it, and measure it. Philip Dick called it VALIS but he understood it only vaguely, from the depth of his sacred delirium. Yet the quest could continue along rational lines.

Hyde Street. Friday 14 October 1988.

Janine is back. Tonight we turned on our little television set, crawled into bed, pulled the blankets up to our noses and watched with increasing disgust a show long-awaited among Alien amateurs, the *Cover-up* documentary produced by Seligman. Never was I so elated to have turned down participation in a television program. It was a circus, poorly filmed, poorly prepared, with Bill Moore's fake "intelligence agents" (Condor and Falcon) telling absurd tales, hidden by a screen. I was sorry for my friend Dick Haines, who had flown to Washington to be part of that fiasco. Even Colonel Friend, a well-informed, intelligent officer, was made to look stupid. A ludicrous musical score ran gaily through the dialogue.

New plans: in two weeks Janine and I will be in London and from there we go to an international ufology meeting in Brussels. A Soviet scientist is supposed to attend, for the first time at such a gathering.

Hyde Street. Saturday 15 October 1988.

Several commitments are keeping us in San Francisco this weekend while the Blue Angels fly overhead in their annual demonstration of air power. This afternoon we will attend Bob Johansen's party for his new book *Groupware*, which he has dedicated to Doug Engelbart and to me (**3**).

On Thursday afternoon I went to SRI for a "debriefing" session with Security, filling out questionnaires. I saw Ed May, who had something new to tell me. To put it bluntly, he said, the paranormal project is entering a terminal phase. The $2 million promised under his contract with the Army have been withdrawn by a new project manager. Jack Vorona at DIA, an old friend of the team, has located another million somewhere to keep the project afloat, but he naively asked Darpa to supervise the spending. The cake fell into Craig Fields' lap. Always the crafty manipulator, he confiscated the money by playing a bureaucratic game: "Your project fascinates me," he told Ed May. "I will finance it without any limits if you pass a simple test which I will give to you."

Fields proposed a task that would not have proven anything. Ed offered a different test; Fields did not accept it... Ed would be happy to take his project away from SRI tomorrow if he could.

Ed described to me the experiments he was doing with the magnetic localisation of brain sites that seem to be responsible for psychic activity. In these tests a light (A) is turned on randomly in a remote room while the brainwaves of a subject are recorded. Theoretically there should be no unusual peak at that point since the subject doesn't see the light. Instead of an electro-encephalogram registering mere surface currents on the skull, Ed May uses a newly-developed magnetic detector aimed at a few clusters of cells deep inside the visual cortex. A few seconds later another light (B) is turned on in front of the subject, giving the usual evoked response. The interval (A-B) is fixed. Ed claims that experiments with Gary Langford, Joe McMoneagle, and Ingo Swann have given significant results, with defined peaks whenever the (A) light is turned on—an evoked response to a signal the subject cannot physically see.

Spring Hill. Sunday 23 October 1988.

We have carried the last three bookshelves into the tower and installed two stained glass windows in the library. Unfortunately we are without phones again: the squirrels that live down the road from us have bitten through the wires and filled the relay boxes with nuts!

A week of travel and lost sleep: New York on Sunday night, and breakfast at the Algonquin with Ned Leavitt. From New York I flew to Washington to see Bob Chartrand, who received me warmly in his office at the Congressional Research Service. Rain was falling hard when I took a cab to Silver Springs where I met Dr. Bruce Maccabee at the Naval Surface Weapons Center. We had a friendly lunch and spoke for several hours about the *Cover-up* show and the Gulf Breeze sightings (**4**). He told me that the television program, as bad as it was, had generated 60,000 calls from the public, of which 3,600 were new abduction stories.

Bruce is certain the Gulf Breeze photographs are genuine but he could not convince me: if the objects are seen so often and are so bright, why was there no attempt to get better evidence, such as a spectrum? And what is the source of the external illumination for the objects on the photos?

Bruce also states that Mr. Ed was recently abducted, and that the little men who took him away used a helmet with four electrodes to transfer his emotions to their "News," the freshly-hatched little Gray hybrids... The symbolic and possibly fictitious character of these events is never mentioned. In line with the new ufology of Hopkins and Jacobs, anything that comes out under hypnosis becomes Gospel to be accepted literally. This kind of conversion pathology in otherwise intelligent researchers amazes me.

I went to Detroit on Tuesday night. Kit was at the airport. We spoke for a long time: in his car, over dinner (at the restaurant from which the Mafia once kidnapped Jimmy Hoffa) and at his new house, actually a mansion overlooking a lake. He assured me that there was indeed an MJ-12, which had employed the list of scientists quoted by the ufologists, including Menzel, and that it had reported to Truman and to Eisenhower. But that project had nothing to do with UFOs: it was a vast program to study impacts and possible reactions against a psychological warfare attack directed at the United States. The story is right out of my novel *Alintel*. This version of MJ-12 still exists, he conceded when I pressed him. Someone has been spinning it through the UFO rumor mill as if it was part of the government's Alien coverup, but what is the purpose of this manipulation?

Maccabee has the reputation of a good physicist, but his unproven claims about Gulf Breeze have turned off a lot of people in Washington: "When the Mr. Ed story is finally exposed, UFO research may be permanently damaged in the government. It will be useless to bring it up again for ten years or so," Kit says.

Bob Weiss and I are making progress on the movie project. On Thursday we will meet in Hollywood with Joe Dante and scriptwriter Tracy Tormé in the offices of Universal. Tracy is finishing a script about Travis Walton's abduction.

Hyde Street. Thursday 27 October 1988.

This evening I attended a rare lecture by Colin Wilson at Cody's bookstore in Berkeley. He was erudite and pleasant, but his talk centered on a model of levels of consciousness that seemed arbitrary and facile. It led to a barrage of pseudo-philosophical questions on the part of Berkeley's eternal students. I had fun watching him field the kind of sticky, ill-defined inquiries I have so often gotten from such people–ludicrous questions like: "If Nietzche had been able to read Huxley, would he have agreed with the existentialists about the concept of *Nausée*?"

When he was challenged about synchronicity he asked, "Is Jacques Vallée in the room?" Taking me as his witness, he recalled my weird encounter with Melchizedek. When he was recounting this episode while writing his latest book, back in Cornwall, a volume fell from a shelf near him. It was a mystical treatise, he said, open at a page called "Melchizedek teachings!"

Before leaving California I drove down to the semiconductor plant of Silicon Valley Group to consult a colleague and called Hal Puthoff in Texas to find out how his super-electron project was doing. In France, Pierre Aigrain's group at Thomson has not signed an agreement for the flat panel technology that was Jupiter's primary hope, beyond Hal's bright theoretical insights.

London, Bloomsbury. Wednesday 2 November 1988.

We rediscover London with delight in a sunny, fresh, crackling atmosphere, exceptional for November. In Regent Street workers are pulling Christmas decorations out of open trucks to hang them up and brighten the city. Young, carefree people dance in the streets of Soho. It is a great pleasure to be here with Janine in a place where I have often walked around in loneliness.

My British publisher is Ernest Hecht of Souvenir Press, a genial Czech who has kindly placed the company's flat at our disposal, a couple of blocks away from the British Museum. Between interviews (the *Daily Express*, the *Scotsman*, four regional radio stations, and a live talk show at LBC) we came back to the apartment as the jet lag caught up with us. Over dinner at White Tower, Ernest Hecht bombarded me with questions about my books. He admits to being a soccer fanatic and an inveterate womanizer. His knowledge of theater seems to be encyclopedic.

Yesterday I finished reading *The Secret of the Unicorn*, by Steve Levy, heavy with recollections of Ira. It makes me sorry I did not pay more attention to Holly Maddux whom I met twice: once at Stanford, another time in their Philadelphia apartment. I do feel irritated when Steve Levy mentions "The Sixties" with awe as if he spoke of such cultural epochs as "The Hellenistic Period" or *Le Siècle des Lumières*.

The Sixties never aroused in me any vast enthusiasm or deep respect. It did mark the healthy rejection of many prejudices for a generation of Americans who finally shook off their parents' hypocrisy and tired cultural attitudes, hurrah! But they immediately fell back into everything that was worst about the old Establishment while pretending to reject it. The drugs that are now plaguing their adult life and ruining their kids were invented by the military complex they despised; they adopted a pseudo-mysticism that has sent their generation into the dreamland of the New Age; their call for sexual liberation was wonderful but the outcome was superficial and pathetic; their attacks against the industrial and financial infrastructure have produced no visible reforms. Against this background there were hundreds of nice harmless girls like Holly: lost, ethereal, a bit masochistic. You found them on every campus.

The portrait of Ira drawn by Levy is excellent, even if he has failed to develop the most significant aspects of "the Network" and the deeper nature of Ira's power. He has not gone far enough into the paranormal milieu to give an accurate description of the small but intellectually powerful world that supported Ira.

Today I have more interviews scheduled in London, and this evening a lecture at Oxford University.

London, Bloomsbury. Thursday 3 November 1988.

Gordon Creighton met us for a pleasant lunch at Hotel Russell with his wife Joan, who unfortunately suffers from acute emphesyma. Then a good meeting with Hilary Evans, conversations on the phone with Jenny Randles, and a raiding expedition against Watkins' occult bookstore. The *Daily Express* has published a favorable review of *Dimensions*, much to Gordon's astonishment: for years they consistently ignored his *Flying Saucer Review*; the magazine came close to halting publication when Charles Bowen died. It would have disappeared if Gordon had not agreed to carry the torch. He stabilized the losses at a time when they were dropping 200 readers per issue out of a total of 3,500 but he's unable to increase the readership again. I am not surprised at this, given the vitriolic, often rambling tone the articles have lately taken.

My Oxford lecture was organized by astronomer Michael Shallis, a pleasant man who related to us some extraordinary paranormal English observations.

Strasbourg. Monday 7 November 1988.

The professional whirlwind carries me off to Alsace. The last smile of Janine, who accompanied me to the train at *Gare de l'Est* remains with me, her laughing eyes, too. Strasbourg is hard, gray, cold, and its black, grandiose cathedral is blurred in the fog beyond the rooftops. I am taking part in a day-long international investment seminar that gathers entrepreneurs and financial managers. In the train I have continued to revise the translation of *Dimensions* and begun reading Jenny Randles' book on abductions, a subject that leaves me amazed with the naiveté of many would-be researchers about hypnosis: the twentieth century may have found its witchcraft and its sabbaths, as well as its Inquisitors like Hopkins and Jacobs, even if they use hypnotic trance rather than torture to extract prefabricated confessions from the victims.

Paris. Monday 14 November 1988.

At my partners' office on *Rue de Monceau*. I barely had time to unpack my bags after Strasbourg to catch up with colleagues, and Fred Adler was landing for two days of abrasive confrontation. He arrived tired and furious against everything French. I took a seat, on purpose, under a portrait of Guillotin. Before the group, which included Jean-Jacques Chaban-Delmas, Fred unfolded his grand stra-

Fig. 13. With Dr. Bounias and the witness in Trans-en-Provence

Fig. 14. The observatory at the Spring Hill Ranch

tegy. The next day we paid a visit to the president of *Electricité de France*, Mr. Delaporte, whom we attempted to dazzle with technological generalities. On Friday night Janine and I fled to Brussels for the European UFO Congress. From the train window she enjoyed watching the great wide fields she likes so much, the upturned dirt where birds pick at food, the sun setting behind the darkened steeples of country churches.

We found a well organized research society in Belgium. Sobeps (**5**) has its own building, a full library, and a conference room. The French were there, represented by Bertrand Méheust and Pierre Lagrange, Thierry Pinvidic and Michel Figuet. There were five Italians, many Belgians. John Spencer and Hilary Evans had come from England, Walt Andrus and Dick Haines from the States and Vladimir Rubtsov from the Soviet Union (actually, Ukraine).

Following a breathless buildup Walt Andrus, head of the Mufon group, gave us an exhaustive after-dinner lecture about the Gulf Breeze sightings, complete with crude jokes, slides of Mr. Ed and a picture of paunchy Andrus himself wearing a UFO T-shirt. Then he stood at the lectern, beamed at the European researchers assembled in the room and said with the tone of a specialist who has just demonstrated his utter mastery of his subject: "Now I will do something that never fails to amaze my audiences; I will ask all of you to raise your hand if you are now convinced of the facts!"

I looked around: not one hand had gone up. Dick Haines told me that at that moment he was ashamed to be American!

Same day, aboard the TGV going to Lyon.

This morning we were invited (through Jean-Yves Casgha) to the apartment of a Paris journalist named Didier Hyiah. He wanted our opinion about the first video scenes ever transmitted from the Great Beyond. These tapes have been recorded in a Luxembourg laboratory run by a schoolteacher and her husband. Their equipment includes a television set, a camera pointed at the screen to create a "feedback loop," a videorecorder, an infrared light and an ultraviolet source, an ultrasound generator whose purpose is undefined and a curious antenna shaped like a five-pointed star. A low voice allegedly triggered by a signal generator stated a series of platitudes about death, in a suitably depressing tone.

The images themselves were fairly clear. Remarkably, they showed a young woman, supposedly from another planet, strolling among the ghosts who rambled on about their happiness on the Other Side of Death. We caught glimpses of a dark city where transmitters were allegedly being built for a closer link with the living... The whole affair did have a poetic overtone, yet I could not refrain from laughing as we watched a man who spoke to us from the eternal tomb, wearing glasses and a tie. I pointed it out to the journalist: "The poor fellow's lot has hardly improved; he still has the same infirmities with which he was burdened on Earth..."

He shrugged: "Perhaps it's all a hoax. But they tell us the Dead can assume any shape they want. Naturally they take one that's recognizable to us."

TWA flight from Paris to Boston. Tuesday 22 November 1988.

A week of hard work analyzing business plans, although Fred Adler will probably veto any investment we propose in the near future. On Thursday Janine came to Lyon with me. Unfortunately she had fallen ill in Normandy, where she and Annick had paid their last respects to their mother, seeing her ashes dispersed over the rough ocean off the coast of Brittany. She was sick, grieving, depressed, and tired. We slept at the Roosevelt and the next day drove to Grenoble to verify the precise features of the celebrated UFO landing at Trans-en-Provence, the best-documented event in the French files. The rain and the heavily industrialized landscape depressed us further; the fog was so thick we were unable to go beyond Sisteron that night.

I had forgotten that magnificent site, with the Citadelle overlooking the Durance and the rocks towering above the road. We spent the night in a small hotel that had only one other guest. On Saturday we met Professor Bounias in Aix and he drove us to Trans-en-Provence. He's an interesting man, an expert botanist full of ideas on physical models of consciousness... He promised to send the manuscript of his book, *Le Rouet de la Génèse*. His theories explain a bit too much; but as we discussed them in his white Land Rover on the sunny Esterel expressway or in the great dining room of *L'Orée du Bois*, he succeeded in communicating his enthusiasm to us.

At the site, with Mr. and Mrs. Nicolai, we examined the place where the famous discoid object hit the ground in January 1981. We interrogated them at length without finding any contradiction in the story. Some doubts remain, of course, even when Bounias' work on the aging alfalfa plants is taken into account. (**6**)

We drove on to Marseille in the cold Mistral and went to sleep in the high-tech décor of a brand new, expensive hotel, all plastic and neon tubes. On Sunday we came back to Paris on the TGV. The sun came out briefly over Avignon, but the clouds closed in when we reached Vienne, giving the French countryside a peculiar silvery tone, which went well with our mood. By the time we reached Paris it was raining again. The journey was intense and tender.

Annick de Scriba, who is translating *Dimensions* for publisher Laffont, came over to meet me on *Rue de la Clef.* Maman offered her some tea. We discussed the wonders and pitfalls of translation work. She told us the very funny, yet real story of the famous General Staff who won World War II, according to the French version of an American history book. An ignorant French translator thought "General Staff" must be a General named "Staff," so that this fearless officer was everywhere at once, sometimes at the service of Russia, sometimes American, British or even plotting strategy on the German side! Brave "General Staff" led every important action.

On Monday I attended a Board meeting of Photonetics, a laser company in Marly-le-Roi that is our first investment. Before leaving France I spoke to Aimé Michel again. He has now moved to Charmes, near Epinal. It was my last memory of the trip: his joyful voice, his mind alert again.

17

Spring Hill. Friday 25 November 1988.

Thanksgiving: we took advantage of the holidays to run away. My life will soon be at the half-century mark, so it is time to review the early parts of these Journals. As I work through the early text I fill in a few holes, cutting long discourses, weeding out tirades and redundancies. Is it worthy of being shared with unknown readers? I have no way of knowing this. But it's an invaluable exercise for me, to live some of those episodes again and try to learn from old weaknesses, passions and follies, from visions that were fulfilled and those that exploded and vanished into nothingness.

It is said that at the time of death a person often watches a forced review of the details of the life just completed, without judgment or censure, like a fast movie. What I am doing is of the same order, except that I don't intend to wait for the hour of death to think critically about my own life. This is a deliberate examination of my progress and mistakes, a summary of what I have learned, compiled before old age makes these lessons useless.

Spring Hill. Saturday 26 November 1988.

Yesterday I pulled out the fence posts of the old corral. Under the drizzle of November the pond overflows through the grass. Wild mint grows at the foot of the willow tree. Birds and frogs are everywhere. I find salamanders, lizards, and big ugly insects hiding in the rye.

Hyde Street. Sunday 27 November 1988.

Among the mass of mail that brings book catalogues, bills, letters from readers of *Dimensions* who claim they've seen the "Visitors" I find an emotional card from Diane LaVey. Her divorce is not official, but the affair has already exploded into the newspapers, from the *Wall Street Journal* to the trashy supermarket tabloids:

> Over and above my workload, the emotional distress and the anxiety caused by the media attention have been terrible: I felt threatened in every aspect of my life, my work, my family (my parents had no idea that we were not legally married) and my lodging.

In spite of all this she hasn't lost her keen sense of humor:

> On the day of Halloween I went to work at UCSF dressed as a Fallen Angel, with the dress I had been wearing at the opening of *Rosemary's Baby*, sporting wings and a halo, bandaids on my knees and scars everywhere... The kids hospitalized in the pediatrics department were tickled when they saw my costume.

Hyde Street. Sunday 4 December 1988.

Fred Beckman, riding the wave of the latest gossip, came here for dinner Monday night with bizarre new stories: The little world of ufology, swept along by abduction zealots, is buzzing with new tales about Alien physiology.

He brought a fancy Italian slide projector stuffed with photographs taken from the *Cover-up* TV program, which he finds fascinating, and he regaled us with a formal course on the biology of the little creatures.

"Do you really believe all that?" I asked in astonishment.

"It does sound far-fetched, but look at the quality of these computer simulations! This comes from a professional place," he answered.

"Of course, Fred, wake up, it comes from Hollywood!"

"You don't understand... the tape wasn't supposed to be in the show, it appeared at the last moment. A motorcycle courier brought it to the studio. Nobody wants to tell me where it came from. I don't think the producers themselves know."

This is another clear indication, according to his ufology friends, that we are dealing with serious information deliberately leaked by a very deep source. The implication is that the Alien cadavers do exist, even live ufonauts, in the hands of the government! Our skepticism did not deter Fred. He has spoken at length on the telephone with Hal Puthoff, who reportedly hinted that his high contacts were convinced of the genuine nature of the photos. Hal requested 15 sets of slides! Dick Haines himself is supposed to have remarked, after seeing them: "I have learned more about the UFO problem in the last 10 minutes than I did in the previous 10 years!"

Have all our friends gone crazy? These graphics could be made by any kid with a workstation. They show unspecified organs surrounded by acronyms that the operator could have inserted, based on his own imagination. There may or may not be actual Aliens, but all this proves nothing, yet our "researcher" friends are swallowing it without any critical thought. This realization depresses me. The last spark of rationality seems to be dying.

After hearing all this craziness Janine and I were eager to get lost in the woods. I finished putting the books in order, and I designed a new stained glass window, an occupation I find more relaxing and pleasant than discussing Alien intestines.

Hyde Street. Sunday 11 December 1988.

Two days in New York with Fred Adler this week, and a new discussion with Kit who has found a medical doctor allegedly involved in an actual Alien autopsy. He heard of him through Dr. Richard Neal of Los Angeles. Unfortunately the doctor in question doesn't want to talk to anyone because he allegedly receives pension checks from the government.

Like Fred Beckman, Kit has seen the *Cover-Up* documentary and was impressed by the section on alien physiology. We disagree about that as we now disagree about many other things. What I saw on the film seemed like a cheap fabrication on the same sad level as Ummo.

The two “secret agents” in the documentary, so-called Condor and Falcon, are none other than Bob Collins, a technical consultant in Albuquerque, and Sergeant Doty, the shadowy fellow from the Air Force Office of Special Investigations—fringe elements of a rogue security apparatus that is out of control.

Magonia Tower. Saturday 31 December 1988 (New Year's Eve).

We found patches of ice on the roof and the road covered with snow. Our daughter is here with John, her Filipino friend. Olivier, who spent Christmas with us in the City, has gone back to San Diego where his new Japanese girlfriend is waiting for him: our extended family now spans the Pacific Rim.

In our retreat we tackle unfinished work: Janine has helped me catalogue another 400 books crowded here. To this tower I can come back from busy Paris or dirty New York, and look at the stars again. In front of me is the marvellous statue of a golden winged angel. Who is this divine being: Lilith? Isis? Sophia? Nature herself inviting us to dance?

The windows I have painted in the stained glass style are in place, too. On the left side of the library are Mélusine and Merlin the Enchanter. On the right, Melchizedek holding the Grail and Dr. John Dee talking to a green angel in his crystal: four guides to the higher world. These two windows show a system of the universe symbolized in two interconnected triangles. I have special reverence for Saint Agobard and prophet Ezekiel, represented upstairs. A more complete tribute to earthly and heavenly masters should include Paracelsus and Nicolas Flamel, Nostradamus and the Count de Saint-Germain, Giordano Bruno and Trithemius the Abbey of Sponheim, and of course Casanova and the Cardinal de Bernis, with a background of happy nuns frolicking in the heather... I just don't have enough windows.

There is much to learn still, from nature herself, so I watch the stars in the cold crisp night: Orion rising in the East, the Pleiades overhead. Last week we celebrated the Solstice in Diane's little house, gossipping happily about occult figures from our past.

Fig.15. The Victorian house on Hyde Street, San Francisco

Janine had brought walkie-talkies as a gift for eleven-year-old Stanton, LaVey's grandson. Now I slide into the warm bed, letting one more year fade into the past.

Hyde Street. Monday 9 January 1989.

Luisa Teish spent the weekend with us in San Francisco, working on her next book that started out as *Eartha's Pass* and will now be called *Carnival of the Spirit*. She has wonderful stories to tell. Her intelligence is sharp, her stories full of funny, incisive observations about people. I wish she would capture them and save them for her book: they would make a splendid series of portraits.

Hyde Street. Tuesday 10 January 1989.

"Are you a producer?" asks the Mexican cab driver at Burbank airport when I tell him to drive to Paramount Studios.

"No, I'm just an engineer," I answer. That puts a stop to his interest.

Tracy Tormé has sketched some ideas about our story, which we debate around Bob Weiss' cluttered table. Bob is in the process of closing down his office at Paramount where his latest farce, *The Naked Gun*, continues to earn millions.

A fresh current of insanity flows steadily through the teapot of ufology. The editor of *UFO Magazine* believes she is under surveillance. By the Aliens? By MJ-12? By CIA? Nobody knows. Tracy tells me that two Men-in-Black showed up ominously at the magazine's recent Christmas party, confirming the worst fears. They were of pallid complexion, wearing dark suits and dark glasses, black hats. They spent the evening staring. No one had seen them enter the apartment! They were actors, paid $70 each for the job.

Over lunch at the Paramount commissary I asked a friend about the simulation of Alien bodies in *Cover-up*. That question continues to fascinate Fred and other ufologists, building a skyscraper of theories to account for the complicated notations and arcane body structures represented on the screen. Several scientific colleagues have even confided to me they were astonished at the sophistication of the images. My Hollywood friend laughed: Kurt Brubaker had hired Mr. Film, a local computer animation company, to build the models to his specifications. He let his imagination loose when it came to technical-sounding acronyms.

Now Stanton Friedman and others are wasting their investigative talents and the money of the Fund for UFO Research trying to correlate this gibberish with the hypothetical MJ-12. It is hard to remain serious in the face of all this childishness.

New York. Hotel Algonquin. Tuesday 17 January 1989.

A cold, bright night in New York. I am alone in my little room with a tiny television set that barely gets one clean channel, and only in two colors: green and red. I don't mind. I brought my old Journal that I intend to edit between business meetings. A woman is moaning with pleasure in the next room. Most males would be exploring the discotheques and clubs of Manhattan on this fine evening. This solitude in which I reside is anything but virtue. New York just doesn't inspire me. There is an emptiness here that makes me wish to stay in my room and work.

Tonight I had dinner at the Union Square Café on Sixteenth Street with Whitley Strieber and his wife, both relaxed and friendly. Whitley was very much the affluent gentleman farmer in his camel hair coat and beige hat, driving a brand-new black Jeep Cherokee. He is buying a new place upstate, with dirt roads and a large field where he claims local people have seen objects coming out of the ground, leaving burn rings. He came into the restaurant carrying one of the new wireless phones, which he proceeded to use to call his associates during our dinner, explaining gravely that he was seeking distributors for his movie, and that timing of the "deal" was extremely important. People at the next tables looked at us with disapproving stares. He sounded like some of my colleagues in venture capital but it occurred to me that Fred Adler, who is worth many millions, would never be seen walking into a fine restaurant carrying a telephone, no matter how critical "the deal" was: real tycoons have competent underlings who carry their cell phones. Nonetheless we had a pleasant dinner.

Whitley told me he still saw the Visitors but the interaction was more "subtle" than before. Does this mean there is less physical content? "There is no limit to the weirdness of the Visitor experience," he told me. "*Communion* had not gone far enough."

On this score I believe he is correct. I told him about Trans-en-Provence and promised to send him my paper on remote viewing (**7**). We discussed hypnosis and Budd Hopkins, who continues to spread bitter rumors trashing Whitley. Later, at his apartment, he showed me the thick file of letters he has received from *Communion* readers.

Ann has taken a lead role in analyzing the letters from Whitley's readers; she will edit the Foundation newsletter. Their son is a bright little chap, full of energy and humor.

New York. Hotel Algonquin. Wednesday 18 January 1989.

Meetings at Ballantine and William Morris. Last night, a friendly dinner at the *Captain's Table* near the United Nations with Shel Gordon who has now left Shearson Lehman to set up a small financial organization. A few years ago it is Shel who quietly engineered the merger of Shearson American Express with Lehman, but he did not intend to stay with the huge firm.

Shel asked me if I had read Steven Levy's book about Ira.

"I read it, but I declined to meet the author or to contribute any material," I said.

"So did I. I haven't even read the book."

"You'd find it well-researched, although he didn't give Ira full credit for his ability to trigger deep attitude changes among people, especially business executives, and to remove their mental blocks."

"Apparently Ira just came within a hair of being arrested again, in Stockholm this time."

"He must have people warning him," I said.

"Yes, part of his network, still in operation after all these years." A pause, then: "What would you do if you were in Paris some day, and you recognized Ira staring at you in the Métro?"

I thought about that, looking out the window at Second Avenue, now bleak and deserted.

"I'd have a lot of trouble going up to him, shaking his hand. It would be different if he had confessed and faced trial. I do believe that he killed Holly. I've thought very hard about every possible conspiracy theory: they all collapse under their own weight. Any man can make a terrible mistake, lose control. But why deny it?"

"There may be something to the idea that he really didn't know he'd done it, that he erased it completely from his mind, because it was so enormous," Shel said. But what about the body?

Shel's limousine was waiting outside; it took me quietly back to Sixth and West 44th.

Hyde Street. Friday 20 January 1989.

Morgane brought us her first set of greeting cards today, a joyful creative explosion. They show a mad dog with half his face sunburned by a UFO, happy sacred cows dancing in the moonlight, Shamanic Dogs having attacks of astral cats, and the Second Coming of a sheep returning to his flock. They are irreverent, funny, and full of color and vitality. She says my weird humor inspired her.

We had another working session with Bob and Tracy at Hyde Street. Over lunch we discussed psychological warfare and belief systems. Bob told us about the time when the Pope came to bless the *Blues Brothers* set in Chicago. They were shooting the movie with John Belushi and Dan Ackroyd when the Pope, who was known to be visiting the city at the time, made an impressive entrance on the set, followed by his retinue of cardinals.

"All the Catholics in our crew just hit the floor," recalls Bob. "It was amazing. The Pope went towards John Landis and extended a hand so he could kiss the ring. Landis saw through the whole thing, grabbed the Pope by the balls and pandemonium erupted."

It was Bob who had hired the Pope, a white stretch limousine, a black car and a fancy troup of Cardinals. Just as Tracy has been hiring Men-in-Black to spook ufologists.

Hyde Street. Sunday 29 January 1989.

Kit tells me he is getting some interesting mail: anonymous copies of AFOSI secret reports of near-landings by UFOs at various military bases. These papers, he says, are authentic, as opposed to the alleged MJ-12 documents, which have the classifications in the wrong places and format. Kit has taken those papers to CIA specialists who are quietly following the field. They have decided it would be futile to try to track down the authors of the leak.

"Who are your mysterious 'friends' within CIA?" I asked him.

"They are serious, intelligent, highly skilled scientists—like you and me," he adds with a wink, spooning up large quantities of Borsht at the local restaurant where we are having dinner. "They have a good sense of humor and a real interest in the whole matter. They've dropped the Gulf Breeze story. They got disgusted with it when they heard of the witness having telepathic contact with Aliens and Budd Hopkins doing hypnotic regression of Mr. Ed."

"What do they know about the history of the problem in general?"

"Next to nothing, alas. They're trained to react to specific information. One of the key guys specializes in undersea objects. These are people who worry about the submarine warfare of the year 2020, about the stealth technology of the next decade. They don't read history, anthropology, or folklore. They don't keep records. When I used to work there, the FOIA attorney kept telling us not to keep any files marked with the UFO label."

So much for that hope: his friends are not those I'm looking for. No names, nothing precise.

"How are you doing with your investigation into alleged autopsies… The doctor you heard about?"

"It turns out the doctor in question exists; indeed he was hired by the Government for consulting work, but he never did any autopsy. He only reviewed some alleged results consistent with reports dating back to Leonard Stringfield, stating that the Aliens have two floating ribs in their chest. He's a thoracic surgeon, with all the right clearances. He spent a month somewhere on a highly classified project. Now my guys are trying to find out if he's really getting a monthly check from the U.S. Treasury."

In the meantime Hal Puthoff has quietly pursued MJ-12, meeting with senior people like the director of DIA, the deputy director of CIA, and even Robert Gates, deputy director of the National Security Council. Hal claims to find serious interest, indications that some of these men's underlings have worked on what they thought was Alien technology of some kind. Kit doesn't believe it.

"The curious thing is, these guys speak openly. As if they wanted the news to get out... or to confuse everyone."

Kit spent last Thursday in Washington for the inauguration of George H. Bush and went to the White House to meet with the transition team. They gave him a choice of three positions, but "they didn't offer me the job I wanted," he says.

Eldon Byrd, a former Navy Intelligence officer, has been fired for "invading the privacy" of the Amazing Randi the magician, wiretapping the well-known skeptic and allegedly leading him to make compromising statements on the record.

Hyde Street. Wednesday 1 February 1989.

Tomorrow Janine and I fly to Hollywood in celebration of thirty years spent together. We will combine my professional visits to several technology companies with another session with Bob and Tracy: four nights away from home. Then we'll go on to San Diego to see Olivier.

Janine feels worried, unsure of our priorities, still grieving after her mother's death last year. She brushes off the information I brought back from my trip, saying wisely: "When you get secret garbage from the CIA, it's still garbage."

Hyde Street. Monday 6 February 1989.

This is the coldest winter in California history; a mass of Alaskan air is sweeping through, leaving snow and ice on the hills. We came back from L.A. with a draft of the first act of *Messengers*, hammered out with Tracy Tormé in Bob Weiss' apartment high above Hollywood boulevard. Janine and I spent the next evening with Bob Emenegger and his wife Margaret. He told us that *UFOs: Past present and Future* had been paid for by the John and Catherine McArthur Foundation, which declined any credit in the final result. There is speculation about the Foundation as a conduit for CIA, but Bob sanely laughs at the gullibility of people who see agents everywhere.

We slept in the bedroom of Bob's daughter Ashley, off to college. Downstairs, in the dense room of dark wood adorned with medieval artwork we spoke for a long time of Norton Air Force base and General Miller, of death and destiny. We speculated about the strange motivations of those who are manipulating the belief in extraterrestrial visitors.

On Saturday we had lunch with Professor Douglass Price-Williams at an Italian restaurant near UCLA. All around us Westwood was pounded by cold rain. We talked about the way ufology had turned from the study of physical phenomena to an obsession with unreliable stories dredged up under amateurish hypnosis. In contrast, many genuine letters from readers of *Dimensions* would be worthy of detailed follow-up. Here is a remarkable report I have received from a woman who lives near Los Angeles:

> In 1976 I woke up in a dream to find myself lying on a table. The room was dim and gray but I could still see. Standing between my legs was this thing: He had my legs slung over his arms. It was hard to tell how tall he was, maybe about 5 feet 10 inches or a bit taller. His head was covered with dark reddish brown fur down to his neck. The rest of his body looked human, he had pointed ears and a nose like a dog... the color of the skin was a healthy flesh tone, Caucasian, only there were red stripes or ridges on his buttocks, sex organs and lower abdomen. He was fully erect. Please forgive my bluntness, this is how it was. We were both naked.

She felt disoriented, confused, and started to struggle, which seemed to make him angry. He never said a word but stared into her eyes. She was unable to look away:

> His eyes began to spin around faster and faster like marbles in a bowl, then his tongue shot out of his mouth straight at my face. It was long and thin. I felt such fear and panic that I thought my heart would stop. I fainted, but jolted awake in my own bed, drenched in sweat, heart pounding... Then about a month after the dream I realized that I was pregnant. I had a normal pregnancy. No more dreams of that nature, I was healthy and fine. On —-, 1977 I delivered a healthy normal baby boy.

She never told the boy about her dream, but on 23 August 1988 she got a Time-Life book of "Mysterious Creatures." Her son, now 11 years old, browsed through it, pointed at a picture of a bronze statue from Egypt and said: "Hey Mom, I see this guy in my dreams every once in a while!" The mother came over to look at the picture:

> It was a dog-headed statue named Anubis, who looked just like the being in my dream. I know nothing about Egypt and have never been interested, and I had never seen that statue before... I think the blood must have drained from my face and the hair stood straight up on the back of my neck. How can this be possible? I carefully questioned him and I did not lead him in any way. I asked him what he looked like: the statue had no color to it. He told me that the head was reddish brown fur, his skin was peach color and he wore a skirt thing that was red. He said he had had this dream three or four times... He was walking into a pyramid and this guy (Anubis) stepped out from behind a wall and started to talk to him, but he couldn't remember what he was saying.

So much for short gray Aliens!

In San Diego the sun finally came out long enough for us to drive off to Mexico for lunch in Rosarito with Olivier. Today the scenery was magnificent, the air clear from La Jolla to El Cajon, with the turrets of the Del Coronado hotel blasting red into the blue sky. We paid a visit to the Unarius Academy of Science, a garish place decorated with Greek statues, artificial grass, plastic spaceships, and visionary paintings of Ruth Norman, self-appointed Queen of Heaven and channel for Alien entities.

We had another quiet lunch with our son in a small restaurant overlooking the beach. He looked at us in awe: "Thirty years you guys have been together... What an achievement!" Yet there is no habit in our facility with each other, and never the slightest inkling of boredom.

Hyde Street. Thursday 9 February 1989.

All week we've been fighting the weather: the pipes froze at Spring Hill where our tenants were without heat. The atmosphere has gone crazy, with snow in Los Angeles and ice on Nob Hill.

Through the rain I went to see Ed May at SRI today. He told me again about his concerns for the psychic project: they run out of money in October. What will happen when old friends like Jack Vorona at DIA retire? Ed may have to disband the team. He briefed me on the findings of their magneto-encephalogram experiments and on two of their remote viewings aimed at the Lawrence Livermore electron accelerator and at a facility in the desert of New Mexico that produces massive microwave bursts. Both gave outstanding results. I pointed out again that this may be due to the spectacular changes in entropy they generate. Yet my own experiments at Spring Hill continue to give no clear result: hundreds of hours of watching the sky have brought us nothing more than beautiful views of comets, planets and the moon, the occasional satellite, and peculiar airplanes with very strong flashing lights that may be drug surveillance planes.

We went on to discuss his clever theory that precognition must be a stochastic process in order not to violate the second law of thermodynamics.

"Will you be able to convince your sponsors that the theory deserves to be tested?"

"I'm certainly going to try," he replied. "The traditional approach of the advocates of parapsychology in the seventies has been to cry to the world, 'Wow! Wait till you see this! Our results are so extraordinary that all the laws of physics will fly out the window! Your paradigm is going to shift!' I don't think that's an adequate presentation. What we observe here doesn't violate physics...."

"Why not repeat these experiments with informational events rather than large energetic ones?" I asked Ed. "If energy and information correspond to each other, you should be able to get similar results from a unique collection of objects or an exceptional database"—or a well-appointed observatory in a quiet forest, with a unique library, I thought to myself—an information singularity.

Ed also told me that the "missing" frames of the super-classified film taken by outer-space sensors (the film that disappeared from its locked, top-secret cabinet after Joe McMoneagle saw it) had been found again and examined. It showed... a weather balloon.

"That doesn't make much sense," I pointed out. "There must be 10,000 weather balloons aloft over the earth this very minute. The analysts are able to recognize them!"

"I know, but that's a genuine conclusion. I wonder what that means for the viewing session that disclosed saucers and little men..."

Hyde Street. Sunday 12 February 1989.

All day I edited and typed Volume One, the Chicago Journals. I emerge from this work in a tender and somber mood: I love Janine so much... Reliving that period moves me and gives me pains I cannot describe.

We walked down Polk Street today to bring the first pages of *Revelations* (written yesterday at Spring Hill) to my friend Emery Reiff, always thrilled to start typing a new manuscript for me.

We had coffee and croissants across the street from Fields, my favorite bookstore. I felt sad. Is my interest in the paranormal a distraction from a honorable career, a regrettable flaw to be crushed mercilessly, or one of those bright fantasies that give meaning to life itself, and make me different from my robotic colleagues in business? Is it what makes me able to take every new moment with full awareness? Janine is the only person who gives depth and worth to my life. Sometimes I am disappointed to be a human, among humans. It is so damn clear that we could be much more!

Hyde Street. Monday 13 February 1989.

More letters from readers today with remarkable photographs from Bertrand Méheust and a letter from Guérin, with whom I had not corresponded for a long time, a warm letter for once:

> We now have the proof that Gepan was only created to mislead and keep public opinion quiet. It served as a screen for the Army to study physical effects observed on vegetation and MHD models of atmospheric propulsion. While Esterle was being pushed away by Curien and his private adviser because he dared publish the results of biochemical analyses about Trans-en-Provence, simulations were conducted to reproduce the pigment alterations at a Toulouse laboratory. Attempts were also made to study Petit's MHD model, without his collaboration. I know through some leaks that the alfalfa of Trans did suffer microwave irradiation.

He concludes from all this that we're wasting our time trying to prove the existence of the phenomenon, and that "in high places" it has long been known to be real, an observation with which I agree. Yet Hal Puthoff doesn't believe the senescence of the alfalfa in Trans is due to microwaves at all, but to relativistic time acceleration.

Hyde Street. Wednesday 15 February 1989.

Last night I was kept awake by some remarks of Richard Niemtzow, who had called me from Texas earlier in the day. He was thinking of leaving the Air Force, where he is tired of doing radiation oncology in an environment of insufficient budgets. When the conversation turned to the possibility that the U.S. was hiding Aliens in its freezers I was surprised to find him ready to believe the undocumented anatomical descriptions circulated by Stringfield.

Richard assures me he was once within one phone call of a doctor who had done an autopsy of an alien. Of course, "being within one phone call" means nothing: as Kit had told me, the doctor in question had not done an autopsy but was only asked to review the alleged results, quite a different thing. But Dr. Neal, who knows the guy, told Richard that he started shaking visibly when the subject was brought up and that he asked to be left alone. That still doesn't prove anything. There could well have been a secret project to manipulate the public belief in UFOs and to use them as a cover for other sinister endeavors, even scarier than any rumors of Aliens (note *). The reality of that betrayal of public trust could be the real secret that makes old men tremble.

Hyde Street. Monday 27 February 1989.

The rage in the media now is "trash television" with a tabloid format. The market leader in this new genre is *A Current Affair*, and it has just exploited the Ira Einhorn case, capitalizing on Levy's book *The Secret of the Unicorn.* There was not much there, except for confirmation that Ira had indeed evaded the law again in Stockholm.

Ned Leavitt just called from New York to say that Random House (Ballantine) was very pleased with *Confrontations.* I have completed a foreword for Linda Howe's next book, a paper about Brazil for the Mufon meeting and a revised article with Dick Haines about the Costa Rica photograph: I am getting drawn into this research again.

Note *: See the note on p.304. A secret group had gathered in 1987 at the Albuquerque home of retired Air force Lt.Col Ernie Kellerstrass to discuss the same issues. Kit Green was there with Rick Doty, Hal Puthoff, Bill Moore, Jaime Shandera and Robert Collins. They assembled again for a follow-up meeting at an Albuquerque hotel in 1989.

18

Spring Hill. Sunday 5 March 1989.

Dreamy time under the rain, blankets of fog closing in around us. Our world is made of books and quiet talks. In the morning, sitting by the window, I finished writing the second part of *Revelations,* the last volume in the Trilogy.

A beautiful bird has come down from the sky and alighted in the prairie. He claimed the pond as his domain. He is a tall wild Chinese gander, majestic and proud. We hope he will stay, blessing us with the beauty of the wilderness whence he came. The creek is full, bounding from stone to stone and across the tree trunks uprooted by the recent storm.

Hyde Street. Saturday 11 March 1989.

While rumors continue to sink into absurdity our *FastWalker* movie project is mired in missed appointments and wasted opportunities. Bob has started work on a new comedy called *Crazy People* that will take him to the East Coast for the spring, and Tracy is making no progress on the new treatment, so I think the project is dead.

Hyde Street. Monday 13 March 1989.

My new French partner, biologist Gabriel Mergui is in town for a week of visits to our portfolio companies and meetings with investors. He is a pleasant man with a balding head, a Moroccan Jew with solid experience in biotechnology, a field I am eager to understand better.

Last night Fred Beckman brought John Lear to dinner. John is an authentic hero of modern aviation with radical notions about the world. He is convinced that an amateur film made in Dallas on that fateful day of 1963 shows Kennedy's chauffeur turning around in the limo and shooting him in the head! Whether the subject is Kennedy or UFOs, John keeps jumping to conclusions for which he has no proof. He is convinced not only that some saucers have crashed on earth but that little Aliens have come out and are still here, alive and well, working side by side with our scientists under a pact that allows them to commit abductions with immunity. The man who revealed this to him, a fellow he calls "Dennis," works at Nellis Air Force Base. He's sure he saw an Alien at a meeting with two humans, through a glass porthole and from the back!

John Lear speaks regularly to Robert Collins, the engineering consultant who goes under the ridiculous code-name "Condor," and to Richard Doty, who goes by the name "Falcon." These men are spreading stories of underground bases full of gray Aliens, tales that were planted with physicist Bennewitz at Kirtland with assistance from Bill Moore. According to these stories the CIA holds Alien technology, which our pilots are busy trying to master...

There is no question in my mind that these allegations are spurious, because they match nothing in any database of genuine reports. The only mystery is their origin: are we simply witnessing the spreading of a delusionary virus, an epidemic of absurdity among men who have spent too long in the musty atmosphere of classified technology, or is it a new set of "memes" being planted among New Age zealots either as a social experiment, as a counter-intelligence scheme, or to befuddle people who want to conduct real research?

There are other participants in this great new charade, like retired military man Bill Cooper whom I tracked down at Hollywood Technical College. He claims he saw a copy of an alleged *Grudge 13 Report*, a fully detailed, 600-page book about the cover-up, with Dr. Hynek's signature! Fred and I jumped up at the absurd suggestion that Allen could have witnessed autopsies and approved a diabolical plan to cover-up the Alien presence on earth... Another man named Bill English says he independently saw a report called *Grudge 13*. John Lear claims that gray aliens are fond of human flesh and are responsible for animal and human mutilations. There are 70 kinds of

Aliens, he states in a matter-of-fact way, evading criticism with generalities like a priest teaching catechism to a group of toddlers.

After John Lear's departure Janine and I looked at each other and shrugged. It was easy to forget the "horrible truth" that the earth had fallen into the clutches of a race of ugly little gray Aliens who engineered human evolution, setup Jesus as their fall guy and now lived underground in the caves of New Mexico. The only reliable, sad fact is that a lot of people now believe this tale.

Hyde Street. Wednesday 15 March 1989.

Kit called this afternoon, with new information. The FBI has interrogated Doty/Falcon, demanding to know under whose authority he was disseminating seemingly secret government documents.

"It turns out the papers in question are of two possible types," he said. "Either they are government items that have been declassified and released a long time ago, or they are pure fabrications. There is no violation of federal law involved in either case. It also turns out Doty is not with the Office of Special Investigations any more and doesn't really work at Kirtland Air Force Base..."

Hyde Street. Sunday 26 March 1989.

All the objectives of my New York trip were achieved this time. We considered several new biotechnology investments in France. I spent two hours on Wall Street with Shel Gordon. As usual I saw Ned Leavitt at William Morris and Joe Blades at Ballantine: we began to discuss my idea for the Alien Contact Trilogy.

Hyde Street. Thursday 30 March 1989.

Determined to get to the bottom of the ongoing charade, I offered to Bill Cooper, extreme ufologist and anti-goverment militant, to meet me for dinner on the Queen Mary. He came over with a Chinese woman named Annie of whom he seemed greatly enamoured. She is fortyish and charming but she did not say more than ten words all evening. Bill is a big fellow with a fleshy face marked by a scar on the right side of his forehead and another scar down the length of his nose. We ordered drinks: he started with a Chivas Regal and I with a Perrier, and we jumped into the subject of the Aliens.

"I've read your recent interview, where you say you don't believe in MJ-12, so I wonder why you wanted this meeting," he began.

"The interview was done before I met John Lear," I replied, "but my position hasn't changed that much. I believe there's a UFO phenomenon that is absolutely physical in the usual sense, and it can manipulate space and time in ways I certainly don't understand; perhaps there are people around who understand it..."

"They do," he stated with sanctimonious confidence, "but go on."

"I further believe the U.S. Government must have been studying it for many years. That doesn't mean that MJ-12 is real. I talked to Linda Howe who recommended that I listen to John Lear, and he said I should talk to you, and here I am."

The waitress brought our drinks, Cooper and his lady friend lit up their cigarettes, and he began telling me his story.

"I became involved in the UFO question as a Naval Intelligence man," he said in a matter-of-fact way. "In the period of 1971-72 I was ordered to brief several high-level officers about the Alien problem, and our agreements with them."

"Why would the Aliens go to the trouble of entering into a treaty with us, if their technology is so far ahead of ours?"

"They needed the Government to keep their presence secret. Remember, we had one of them in our custody. Somehow our radar affected their navigation system and threw their craft off-balance."

I didn't tell Bill that I had spent the afternoon in Huntington Beach with an electronic warfare company that was looking to us for possible financing. They made a radar simulator among other military products. The idea that our primitive radars of 1947 would have repeatedly knocked Alien spacecraft out of the sky was utterly ludicrous. Our own aircraft carry a device known as a "DERFUM," a little bigger than a shoebox. It has the capability to learn the characteristics of electromagnetic sources that are operating in its vicinity and to respond to them with false information. For example it can paint a fleet of airplanes miles away, or make the ground radar see an innocent Piper Cub instead of a bomber.

Our food had arrived. Bill attacked his steamed clams with gusto. I had a choice: I could either challenge Cooper on the outlandish statements he had just made, patently at variance with reality, or I could just keep going. I decided that a challenge would lead nowhere and only get him upset, so I went on with my questions. Once you hold an extreme belief everything falls into place: any small detail of history can be explained by bizarre twisting of the facts.

"How did Bill English get to see the documents?"

"He was a Captain in the U.S. Army, Special Forces. He was assigned as an information analyst at a British base. The document came in the regular pouch. He wasn't supposed to see it, it was an error in routing. So he was kicked out. Attempts were made on his life. He was ridiculed. Even Bill Moore said he was on LSD. Perhaps I shouldn't say this, but Bill Moore is a strange fellow, do you know he showed Jim Graham a card with his picture on it, but it had a different name, and it was an official credential issued by the Defense Intelligence Agency?"

So I had in front of me an old Navy Intelligence man telling me not to trust Bill Moore because he worked for the DIA. I let it slide. I was listening to a bad spy story, yet Cooper obviously believed it. When he left after another series of stiff drinks he was still suspicious of me, because I hadn't shown the unconditional enthusiasm he was seeking.

Hyde Street. Thursday 6 April 1989.

Last Saturday Morgane gave an All Fools' Day party at her new house on the slopes of Mount Tamalpais, everyone dressed in white except for one attorney who naturally came in black. She had asked her guests to bring samples of their work, so the evening involved a colorful cross-section of Bay Area talents, from painters of mandalas and makers of encrusted belts to software experts, builders of slimy creatures for Lucasfilm, authors of children books, carpenters, and engineers. It was a sweet, relaxed evening, a welcome break.

Tracy claims that among members of Congress who became interested in the issue following *Cover-up* were Senator Christopher Dodd of Connecticut and Senator John ("Jimmy") Exon of Nebraska.

Spring Hill. Saturday 15 April 1989.

Yesterday I came back from Washington. This is our last weekend at the ranch for some time: we fly to New York and Europe on Thursday. I have set aside *Revelations* and I am working hard editing the Journal. I am moved by the memory of those Chicago years with Janine, very proud to have her still by my side. Yesterday Joe Blades sent us the first paperback copies of *Dimensions*, as well as the re-issued edition of *Challenge to Science*, twenty-two years later.

In Washington, my business done, I met with Kit for a few hours in Virginia. He has an indirect contact with Doty, alias Falcon. Until recently Doty was a willing participant in the game, circulating both genuine and fake information to people like Bill Moore and Linda Howe. But his federal employers were telling him which was true and which was false... until the MJ-12 documents, where allegedly he got caught in his own lie. Now he claims he's furious, and that's why he is talking. He has provided information—names, ranks and office numbers—which Kit will check out the next time he is at the Pentagon.

The FBI is fed up with these little games, too. They've told the Air Force to go to Hell with their complaints about leaked secret documents: "Every time we look into it, it turns out these documents either weren't secret in the first place, or they have been declassified a long time ago, or you just made them up! We don't know what game you're playing, but don't ask us to get involved in the future!"

The doctor who is said to have reviewed the alien autopsy data is a Dr. Crowley, a thoracic surgeon who lives in Lancaster near Los Angeles. But it turns out he isn't receiving a monthly check from the government after all. Again, who is lying? A new name has come up: Dr. Ron Pandolfi at CIA is one of the technical people who are involved in all this. Kit and he have compared notes: what is surprising is the number of high-level individuals who are either contributing to the MJ-12 charade or letting it happen with a thin smile. Someone is hijacking the fantasies of the UFO believers to cover up something that has nothing at all to do with extraterrestrials.

At Spring Hill where none of this reaches us, spring is bursting with delicate lilacs, pink and mauve tamaris, deep purple irises, and a thousand shades of green. Our apple trees are covered with white petals. The first rose is blooming by Catherine's window. The fields are covered with blue flowers; the riverbanks are spotted with bursts of yellow and orange. Our handsome gander remains on alert, protecting the ranch, hissing and cocking his head watchfully to one side whenever someone approaches "his" pond.

I am reading Mircea Eliade's autobiography, marvelling at the subtlety and depth of intellectual life in Romania before 1939, wondering about all the simple, straightforward secrets of the mind and the heart we have lost in the name of rational triumphs and scientific progress. I am touched by his description of that supreme agony, loving two women who both return his love and thus make his life impossible, in that little attic of his in Bucharest.

Hyde Street. Tuesday 18 April 1989.

We are packing for our trip to New York and Paris. Under my care the Fund has made two investments since the beginning of the year and I will propose three more to our investment committee, while Gabriel Mergui has several good leads for biotechnology firms. Most importantly, Olivier has completed his bachelor's degree in physics at UCSD, a real accomplishment, and Catherine only has another year to go in Boulder.

TWA 800, over the North Atlantic. Friday 21 April 1989.

Stories continue to build up about the supposed Aliens. They get increasingly confusing. Now a truckdriver has seen several disks and a blue sphere on the ground at Deep Springs Ranch (Route 168, close to the California border) near two Navy high-altitude research installations, according to Fred who got this from Dr. Ron

Blackburn, a microwave specialist formerly at the Lockheed Skunk Works. Blackburn hinted he was working on UFOs, or the Secret Onion, or perhaps on Stealth? Nobody is sure of anything any more. The only interesting fact in all this is the observation that the confusion is deliberately engineered.

Janine and I met with Ned Leavitt at the Algonquin, to sign the Ballantine contract. Today, lunch with Ingo at the Cloisters. In his artist's basement we met Bernard Gittelson, the author of *Intangible Evidence*. Ingo told us about his own UFO, seen at age nine at Camel Garden in Colorado. A few years ago, he also watched an orange ball flying over Manhattan. He now thinks his earlier sighting was an abduction: a man wearing a white gown open in front on a powerful chest put him to sleep and (Ingo believes) raped him. Scrapings of his fingernails and blood samples were taken from him. Was the UFO a screen memory?

Paris, Rue de la Clef. Saturday 22 April 1989.

Quiet, sleepy afternoon. Upstairs a pianist plays *The Trout*. I called Pierre Lagrange about the news of an upcoming meeting of French ufologists in Lyon. He confirmed that Bill Moore had been invited to talk about MJ-12 and the Roswell Crash. The French pay the bill.

For old time's sake I also called Guérin. His voice was excited and vibrant as always. He has jumped to all sorts of new conclusions. He will not attend the Lyon meeting because "it's controlled by psycho-sociologists who are manipulated by the rationalists." In five minutes he managed to rattle off a rabid commentary on everything that was wrong in the world.

Paris, Rue de la Clef, Sunday 23 April 1989.

In person, Guérin was rather kind to me in spite of his formidable verbal barrage on the phone. He even appeared moved again by our old friendship. He told us about Aimé Michel's disappointment with his children, his multiple operations, and his wife's mental illness. One winter Aimé found her in the kitchen, utterly distraught, surrounded with candles, performing a strange ritual. Then she went out on the mountain and did not return. He went into the night to look for her, hobbling on his cane through the snow. She had lost her way in the blizzard, her feet frozen. After they separated he received crazy letters from her. Aimé is now back in the Alps and seems to enjoy better health at last.

We also discussed Poher. Guérin thinks he got discouraged because he expected too much, too soon; he wanted Gepan to quickly elucidate UFO technology. He also confirmed that the French military had been redoing Petit's experiments without him, irradiating plants to simulate what happened at Trans-en-Provence, and researching microwaves.

Esterle was removed because he published too much about Trans: the military demanded control. Guérin has had no further contacts with the French secret services since Aimé's failed attempts to get them interested, many years ago.

Pierre will retire in two years. He doesn't care any more what his rationalist colleagues think about him. He is happy and proud because he recently obtained some of the finest photographs of Mars ever taken, from *Pic du Midi* observatory.

Lyon. Hotel Roosevelt. Saturday 29 April 1989.

French ufologists are congregating in an ugly modern building, part youth hostel, part conference center. Janine and I found the first few lectures worse than anything Guérin had predicted. A local astronomer named Ribes presented all the possible causes of mistaken identification, from satellites to meteors. He only forgot to mention the Moon and the Sun. Our friend, investigator Michel Figuet, sweetly smelling of onions and garlic like a vegetable garden in Provence, pointed out the mistake with his usual acerbic style:

"What about the *Bradytes*, Professor Ribes?" he asked to muffled laughter in the audience. "What were those slow meteors that so many noted astronomers observed early in this century?"

Bill Moore did arrive with an American named Severen Schaeffer who lives in Paris and allegedly teaches general semantics to medical students. He represents Mufon in the pompous position of Continental Coordinator for Europe, smokes constantly and is periodically seized with fits of coughing that sound like an advanced case of emphysema.

Moore agreed to have a private discussion with us over dinner, so we took him to Old Lyon, an area of narrow medieval streets worthy of the Blessed Saint Agobard, and we ate a hearty meal at *Pique Assiette,* where they gave us a quiet table and left us alone.

Moore leveled with us right away. He said he knew that we had connections as high as Hal Puthoff and Kit did. Still fishing, he said that my reputation in "those circles" was impeccable. "You should know that I have been used as a source or as an informer. I was never on the payroll; they always paid me in cash."

"Did they ask you to provide data on cases, or on individuals?"

"They mainly wanted information about people in the UFO movement. People like you and Fred Beckman."

"Where did the information go?"

"It went up to the Pentagon through people like Barry Hennessey and Bob Gates who is now on the NSC," he answered matter-of-factly. "What puzzles me is that they also used me to put out false information into the community itself. They were disinforming their own counter-intelligence folks, all the way up the line! I still think about that; it makes no sense."

"What about John Lear, Bill Cooper, and all those obviously fabricated Alien stories I hear?"

"It all comes from a single source, and that single source is Paul Bennewitz at Kirtland." (*)

"The rumor is that Bennewitz is deluded."

"They don't say how he got that way, do they? That's the interesting story. Bennewitz runs a little company that makes thermocouples for the Air Force. He became interested in UFOs and interviewed a woman who had seen something flying around. Under hypnosis she said she'd been abducted. Not only was she abducted with her son,

(*): We later learned that Paul Bennewitz was targeted by AFOSI because he was intercepting classified biological signals. He had also photographed tests of secret prototypes over Kirkland, thinking they were UFOs.

but she revealed they were taken underground to a facility where they saw vats of fluid where parts of human beings were floating. Convinced that she was receiving genuine communication, and that he was onto some horrible secret, Bennewitz kept studying the woman when she did her channeling and pretty soon, *bingo!* his equipment started picking up something physical."

"You mean an actual transmission?"

"It was an electronic signal and it came over in the ELF range. When the Base security people found out he was recording that signal they freaked out, because he was accidentally eavesdropping on a genuine secret military communications experiment of theirs that had nothing to do with UFOs or channeling."

"They could have told him about his mistake," I pointed out.

"They tried! They spoke to him under conditions of secrecy, but the more they told him that there was a secret project going on, the more he became convinced he was really onto something big, and that the government actually knew all about UFOs."

"So he freaked out even more?" I asked.

"Naturally. The counter-intelligence people got involved, and the Office of Special Investigations too. They decided, 'this guy is already half nuts, we'll drive him completely nuts.' They used me and others to flood him with insane stories; he believed them. He once took me to a hill from which he showed me some lights he said were UFOs abducting humans; they were just helicopters practicing rescue missions!"

"And you think Bennewitz started the whole rash of the new stories single-handedly?"

"All I know is that John Lear believed him. "

"What about the alleged *Report 13*?" I asked, summarizing my talk with Cooper.

"I think there may have been a *Report 13* at one time that reached positive conclusions about UFOs so it was hushed up and *Report 14* was released instead, with sanitized recommendations."

That made sense. I thought about Battelle and the Pentacle letter I had uncovered.

"What about Bill English's statements? Do you really think there are Alien bodies somewhere?"

"All I can say is that I have spoken to people who claimed there were Alien bodies."

Lyon. Hotel Roosevelt. Monday 1 May 1989.

Bill Moore has given his talk, establishing that something indeed fell on Roswell and was covered up by the military, all of which we already knew, but it doesn't mean it was a disabled Alien spacecraft. Nor does it mean that bodies were found. But Bill Moore points out it is unlikely that a military experiment was involved: They would have intervened a lot faster, looking for their crashed equipment. On that point too he is right, so I still don't know what to think.

There we were, on Walpurgisnacht, the night of the witches, discussing Aliens flying through the sky. Marie-Thérèse de Brosses took us all to lunch the next day. She breathlessly told us she had nearly been abducted and had "lost" two hours waiting for a UFO with Gendarmes who also experienced a memory loss.

Janine was amused by one scene she witnessed in the lobby where the French Magonia group from Marseille, who plan a new, massive and characteristically impractical database project, were arguing with acerbic Englishman John Rimmer, editor of *Magonia* magazine, about who owned the rights to the name Magonia.

"You'd have enjoyed the argument," she said, "the absurdity of it."

"As far as I'm concerned, anybody has a right to the word," I said. "It's been in the public domain since the 9th century! They really shouldn't be seen fighting about Magonia here in Lyon, the town of Saint Agobard!"

We stayed in our big soft bed all morning, and then we got up lazily to visit the *traboules* on the hillside above the Saône. Most shops were closed because of the French Labor Day. In the afternoon Joël Mesnard came to see us with his wife Hélène and Roger Chéreau of Montigny, a serious researcher. They have taken over the editing of *Lumières dans la Nuit*, and thus made enemies within the psycho-sociological chapel. They didn't attend the Lyon meetings, but they were driving through the region and stopped to speak with us. They gave us good news of Lagarde and Veillith, both retired in the quiet countryside. We spoke about physiological injury cases in France.

London. Adeline Place. Friday 5 May 1989.

In Soho Square, at the William Morris office, I just signed the British contract for *Confrontations*. The weather is warm and slightly smoggy in London. The only problem is to find something resembling a coffee shop in this city of pubs, old clubs and stuffy tearooms. We walk everywhere.

Last Wednesday night, after I flew back from Marseille, we went out for dinner near Montparnasse with Shel Gordon and his wife Judy and with Michel and Liliane Crouhy, both of them economists and professors at HEC.

"As a French economist," I told Crouhy as we walked back in the quiet night, "perhaps you can explain to me why France, where nobody seems to be doing any serious work, appears to be doing so well while the U.S. works so damn hard and is so gloomy."

"France is benefiting from the restructuring and consolidation it has been forced to do over the past few years," he answered. "Productivity is actually going up. And people do work hard in the services area, if not in the government sector. The statistics don't show this. There's a liberal wind blowing in government; the Unions have lost much of their power. The result is a steady gain in productivity." Shel told me France should do well in the future: "Paris can become the center of Europe. Brussels and Strasbourg are too far, London too eccentric. And who wants to live in Dusseldorf?"

London. Adeline Place. Monday 8 May 1989.

We met with Jenny Randles at the Hotel Russell. She came with three other researchers and we had a long friendly talk, although I still found it disconcerting that her eyes were always averted when she spoke to me. Later we went to lunch with a young English hacker, Edward Singh, a friendly and genial fellow with many shadowy achievements to his credit. From a school terminal in England he managed to compromise nearly half the computers on Telenet. Scotland Yard had to release him when they realized he had committed no crime in Great Britain. Prime Computers did try to entice him to come to the U.S. as their consultant, so the FBI could arrest him in New York, but they organized the whole entrapment on their electronic mail system, on which he was spying regularly, so he did not fall into their trap.

We have played tourists long enough: today we fly back to Paris. The advisory board of our Fund meets tomorrow. On Thursday we pick up Fred Adler at the Ritz and we convene the investment committee. On Saturday morning we go back to California.

Paris. Rue de la Clef. Saturday 13 May 1989.

Maman reminisced about her childhood as we sorted out old books this afternoon, helping her clean out her apartment. "When I was ten or eleven my parents would give me money to go and buy some soup—the brand was *Potages Maggi*, my favorite—I always bought two more packets and left them on the doorstep of some poor people, without telling anybody... I never found out if they appreciated it. I certainly wouldn't do that today, not with all the things that are happening. You can't tell if people are really in need."

People in the shops ask her if she comes from a military family, because of her impeccable bearing, her straight back.

"Well, my parents were Protestants..." she says proudly.

"That's it, that explains it!" they reply.

Hyde Street. Tuesday 16 May 1989.

We are back in this house, our true home in spite of the pleasures of Europe. Letters and packages had accumulated at the mailing service: admonitions from readers of *Dimensions*, the first issue of the *Communion* newsletter, a signed contract with a check from Universal Studios were notable items, along with magazines I will never have time to read.

Work was intense right away: we are investing in two new companies, one that makes a revolutionary laser for high speed fiberoptic communications, the other a franchise selling an environmental cleaning product based on bacteria.

I escaped in the afternoon for coffee with Fred Beckman at the *Perfect Recipe*. He said John Lear got close enough to Area 51 to get arrested by the base security people. There were aerial tests that night, and what looked like disks rising from the base with an orange glow. The man who was with him, known as Dennis, turns out to be a 30-year old fellow named Bob Lazar who claims to be a physicist "close to Edward Teller." He is the secret informer John Lear mentioned (without naming him) when he had dinner at our house. Fred finds all that fascinating and resents my skeptical reaction.

When we got to the parking lot Fred looked at my white Dodge convertible and joked:

"I see you're still buying American cars".

"I've always regretted that little blue Buick in Chicago."

"I remember it well. The first time we met, you put the top down and we drove to the Red Knight Inn for lunch...That was the beginning of the Invisible College…"

Hyde Street. Thursday 18 May 1989.

Crown Prince Hans-Adam von Liechtenstein was in town yesterday with his consulting engineer from Toronto, a man named George Hathaway who helps him study the phenomenon with the hope of discovering new forms of energy production. Hathaway had written to me during our trip to Europe. He has spoken to Fred Beckman with whom they spent the afternoon.

"You've never met this Prince?" Fred asked me. "He's one of those people who are still looking for propulsion systems, advanced spacecraft and the like."

"Perhaps he's right," I replied. "There's no question in my mind the phenomenon is physical. But the real answers may come from other directions, like cosmology and particle physics, rather than beating the bushes looking for flying saucers."

"Unless, of course, we become much a lot more clever in the way we're doing it, without preconceived notions," Fred reminded me.

Hyde Street. Wednesday 24 May 1989.

Kit assures me he has never spoken directly to Bill Moore. He's skeptical about any relationship between him and Bob Gates. He is following a new trail: during my last trip, did I meet a Dr. Leon Evissa or Yvissas from Saint-Pourçain, he wanted to know? He's another doctor who is supposed to have been involved in autopsies. That name means nothing to me.

Hyde Street. Monday 29 May 1989.

Memorial Day. It turns out there is in fact a Dr. Léon Visse (not "Yvissas") in Saint-Pourçain. Kit confirms that Moore and Doty were in England seven years ago trying to sell a novel, the story of what has become known as MJ-12. They couldn't get it published. Doty isn't in the Air Force any more; he has become a New Mexico State officer, reportedly in a narcotics unit.

Robert Gates is unlikely to be involved in any of this, contrary to Moore's claims. He's known as a keen analyst, a skeptic trained in political theory (PhD), leery of counter-intelligence folks.

We have just spent the weekend at Spring Hill with Morgane. I resumed work on the observatory dome and ended up constructing most of the shell. Morgane helped me valiantly in getting the heavy sheets of plywood up above the crenellated walls. We debated channelling, and the magical books of Dion Fortune.

Hyde Street. Monday 5 June 1989.

The observatory acquired its inner structure and its roof this weekend. At night, after a fine evening of swimming and reading, a thunderstorm rolled over, reverberating along the canyon.

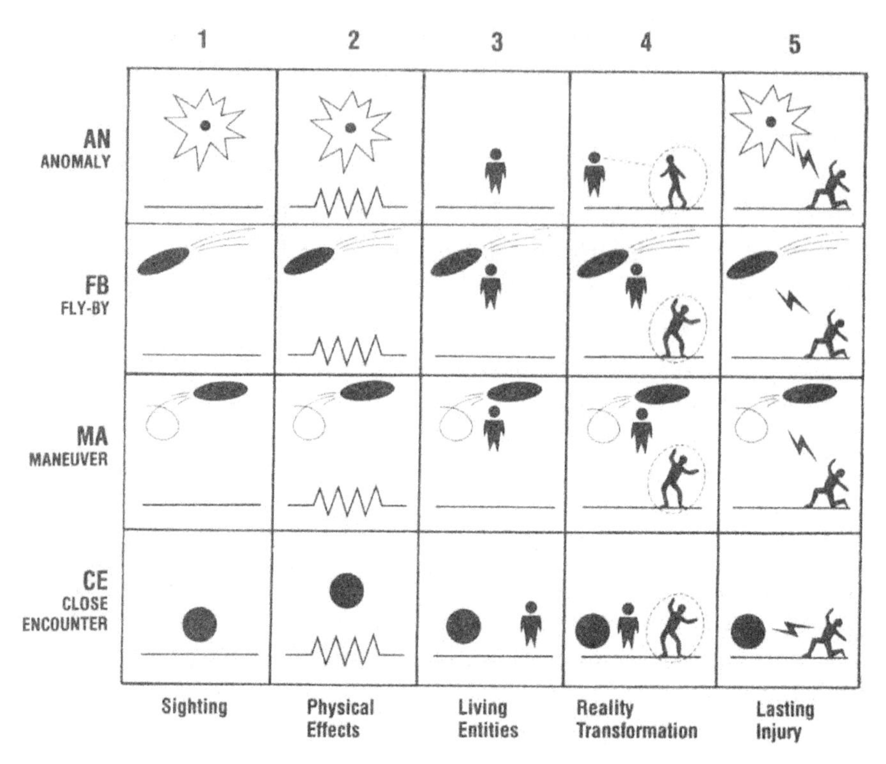

A classification system for anomalies

The noisy radio brought us the scratchy voice of a reporter in faraway San Francisco reading historic news from China: after weeks of demonstration by thousands of students clamoring for democracy, the government's tougher faction won the day: tanks have rolled into Tiananmen square. A bloodbath has started in Beijing. In Iran the Ayatollah has died, replaced by yet another religious fanatic.

In Mendocino County the living is easy. Roses cover fences and overflow from every garden. The roads are filled with motorcyclists in black leather riding to their annual spring orgy on gleaming black and chrome machines. They cluster around every beer garden from Hopland to Oregon like fat insects near a pool of sugar water.

I had a long friendly talk with Richard Niemtzow, about to be promoted to Lieutenant Colonel in the Air Force. He continues to be puzzled by the advances made to him by the French: Jean-Jacques

Velasco makes it a point of paying him a visit later this month after the Boulder conference of the Society for Scientific Exploration.

"Why is he coming, if Gepan is getting disbanded?" asks Richard. And what about the team of microwave experts who visited him a few months ago, bringing with them a man from French Intelligence who is now stationed at the embassy in Switzerland?

"Why me?" Richard wonders. "I'm not a microwave expert. They have more qualified people over there. Could it be that they're coming because of my UFO interests?"

The answer seems clear: twenty years ago those few secret studies of UFOs that were under way were aimed at understanding propulsion systems. Today technology has moved forward, the newer secret studies try to crack the radiation characteristics of the phenomenon, under a suitable cover of denial. But no one researches the phenomenon itself, only its exploitable effects.

The UFOs, whatever they are, do a good job of taking advantage of the fallacies in our own technocratic culture, unable to integrate or perceive anything that isn't parcelled out into specific compartments.

In the magnificent words of Ingo Swann, talking about the scientific approach to psychic phenomena: "They grind the diamond into dust to capture the sparkle."

Hyde Street. Wednesday 7 June 1989.

Lunch with Ed May and Nevin Lantz, a member of the SRI team of psychics, who is now taking the Stanford course on lucid dreaming to become an "oneironaut."

We discussed Hal's technology: Ed compares Hal's super-electrons to cold fusion, a fascinating phenomenon that may be worth only a footnote in future science books. We went back to the lab, where the team was excited about their new magneto-encephalography results. The stimulus they now use in their psychic experiments is not a light bulb anymore but a lighted square on a television set, and the pseudo-stimulus is the absence of light, no square at all. The results show up on the phase difference. They have now processed six subjects and will do more if they find the money, but the budget is in question again. The man who gave them their last big grant when he was in charge of Army biotech, General Rapmund, was in my office earlier this week, to compare notes on new investments. Recently retired, he has joined Flow General in Virginia as their chief scientist.

Hyde Street. Thursday 8 June 1989.

Bill Cooper called me and, after some pleasantries about a book whose reference he had given me, casually said: “I understand you're going to speak at the Mufon conference in Las Vegas about the human mutilations you've investigated in Brazil?”

I had to laugh at this. “I did go to Brazil, but there weren’t any mutilations. I did look into cases of human injuries, but we found none of the evidence that had been alleged about UFOs directly causing deaths, or bodies being drained of blood.”

There was a silence, and then Bill asked in a threatening voice: “Are you trying to hide the truth? I know who you're working for!”

All this is finally getting to me. I blew up, called John Lear, and told him I never, ever wanted to talk to his friend Cooper again.

Hyde Street. Sunday 11 June 1989.

Cooper has apologized to me through John Lear: He confessed he had too much to drink again the other night, embarrassing everyone.

Jean-Jacques Velasco has just arrived in San Francisco. Janine retained a hotel room for him nearby; we expect him for dinner tomorrow with Fred Beckman and Dick and Carole Haines.

At Spring Hill we swam, after “saving” a dozen baby frogs foolishly drowning in the pool. The observatory makes a fine little shelter where we can hide from the sun, read a book, smell the wood, feel the breeze from the forest and look at blue infinity above. I have reworked the first part of *Revelations*, after nearly throwing the whole manuscript into the garbage, so disgusted was I after the altercation with Cooper, and evidence of a spreading delusion.

John Lear gushes about new claims. “Dennis” (Bob Lazar) has assured him again that flying saucers were being flown by American pilots out of the base: the saucers are powered by antimatter reactors that generate negative gravity. They fly after sunset, he claims, “When the Q clearances have gone home.” It takes a higher clearance to be allowed to see the devices, “Majestic” being the very highest. When I tell him all this is baseless, Lear says he “just wants to get all the information out,” after which he looks forward to returning to gardening. I have no such luxury: this week I must travel to Boulder for the meeting of the Society for Scientific Exploration. On July 1st I plan to be in Las Vegas with Janine to observe the Mufon meeting where many of these tales may come to a head, another storm in the ufological teapot.

Menlo Park. Monday 12 June 1989.

A typical phone conversation with Fred Adler, who calls me out of the blue from New York: “Write this down,” he yells without any preliminaries. “Guy named Fritz, gonna call you. Medical laser company, still unlisted. We used to chase women together in Paris. Cyanamid is gonna dump their holdings. Somebody could pick up 70% of the company for two million bucks. I told him to send you his business plan.”

“I'll take it with me to the Monterey conference; the American Electronics Association has a meeting...”

“Waste of time. You're not gonna learn anything from AEA. Bye.”

“Wait! Did you see my memo about Mercury Interactive, Aryeh Finegold's new start-up? I turned down his earlier plan for a training company but this one's good... Could we put in half a million?”

“All right, all right. Do it if you wanna. Good bye.”

Hyde Street. Tuesday 13 June 1989.

Last night we had dinner with Jean-Jacques Velasco. I had spent most the day with him. He told me the story of the “meteor” that turned out to be a bouncing cometary body over the Pyrénées (where the whole staff of Pic du Midi observatory saw it pass by at dinner time) and the UFO that was an old German shell that exploded out of the ground near Royan. It almost hit a farmer who saw it coming out of the sky and dived away in time. It is thanks to excellent detective work on the part of the Army laboratories that they were able to identify it: the man who called Velasco over had the device in pieces on his bench: on the cylinder was clear Wermacht identification!

We went over to Neuron Data in the afternoon to fix some bugs in the Ovnibase expert system, and Jean-Jacques gave me a copy of the Gepan database. He confirmed that some of the French teams interested in microwave weapons wanted to talk to Niemtzow, notably the shadowy Gilbert Payan who works with ETCA (*Etablissement Technique Central de l'Armement*).

Over dinner with Dick and Carole Haines and Fred Beckman we debated the many issues that are agitating researchers in this field. Are there abductions in France? Have they been reported to Gepan? No, says Velasco. But what about the Pontoise case? I ask. Well, the Pontoise case was obviously a hoax, says Jean-Jacques. But a hoax by whom? That's the question. Throughout this discussion Fred kept complaining that the wine brought by Dick Haines was a poor choice and an insult to his expert palate.

I have tracked down Len Stringfield, who has been researching the "dead Alien" angle for 12 years. He confirmed to me that in 1978-79 he was in touch with two doctors who alledgedly did some autopsies, but he's unable to get anything from them anymore:

"They're retired and they just won't talk," he told me. He claimed he had no less than 37 first-hand sources who either saw crashed disks or bodies, but none of that can be seriously documented.

Boulder. Friday 16 June 1989.

On the flight to Boulder Jean-Jacques told me about his life near Toulouse. He has been reelected as mayor of his town, on the socialist ticket, and in that capacity he has often met with Jospin, whom he knows well, and once with Mitterrand. At a formal political reception, when Jospin introduced him and mentioned to the

President that Jean-Jacques was in charge of the UFO project at Cnes, Velasco added that it had to do with "unexplainable" observations. Mitterrand corrected him: "Surely you mean *unexplained*, not unexplainable," the President said.

When a strange light phenomenon was seen over Kourou last year, Jean-Jacques was sent there. It turned out the object had been a satellite reentry. The commander of the frigate guarding the coast was sure he was being attacked by a submarine launching rockets, and the man in charge of security was ready to go to war.

Last night my daughter (more strikingly elegant than she would admit, in pointed shoes and leather jacket, an Egyptian amulet around her neck) accompanied me to the informal reception for SSE members, where I cornered Hal.

"Do you realize how long it's been since we last spoke?" I said.

We walked all the way to Denny's and he brought me up to date about his contacts while I told him bluntly what Bill Moore had said in Lyon, about being in touch with Kit and Robert Gates.

"The man's on a fishing expedition," I said. "Did any of his information ever check out? Have you found any source that has in fact seen an Alien, or done an autopsy? I hear that you took Condor and Falcon to Washington to see a Congressman..."

He stopped me: "That's another silly rumor. I have not taken anybody to Washington. There's a Congressional aide who's willing to talk to Falcon or Condor if they have serious information to offer, but so far nothing has happened. I did talk to a number of people, in part thanks to Moore. They all tell extraordinary stories, but when I ask them to report only about what they have seen themselves, the data evaporates."

He added: "There is only one guy they call Hawk, who's a consultant at Wright Field; he claims he's observed something remarkable. He was on a military exercise in the Pacific when a fighter pilot said on the radio that he saw an object with a blue beam. A voice came on the communication channel, instructing the pilot to get out of there in a hurry if the beam turned green. The pilot did report the beam turning green and that was the last that was heard of him. The plane never came back. So who was the guy on the radio, and how did he know what the beam would do?"

Hal assures me he has checked Hawk's credentials with a former monitor of one of his SRI projects. He has learned a few other concrete things. Richard Doty, who is undoubtedly Falcon, did work at AFOSI under Hennessy, who has an office in the Pentagon. He says that he was indeed shown a training film when he was indoctrinated, but it was a disinformation job he was being trained for! Allegedly Doty blew Hennessy's cover when he passed out information that was false while he was told it was real, a violation of the understanding under which he worked.

"That sounds bizarre to me," I said as we strolled across the little bridge over Boulder Creek that babbled in the dark. "Here is a guy who is on the payroll of the lie-steal-and-cheat department, yet he's so full of upright moral principles he has to spill the beans to a free-lance reporter the first time they feed him some bullshit? Come on, Hal, you know better than that!"

He laughed and had to admit it was far-fetched.

The Secret Onion project is still headed up by John Alexander, now a project manager at Los Alamos. He attended the SSE meeting in Boulder. It did get off the ground, as it turns out. Its first step was to go out into the desert with an infrared camera, and they did record a V-shaped object similar to the Hudson Valley craft. But everything stopped when they setup a second camera, and eventually the effort was disbanded. In my opinion it was doomed from the beginning: too obvious, and starting from false premises.

One evening in Boulder Hal attended a hypnotic session run by Jim Harder. He told me about it, shaking his head: "It was as bad as anything you had warned me about... All sorts of leading questions about the Alien civilizations the witness had visited, a sad joke."

United Flight to San Francisco. Saturday 17 June 1989.

At the SSE conference I met Professor Joachim Kuettner again (Fig.16 on p.406). I hadn't seen him since the days of the Condon committee. He deplored the passing of Hynek and McDonald, commenting on the loss they represented. He spoke of the mysterious circles found in the wheat in England, which have created much excitement in newspapers, including the *Wall Street Journal*: "Perfectly explainable," he said; "they are just micro-tornadoes, a newly-discovered phenomenon."

I doubt that explanation, unless the micro-tornadoes are endowed with a great deal of geometric genius: some patterns show concentric circles with four smaller perfect circles forming a square around the primary ones! Instead I suspect a technical military project.

Jean-Jacques Velasco spoke before the group, explaining the mission of Sepra, which now supersedes Gepan. He is running my "Ovnibase" expert system against their growing database. Nobody asked any questions: ufologists are always ready to jump to exciting conclusions about supposed Aliens from other planets, hidden away by the Pentagon, but when artificial intelligence is applied for the first time to the task of screening UFO reports, under the auspices of a major national government, nobody takes notice! Yet what we were reporting was a big step forward in methodology.

After the conference Catherine drove me to the airport in her green Subaru. I have shared her student life for three days, having breakfast over her makeshift table in her dark, "industrial art" apartment where the stereo hums along with her big fishtank.

Marcello Truzzi was at the meeting. "Do you ever see Anton any more?" he asked me. I told him no, but we had been wondering about him, too. Apparently he is becoming very reclusive: "When Diane left he lost his backstage support," Marcello said.

Last evening I spent six hours with Linda Howe, who came to pick me up at the conference center in her red Honda, wearing a red dress and red heart-shaped earrings. She gave me a copy of her fine self-published book, *Alien Harvest*, filled with color photographs that should force the issue of the reality of mutilations. She, too, has been approached by all kinds of people, notably a fellow named Gordon Novel who works with George Uhlig, director of R&D for Hercules Aerospace in Salt Lake City. Novel has allegedly developed some fancy weapon systems. But I know nothing about weapons.

On the terrace outside the Boulderado hotel where we had dinner while watching the full moon rising, we discussed witchcraft and Whitley Strieber. Whitley operates by deliberately placing himself in situations where he is likely to have ambiguous or borderline experiences. It is the kind of writing that literary analyst Virgil Thomson describes, placing people "into situations where they take on memorability." Not a bad technique for a novelist. In the process he creates the very "reality" he is trying to investigate.

Linda is worried about John Lear, who drinks an awful lot and has a house full of guns. One room of his house is covered with pictures of John with his father Bill Lear, with whom he was in fierce competition. Bob Lazar, who supposedly saw the Alien at Area 51 and gave Lear information on the schedule for the UFO flights, doesn't check out at all: No one at MIT remembers him, and he certainly did not graduate from there.

Linda told me an amazing story of a sortie in the desert near Roswell in Lear's truck: "He had this big gun on the seat next to him, and a rifle hanging behind us, and they were both loaded. When we approached Roswell I saw a dead cow and I asked him to get the truck into the field, but he wouldn't come out and I realized he was genuinely scared. So I went out alone and I found more dead cows, and more feet sticking up in the air, eleven in all! I got John to drive me to the farmer's house. The man didn't seem to be concerned at all over so many dead animals. He said it was probably blackleg, and he didn't care if his ranch was quarantined. We got to talking about the Roswell crash; he gave me the name of a neighbor who still had a piece of the metal. When we got back to the main road a big black triangular jet came roaring at us just a few feet off the pavement and veered to our right just before it seemed inevitable it would hit us. John was waving his gun at the jet, yelling "they" were after us. I admit I was pretty shaken..."

Hyde Street. Sunday 18 June 1989.

I just spoke again to Richard Niemtzow. I told him that Dr. Richard Neal was trying to reach him. We ended up talking about France.

"Whenever Velasco comes here to talk about UFOs, all kinds of other stuff happens," he said excitedly. "I've just had another call from Dr. Bernard Veyret, who is doing research on electromagnetism at the University of Bordeaux. He's the one who is trying to validate the Prioré machine and the use of microwaves in cancer treatment."

"Jean-Jacques did tell me about that."

"Well, this Veyret is open-minded about UFOs, but I don't think that's his real interest. He mentioned it might be possible for me to work half time at Sepra in Toulouse and half time in Bordeaux. Does that sound reasonable?"

"Yes, that's interesting. Things are changing in France, you know; they are much more pragmatic today than just a few years ago."

"Veyret tells me I should meet with Gilbert Payan, have you heard that name before?"

"Jean-Jacques did mention him: behind-the-scenes guy, especially interested in microwaves."

I didn't tell him that Jean-Jacques had told me, in the plane going to Boulder, that Payan was working closely with the military at ETCA, like our friend François Louange, and that he was the one who had ordered the Petit experiments redone, *sans* Petit of course.

"*Payan aime le secret*," were Velasco's exact words.

In the last few days I have been able to close many of the loops left open by our last trip to France and our discussion with Guérin.

"Payan is a consultant with the *Défense Nationale*," Niemtzow went on. "Apparently he's highly respected. They say he can get me a position in France. Jacqueline would also have a job."

The fact remains that Richard is subtly being recruited to work in France on secret microwave projects, and I cannot shake the impression that Poher is aware of all that, although Velasco is always quick to answer that he "never sees and never talks to Poher." According to Richard, Payan is in contact with a Monsieur Cannon, or Cannone, supposedly with French Intelligence at the Embassy in Switzerland who travelled to the U.S. to see Niemtzow on a mission hurriedly arranged by the *Quai d'Orsay* last year.

Hyde Street. Tuesday 20 June 1989.

This morning I tracked down Dr. Visse in Saint-Pourçain. An older woman put the Doctor himself on the line.

"I'm calling from San Francisco. Perhaps you've received my letter?" I asked. "I'm a French scientist who works in the U.S...."

"And I'm a French scientist who works in France..." he replied humorously.

"I often work with biologists interested in advanced research," I went on. He knew what I was driving at, because he cut through my explanations:

"There's a mistake here, Dr. Vallee. I wasn't the man involved in this affair."

"Have you ever worked in the United States?"

"Never."

"Have you had occasion to work with American teams?"

"Yes, but *not on this issue*."

"Have you ever met a man named Bill Moore?"

"I don't remember that name."

Hollywood. Hotel Roosevelt. Friday 23 June 1989.

A cool gray morning. From my window on a high floor I can see people lining up in front of the Chinese Theater to catch the first showing of *Batman*. Tracy Tormé missed our appointment last night, so I went out to dinner alone, at the *Melting Pot*, and came back on foot along Santa Monica Boulevard decorated by various interesting characters, macho Mexicans driving noisy boomers, among office workers waiting for their bus.

At midnight I called Tracy, who complained that in my *FastWalker* story the Aliens seemed to come from Earth:

"We can't show this multi-dimensional stuff on the screen," he complained. But we can! Bob and I spent hours explaining multiple dimensions, even showing him Carl Sagan's clear explanations in *Cosmos*, all in vain. (**8**)

Hyde Street. Monday 26 June 1989.

George Hathaway, the Canadian engineer who works with Liechtenstein, tells me he has been making contact with all leading UFO researchers who had ideas about energy or propulsion systems at the request of the Prince, who is also quietly sponsoring studies on abductions. That group tends to discount me because I have written *Dimensions*. My views on the subject are mis-represented: Jerome Clark and Budd Hopkins have told Hathaway, “Vallee doesn't even believe that these things are physical!” So I found myself having to explain to him I did believe that UFOs represented a physical technology, just like movie projectors are a technology; which doesn't mean I believe in Bambi, Batman, and the Creature from the Black Lagoon when they come out of the projector. Why is it so hard to explain to people how the phenomenon works? Why can't they see that it is a meta-system?

“But you did say they were multi-dimensional, rather than physical?” Hathaway countered.

“You and I are multi-dimensional, aren't we? Does that mean we’re not physical?”

He finally understood the point but stayed on his positions. He gave me some insight into his (and the Prince's) theory: there is an extra-terrestrial force that is monitoring and controlling man's drive into space: “It's a question of how far we'll be allowed to go before some other entities put the lid on what we do with our little rocket firecrackers. We have to be prepared for certain pressures. Space is not the beckoning, wide open, new frontier people dream about...”

The Prince seems to be aware of covert studies going on “at his level” (that is, at Head of State level) around the world. Hathaway, in the meantime, investigates Tesla phenomena and alternative energy devices, and lectures on such topics.

Later the same day.

Hal Puthoff tells me that he's met a couple of times with the Prince, a sophisticated aristocrat in his late forties. Liechtenstein is excited about energy concepts, to the point of setting up a corporation to which inventors of alternative devices can sell their patents and obtain royalties, free from military considerations of their respective countries. One of the times when Hal met Prince Hans-Adam was at the SSE meeting in Cornell, where the Prince argued knowledgeably with Carl Sagan.

Hathaway is an engineer (EE) who has worked in collaboration with the Planetary Association on Clean Energy, a group that brings back memories of Andrija Puharich.

I also mentioned John Alexander and the Secret Onion project.

"In my conversation with Alexander," I pointed out to Hal, "he didn't ask about any of my data. We spoke about parapsychology, the recent study by the National Academy of Sciences, dolphins..."

"They started with an ETH model," Hal said. "Alexander lined up several labs for material and photographic analysis. He had experts rewrite NORAD software to inventory all objects flying on trajectories that didn't match ICBMs. But he didn't have a theoretical framework."

"That may have been part of the problem," I said. "How did the whole thing collapse?"

"He was only serving as the action officer for heavy-weight people, higher-ups in aircraft companies, industry, government, and the national labs. A lot of people had been briefed and had agreed to cooperate. But all of a sudden he was re-assigned as part of a move that affected 40,000 people in the Armed Forces. He was sent away to Los Alamos. He lost his power base."

That left me unconvinced: "My experience is that if someone really high up wants something done, it gets done. Surely they could have prevented one person out of 40,000 from being re-assigned."

"The plan may have been killed by someone deciding that the timing was wrong, or they were the wrong people, or the approach was bad," Hal conceded, vaguely.

"How do we know that nothing got done?"

"Only one project got started, because it could spend year-end money, a small investigation into some electromagnetic and gravity effects. Another project, which had to do with potential detectors, never got off the ground. The group that backed the whole idea is still there. I would know if anything concrete had developed."

Hal said his super-electron devices were advancing rapidly, with briefings at Boeing, Dassault, China Lake, the Secretary of Commerce and the President's science adviser. People seem especially interested in the radar applications of the technology.

Hyde Street. Tuesday 27 June 1989.

Kit has discovered that Scott Jones was the aide to Senator Claiborne Pell who listened so intently to Doty/Falcon. He was also deeply involved in the study of electromagnetic effects (as described in *Maze*, by Larry Collins) as well as the MJ-12 affair.

It turns out that Bob Chartrand, who came to dinner last night with his wife Ellie, knows Claiborne Pell very well. At my next trip to Washington I should meet Pell's staff, as well as Art Lundahl.

Today, at Chartrand's request, I gave a luncheon address at a conference on Executive Information Systems attended by experts from the largest companies in the country and Canada. Several of them wanted to talk about UFOs after the presentation, and there was a former Air Force officer with stories of unexplained lights in formation and of unidentified radar trackings in Alaska.

The Mufon conference starts in a few days in a Las Vegas casino. The symbolism is appropriate: the Aladdin hotel is on the verge of bankruptcy, under investigation by the Gaming commission and on a cash-only basis with its creditors. Thus it is in a grotesque atmosphere of Vegas-style make-believe, hypocrisy, and fakery that ufologists from all over North America will gather there.

Las Vegas. Sunday 2 July 1989.

This Annual Mufon Conference is a fine tribute to man's paranoia. Last night Bill Moore scandalized the audience by repeating what he had told us in Lyon, namely that he was a willing contributor to the deception that pushed Paul Bennewitz to the verge of insanity. I was tempted to take the first flight back to San Francisco.

Las Vegas. Monday 3 July 1989.

Thankfully, the Mufon conference is over, a complete fiasco. Perennial critic Philip Klass, the butt of all the jokes, enjoys the last laugh. He now has enough material for another book about this crowd of believers in Alien cadavers stored below the Pentagon. Over multiple rounds of drinks Klass has told Fred he worried about John Lear's sanity and recent comments.

Lear showed the film of the Kennedy assassination, claiming he could see the driver killing the President. We could see nothing but random spots of shadow and light. Later I met with Budd Hopkins, nervous and disorganized, who couldn't stop talking about "his" abductees and the endless hypnosis sessions he arranges for them.

Before doing hypnotic regression sessions people like Jacobs, Hopkins, Sprinkle, and Harder would do well to study the chapter on "The Jet-Propelled Couch," in *The Fifty-Minute Hour* (**9**), the book where psychiatric expert Dr. Lindner explains why he decided not to use hypnosis to bring a difficult patient back to sanity: if the victim suffers from a fantasy, Lindner asserted, hypnosis will only reinforce the delusion, and it will become glued to his reality forever, causing irreversible harm to the human subject.

In most claims of Alien abduction we must start from the hypothesis that some or all of the experience may be fantasy-based, making it imperative to strike hypnosis from the list of primary investigative techniques, and reserving it only for the elucidation of details in the most reliable cases.

Hyde Street. Wednesday 5 July 1989.

Kit was aware of Bill Moore's speech when he called me this morning at my Silicon Valley office. We agreed there must be twelve laws on the books against what he did. Yet he claims he did it as part of a government job.

Kit has spent two days at Area 51 on official business and did see interesting craft, but nothing resembling a flying saucer.

"By the way," I asked him, "you never did tell me what got you interested in these rumors about Alien bodies in the first place."

"It goes back to the seventies," he answered. "When the first alleged autopsy pictures came out, all that stuff by Len Stringfield."

The pictures turned out to show bodies in coffin-like boxes with wires and pipes running into them, a bad joke. Next, we discussed Larry Collins' book, *Maze*, which goes over some of the government's psychic work. It mentions Keith Harary and Pat Price.

When I asked Kit whether he had ever shown the injury photos I had brought back from Brazil to a dermatologist he seemed taken aback and finally confessed he hadn't done anything with it, "because the spot just reminded him of ringworms." Ringworms? Why not swamp gas? It is only the political aspect that fascinates him: who knows what, and who does what. He did tell me once that he thought UFOs were explainable as anthropological phenomena. I measure every day how rare minds like Hynek's are among scientists. Yet, even Allen could lose his research focus.

When Janine and I had dinner with Tina and Brian they told us some things we had never known about him. He didn't want to call me to Arizona after he settled there, for example, because he didn't feel like sharing the favors of his new protectors, from whom he expected untold millions. Tina kept insisting they had no new ideas for research, while my books contained a mine of such material: why not bring me over? There was a sense of jealousy toward me at that point in Hynek's mind.

Their little organization, Icufor, has now convinced Larry, the Lorenzens'son, to turn over the Apro files to them. Other ufology groups are livid. In the old tradition of friendly collegiality and cooperation in honest research, Cufos is even talking of suing.

Monterey Hyatt. Tuesday 11 July 1989.

Yesterday I had a pleasant and studious lunch with Dick Haines. We sat outside at the Gatehouse restaurant that features nice baskets of

Fig. 16. With Dr. Joachim Kuettner and Jean-Jacques Velasco at the SSE conference in Boulder, June 1989.

Fig. 17. With Fred Beckman in Las Vegas, July 1989.

flowers and a wonderful waterfall. I gave him the Canadian photograph someone had shown me in Las Vegas and two more years of the *Flying Saucer Review* for his pilot sighting catalogue. He had not attended the meeting on abductions sponsored by Prince Hans-Adam a couple of months ago, but he heard that a woman named Rima Laibow had been put in charge of the group. Unfortunately she has no training in hypnosis.

Tonight I spoke with Hal again: "When you know the people inside, as I do, you may not be able to find out what a black program is about, but at least you know it exists," he said, "because you bump against the box.... With UFOs there just isn't any such evidence; there's no box! Nobody with any brains seems to be tracking this."

I disagree with him: where did those hundreds of Brazilian pictures go? Who was giving instructions to "Jim Irish," the man who took infrared photographs on orders from Washington?

According to Hal, John Alexander did go out to Dulce with night vision super-scopes and saw strange devices, but he doesn't believe they had anything to do with Aliens.

Hyde Street. Tuesday 18 July 1989.

In Los Angeles, where I was visiting a robotics company today, I took a couple of hours off to have lunch with Dr. Richard Neal, the African American gynecologist interested in UFOs and their physiological effects. I was surprised to find that he was an ardent believer in the Extraterrestrial Cause and everything Budd Hopkins had stated about sexual interaction between human witnesses and their alleged abductors. It is only recently that he began to doubt these claims. Having co-founded the Los Angeles abductions research group, he finally realized that no tangible medical details were forthcoming from witnesses who claimed contact or from the ufologists who propagated their claims. He tried in vain to get them to agree to a screening protocol: David Jacobs insisted that a five-minute preliminary interview with abductees was sufficient to convince him they were genuine!

Disgusted with such disregard for standards and with constant feuds among UFO factions, Neal resigned. He said that his only serious lead for a doctor who may have done autopsies was the Lancaster doctor already mentioned to me by Kit: he went to his house and the man refused to talk, obviously embarrassed, claiming the need to keep his government pension secure. Kit can find no trace of such a pension. But Neal's information comes from Len Stringfield, who still claims he cannot release any names for fear of some dreadful consequences, and so on…. A waste of time.

Hyde Street. Thursday 20 July 1989.

A call from Bob Weiss just brought sad news, the death of our mutual friend George Koopman, president of the American Rocket Company. He died in the desert at Edwards Air Force Base. He was visiting the site of an engine test in preparation for the company's first launch. He was using his cell phone, shuffling papers while driving. It seems that he just drifted off at high speed, and couldn't control his car on the gravel on the shoulder of the road.

Hyde Street. Sunday 30 July 1989.

Last Friday Dick Haines invited me to observe a hypnotic regression session in Sausalito. The witness, a talented musician, was 23 at the time of the suspected abduction that involved strange bands of light appearing in front of his car on the freeway from New York City to Albany, where his parents lived. He had reached a point close to Ossining when he felt the car levitating. The next thing he remembers is seeing some deer on the road, with their big black eyes. Under hypnosis, he has previously recalled looking down on his car, seeing some beings around it, and watching two silver eggs in the sky through a rectangular window.

The hypnosis session, which Dick conducted well but without all the safeguards specialists would employ, resulted in considerable stress and pain for our subject, who struggled on the floor moaning and writhing for some 20 minutes before he was able to get out of the trance. This episode left me unconvinced about the relevance of hypnosis in such cases, except under the most stringent conditions of medical control.

A friendly letter has arrived from Guérin. He plans to write a book after he retires, “to expose the cover-up.” He now seems to agree with me that the first-degree ETH is dead, and he moves on to my second-degree version that implies the objects emerging out of a multi-dimensional manifold. Once they have emerged, he argues, why shouldn't they have accidents and fall to earth in Roswell, to be picked up by the Pentagon? That logic is impeccable, if one forgets all the ancient cases of “airships” and flying vessels. The fantastically complex nature of the phenomenon is always swept under the rug.

Maman has just sent me an art magazine with an article about Jean-Francois Deluol, who has dedicated to me his 1983 painting *The Interrupted Journey*. **(10)**

Later the same day.

Conversation with Richard Niemtzow: he left a message on my machine this week-end, stating he had just flown back from France where he had met with Jean-Jacques Velasco and “people within the hierarchy” representing the French government's interest in the UFO question. When I called him back he first told me he had just been promoted to Lieutenant-Colonel in the Air Force and was still trying to decide whether or not to take a job in France. He did interview for a position where he would head up oncology clinical trials but he was disappointed at the offer, so the move does not make sense.

He went on to Paris where he met Gilbert Payan and Jean-Jacques Velasco. Payan invited them to lunch at his apartment so there were no witnesses to their discussions of UFOs and physiological effects of microwaves. Although Payan presented himself as a high-ranking official of the Ministry of Research, Richard suspected he was a specialist in scientific intelligence using the research ministry as a cover. He kept Richard and Jacqueline most of the afternoon, asking many questions but providing few answers himself. He was evasive when asked about the future of the French program at Cnes.

During the lunch, which was formal, with Payan keeping his jacket and tie in spite of the sweltering heat (I joked that he could not take them off because his tape recorder was inside his breast pocket, his tie hiding the wire) Payan mentioned that France was making progress on ionic propulsion systems. He had also been associated with Poher's project to camouflage automated UFO detection devices into atmospheric monitoring stations, an effort that went nowhere.

Payan asked Richard numerous questions about microwaves: would they interfere with recording equipment? No, replied Richard with the impression Payan already had the answers. The apartment held an excellent UFO library: Payan knew my work and had read all of Niemtzow's papers. He clearly occupies a position of clout in the administration, from which he plans to retire in a few months, but Richard had the impression he did not know much more than we did on UFOs, while he was very up-to-date about the aerospace industry, both French and American. Space travel seemed to be his dominant interest, along with sophisticated weapons: his interest in UFOs is linked to the desire to manufacture a "ray" that could paralyze people at a distance like these objects do. Dr. Cannone, of French intelligence, was again mentioned as his "collaborator." And Payan considered the idea of hiring Richard as a consultant on these issues.

Whenever they discussed UFOs it was the medical aspect that came back. Would certain types of radiation be useful in paralyzing muscles? What was the effect of microwaves on tissue? At what frequencies? Those were the topics he wanted to discuss. They correlated closely with those asked by Dr. Bernard Veyret of Bordeaux University Medical School, himself an expert on radiation impact on human tissue who recently visited Richard in Texas.

This brought up an interesting point about Velasco that did not escape Richard's attention. At one time Velasco said that he had only spoken to Payan once or twice, and that he did not know of Veyret's visit to Texas until after it happened. Yet during lunch he mentioned earlier conversations with Payan about Veyret's imminent visit. Richard felt sure that Velasco and Payan had in fact spoken of it frequently. Another incident threw their relationship into a different light, when Payan casually mentioned that both CIA and the KGB had gone through the Gepan files in Toulouse. Velasco's mouth opened in shock: “What do you mean?” he managed to say. His question was answered by another question: “What did you expect them to do?” asked Payan.

Velasco had told Niemtzow about a highly confidential French government paper on microwave activity that mentioned work at Brooks Air Force Base, among other things. We agreed that Velasco would never do such a thing under his own initiative. When Richard asked Velasco if he ever saw Poher he was told that they had not met for a long time. I told Richard I did not believe that: The last time I saw Poher he was busy designing microwave experiments and developing theories of effects on muscle tissue. Perhaps, behind the scenes it is Poher who is pushing to bring Richard back to France.

This led us to a wide-ranging discussion of the role of various agencies in the UFO business and we came to talk about Kit. Richard reminisced about the time when he and John Schuessler were almost “recruited” by a woman who claimed to be working for a private investigation service in Houston. When they came to her office for a meeting about UFOs they found a dozen people working behind desks which were so neat and devoid of paperwork as to seem unnatural, and they quickly came to the conclusion the whole thing was a setup.

“Was that woman named Valerie Ransone?” I asked Richard.

He seemed puzzled to find that I knew her and her operation.

“Did you ever find out who she was working for?” he asked. I confessed that I did not.

“Schuessler tracked her down through his channels at McDonnell-Douglas. It turned out she was an agent for NRO, working with the Navy. Kit, who took care of her medically, once told me that she was amazing; she knew four times as many people as the both of us did.”

I laughed at that: “She also looks a lot better than both of you guys,” I pointed out. “A woman as beautiful and articulate as she was would have had no difficulty being invited to lunch by any company president. That didn't necessarily mean she had access.”

"There's something else, Jacques. When I revealed to Kit, over lunch, that I knew her affiliation, he practically choked on his food. He told me not to mention her again at the restaurant. I've only had that reaction from him twice in all the time I've known him."

"Let me guess: the other time was in connection with Len Stringfield and the doctor who had done the autopsy?" I suggested.

"Precisely. Have you heard of a Dr. Ron Weiss at McDonnell Aviation? He was a higher-up that Schuessler sometimes consulted (**11**). Whenever they discussed UFOs, Weiss would take him into the parking lot, so paranoid was he about people snooping around the subject; a subject that isn't even supposed to exist!"

Hyde Street. Monday 31 July 1989.

Richard Niemtzow is puzzled: Velasco has left a message on his machine asking him again to send his biography urgently "as Cnes was considering making him an offer for employment."

Payan has to be behind this move. Richard wonders if he should take the job in France to see what is going on, and if he should tell Kit about all this. We agreed that I would go see him in Texas: This seems like a good time to visit the cancer research center in San Antonio, and see their 3D computer simulation of complex molecules. This is a medical area in which I came close to recommending a couple of investments during the last year.

I also continue to research the Battelle letter. The Air Force has given an evasive response to my FOIA request for all correspondence between ATIC and Battelle in January 1953: "Most records with a date of 1953 and earlier would probably be destroyed or retired to the appropriate Federal Records Center."

Would secret papers have been automatically declassified? My attorney and I are filing a detailed answer, pursuing the probe.

Hyde Street. Tuesday 1 August 1989.

Going to lunch at my favorite Chinese restaurant in Menlo Park on El Camino, I found Ed May there with remote viewer Nevin Lantz, soon to leave for Pennsylvania where he has a 14-acre farm and will open a practice in clinical psychology. Ed told me that he was as disappointed as I was with the poor level of the SSE Boulder conference. He also said he now expected to get funding for the next three years, thanks in part to Jack Vorona of DIA who, in spite of being close to retirement, has been able to open some important doors. The key factor is that the program claims theoretical and operational success, so the briefings are increasingly impressive. He invited me to come back for an update and possibly to resume my consulting work.

The name of Dave Saunders came up in the conversation. I learned that he had just moved to a retirement community in South Carolina with his wife. I had not realized that Dave was 65, which is not that old. He now intends to write the definitive book on personality analysis.

In the afternoon, coming back to San Francisco and checking my mail I bumped into Keith Harary on Polk Street. Keith told me that he had launched into new psychic exploration, a book, and film ventures that revolve around shipwrecks in the Caribbean and forgotten mines in Arizona.

Hyde Street. Thursday 3 August 1989.

We are ready for another meeting with Tina and Brian, with whom we had dinner last night at Maxwell's Plum in Ghirardelli Square. We started out by exchanging gossip. They told us that following Bill Moore's depressing confession in Vegas, Vicki Cooper was thinking of dropping her magazine. The field is going through the kind of psychic trauma I first noticed when I was investigating "The Two" and other cults, and the disease keeps expanding.

Tina and Brian are engaged into a successful program of art exhibits with a "Contact" flavor that meets with good public response. The change may come from George H. Bush's decision to push Nasa towards a Moon base and a Mars expedition over the next 25 years. I see the proponents of aerospace technology using the Alien theme to inject drama into what threatens to be another boring technical program. Nasa has already released an expensive television spot in which one of their probes is depicted bearing the letters "UFO," floating in an alien planetary atmosphere.

Linda Howe tells me that John Lear has been fired from his job following the Mufon conference. His boss had on his desk a newspaper quoting Lear's statements. He told him he couldn't have that kind of thing associated with the airline.

Today I closed our fifth Euro-America-I investment in Mercury Interactive, headed up by Aryeh Finegold, of Daisy fame. They design a "pixel grabber" that could revolutionize software testing. Their plan reminds me of my long days and nights of database testing at RCA and Stanford: I have no doubts about the market for their product, if they can build it. (**12**)

I invited Tina and Brian for lunch at *L'Olivier*. They urged me to work with them: I would move to Arizona and pick up where Allen left. The idea of helping them on short, specific projects like the Apro database appeals to me, but anything else would be foolish. Tina enjoys managing things and people. Brian, on the other hand, an idealist who left college to study yoga and psychic massages, wants to "help mankind" in a general and engaging way. I told him I could think of many things that would help mankind more than UFO research. Both are impressed by the new "contactee" movement. They dress smartly, in flowing white, and they exude enthusiasm.

Spring Hill. Saturday 5 August 1989.

Last night we had dinner with Keith Harary and Darlene. We went into their living room between two long stacks of cardboard boxes: they are moving to Los Angeles, where she expects to earn a higher salary and find lower rents. Indeed San Francisco is becoming unaffordable. New Chinese and Japanese money flowing into local real estate propels rents and property prices beyond the means of most residents, while decreased support for public welfare and the mismanagement of federal housing have thrown into the street hundreds of people who should be under treatment in mental hospitals, in rehabilitation centers, or getting help to get back into the world of work. They sleep in doorways, defecate on the sidewalk.

"I don't have anything against these miserable people," says Keith, "but given a choice I will move to a place where I won't have to sweep garbage and beer cans from my front steps every morning, and have my wife threatened on the street."

Keith is publishing two books, one on lucid dreaming, and the other on out-of-body travel, co-written with a senior editor at Omni. He is also participating in the search for sunken Spanish galleons. He is full of energy and humor.

While the field of paranormal research stalls or, like ufology, sinks into the swamp of irrational belief, my professional life is fortunately grounded in hard science domains in full expansion. High technology in Silicon Valley has never been more vibrant. When we left for a two-week holiday at the ranch, the closing papers for the financing of several companies were ready on my desk in my Sand Hill Road office. They included the final documents for Mercury Interactive and investment memoranda for companies with evocative names like Cryogel, Polaris and Sangstat Medical. I told my secretary not to give away my phone number.

It is only in my spare time that I can continue to meet with my old friends. Over lunch at the Gatehouse Fred Beckman told me of his new concerns for John Lear, who intends to go to Egypt "to clear his head." Lear could easily be assassinated while in Egypt, he said. I was unimpressed by this ominous statement: why would anybody want to eliminate John Lear? Nobody takes seriously the so-called "revelations" of Bob Lazar about his meetings with Aliens.

Fred looked tired and drawn. "This phenomenon is so amazingly large and varied that it is impossible to keep it all inside one's brain," he said when I urged him not to fall victim of the paranoia in the field: "You have to go up a level and look at the big picture," I said.

"That's what you wrote in *Dimensions*. But none of the ufologists I know understands your book."

I laughed: "That says more about them than it says about *Dimensions*, because the general public certainly understands it. I get letters every day from people who obviously find it pretty clear."

"How do you state your position, then?"

"Very simply. Here's my elevator pitch: *The UFO phenomenon is a meta-system, not a bunch of spacecraft. It adapts to its environment, like the cinema does. Think of the movie industry as a meta-system. We just need to find the projector*."

"You never explained it this way, so clearly."

He thought about it and went on: "To me the phenomenon is interesting because it brings into question two fundamental aspects of human life: our history on this planet and our understanding of reality. If and when we understand UFOs both of these aspects will be revolutionized."

I hope that Fred, now close to 60, will remain active in the field without slipping back into bitterness. He has a subtle, enquiring mind, and a good sense of humor: "Allen used to get me to answer his mail," he reminisces. "That was my punishment for..." he searches for the right word... "for being like I am."

A few hours later I had tea with Peter Sturrock at the *Perfect Recipe* in Palo Alto. We spoke of the next SSE meeting to be held at Stanford. He told me about Bill Tiller, a professor of material science who has built a gas discharge device to test whether it reacts to psychic influence.

"When Bill came back from a recent trip he found his lab taken away from him."

"How was that possible? Isn't he a tenured Faculty member?"

"Quite so, but his department allocates the space, you see. Not very nice. Not nice at all."

Things haven't changed much in Academe since the days when Dean Cooper refused to sign my proposal with Hynek for UFO research at Northwestern. This little story made me glad I never took the job I had been offered as a Stanford professor.

Peter reminded me that Chandrasekhar, when he first proposed the idea that some stars were white dwarves, was given the cold shoulder by polite colleagues in astronomy and howls of laughter from the more demonstrative ones. Instead of arguing he just let time go by, worked on other things and established his scientific credentials.

Twenty years later the evidence for white dwarves had simply become overwhelming.

Spring Hill. Monday 7 August 1989.

Breakfast in bed. I work on a manuscript while Janine reads the draft of *Forbidden Science* and tells me: "Twenty years ago we were doing the same things... You write in this diary that you are in bed working on a new book, and I'm proofreading the earlier chapters. See, our life hasn't changed much!"

After she got up and I finished writing my daily chapter I went into the pool to clear my body of last night's episode of asthma. A fawn was shamelessly eating our juicy grapes just outside our bedroom window. Last night we looked at the sky from the flat roof of the tower. Saturn was in the south, splendid with its rings clearly visible in my refractor. Deer came out of the forest, barely seen in the darkness. Janine caught four Perseid meteors, but we still fail to observe anything out of the normal range.

Now there's an electric storm to the South, with spectacular lightning. I installed the refractor inside the observatory shelter to look at the crescent moon in the Southwest sky and to take some measurements of height and clearance for my future telescope.

Spring Hill. Wednesday 9 August 1989.

Quiet times: We are waiting for Catherine. Olivier will join us at the end of the week, bringing my nephew Denis and his wife Pascale. I have started work on my last stained glass panel: Giordano Bruno and the fascinating figure of Trithemius, Abbey of Sponheim.

Spring Hill. Saturday 12 August 1989.

One year ago Janine's mother left us. In the bright sunshine and the joy of Spring Hill, where we play with Denis and Pascale, Olivier and Catherine, it is impossible not to reflect on how happy we are, while we also feel quiet sadness about the past, and the memories along the way.

The fact that I am working on the manuscript of the early diaries makes them even more vivid: I remember the quiet gray mornings at Marigny and Bayeux when I would borrow a volume from Mamie's library of historical stories and read it while listening to the soft sounds of the household around me.

Spring Hill. Wednesday 16 August 1989.

Bob Emenegger called: he is thinking of a new documentary and wants to use me as a pivot. Bob has determined that the Bentwaters object was not a real UFO but a holographic projection, combined with other props for a psywar test. Paul Chartle had investigated such technologies when Alan Sandler was pretending to be interested in Pentagon technical developments "as a cover for our UFO documentary." This is the first time he has admitted to me that their other shows were pure interference.

Spring Hill. Thursday 17 August 1989.

The wind carries yellow leaves into the pool; the sky is swept by wispy white clouds, first signs of approaching fall. I started reading the Diary of Andy Warhol, and soon put it down: what a boring world, all those glamorous Manhattan people with no brains, staring day after day at one another's clothes, counting their pimples…

Last night, between 21:35 and 22:00 we watched the end of the total lunar eclipse from the observatory: Arcturus just above the trees to the West, Vega close to the zenith.

Today I called Aimé Michel in Epinal. He answered in a low tired voice, and then perked up when he realized it was an old friend calling him from California. He felt as I did about all the rumors of saucer crashes and the insanity sweeping the field: "The problem is, there's a new audience," he said. "The people we used to call "enthusiasts," folks like Jerry Clark and Stanton Friedman, may have been misguided but they were sincere. While the new amateur communities feeding the rumor mill... they don't give a damn about truth; they've never heard of Hynek. They are just starved for Hopkins' stories of ugly little Aliens abducting people, tortuting women..."

He went on, fully alive now: "Even in rational France there are people with good minds who are ready to believe all that trash. You know as well as I do that they will end up swallowing it."

Spring Hill. Friday 18 August 1989.

Ray Fowler, an old-time researcher of the mystery, calls me to say he is about to resign from Mufon, upset at what happened in Las Vegas and sick of the Gulf Breeze case: "In the old days, a case like this would never have been followed up, because there are so many questionable points about the witnesses. The skeptics are going to tear it apart." Later I called Jenny Randles in England to verify some details about Bentwaters. She told me she was coming to San Francisco next month, so we made plans to have dinner together.

Spring Hill. Saturday 19 August 1989.

At night I wake up, vaguely depressed and anxious, wondering about the wisdom of publishing *Forbidden Science*. I reflect on InfoMedia and other failures in my life. They can be traced to two weaknesses: my lack of a sense for marketing and my lack of skill as a negotiator.

Marketing is the ability to recognize what people want and to find ways to provide it to them. I am not apt at teasing out the interests of others. InfoMedia was a classic example. I can inspire loyalty, even enthusiam, so I got a small movement going, but it didn't match any genuine "want" in the real world. We were too early trying to build network communities around urgent themes and projects. The concept will succeed but it will have to be implemented in other guises, in a different economic environment.

The lack of negotiation skills is evident in my current position: I could command a higher salary and more responsibilities but I have traded all that against the freedom to write, to enjoy my family and to pursue other interests. In the end I may well be the winner, but it doesn't feel like it at the moment. It is true that negotiating with Fred Adler is a challenge in which far greater businessmen have lost both their patience—and their shirt!

I do not know what to do with *Revelations*. The phenomenon still looms large over us, but my research increasingly points to the fact that it's not a recent problem. It relates to the deepest levels of our consciousness; it invokes forces from the dawn of history, from the depth of magic, beyond human life and its slavery to the time dimension.

At the same time the secret services of major nations keep feeding the Undercurrent for their own sordid purposes, simulating close encounters, using their puppets to spread stories of live Aliens in Pentagon cellars, intimidating witnesses, covering up data and experiments, and expending big efforts to create confusion: Why are they doing this? Probably to hide some strategic operations and to take our attention away from their weapon development projects.

There is a striking contradiction here. If the phenomenon lurks in the deeper recesses of consciousness where nightmares reign and leprechauns roam, why is the military so frantically interested in its implications?

19

San Antonio. Wednesday 23 August 1989.

Hotel Windham. From my window on the tenth floor I see the vast plain, the wide Texas skies I've always admired. The jets from nearby Brooks Air Force Base roar out of nowhere to burrow their way through the hot, muggy air. Tomorrow, a visit to an advanced project in molecular modeling at the local cancer research center.

Richard Niemtzow (in Air Force uniform, with his new Lieutenant-Colonel insignia) picked me up at the airport. We had the whole evening to discuss topics we hadn't been able to voice over the phone, notably the puzzling developments in France and our mutual relationship to Kit. Richard showed me the latest letter from Gilbert Payan (from Boulogne) inviting him to France. It suggested that he contact a woman named Annie Wolff who seems to be his assistant. As he had told me before, it hinted that they could help him secure a job at Hoffman-LaRoche while he would be supplementing his income working for "them" as a consultant. But who is "them?"

Another document Richard gave me answered the question: it was an excellent summary of biological effects of weak microwaves written by three scientists from Bordeaux University on behalf of the SGDN, the General Secretariat for National Defense (**13**).

"Clearly the French are moving towards the development of what they call MOPAP weapons, Anti-Personal Pulsed Microwaves," he said. "Do you think I should go there and join their project? See where it leads? My wife is French, we could easily move back. Payan has hinted I could work with Velasco in Toulouse. I could become active in their UFO work... I have good contacts with amateur groups in France."

I know he is asking me this out of friendship, but he puts me in an awkward position. I have to caution him: France has indeed changed for the better in the last five years but it remains an irritating, inefficient country, where he will be subject to all the vagaries of another bureaucracy.

"It all depends if you're going there to help the French build a death ray, or if you're going there to study UFOs," I said. "I love France, but frankly, even if they tripled my salary and guaranteed my retirement I wouldn't go back there to build a death ray."

The notes from Payan indicate that the Pentagon review, *Soviet Military Power* repeatedly stressed that the Soviets had studied MOPAP weapons and were in a position to manufacture them. An ETCA mission to the U.S. (arranged in part by Niemtzow in July 1987) brought back data on American progress in this area. Payan quotes articles from *IEEE Spectrum* and Heracles International that indicate that microwave beams can paralyze or injure fighting troops by acting on the nervous system (**14**). That made me think back over our experiences in Brazil. But Richard had other concerns:

"If I go there, should I tell Kit what's going on? Perhaps he would want me to gather information for him..."

Payan is no dummy. He must know quite well that Niemtzow has to report on such contacts.

"I don't think you or I are under any obligation to provide details at this point," I replied. "If they do their job, Kit's colleagues must be aware of the French mission visiting American research centers preoccupied with microwaves," I pointed out.

"Not necessarily," he answered with a smile. "Those people are clumsy; they screw up the simplest jobs. When the French came here, I arranged their trip and then contacted AFOSI, our own Air Force Intelligence, to brief them on the visit. They didn't want me to come to their office because that was too obvious. So we met at a restaurant; they told me they had a special budget, and this was an important occasion. So we got there in their big secret unmarked car, very noticeable with all its antennas sticking out. It was another joke. One of them had a knife and a gun in a holster, which I could see when the wind caught his jacket. They had a woman with them, supposedly a Soviet expert. We ordered the appetizers and I turned the file over to them: the letters from France, the scientists' background, the itinerary, and the technical summaries.

Suddenly one of them said, "Have you noticed those guys, at the corner table?" I asked what it was about, wondering if we were being spied upon by foreign agents. They told me, "it's none of your concern, but we've got to get out of here right away." So I said, "We haven't even paid for the food!" They told me not to worry about it. The bully with the gun practically carried me out. Once we got to the car I asked them where the file was: those idiots had left it on the table! They rushed back inside, it was gone. The whole scene was like something out of the Three Stooges. It'll be a long time before I deal with AFOSI on a confidential matter again!"

We laughed about the incident but I urged him to be careful. "Look, these people behave like drunken cowboys. But the French may be dangling out this job to flush out the intentions of the U.S. Government on UFOs."

A young woman who studies to be a nurse and is Richard's occasional housekeeper, brought us some food and we pursued the conversation until another guest of his arrived, a fellow from Brooks Air Force Base named John Simmon, a top Air Force rheumatologist. I told them about our trip to Brazil. They had the same reaction as many people to whom I have described our experiences: "Can I go back there with you next time?" After dinner Richard showed us his radio amateur antenna system in his backyard, a very professional arrangement of four very tall masts in a large square.

San Antonio. Thursday 24 August 1988.

A Texas-class thunderstorm hangs over us. I am delayed, waiting for plane connections. I was able to spend more time with Richard today. I told him I had been disappointed in the superficial way our friend Kit had dealt with some of the best data I had brought to him, notably the "ringworm" incident. It was almost as if he was interested in a different UFO phenomenon from the one I am studying.

Niemtzow ran his hand over his balding scalp and said forcefully: "Make no mistake about it, Kit has been studying this subject deeply, in an official capacity. In the seventies, when McDonnell-Douglas had a secret study of UFOs under way, who do you think was showing up regularly from Washington to monitor their progress? It was Kit, sent by CIA on official business. He came over whenever one of their aircraft had a sighting. John Schuessler told me that. I found that communication with him was always a one-way street. Those guys are trained that way."

"Whatever happened to the McDonnell study?"

"All they got were some pieces of metal, and they couldn't learn anything from the analysis, it was futile. Of course, being an aircraft company, they thought they would quickly crack the design, the propulsion system..."

Kit's involvement also appears in connection with Valerie Ransone. According to Niemtzow he was her medical handler. It is through her that Niemtzow met Kit; she put them in touch with each other! Kit subsequently helped Richard get into the Air Force. There followed the famous episode in which Schuessler and Niemtzow found themselves being recruited by Valerie's outfit in Houston. Some time later they met with a higher-up from McDonnell, the fellow named Dr. Weiss that Richard had mentioned to me before.

"We went to a motel where we were going to discuss the whole episode," Richard recalled. "This was in Saint Louis. The man at the desk told Weiss that a phone call had been made to move him to a different room, but he could not tell us who had made the call. Weiss just laughed. He told John Schuessler that he wouldn't fall for such an old trick as being moved to a bugged room; we would have our meeting in the parking lot. He warned us against CIA recruitment: once you are in their clutches, he said, you can forget about the rest of your life as a human being."

During our discussion at Richard's house the phone rang several times, and there was no one on the line. "You see what I mean?" he asked. "Happens all the time, whenever I discuss the subject with someone."

Spring Hill. Saturday 26 August 1989.

The trip to Texas has left me worried and confused. Fortunately I had manual work waiting for me at the ranch: I fixed the roof and made gutter repairs while Janine cleaned the garage and our workshop. The chores shook me out of my concern. We are happiest, it seems, when we work hard: carrying things, fixing, building, cleaning, and hacking away. Tonight we plan to watch *Rosemary's Baby*, and then perhaps we'll go for another swim under the stars.

Last week I spoke on the phone to Gretchen, on her way to Red Bluff to see her parents. She told me about her new life in Michoacan, her pride in her five-month old son. Then she gave me some bad news about Bill Murphy, who has been diagnosed with cancer and hardly leaves his house in Mount Shasta City any more.

Spring Hill. Sunday 27 August 1989.

Janine tells me I have a duty to publish *Forbidden Science*, given all the confusion about the phenomenon and the misconceptions about the Air Force and Allen Hynek. I am one of few surviving sources of primary data that others will need to make up their mind, whether or not they agree with my interpretations, she says.

On Friday I had lunch with Ed May at SRI. He gave me a briefing on the project, miraculously restarting with a major budget from classified sources. Briefings to Admiral Marriott, to the Military Intelligence Board, to Secretary of State Howard Baker and various senators, including Pell and Gore. The results are now so good that Darpa itself is interested. Another development is the departure of Jim Salyer, recalled after ten years of residency as a security watchdog for the psychic program at SRI.

We discussed my theory that consciousness effects are linked to entropy variations and are thus regulated by the magnitude of a physical quantity (ds/dt). He feels that success in detecting large physical events such as atomic explosions do support this theory, but he is worried about shielding against electromagnetic leakage.

"Why not move over to the digital domain?" I asked him again as we were messily eating hamburgers at a restaurant behind the Menlo Park railroad tracks. "You can setup an entropy variation inside a computer memory. You could even make it portable."

"We never thought of that," he said. "We could get a big memory to go suddenly from a random state to all ones, or all zeroes."

I pointed out that all anecdotal evidence about psychic phenomena indicated they were primarily informational. Therefore a digital event might be more likely to be "noticeable" in psychic space than such physical acts as pouring a bottle of liquid nitrogen on the ground, as Ed is proposing in one of his experiments. It is in the same vein that Janine and I have created the Spring Hill observatory as an informational focus, a discontinuity; so far we have recorded no unusual phenomena, other than occasional sightings of peculiar lights on the ranch and a few UFO sightings in the vicinity, but I plan to expand our experiments next year.

Hyde Street. Tuesday 29 August 1989.

At the *Perfect Recipe* this afternoon I met with Ron Blackburn and Fred Beckman, who had hinted that Blackburn was particularly "in the know" about UFO technology and devious government plots. In fact Blackburn, a PhD and consulting engineer for Advanced Systems Technology at Lockheed, presents himself in a humble, even shy fashion. He spent 21 years in the Air Force, was a Lieutenant Colonel when he retired, with assignements in nuclear weapon safety. He joined Lockheed, worked at the famous "Skunk Works," saw that reality was not quite up to the glamorous legend, and moved to Palo Alto.

Here too, he has complaints about the bureaucracy. He was almost thrown out of his supervisor's office when he suggested that cold fusion effects might have something to do with zero-point energy, an idea he picked up from Puthoff's papers. So we are a long way from little Aliens in secret bases.

We learned nothing specific, except that John Lear is now flying cargo in DC-8 aircraft for an outfit called Rosenbaum out of Detroit. Blackburn knows nothing more than anyone else. I was occasionally disturbed to find his lizard-like eye gliding in my direction during Fred's tirades.

Blackburn's ambitions in UFO research are very classic: He wants to compute mass and acceleration for physical UFOs, knowing the observed weight on the ground traces—the usual, solid engineering approach. It's a good plan, but would he bother with such hypothetical stuff if Lockheed held the real thing in a lab somewhere?

Spring Hill. Saturday 9 September 1989.

Bill Calvert and his family have joined us here for the weekend, so we have resumed our long discussion on the paranormal. Brazilians are closer to magic than any other culture; their experience provides a frame of reference that is lacking in North America and Europe. In that frame of reference, many phenomena that find their way into the

UFO literature are only manifestations of what occultists call the "lower astral," for lack of a better term.

Janine and I have just had a vivid example of it in our discussions with a woman from Budd Hopkins' inner circle. She came to me with stories of multiple sightings, Aliens in the bedroom, audio tapes filled with messages from strange entities, and her "Alien" daughter. We saw pictures of the girl, we heard the terrifying tapes. In other times this would have been treated as witchcraft, but how do such phenomena manifest in our rational age?

Bill thinks there is something demonic about Strieber's visitors, too, possibly explained by his witchcraft background. Where does one draw the line? Some of the women in Hopkins' group are increasingly disenchanted with his ministrations and seek my advice, in search of real psychiatric treatment. Hopkins is only interested in those stories that match his preconceptions, while I leave the door open to larger experiences in the lives of these witnesses.

Now "Kathie Davis" herself, the star of *Intruders*, the book that started the whole movement of public fascination with abductions, has written to me under her real identity, sending along a tape of her actual ordeal that describes the episodes Hopkins has not wanted to use in his book.

After mentioning the regard she retains for Hopkins, she writes:

> You know, there is so much that isn't in that book… In order to maintain a kind of order, to keep the readers from getting confused, much of what Budd considered 'peripheral' was omitted, and I feel that *all of it* is important in one way or another.

She goes on to relate "one particular incident that was left out of the book," a key encounter that changed her life: A man approached her on the bus ride home from New York after she visited Hopkins for the first time (which places it in October 1983). She describes him as "a really strange character who mesmerized me." For instance, at one point in the 17-hour bus ride they stopped to eat, and she discovered that he didn't understand the menu. He ordered one of everything, and she had difficulty explaining to him the difference between sausage and bacon. He was tall, six foot four and perfectly built, with short length, wavy blond hair, steel-blue eyes, and a strong jaw. His skin was very soft and even by the end of the trip he had no sign of hair on his face. He was "breathtakingly handsome."

After she came home she saw him again twice, each time for conversations in which the man displayed much technical and medical knowledge as well as apparently paranormal abilities.

My first-order analysis of all this, given the obvious sincerity of "Kathie" and other abduction witnesses, leads me to the conclusion that many of them have undergone a profoundly disturbing, sometimes life-changing experience. But I also have to conclude that (1) subjecting them to hypnosis is tantamount to torture and, like torture, is unlikely to provide any insight into what really happened, (2) the approach used by the ufologists has the effect of reinforcing a fantasy designed around a crude approximation of what an extraterrestrial invasion would be, further injuring the mental state of the witnesses and (3) the extreme reaction of the leading abduction researchers, expressed by the utmost rage and a barrage of insults and threats against anyone who questions their methods, belies the outwardly warm, paternalistic, concerned and scientific image they are trying to project.

Now I am invited to a conference about "Experienced Anomalous Trauma." A bevy of ufologists with no background in clinical psychology who seem to have become instant experts on trauma will lead the discussions. The organizer is Dr. Rima Laibow, who approaches the subject with a mix of enthusiasm and credulity I find alarming. I declined participation since my views, even if I was allowed to speak, would be unwelcome and probably censored.

New York. Tuesday 12 September 1989.

A writer named Lebelson, who used to cover the paranormal for *Omni*, has tracked me down at the Plaza, seeking an endorsement for a book on crashed saucers and Alien bodies. He knows a media figure in New York, "someone whose name and face you'd recognize immediately" who once interviewed Richard Nixon. They spoke on the record about Gorbachev and world developments, after which they relaxed and Nixon informally asked what interested him in life. The man said that as a child he'd seen a UFO over an oil field in California. "Do you believe in them?" asked the former President. "Of course I do," was the answer.

Nixon is said to have walked over to a file cabinet and extracted four pictures of body parts, heads and hands in Mason jars, clearly non-human entities preserved in formaldehyde.

"There's a place where we keep these, and the Russians and the Chinese send us their specimens. It's a storage facility near Dulce, in New Mexico," the President reportedly said.

I asked Lebelson how I could stay in touch with him. He pretended he didn't have a phone, and would only give me his post office box number, so I had to assume the story was just another dangling "meme" or an attempt to send me into blind alleys.

Last night, as soon as I landed, I arranged for dinner with Shel Gordon and his wife at the Manhattan Ocean Club. He shared my analysis of the Soviet situation: all the fine plans that are made for Europe, all the beautiful financial projections and stock market extrapolations could easily come crashing if Gorbachev is unable to push his reforms through.

Today I was on the phone all morning with France and Israel, where Dan Tolkowsky is ready to move on several joint investments. I spent part of the afternoon with Fred Adler who was uncharacteristically warm and paid me some rare compliments. We decided we would not pursue a laser photometer deal with General Motors because we don't seem to be able to find any common ground with their attorneys.

Washington. Arlington Hyatt. Wednesday 13 September 1989.

Before I left New York I had a sad meeting at William Morris when Ned Leavitt told me the news about Bill Whitehead who had been my very bright editor for *Invisible College*: he died of AIDS a few months ago. Walking back towards Central Park (the weather was sunny, putting a twinkle in every girl's eye) I met with Bob Weiss for a quiet working lunch at the nearby Jockey Club. The air is muggy and thick. On the positive side: Bob Chartrand has promised to introduce me to Art Lundahl.

Washington. Thursday 14 September 1989.

This afternoon I met Bob Chartrand at the Friendship Heights metro station. He drove us over to Art Lundahl's house in Bethesda. It is an encounter I won't forget.

Art Lundahl is a hero of the cold war whom CIA director William Colby called "one of the seven greatest spies of all times." Allen Dulles said of him, "He has done as much to protect the security of the nation as any man I know." Now a crippled who needs help to get dressed and can only move in a wheelchair, he has fallen victim of an advanced form of arthritis. He is warm and cheerful in spite of his disability, and his mind remains keen. Lundahl put me at ease immediately, stressing that *Anatomy of a Phenomenon* had been the first sane book he'd read about UFOs.

I had not realized to what extent Lundahl was interested in the topic. While other Intelligence experts like Tom Belden and Frank Pace had only given me encouraging but superficial comments, Lundahl leaned forward in his wheelchair, intertwined the gnarled fingers of his hands and proceeded to tell me of his analyses of the famous Mariana and Newhouse films, of his testimony before the 1953 Robertson Panel, and of his participation in every attempt by the government to analyze the problem. He looked down with skepticism on the various "explanations" provided over the years by academics. The Newhouse (Tremonton) film was certainly not of seagulls, he said: some objects circled the others; one of them left the group, returning at high speed to resume its place. The Mariana (Great Falls) film was also unexplained, he said. The two objects were certainly not aircraft, contrary to the official statements.

It is also in Art Lundahl's office that the famous scene of contact with the AFFA entity took place in 1959. There too, he gave me some new information and denied the story that is circulating in some magazines, notably in Fate:

"It wasn't a *séance* at all," he insisted. But he also stressed something I'd missed: the medium, Mrs. Swann, had met a strange man one morning at church, and that same man had called her later in the day to tell her: "We have chosen you..." He didn't explain what he meant, but the automatic writing started that same day. It is the Vintras pattern again, also the pattern described by Bettina Zerpa and Kathie Davis: absurd, paranormal phenomena centering on one person, triggered by a meeting with a peculiar individual. I despair of ever being able to study this mechanism objectively.

Art has nothing but contempt for Professor Condon, who once came to visit the National Photographic Intelligence Center (NPIC), Lundahl's creation, the legendary institution responsible for the processing of the U-2 pictures that revealed the presence of Soviet missiles in Cuba, among other things.

"Did Condon ask you what you thought of the UFO problem?" I asked Art.

"He wasn't interested at all," he answered with a shrug. "You could tell that he and his administrative assistant, Bob Low, had already reached their conclusion. Condon even said he was going to start with the craziest cases, because they would be the easiest ones to cxplain. That's why he loved to hang around the UFO groups, the weirder the better."

Art was impressed with McDonald, although he quickly recognized that his interest in the subject had turned into a dangerous obsession.

After the Cuban missile crisis, when Art Lundahl personally brought the photographs to Kennedy, he received numerous honors, including a knighthood from Queen Elizabeth. His colleagues humorously dubbed him "Sir Arthur of the Light Table." He also told me the story of his visit to De Gaulle:

"I was sent to the Elysée Palace to show him the U-2 photographs in advance of Krushtchev's visit to France, since he was raising all kinds of hell about Gary Powers, and there was no way we could deny what the plane had been doing over the Soviet Union. De Gaulle was a remarkable man. He remained standing during the whole hour and a half of my presentation. He was alone with me, which surprised me. He did not trust anyone, had not even invited his Intelligence experts into the room. When I left the palace the Soviet limousines were coming in through another entrance. The next day I was told that De Gaulle had asked Krushtchev, "Why are you making so much fuss about that American plane you shot down, when you send all kind of spying equipment over France every day and I don't make a big deal about it?" To which the Soviet leader replied it wasn't so much the aerial photography he was mad about, it was the fact that the aircraft was manned by a human pilot. He thought that made it too efficient, which shows how far behind he was in understanding robots and remotely-controlled devices."

I showed Lundahl the Costa Rica photograph. I held my breath as he looked at it with a magnifying glass, thinking "he's going to tell me it's a picture of a hubcap that fell from the plane's wheel," but he simply handed it back to me with observations that matched what Dick Haines and I had determined after studying the negative.

Lundahl also told me about UFO hardware collected by the CIA. A colleague of his at the Agency had custody of a strange piece of metal that fell from the sky during the 1952 UFO flap. It was smooth on one side and bubbly on the other. The National Bureau of Standards only determined it was "an uncommon alloy." The fellow kept it in his house, wrapped in newspapers. One day, returning after a weekend away from home, he found the paper torn up all over the hallway and discovered the metal was gone, although there was no sign of break-in.

Washington. Friday 15 September 1989.

Today I had breakfast with Ed May (staying at the same hotel) who took me to meet Scott Jones at the Russell Senate office building. We found him in a large office with beautiful red wallpaper and bookcases with glass doors and curtains. There were piles of magazines on the floor. The air conditioning system was broken, so the atmosphere was muggy and uncomfortable. Jones is a tall, distinguished man with white hair, a former Naval officer with a

PhD who can discuss with you the scope of the Pentagon budget, wearing a banker's suit in his Senate office, but will next be found in blue jeans at gatherings of parapsychologists arguing about telepathic communication with dolphins.

I presented Scott Jones with my paper on “Five Arguments” (**15**) and told him I wanted to offer my free services as *Amicus Curiae* (“friend of the Court”) if new Hearings were planned. He didn’t take me up on this offer. Instead he spoke about his experiences in Peru, where he spent time with a group that claims to communicate with Angels: a great wind and the noise of vast wings were heard, he said, after which someone spoke telepathically to an invisible presence.

“Let me ask you a philosophical question,” he said, coming back to our subject. “If the Government has data about UFOs, do you think they should make it public?”

“Data is just data,” I said. “I wouldn’t be surprised if within ten miles of this office there was a building full of records, tapes, photographs, films, and other relevant documents. That doesn't mean that the government has any answers. The ideal scenario would be to first release that data to selected scientific groups.”

“It might be an impeachable offense for the President to keep such knowledge secret from the public, and certainly from Congress,” he went on. I doubted this: “The reality is that any President would demand to know what his options and priorities were before releasing such data. Until now, as far as I can tell, science has never been applied to the phenomenon. That should be the first step. If it has to be done secretly, so be it.”

Scott Jones seemed to turn the question around in his head, and then he said: “Other countries could make it public if they wanted. Or the UFOs themselves....Nobody has ultimate control.”

“The problem with secrecy is that under the classified umbrella it’s too easy for anybody to play games and hide mistakes or ludicrous pet projects. And that's exactly what's happening with those rumors of crashed saucers and gray Aliens,” I pointed out, knowing that he had met Condor and Falcon.

“Disinformation is unavoidable,” answered Scott Jones. “If there's an official project, it must involve a cross-section of humanity, four-star generals to privates, drunks and crooks. They would have to be given a cover story so simple that even the most truthful of deathbed confessions could be discredited, or would lead into blind alleys."

"The deathbed confessions can be manufactured lies, too," I said.

Dale Graff, current DIA monitor for the SRI project, arrived and took a seat near the door. I excused myself and went upstairs to see Orlando "Lan" Potter, Senator Pell's first assistant (in room 335, which was mercifully air-conditioned). I conveyed the greetings of his friend Bob Chartrand, and then I left the building.

Spring Hill. Saturday 16 September 1989.

Another thunderstorm woke me up. It brought the first rain, blue flashes around the tower, the sound of cascades in the new gutters. We got up late and read the accumulated mail: a long letter from Prince Hans-Adam, a request from Rémy Chauvin for Mars pictures, remarks from Gordon Creighton on multi-dimensional models, and lamentable trash from an assortment of New Age magazines. The sky is low, gray, hanging over the observatory like a dripping rag. To put myself into a writing mood I listen to Shostakovich's trio in E Minor, played by Rostropovich.

Last night I flew back from Washington with Ed May, who explained to me his model of paranormal statistics. It leads him, surprisingly, to reject psychokinetic results as chance occurrences, leaving remote viewing as the single psychic phenomenon of scientific interest and applicability today. I brought up Bill Tiller's device based on a gas tube that lights up in response to a thought. He was skeptical: "Those things are so unstable that anything triggers them, even a slight variation in current. Forget any instrumentation that plugs into the wall! People keep designing super-sensitive devices to exhibit psi. They forget it magnifies the physical artifacts."

He is obviously right. When I described to him my meeting with Art Lundahl and reviewed what Scott Jones had said, I reflected that even if some data were released by the President, Congress would have a hard time funding any formal study of UFOs: "The religious groups would never let them get away with it; they would scream about Separation of Church and State!"

"That's what happened with the *Spoonbenders' Bill*, the nickname they gave a few years ago to a similar attempt to get research on the human potential funded through Congress," Ed commented with a chuckle. "It was brought down by Fundamentalist Christians who were leery of Uri Geller."

Ed told me that the psychic project, which has brought SRI an average of $750,000 a year for the last 17 years, is only funded through next February. He is assured of $250,000 and there is another $1.5 million in a budget that will be proposed but may not pass Congress. I admire his patience. Ed is a Jew from Hungary with a keen sense of humor and an ability to manipulate complex statistics that fly beyond my grasp. He wants to move the project out of SRI.

Hyde Street. Sunday 17 September 1989.

Now I look back at my meeting with Lundahl, who probably has the highest clearances of anyone I know, with the possible exception of Paul Joyal, in charge of security for the Senate Select Committee on Intelligence, the fellow who served the subpoena on Colonel Oliver North. Art is a man whose professional activity consisted in scanning the remote corners of the entire planet to pick out anomalies, a man who was open-minded enough to realize that the UFO phenomenon was a reality: wouldn't he know if there was a secret project dedicated to its study? And if so, wouldn't our conversation have taken a different turn? I wouldn't expect him to come right out and tell me I'm wasting my time, or reveal any secrets, but he might have avoided the subject altogether; or he might have hinted that he didn't want to discuss certain things.

If Lundahl is unaware of a black project, if Kit has come up with nothing, if Admiral Houser and General Johnny Johnson strongly deny ever being briefed about any high-level UFO threat, that leaves me with no evidence, not even the hint that a black project is active. But what about "Jim Irish?" Who was he working for? What about

Valerie Ransone? What about the people who brought Castillo to the United States and grilled him for several days about his experiences?

Perhaps there is a project so black it could operate without a need for the extraordinary skills of Art Lundahl, the arcane knowledge of Kit, the military lines of command of Houser and Johnson? But the latter was also in charge of all communications for the White House for several years, and it's hard to believe he would not have been aware of something, even in the absence of any direct military threat.

I am as puzzled as ever: there is evidence of a large disinformation campaign. It must be designed to cover-up something, but when I peer behind the fence I can find no trace of what it is supposed to be covering up.

The "Jim Irish" task force could have represented a data-gathering effort on the part of AFOSI or NSA. The Castillo interrogation could have been a simple NRO or CIA rogue operation. There is no evidence that any American data-gathering effort was active in Brazil at the time of Project PRATO when UFOs were performing near-landings at Colares every night.

If there were an Alintel, thousands of people throughout the military and intelligence community around the world would have to be alerted to channel UFO information in certain directions. It could not function in a vacuum. By now, we should see some external evidence of it. Even John Alexander has found nothing.

Hyde Street. Thursday 21 September 1989.

On Wednesday night Jenny Randles had dinner at our home. I had invited Fred Beckman, so we spent an enjoyable evening catching up with various events and discussing the Bentwaters case. Most interesting was Jenny's story of being approached to leak certain documents that were eventually published by Timothy Good. They included tales about Aliens and autopsies performed by a certain doctor named Houser.

Today I called Kit about a business question and we ended up debating last night's *Unsolved Mysteries* television show that once again hyped the Roswell incident. The story is full of contradictions:

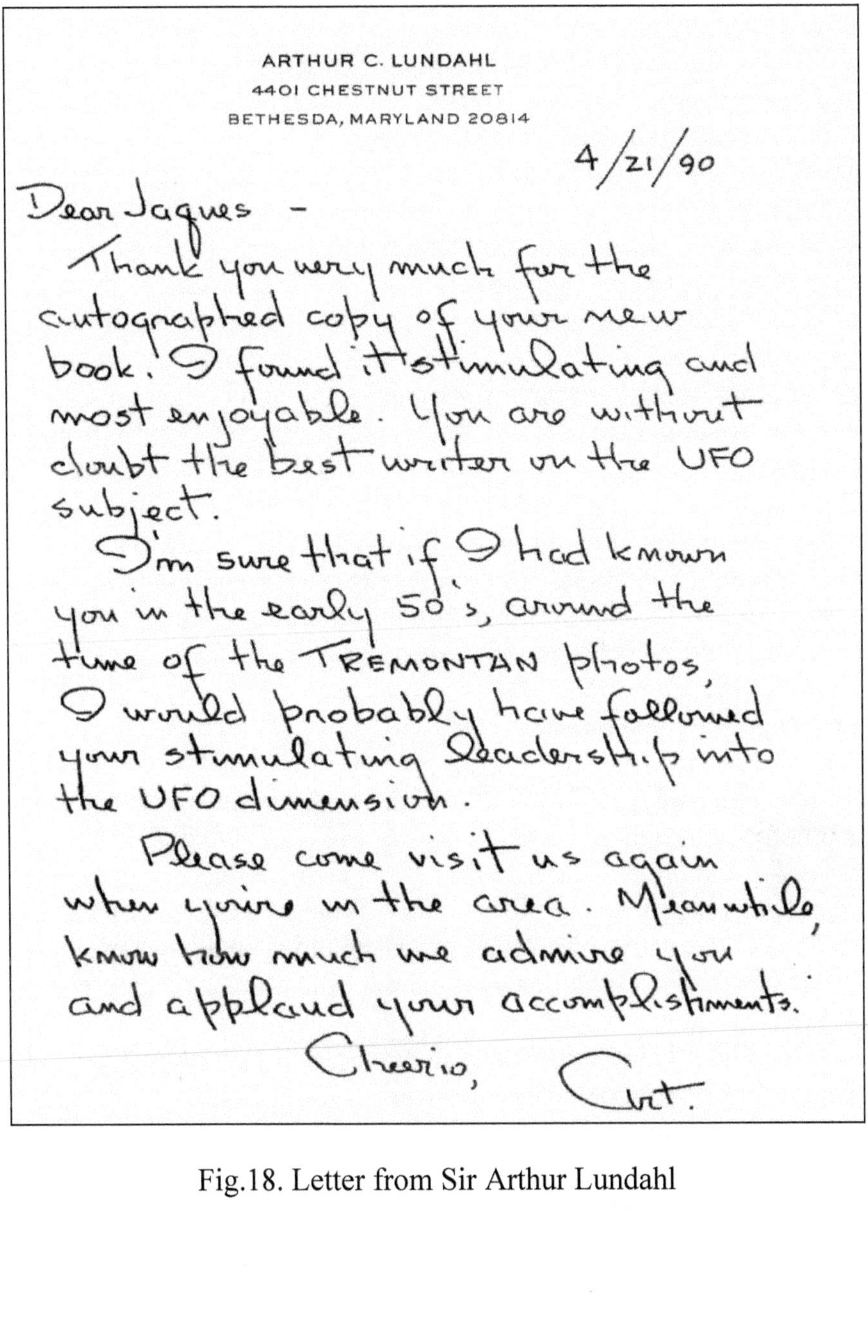

ARTHUR C. LUNDAHL
4401 CHESTNUT STREET
BETHESDA, MARYLAND 20814

4/21/90

Dear Jaques -

Thank you very much for the autographed copy of your new book. I found it stimulating and most enjoyable. You are without doubt the best writer on the UFO subject.

I'm sure that if I had known you in the early 50's, around the time of the TREMONTAN photos, I would probably have followed your stimulating leadership into the UFO dimension.

Please come visit us again when you're in the area. Meanwhile, know how much we admire you and applaud your accomplishments.

Cheerio,
Art.

Fig.18. Letter from Sir Arthur Lundahl

One site or two? Bodies or none? Kit was struck by the fact that none of the people who claimed to have seen and carried cadavers mentioned any odors. In his forensic experience the stench is the overwhelming feature of all disaster sites. The most important thing Kit told me concerned his follow-up of the information he had been given about a certain project inside the Pentagon.

"Either I have solved the problem, or I have found the cover story," he told me. He did go to the office he had been encouraged to visit.

"It's on a back corridor, in an area where the signs on the wall read 'your person is subject to search and seizure. Deadly force authorized.' There's an office that serves as the entrance to a suite of about 40 rooms over 3 floors, with a hospital unit at the bottom. A vertical column links these three floors and there is no other access. None of the personnel are listed in the Pentagon directory, except for one fellow, a Captain, who appeared in 1983 with his correct function, and it had nothing to do with UFOs..."

In the maddening complexity of the story, one could argue that this "black" program, which relates to the Air Force space ventures including stealth technology and low-observable objects, could easily be confused by believers for a secret extraterrestrial project. Is this under Petraski?

At the same time, if someone had an Alintel-type program, the best way to camouflage it would be to put it within an Air Force space project that is already classified at a high level and has existed for some time, just like the Glomar Explorer was camouflaged within ocean mining and mineral exploration.

Kit has confronted two high-level (sub-Cabinet) people, members of the Board overseeing the program. They didn't laugh when he said, "There are folks out there talking about your work having to do with UFOs."

They told him, "There might be something to that," adding they didn't know what to think, they had heard rumors from the inside, they didn't have information, they didn't know if it took a special clearance...

Playing games with him.

Hyde Street. Saturday 30 September 1989.

It is time I simplified my life. We had another example of the world's bitter absurdity when Diane came here last Wednesday and told us her story. We were shocked to find her changed, tired and weary. She was visibly upset when she described her situation with Anton and Zeena, although her daughter manages to keep good relations with both of them.

Diane left Anton five years ago. His attorney now claims "she was never more than an employee of the Church, whom Dr. LaVey was kind enough to shelter. It is thanks to him that she has met the important people who have provided her with employment..." When she ran away, she did get a job from David Werby, a San Francisco real estate man who was one of Anton's close associates.

We went over to noisy, youthful TGIF for dinner. Over pot stickers and burgers, Diane told us she had brought many boxes of notes to her new home and was busy sorting them out. She thinks of compiling a book of memoirs. Janine advised her to secure her papers, to take precautions. She wasn't worried, she replied, not afraid of Anton: "I believe, as he does, that curses only work against those who deserve them!"

On Thursday afternoon I had coffee with Loren Gross, a teacher turned auto mechanic whose real hobby is history. He is compiling the most formidable, scholarly, documented encyclopedia on the UFO phenomenon, starting in 1896.

Yesterday, before an Interfax Board meeting, Paul Baran pulled me into his office. Steve Millard had sent him my paper on *Five Arguments*. Now Paul is drawing some clear conclusions: the nocturnal distribution of close encounters and abductions clearly points to the dreamstate as the important factor in these sightings, he says. Furthermore, what about globular lightning? He saw such a phenomenon as a kid and has never forgotten it. I replied that if UFOs were ever studied scientifically one might indeed find that chunks of the phenomenon could be explained through psychosocial factors including dreams and visions; a few others would turn out to be earthquake lights or plasmas. But I contend there would be a hard residue of real UFO stories. The challenge is to find them:

"If you came to this planet and you only had a sense of hearing, how would you ever find that there is such a thing as classical music? You would catalogue the noises of rivers, storms, wind, helicopters and jets, people talking, birds singing..." I said.

"You could detect intelligence," answered Baran. "Any periodic or non-random sound would suggest purpose. The sound of a jet indicates intelligence. Of course you'd make mistakes. When pulsars were first detected, they were thought to be artificial beacons."

"But how could you tell that the noises around an airport are culturally different from Mahler's *Fifth*, from Varèse, or some of the cutting edge heavy metal rock music?" I asked.

Rear-Admiral Houser joined us. The most interesting fact for me was the observation that here were two of the men I would want to have on my board if I ran an official UFO study, yet how little they knew of the real state of the problem! I despair of conveying the meaning of the experience to someone who hasn't gone through it.

Later I had a phone conversation with Hal, who was returning from Palo Alto where he had met with Lockheed physicists, including Blackburn. He told me his super-electron project was "ready to go big time." He was invited to brief a high-technology committee of the Defense Department, the same group that was responsible for initiating stealth technology. They decided that Hal's proposals would take precedence over optical computing. In October he will brief the inter-agency technical assessment group about his experiments, including energy production.

One of the factors precipitating this decision is the observation that the Soviets and the Bulgarians are on to the same thing. They've experimented with plasma streamers at various energy levels and they have found the same kind of Casimir compactification of the charge detected by Ken Shoulders, a phenomenon Puthoff explains in terms of conversion of vacuum energy. There is some suspicion that the Soviets are planning to put a gigawatt generator into orbit using this principle, so Hal cannot continue to sit on the "confidential" applications of his ideas.

There is a project brewing that will link China Lake Naval weapons with Darpa and Hal's Jupiter group, with an initial contract of a few hundred thousand dollars for replication experiments, initially in the radar domain. Hal is also negotiating with a large private company to pursue the energy idea, under an exclusive agreement. "All the reviews of the technology so far have been positive," he claims. "With less than one milliJoule we've demonstrated we could punch a hole in ceramics, which would exhibit ten times the energy we put in. We're not certain of the precise factor because we don't know exactly how much of the ceramics has been liquefied as opposed to vaporized, but the phenomenon is there in either case."

He wants me to become involved again in finding companies interested in discussing licenses with Jupiter for RF generators in the 90 Gigahertz range, for novel medical X-ray units and flat panel displays. He's convinced that his theory can explain my observations about UFO physical factors, including the differences in size of the disks (the inside being larger than the outside) and physiological effects:

"One simple thing would explain all that," he claims. "If they follow the mechanism I have in mind they must be manipulating the dielectric constant of the vacuum. They could take ambient heat and blue shift the energy into ultraviolet and soft X-rays that would also produce the injuries you describe. The same variations explain the beam and the time and dimensional contraction. All they have to do is shrink the external metric. They can turn a 300 foot craft into a 100 foot object or even smaller."

I asked him what he thought of John Alexander, his beliefs about telepathy with dolphins, dead Aliens at the bottom of the ocean...

"You can't blame the guy for trying everything he can think of," he replied. "Alexander is well-regarded as a good action officer. He has gotten support from people at the Space command and at Norad who agree to join his project if it's ever formed. His new job is to bring Defense money to Los Alamos. The lab suffers from cuts in nuclear work. He deals with real-world stuff every day: armor-piercing charges, super chemicals. It's from that position that he asked me to give a briefing at Los Alamos."

Spring Hill. Saturday 7 October 1989.

All day I have felt pleasantly lazy. This afternoon, as I was cataloging dusty science books in the tower, Janine came over and had no trouble seducing me. The wonderful thing about Spring Hill is a peculiar sense of time created by the awareness that we could survive indefinitely here, without ever returning to the world. The only thing missing here is evidence of phenomena we could put under the scrutiny of a scientific project: I have to confess that my information experiments have not brought us closer to a validation of my hypotheses.

Kit has sent me two reports from Lear's group with a handwritten note penned on the beautiful letterhead of the Hong Kong Sheraton:

> Either this shit is true—or there are very delusional people out there. I read *Majestic*. I'm still banking that Whitley is on the way to not being able to buy coffee at Seven-Eleven.

I answer:

> I agree with you that in a few years Whitley won't buy coffee at Seven-Eleven. He won't have to. His disciples of the Communion Foundation will come and pick him up every morning in a white limousine to treat him to a Champagne breakfast. They will sing hymns to him as he sprinkles sugar on his strawberries, while you and I try to figure out the meaning of the Cosmos at Denny's over soggy sandwiches.

How typical of my friend Kit, that he would write to me on some fancy hotel stationery he picked up in Hong Kong on his way back from Bangkok to tell me the world is crazy, as if I didn't know it!

The report under John Lear's signature again rehashes Bill English's supposed recollections of *Report 13*, including an analysis of Alien autopsies by Hynek and "Lt-Col" Friend. The whole thing is not only absurd but sloppy and stupid: Hynek was never involved in any autopsies and Friend was only a Major in 1953.

My French partners have been in California all week: I flew back with them after spending Monday with Fred Adler in a Fulbright-Jaworski conference room, 42 floors above Park Avenue. We visited several companies, including the laboratories of Harmonic Lightwaves where we saw the first high-precision laser for fiberoptic television transmission.

We met with Paul Baran at Interfax and discussed an investment with Dr. Philippe Pouletty, a brilliant researcher from the Pasteur Institute, the developer of the first French test for AIDS.

The early attempt at an operational launch by the American Rocket Company has been a tragic failure. The device, which carried a Defense Department satellite, developed a valve problem half a second after ignition.

Bob Weiss, who was in the bunker at the time, tells me they tried to shut down the rocket engine but a computer that controlled the steering kicked in three seconds later, injecting hydrogen peroxide into the nozzle. Everything blew up: "The fire went up along the fuel lines, the epoxy started burning. The rocket broke up and fell like a tree in the forest." It will be six to eight months before they can test another rocket.

20

Hyde Street. Monday 9 October 1989.

Columbus Day. My knowledgeable friend, journalist Holly Newman just called from the editorial offices of the *Wall Street Journal* in New York: She was puzzled by a sensational dispatch from Associated Press, originating with their Moscow correspondent, reporting that "Soviet scientists have confirmed the landing of an Alien spaceship carrying giant people with tiny heads (!)"

The incident described in this obviously garbled report is said to have happened in Voronezh, 300 miles southeast of Moscow. The beings were said to be four meters tall and accompanied by a small robot. The craft, which first appeared as a large shining ball, left a depression in the earth. The witnesses were "filled with fear" for days, an observation that may hint at physiological effects. The chief of the local geophysical laboratory, Genrikh Silanov, stated that the depression was 20 meters wide, with four indentations, and that two unidentified rocks had been recovered, resembling sandstone. Mineralogical analysis is said to have disclosed they were "not of this earth." All this is astonishing, coming as it does from Soviet sources, even if the unscientific language ("alien spaceship", rocks "not of this earth") sounds very suspect.

Later the same day.

Some additional insights from Kit, whom I have just alerted to the Voronezh landing: (i) In recent months Tass has run several such stories, but the Western media have not picked them up. He is surprised that this one comes straight from AP.

(ii) The President of Penn State, a highly respected scientist named Eric Walker, is said to have written letters to several people asking them to be quiet about his past role within MJ-12.

Kit is trying to get copies of these letters: which version of MJ-12 is in question here?

(iii) There's nothing new with Dr. William Crowley of Lancaster, who was alleged to have performed autopsies on Alien bodies. Kit points out again that the man is not a pathologist, therefore he could not have done such procedures himself anyway, but he may have been asked to provide expertise as a thoracic surgeon who was also a cleared Air Force consultant.

The autopsies are said to have been performed in the basement of the Guggenheim Foundation in New York City.

(iv) There is supposed to be a meeting on October 18th between someone "very high in the White House" and a mysterious senator and his aide to discuss MJ-12. Allegedly the White House man will be accompanied by Doty, who will bring the mysterious Yellow Book: everything about this absurd business is "mysterious"!

(v) Kit still fails to find any confirmation from the people he trusts within the system, but no one laughs at these questions any more. "A few years ago this kind of inquiry would have been met with suspicion about my sanity. Today what I get is an answer like: 'We can't confirm that there is a study on actual Aliens, and we're not doing any such study ourselves, but we've heard the same rumors'."

I continue to think we witness the spreading of a conversion phenomenon. In Scott Jones' office I was struck by the fervor with which he approached the subject. The same fervor now exists in many people associated with this topic.

Kit told me that a friend of his had recently paid a visit to the secure facility on the fifth floor of the Pentagon. The signs about "deadly force" have been removed. The project, he reported, did what it was supposed to do: aerial coverage against certain types of threats. It had nothing to do with UFOs.

Hyde Street. Tuesday 10 October 1989.

The Voronezh story is having a remarkable impact in the world media. I should arrange to go to Russia and check it, instead of relying on rumors distorted by American journalists. Every newspaper and radio broadcast is quoting it, putting an ironic or negative spin on it. In San Francisco, KCBS placed a phone call to skeptic Paul Kurtz, who mocked the lack of hard evidence: extraterrestrial civilizations might well exist, he said, but the two strange rocks reported by the Russians sounded to him like simple pieces of "outer-space crap."

Elsewhere the story was explained as an unfortunate aberration, a remote consequence of *Glasnost*. A scientific "expert" pointed out that if such an event had actually happened Gorbachev would have announced it personally. For good measure the reporter went on to interview two disciples from the Aetherius Society, formally attired in suits and ties, spewing New Age nonsense.

Spring Hill. Sunday 15 October 1989.

Autumn colors in the trees, glorious sun over the observatory tower. Last night Janine lit the first logs of the year. I resume the catalogue of our research library and the writing of *Revelations*, with the feeling that I am backing into this book rather than facing the troublesome issues it raises. I am puzzled by the Voronezh case, coming as it does at such a unique time in Russian history. My mother tells me that the French media have been silent about the case, except for one report on radio and limited TV coverage.

Whitley recently appeared on Good Morning America, presenting his novel *Majestic*. The network had invited Stuart Goldman, who attacked his credibility in the case of the Texas tower massacre: at the time, Strieber had described the incident in the first person, as if he had been an actual witness. The debate continued with an exposé of Whitley on *Inside Edition*. He reportedly had told "Kathie Davis" he'd seen her severed head on a shelf aboard a flying saucer! Whitley claims this is a dirty lie circulated by Budd Hopkins. Now everybody threatens to sue everybody else...

I prepare our trip to Europe: first, London to see my new publisher, then Holland and France where my work calls for meetings with entrepreneurs in several cities, finally to Switzerland and Liechtenstein at the invitation of Prince Hans-Adam.

Hyde Street. Wednesday 18 October 1989.

Yesterday afternoon Colonel John Alexander from Los Alamos came over to my office in Menlo Park to discuss his UFO research plans following the failure of the Secret Onion project. I found that we had similar, skeptical viewpoints on *Majestic* and the so-called Alien presence. He has reached the same conclusions as Kit and me concerning the rumors spread around by Lear, Cooper, and the others. We spoke about Dulce, the likelihood that there could be a hidden facility in New Mexico, and the sightings his friends had made in the area: they did track an object that disappeared from view with the naked eye but was still visible in the infrared scopes.

As we discussed MJ-12 my office started shaking and we looked at each other: "Earthquake!" I said with the assurance of a veteran Californian, expecting things to return to normal. It was 5:04 pm.

But things did not return to normal at all. The office kept shaking harder, floor buckling, windows rattling, curtains waving wildly. I plunged under the table and John, who had gotten up and braced himself in the doorway, recognized he could hardly stand up and joined me in the fragile shelter of the desk. When the rolling stopped we brushed ourselves off and we decided to get out before any aftershocks.

"That was a good one, I said, between six and seven." **(16)**
While I was trying to look brave and unconcerned, privately I was thinking, "How bad was it in San Francisco? Where is Janine? Is she hurt?" The people who left the building with us were pale and shaking. Large waves sloshed around the concrete fountains outside, much of the water spilled over. In the yard the waterfalls were idle, the pumps had stopped, and everything was silent.

It took me two hours to get home. The freeways were increasingly congested as I neared San Francisco, yet there was no panic, drivers demonstrating extraordinary discipline everywhere. At major intersections where traffic lights were dead, I was amazed to see people motioning politely to each other to insure everyone could pass. The radio stations that were still on the air were assessing the damage.

The picture of the real disaster slowly emerged. Increasingly, as I heard about the scope of the catastrophe, I worried about Janine and the state of our home. A section of the Bay Bridge had collapsed, killing several people. Fortunately I knew the City well enough to leave the freeway and make a big arc to the West, away from the congested business center. I slowly negotiated the smaller streets around Twin Peaks. From the top of the hill I saw an ominous column of black smoke rising to the north. News reporters located it not far from Hyde Street, in the Marina district, where several blocks were burning out of control. I reached our area and parked in front of the house, relieved to see that nothing had moved along our block, which had survived the even more devastating 1906 earthquake.

Janine was home safe. At the time of the quake she had been driving a few blocks away, she told me. She had first thought that her tires had blown up. The only damage we found was a large bronze lamp above her desk, which was thrown onto the floor, its two light bulbs broken.

I thought gratefully of the skills of the architects who built this Victorian out of redwood back in 1901.

We wanted to go out again on foot, talk to our neighbors and be around people, to see if we could help. The phone was out of service, all lights out. We reached the Marina and discovered the full extent of the disaster: leaning buildings, collapsed houses, and exploded sidewalks spewing pools of water and sand, with the smell of gas everywhere. In the darkness people were walking aimlessly or listening to the news on portable radios, simply stunned. Several blocks were still burning when we made our way out of the area, realizing that gas explosions could take place at any time.

We moved over to darkened, stunned Lombard Street and came back home. Janine found some candles. The phone service had been restored but it was heavily overloaded. I waited a long time for the dial tone and called Catherine in Boulder, putting her in charge of calling our family before they could hear the alarming news of the catastrophe on the morning broadcast in France.

Now I write this by candlelight while Janine tries to reach Spring Hill to find out if the ranch has suffered. I haven't gone back to work. The City has the mood of a place under siege. It will be many days before all the bodies are extracted from the twisted cars under the collapsed sections of freeway, weeks before the Bay Bridge reopens, months before all the debris is cleaned up, years before life in the Marina comes to resemble what it was just two days ago.

Full realization of the blow has not yet set in. In the Tenderloin small groups huddle in doorways, police cars and fire trucks race in all directions, their sirens at full blast, their spinning lights blazing along the facades of the dark buildings, crushed glass scintillating on the road in the glare of my headlights. The air is warm and stale.

Smoke chokes the whole region. The unnerving whir of generators comes to us from Fisherman's Wharf.

Hyde Street. Thursday 19 October 1989.

Power was restored to our block this afternoon. Although we rejoice to see life coming back to San Francisco, and thank our good fortune that we came through the event without a scratch, we find ourselves irritable and depressed.

Friendships get strengthened in such an ordeal: Morgane came by during the day to see how we were. Richard Niemtzow was among the first to call. He told me that the French were seriously investigating the Soviet reports. Not only is Jean-Jacques launching an investigation, but the French secret service is doing the same thing. Velasco has seen Payan again: "The more I know this man, the stranger he seems," Jean-Jacques said.

My French colleagues kindly offered to postpone my next business visit but there would be no purpose in my staying in San Francisco: work here will be disorganized for a long time.

London. Bloomsbury. Monday 23 October 1989.

In Ernest Hecht's large publishing office, with its windows facing the British Museum, the news about *Dimensions* is heartening: two English book clubs have re-ordered it massively, the hardcover has been reprinted, and Sphere is bringing out the paperback.

I enjoy the busy, massive little building of Souvenir Press where Hecht hobbles in his white sweater, bossing around a small commando of spinsters. There are theater posters on the walls, porno books on the floor, and whispered claims that frequent poltergeists open and close the doors mysteriously.

Last night we spoke of such mysteries with Hilary Evans at *L'Entrecôte*. With his flowery white beard and long hair, his purple sweater and tales of occult lore he offered an uncanny resemblance to my stained glass picture of Abbot Trithemius, the genial 15th-century scholar, librarian, and occultist. Hilary is one of the better skeptics of ufology, but when we push him he admits that many cases defy analysis and launches into stories that are even weirder than those he professes to debunk: he studies a woman who seems to turn off street lights psychically as she walks down the street.

Janine and I spent the first night at the Hotel Russell. We had fun watching the ponderous processions of English matrons, secure in their gray raincoats, carrying large purses over their shoulders, filing into the carvery like a conquering army.

At the British Museum I ran into the former president of Sector Technology. I had recommended to his board that he be replaced. He was actually enjoying being discharged of his responsibilities, and didn't bear any grudge against me.

The night is mild, with the smell of fresh rain on dead leaves. I write in bed, in one of those beautiful French hardbound copybooks I get from a stationery store on *Rue Monge*. It is finely lined and guides the pen easily to its destination at the end of every sentence. Janine pretends to be reading Morris Berman's boring and confusing book *Coming to our Senses*, but I feel her slowly falling asleep. Nobody knows we are here. We are at peace with the world.

Paris. Rue de la Clef. Wednesday 25 October 1989.

Last night we went out hunting for that rare and wonderful thing, an apartment in Paris. We walked along *Rue du Cherche-Midi* and made our way towards the *Institut*. Older flats here now cost $2,300 per square meter ($230 per square foot) and newer ones reach $430, in the same price range as our house in Belmont.

The weather is delightful; there is a festive smell in the air. The shops offer every fashion, every delicacy, every form of art.

Les Ulis. Later the same day.

In the bistrot near the train station I am waiting for an executive from Gixi, a manufacturer of computer screens with innovative graphics capabilities. Warm, somewhat close weather, no wind, smoke hanging in the air over Paris.

This morning at Laffont they gave me the good news: *Dimensions* comes out tomorrow (under the French title *Autres Dimensions*). They are getting excellent response from the media, with many press interviews scheduled for next week.

Lille. Hotel de la Paix. Friday 27 October 1989.

White haze dragged across the airfield last night when I flew here from Nantes. In a great burst of enthusiasm Gabriel Mergui, my French colleague, has planned visits to companies all over, so we began the trip before dawn and finished late.

When I reached Janine in Paris she told me the exciting news: after looking energetically all over the map she has found an apartment near Mabillon, in *Saint-Germain-des-Prés*. It was past midnight when I reached our banker in San Francisco, instructing him to transfer enough money to cover our deposit.

Another café, another train station, another little square full of sunlight and noisy cars. I am eating a snack before my appointment with Payan at the Armament's technical center. This morning at the *Arts et Métiers* School in Lille I spent several hours with a group of engineers who have patented a clever system of non-circular gears.

Lille has the same majesty I remember from the two years I spent there, 30 years ago, learning programming and astronomy. They have improved the square in front of the train station, with happy fountains and bright flags. A rare sun even made an appearance.

Paris. Rue de la Clef. Saturday 28 October 1989.

We're about to go over to make a deposit on the apartment. We will also pick up our tickets for Liechtenstein, and the first twenty copies of *Autres Dimensions*. At noon M. Chéreau, an investigator for *Lumières dans la Nuit*, will take us to lunch with Joël Mesnard and his wife. He promised we'd drive to Pontoise together.

Yesterday I met Jean-Jacques Velasco at the guardhouse to the *Etablissement Technique Central de l'Armement*, and he introduced me to Gilbert Payan. It turns out he was once the head of R&D at

Creusot-Loire and a member of the Sofinnova advisory board, so we were on familiar territory. We discussed Voronezh. When I mentioned that the object may have sported the Ummo symbol on its side, Velasco and Payan said this confirmed their suspicions about KGB influence over the saga of the friendly Ummites. That may also explain why *Messengers of Deception* is banned in the Soviet Union.

Next we talked about Trans-en-Provence. I gave them the results of our micro-analysis of the soil samples, which proves that Nicolai told the truth and the traces were truly unexplained. We talked about Niemtzow and Poher. Payan clearly has some latitude in military research and is close to the French secret service. After Jean-Jacques left, he took me on a tour of the lab's power lasers. It turned out he knew George Bret, and used some of the research instruments built by his company, which we have financed.

Paris. A bistrot. Sunday 29 October 1989.

A slow, sad weekend. I am eating a snack and lamenting the grayness of the streets. For some foolish fashion reason all the women in Paris believe they must dress in mournful black this year: so much for the *filles de joie*! This is Sunday; most cafés are closed, adding to the depressing atmosphere. This place is full of wicked women dressed like widows, having a quick apéritif to chase away the slight chill of the rain that has replaced yesterday's warm sunshine.

Dusk is already falling. Many people have left Paris. Next week is All Saints' Day, which means time off from school for the kids, big family meals, and fresh chrysanthemums on family graves. Back in San Francisco they're celebrating Halloween. On the phone from Normandy Janine told me she missed Spring Hill.

I went back to Mabillon to take some pictures of the building. Miraculously, Janine has located the ideal Paris hideaway: a one bedroom apartment full of light on the 7th floor, with a small entrance, a toilet, a bathroom, a fairly large kitchen; windows opening on the *Boulevard Saint-Germain* in front, on the towers of Saint-Sulpice in the back; the subway is at the door, next to a taxi station; there are three Métro lines, a Post Office and a swimming pool, all within two blocks, with an ice cream shop right below, the celebrated market of *Rue de Buci* and a bank across the street, restaurants and cafés everywhere... one cannot imagine a more strategic location.

Later the same day.

At lunch yesterday in Brétigny with Joël and Hélène Mesnard and Roger Chéreau, who are doing some of the best investigative work anywhere, we learned that French UFO research is at a low point. No more than half a dozen people are going into the field any more. Most of the work rests with intellectuals like Petrakis, Lagrange and others who represent a subtle form of skepticism, or a few armchair researchers doing nothing but statistics. All the talk, here as in America, concerns speculation about the Pentagon and breathless gossip about the Aliens, ridiculously named *Les Petits Gris*. In French "*petits gris*" designates a type of *escargots*, snails found as a delicacy in the best restaurants.

Later in the afternoon Chéreau took us to Pontoise. We drove to the *Justice Mauve* where we verified it would indeed have been easy for a team on a psychological warfare exercise to use the small tunnel under the road to gain direct access to the parking lot where Franck Fontaine mysteriously reappeared after his one-week "abduction."

We drove back down *Rue de Gisors*, which I didn't recognize at first with all the new construction, and we went up the hill above my old school to the house of Marceau Sicaud, a 60-year old man who told me he had lived in Pontoise since his birth in 1927 and remembered my parents: "I met your father at the Courthouse. Your mother was a tall, active woman who walked very straight, didn't she? She used to go to the same pastry shop where we bought our bread..."

I told him my father was dead but my mother was still alive and living in Paris, even if she walked a little bit less straight today. In Sicaud's living room adorned with copies of Impressionist paintings and a fine watercolor original of Saint Maclou church we spent two hours with Franck Fontaine, the alleged abductee. Another witness, Salomon N'Diaye joined us after the first hour, looking very dapper in a nice brown suit. They hadn't seen each other for six years.

Franck is dynamic, nervous, a bit frail. He wears his black hair in purposeful disarray to demonstrate his contempt for society. He hung his black leather jacket on the side of an armchair. His energy reminded me of the young Uri Geller of SRI days. He insisted that I must address him familiarly as "tu."

We asked Franck how he was doing. He felt some pain when he was around people, he answered, hinting that he had become psychic: he would have us believe that his body interiorizes other people's miseries. We started talking about the case. He earnestly assured me that he had no idea where he had spent the famous week. When Roger asked him if he could have been the victim of a manipulation rather than abduction by true Aliens, he said that was possible. Salomon, on the contrary, completely rejected that idea. He spoke as if he knew more about the phenomenon than Franck did:

"We can't say all the things we know..." he insisted with dark hints of higher knowledge. "Let me put it this way: if I knew you could go to a certain place and have certain experiences I wouldn't say it, because you're not ready."

Across the room Franck was laughing: "We sure weren't ready either!" he said.

I went away having enjoyed the conversation. Salomon's superior airs are irrelevant. Franck is the one with whom I feel affinity. He has some good energy; he is a small-time crook but a very unlucky one: when he "borrowed" a little car to drive home one night he picked a cheap, unnoticeable 2CV Citroën no one would ever miss... But it was the prize possession of a well-known French movie star! Poor Franck Fontaine landed in the slammer the next morning.

Zurich. Hotel Arc Royal. Thursday 2 November 1989.

After our last appointment this morning I left my investment colleagues on *Rue Réaumur*, in that busy area near the Opera where the headquarters of all the big French banks are concentrated and I declared myself on vacation.

I have been working hard. On Monday we had flown to Geneva to review the European telephony market and we had driven back to Lyon for more meetings, phone calls, reports to prepare. Yesterday we were in Amsterdam and Utrecht, under gray clouds and drizzle, visiting biotechnology companies. Europe is awakening to an explosive future. Everywhere we find scientists anxious to build new things; unfortunately there are few financial experts capable of calculating the risks of their proposals, and even fewer managers who can provide the business skills a young company needs.

Paris also was gray today, dressed in proper All Saints sorrow and austerity. I walked along the Boulevards, bought a few books and ordered a lunch of Frankfort sausages and French fries at the Capitole. Next to me were two pale girls with straight hair, wearing pants, early 30s. One of them was recounting a train trip during which she travelled with a handsome man who had his little boy with him. The child played with her; when they reached their destination the man helped her down with her suitcase. On the platform some fellow named Dédé, who had come to meet her, took umbrage at the scene and got mad because she stepped out of the train with this man and his boy, "giving the wrong impression."

She proceeded to repeat this story four or five times, using practically identical terms. The other girl listened patiently, nodding her head. I never found out what happened to "Dédé" but I marvelled that people could become so utterly obsessed in details, absorbed in one little episode. It reminded me of Raymond Queneau's *Exercices de Style*, in which he tells the same story of a tall gangly man seen aboard a bus, a hundred times, in slightly different literary styles. Such is human life, an insignificant story squeezed of its puny content again and again and again.

Liechtenstein. Schloss Vaduz. Saturday 4 November 1989.

Sleep comes easily behind the walls of this massive castle. From our guest room we can see the courtyard, the base of the huge keep (a

12th century square tower, walls four meter thick) and the cannons guarding the valley. To the west, towards Switzerland, the outer wall hangs over a sheer precipice, the town of Vaduz and the Rhine far below. To the east the mountain rises all the way to Austria.

As soon as we arrived there were people to greet us. Prince Hans-Adam appeared, wearing a blue open shirt and beige trousers. We had lunch in the smaller dining room with the family: the Prince's wife, his sister, two of his children. Coffee was served in a drawing room. Conversation about various paranormal topics began over lunch and continued well into the afternoon.

We walked through the garden, watching great dark and light patches in the sky agitated by the warm Foehn wind that blows from Italy.

Janine and I drove down to Vaduz to visit the museum, where the reigning family regularly sends some of its painting collection—currently a large room full of huge Rubens and a series of smaller, but equally gorgeous Bruegels, one of our favorite artists.

At five o'clock Prince Hans-Adam graciously met us again. He offered to give us a private tour of the castle including the large square tower and two huge round towers added early in the 16th century.

The family collections include arms (pistols and muskets and cannons of various kinds, an ancestor of the Prince having set the international standards for artillery some time before the wars of Napoleon), porcelain and glasses, ivory and bronze, and an astonishing room where paintings hung on both sides of mobile partitions, 19 on each side; each one of these panels carried 10 to 20 paintings and would have done honor to the best museums. The room contains the largest collection of van Dycks in the world, as well as some works on fragile wood panels that are never seen outside— notably the splendid portrait of Rubens' sons.

We had dinner at seven, after meeting Hans-Adam's brother Louis who had just obtained his medical degree in Zurich. The Prince's other brother Nicholas joined us in the drawing room after dinner. A fine mist had begun condensing into light rain when we resumed our talks about paranormal phenomena, which lasted until midnight.

Breakfast was served in our room this morning. A silent servant spread it on the table, silver spoons with the arms of Liechtenstein on both sides of each cup. Prince Hans-Adam told Janine he had become interested in the subject of UFOs following a sighting by one of his aunts near Munich in the fifties. A few months later a cousin also observed an unusual object. The most interesting part of the discussion with Prince Hans-Adam had to do with history, specifically the history of secret knowledge. He spoke simply, with a smart grasp of the subject:

"It is as if Mankind, periodically, rose towards a peak of enlightenment and wisdom and then fell again into bloody wars and anarchy," he said.

We spoke at length of the control system idea. Could we ever graduate from such a system?

I measured how little progress we had made in the last 15 years. We do have a lot more data but we have not improved either our ability to organize it, or our theoretical framework to understand it. Those who have made sensational claims of an imminent breakthrough: Strieber, Hopkins, Moore, and Lear, have rapidly disqualified themselves. Hans-Adam listened kindly to the facts I presented to him about the inconsistencies of the extraterrestrial argument.

I mentioned my visit to Lundahl. The Prince told us he had made similar inquiries and came back with the same empty net. Yet when he discussed the phenomenon he still spoke in the same terms as before, heavily biased towards the abductionist view: he insists it seems we are visited by a race that lacks certain vital features. Aren't they aiming at creating hybrids of human, animal, and insect life?

"People listen to you," Janine told me later, "but they go on believing whatever they want to believe, as if you had not given them new evidence to think about…"

Prince Hans-Adam is spending small amounts of money (a few tens of thousands of dollars, he said) validating experiments in free energy that, he claims, are generating more watts than are put in.

George Hathaway, who is well-qualified, is in charge of these validations. I hope it is clear to Prince Hans-Adam that I am not looking for any subsidies for my own work.

"And what about Jesus Christ?" asked the Princess, catching me off guard. I had almost forgotten that ladies of royal blood were still likely to have been raised in a convent or a school run by Sisters.

Catholic religion is the ultimate reference of the aristocracy: "I have my faith," was a statement she made several times whenever our discussion probed the outer limits of man's place in the world. I answered her, quoting the Medugorje phenomenon.

She had gone there three times and was impressed. But Prince Hans-Adam said he had observed nothing physical there.

Same day, Zurich airport.

We left the castle of Vaduz in mid-morning, following our hosts who had driven off in a red Audi on their way to visit their father, ill in a Zurich hospital. As we drove away towards the Rhine and Switzerland we caught a last glimpse of the formidable towers at the base of the fog. There was new snow above us on the higher peaks.

The distances are so short in Switzerland, compared to our frenzied driving habits of California, that we were surprised to find ourselves halfway to Zurich well before noon. We decided to go on a side trip to Hinwil to visit Eduard Meier's place. He is the Swiss contactee who has so strongly influenced Wendelle Stevens, Tina and Brian, Gary Kinder and other American believers in the "New Age."

In Hinwil we didn't find Meier but people did know who he was. The wife of the restaurateur sent us up the hill to yet another restaurant where we had dessert and coffee. The owner spoke French. The actual address of our contactee was 18 kilometers away in Schmidruti, so we drove up in the fog and the drizzle. We found the place at the end of a gravel trail, complete with a parking lot, a garbage incinerator and a neat garden with a tree nursery.

Billy Meier was not visible but we were able to witness the efficient system he has put into place to screen his visitors: a middle-aged blonde German woman took us into a garage where a trailer had been converted into a salon equipped with a television set. Meier's books and photographs were exhibited and presumably sold in this setting, although we were not pressured to buy anything. After signing the guest book, where I found numerous autographs in Japanese and many names of television companies, we had a brief conversation with the blonde woman. It reminded me of my interaction with the cults I researched in *Messengers*: the same pretense to ultimate wisdom, the all-knowing smile, the professions of faith and the same expressions of utter pity for those who are not struck by the blinding beam of unquestioning acceptance.

"How do we know that Mr. Meier is right?" I asked. "In America many groups claim to have similar contacts, but the Aliens they interact with are not your Pleiadians."

"It's for you to search for the truth within yourself," answered the well-trained woman in standard New Age fuzzyspeak.

"What about claims that some of the Aliens are living on earth and that the U.S. Government has recovered some crashed disks?"

"We do not believe such stories."

On the way back to the car she insisted that their group "was not a sect."

It was her turn to ask questions: What did we think? Had we had our own contacts? And it was my turn to be evasive:

"I am only a student."

Later, as we drove down the hillside towards Zurich, Janine asked me: "How can you be so polite when people are so arrogant and insulting with you?"

"Why should I let them get to me? I try to behave as a doctor would with his patients."

The blonde's attitude was a mask: she confessed she had lost her husband when he was only 41, her life shattered until she met Billy. He gave her a reason for living, a place, a purpose. Even if he now keeps all the "contacts" for himself, he has found a convenient setting, a team of disciples to keep his place neat and his plate full, and the dark blue flag of the Semjase Center flying limply in the damp wind over his big house.

We came back to Zurich tired and a bit depressed. Perhaps it is the altitude that drains us.

More likely it is the pathetic spectacle, the endlessly repeated joke of human life groping blindly for some meaning in the dark night of the soul.

Paris. Rue de la Clef. Sunday 5 November 1989.

We're only a few weeks away from the end of another decade, with important changes in our lives and the wider world. Our private interests shift back towards a Europe suddenly inebriated with an unprecedented sense of freedom. Soon we will have our own little place in Paris.

TWA flight Paris-Boston. Thursday 9 November 1989.

Last Sunday we moved to a small bedroom in the *Hotel des Saints-Pères*, in the *6th Arrondissement*, our future village. I left my mother with books dedicated to friends and family, phone messages to relay... She is still active and energetic, although she gets easily tired. It is with more sadness every time that I kiss her goodbye and walk down her four flights of stairs, fighting back tears because I know the day cannot be far off when she will no longer wave at me from her window when I turn the corner of the narrow street.

In the evening we had dinner with my colleagues at Procope and on Monday promotion began for *Autres Dimensions*. Among other media people, I saw Jean-Yves Casgha and the Bogdanof brothers in their TV studio in Arcueil. On Tuesday, more interviews and a live debate on a highly controversial show called *Ciel Mon Mardi!* It is widely watched in France, and run by Christophe De Chavanne.

Cnes authorities had refused to let Velasco participate in our televised panel and Dr. Bounias wasn't allowed to state on the air that he worked for INRA, but Jean-Pierre Petit was there with his usual petulance. I also met Jimmy Guieu for the first time. No longer the ebullient science-fiction novelist of his early books (those I devoured eagerly when I was a poor student on the night train to Lille) Jimmy is a short man with flashy ties, various Egyptian crosses and pentacles dangling from two gold chains around his neck, a gray mustache twitching. He dragged a bag filled with his latest paperbacks that he couldn't resist exhibiting before the camera like a cheap salesman. In spite of that I liked him. He is looking for his own truth and has probably brushed against some deep ideas over the years. Unfortunately he has fallen into the easy pitfall of sectarian belief: The Lazar-Lear legend, still popular in America, is a little too stupid to be taken seriously in France. Guieu was met with laughter from our live audience when he talked about the horrible deeds of the Short Grays at Area 51.

During the show I was sad to see that witnesses were always made to look ridiculous, without time to put their experiences into perspective. Jean-Pierre Petit wasted time arguing against Cnes and bringing up obscure polemics. Before the show he had told me again that the French Army had redone his work without him. He had a copy of their report in his briefcase. He quoted Sakharov.

Petit, who is undoubtedly brilliant, believes he can show that UFOs use artificial black holes to travel between different folds of this universe without using higher dimensions beyond spacetime. He thinks he can prove that the speed of light is a variable quantity that decreases as the universe gets older and the cosmos expands.

The next day Jimmy Guieu insisted in coming over to Laffont to discuss John Lear with me between two interviews. He told me how Wendelle Stevens had shown him photographs of Aliens lying on tables, with their atrophied sex organs and gray skin. Later I had lunch (at *La Foux*) with publisher Robert Laffont, who laughed as he commented on the show, where Petit had presented himself as a misunderstood genius: “As you may have guessed, I am the 'mean guy' who refused to publish his manuscript! The real story is quite different from what he said on the air. I gave him 7,000 francs as an advance, but what he wrote was unpublishable, part unreadable physics and part polemical garbage. It's too bad, because I do think like you that the fellow is brilliant.”

Robert Laffont also told me the financial history of his company, once owned by Time-Life and managed with proper American aloofness and arrogance by a vice-president who never left Manhattan. When their management changed he was thrown into the clutches of Morgan Bank and had to find new investors to rescue the company, a familiar tune! He found an investor but still had to fight insensitive bankers. A few years and a major heart attack later the company is still going, although no longer independent. Now over seventy, Robert Laffont fully enjoys making the editorial decisions and leaving the financial chores to others. I showed him the American galleys for *Confrontations*. He told me over dessert that he wanted to publish the French edition.

In the afternoon we filmed a sequence for *Ex Libris*, another literary show. The producer had the idea of shooting it inside the *Sainte Chapelle*, which I mention in *Dimensions*. The scaffolding that was hiding the Ezekiel panels at my last visit were now gone, the various episodes resplendent under the rays of filtered sunlight that broke through the rain. While we were waiting for the crew to set up their equipment the guide taught me something I hadn't realized: to the right of the Ezekiel panels that show the concentric wheels is a representation of Saint Louis as he looks upon that very same scene. It turns out the King was fascinated by the Ezekiel story because the prophet had received a vision of the celestial New Jerusalem, a place towards which the *Sainte Chapelle* is supposed to be an earthly interface, a passage, a mystical window (figure 19).

In this observation resides everything I have tried to say for years: there is another level of consciousness. Human witnesses are occasionally in accidental contact with it. I admire the panel where poor Ezekiel, fresh from his abduction, tries to carve on a humble brick the plans and measurements of the Celestial City. God is looking over his shoulder to make sure he makes no mistake. I am reminded that King Saint Louis fixed his eyes upon that scene during Mass in his own effort to bridge the gap to that higher world.

As journalist Martine Castello of *Le Figaro* told me, life is wonderful because when it's finished, there's still the whole of death to explore! I discussed Voronezh with Martine, who had hoped that no one else would notice the Ummo symbol on the side of the Russian craft, since she intended a scoop, writing a piece about it. We spoke of going to Russia together: She will fill out an application

Fig. 19. The vision of Ezekiel: stained glass at the Sainte Chapelle, Paris

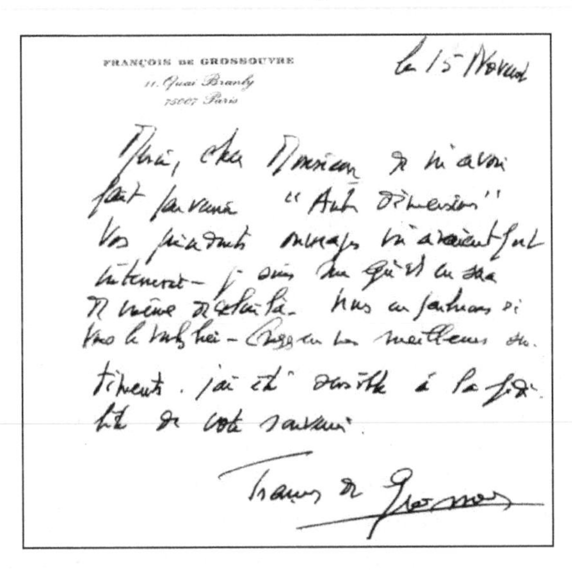

FRANÇOIS DE GROSSOUVRE
11, Quai Branly
75007 Paris

le 15 Novembre

Merci, cher Monsieur de m'avoir fait parvenir "Autre Dimension". Vos précédents ouvrages m'avaient fort intéressé - je suis sûr qu'il en sera de même de celui-là. Nous en parlerons si vous le voulez bien - Croyez en mes meilleurs sentiments. j'ai été sensible à la fidélité de votre souvenir.

François de Grossouvre

Fig.20. Letter from President Mitterrand's advisor, François de Grossouvre

for me at Novosti, the Soviet press agency. I would dearly love to discuss the case with Kazantsev, Zigel, and perhaps even Sakharov.

When I came back to our hotel Janine was waiting for me with Annick. We had a nostalgic dinner at *Brasserie Lipp*. Annick left late at night, then we started packing for the return trip.

Spring Hill. Saturday 11 November 1989.

We're lost in time. My plans at this early hour include a steaming cup of coffee, then a first look at the accumulated mail.

I begin with the thin novel Jimmy Guieu gave me as we stood in the rain in front of *Saint-Sulpice*. In this story, *Les Yeux de l'Epouvante*, he develops an abduction tale full of Alien biogenetic references dear to American ufologists. The protagonists are perfect young Aryans who spend their time strolling naked on the beach. Everybody is nice, slim and sexy, including the “Uranians.” These ideas, reminiscent of the early Nazi, resonate with some ufologists.

At this moment millions of men and women are celebrating their new freedom in the streets of Berlin. Hundreds are dancing on top of the Wall. Eastern Europe is melting like an ice bank in warm spring, sending Stalinist bureaucrats tumbling down into the well of oblivion. Historical events in the Soviet Union and its satellites are accelerating to a blur. My French associate believes the first impact will be an economic boom for West Germany, which may end up dominating Europe: “Former Prime Minister Raymond Barre has told me the instability of the Eastern block was the most important danger looming over the fate of Europe,” he said.

Hyde Street. Wednesday 15 November 1989.

The father of Prince Hans-Adam has died. He never recovered, it seems, from the shock of his wife's recent death.

Literary agent Ned Leavitt tells me that he found *Forbidden Science* to contain “some of my best writing.” Joe Blades pays me similar compliments, yet Ballantine will not publish the book because I am not a celebrity, so there would be few readers patient enough or motivated to take an interest in my private adventures. Well, I have no desire to become a celebrity. I've seen what damage his status with the media did to Allen Hynek when he allowed it to become a major part of his life.

Last night Dan Tolkowsky and his wife Miriam came over for a relaxed dinner. Here is a man who has not allowed his international status to change his sharp outlook on life; or his sober sense of humor.

Hyde Street. Thursday 16 November 1989.

Dr. Rima Laibow, who is organizing the latest abduction conference, has told me her concerns about Budd Hopkins. She cited one episode in which Hopkins had hypnotized a woman abductee who didn't quite have the type of Alien experience he was looking for. According to Dr. Laibow he started yelling at her while she was under the trance. This re-awakened some deep trauma for her as a battered child: she is now in psychiatric therapy – under real doctors.

Dick Haines told me over lunch that the Prince had described to him what seemed to be a landed UFO he had observed from his upper garden when he was young. The object was seen towards Switzerland and was shielded by trees. Dick seems convinced that there is something deeply "evil" in the UFO experience. He also told me our friendship was important to him, knowing that I would give him frank criticism if I felt he went astray. I value our interaction, too, although there seems to be something he is holding back, perhaps because I don't share his religious fervor.

Hyde Street. Friday 17 November 1989.

San Francisco: I found the City again with intense interest, even the Tenderloin through which I drive every day, looking at the derelicts, creatures of a parallel world trying to survive on the margins of our greedy, tough society. These people are real for me. They grab life as they can; they try desperately to hold onto it.

Spring Hill. Thursday 23 November 1989.

Gray lazy foggy Thanksgiving day. I continue to take a perverse pleasure in cataloging our book collection. I find much less pleasure in writing *Revelations*. I must force myself to pick up the manuscript again and again, working one time on this bit and another time on another aspect. Fortunately Janine perceives my distress, puts more logs in the fireplace, and comforts me.

I spent yesterday in San Diego (dinner with Olivier, visit to IRT) and Wednesday in Hollywood with Bob Weiss and Tracy Tormé.

The mail has brought a delightful letter from our long-lost Russian friend Galia, our interpreter during our first trip to the USSR, who managed to move to Denmark. She writes that adjusting was difficult, and she would love to hear from us "now that I can write freely and say what I think without any censorship."

Hyde Street. Sunday 26 November 1989.

The Voronezh case, which I continue to study, turns out to be part of a major wave over the Soviet Union. Coming at the historic turning point of *Glasnost*, that is a remarkable fact. Velasco has spoken to Silanov over the phone: A scientific committee in the USSR has already interviewed 40 witnesses.

Hyde Street. Wednesday 6 December 1989.

Paul Devereux and his wife Charla are coming over for dinner tonight. Morgane will join us as well, to talk of earth lights and megaliths. Yesterday we spent the evening with Mark Rodeghier of Cufos, discussing his thoughts about the Roswell crash. Monday night we had Martine Castello and a friend from *Le Figaro*.

Martine had energetically followed up on our talks in Paris. She told us she hoped to obtain a visa for us to visit the Soviet Union next month, and research the current wave by meeting the witnesses, rather than relying on media hype.

Hyde Street. Sunday 10 December 1989.

Reports of UFOs over the socialist world are continuing. Some now come from Hungary. Velasco confirmed again to me that the Russians had a massive wave with many landings and that physical measurements were being pursued.

A brief conversation with Richard Niemtzow on Friday has brought another surprise. He prefaced it by saying that the Air Force had made plans to send him overseas instead of moving him to Washington, where his family lives. He is now a full-fledged flight surgeon. Accordingly he has approached a colonel who heads up another department at the Base to see if he could transfer to his unit. After the customary interview the man asked him about any other interests he might have. He mentioned UFOs.

"I've had some acquaintance with the subject myself," said the colonel. "So have a number of our pilots, but of course it's difficult to discuss it in the open." After a brief silence he told Niemtzow: "We really ought to have lunch and pursue this UFO thing together."

Then came the shocker: "Did you ever wonder about those little Aliens people are talking about these days? Everybody thinks they're at Wright-Patterson. Don't you think it would be more logical to house them right here at Brooks, where we've got a large facility for irradiation, and for the study of primates?"

He went on, much to Richard's amazement: "Have you met Dr. Robert Bright, the forensic pathologist here? Why don't you ask him some day, about some of the autopsies he's done?"

Today I called Hal Puthoff. "Our technology is taking off like a rocket," he said with enthusiasm. "I may even go to the Soviet Union in a month or so. One of their labs makes a plasma energy device; they've observed plasma concentrations since the early seventies. They've got a model that produces more watts than it consumes. Their theory uses a zero-point energy model. They're ahead of us; they plan to orbit a gigawatt device for the mission to Mars."

Hal is getting together a database of all published papers by the Russians, who have invited him. The U.S. Department of Defense has placed his technology on the list of hi-tech priorities, and he's received several contracts with aerospace companies.

"I haven't made much progress on UFOs," he said, "other than meeting with Falcon, who looks better on closer scrutiny. He claims to have seen a training film detailing Alien physiology, with a live Alien in full view of the camera." Hal has verified that several U.S. Intelligence offices were in fact involved in data collection, but are they actually tracking UFOs, or Stealth technology?

TWA Flight to New York. Monday 11 December 1989.

Valiantly I keep writing, plowing through *Revelations*. How do I know that the Roswell Aliens are not actually here? Perhaps the so-called "core story" is real, not a hoax made up by government spooks for their own dark purposes? Biology is against it, of course. So is everything we know about communications: the Alien story is only one of the skins of an Intelligence onion. It hides something else, but what? Is there an *Alintel*? Could false Alien hybrids be generated in our own labs? Dr. Miroslav Radman, in an article just published in *Nature*, explains how inter-species hybridization could be achieved, but my biologist friends in Paris tell me he is at least two years away from the simplest applications.

Hyde Street. Thursday 14 December 1989.

Kit called me, eager to get together: "As you taught me a long time ago, this is an information game," he said. He assured me he had now received confirmation "from the inside" of an Alien presence. "That doesn't mean I believe it," he said, "but it means I have to make a choice. And it relates to something you wrote."

I am intrigued, but not enough to jump into another plane so soon. There are several burning questions I would like to put to Kit: who was Valerie really working for? Who was paying Bill Moore to spy on ufologists? Where are all the McDonnell reports?

Novosti is ready to grant our travel visas. We would have to go to Russia early in January. The country will be frozen, in the grips of winter, but I will not pass up the opportunity: I learned the true importance of such trips in Brazil last year.

I told Martine we must try to see Alexander Kazantsev. Through *Le Figaro*, which has powerful international clout, she had already made a request to meet Sakharov, but he is absorbed in politics. In my room at the Plaza I had watched him on television, arguing against Gorbachev, urging the end of Communist rule in the USSR.

Now Janine tells me the latest news: Sakharov has just died.

Hyde Street. Wednesday 20 December 1989.

After lunch I went over to SRI to tell Security about my forthcoming trip to Russia. I expected a formal briefing. Instead I was simply asked to sign a few papers and was reminded that the KGB was always trying to recruit new people and might seek to compromise me. “Don't look for bugs in your hotel room,” they said, “but be aware that they're there. The mirrors may be made of two-way glass. Don’t carry any adult magazine like *Playboy* in your briefcase. Don't accept any papers or any letters to be taken back to the West. And if you're detained or taken hostage, stay calm and be very patient until we can get to you. *Bon voyage!*”

Hal tells me he has sources who tracked down two people who claim they were at Holloman Air Force Base in 1964 and did witness a saucer landing. A pilot saw it from above and gave a report to Apro. The rumor states that a Holloman secretary filled out a form for the transfer of the saucer... to Canada!

Spring Hill. Sunday 31 December 1989.

We spent Christmas in San Francisco. Alain was with us, as well as Olivier with his Japanese girlfriend. Now I'm sorting books, papers, and any information about Russian sightings. I hope to hear from Martine that our trip is confirmed. In spite of all the talk about *glasnost* it is still difficult to travel to the Soviet Union. Our visa application has been in process for nearly a month.

At Spring Hill the paths are covered with a carpet of dead leaves. Around the fire last night were Annick and Michel and Catherine. We are rebuilding the water system in the creek bed. We've installed a large table that fills the library with a fine smell of freshly cut wood. When I go up the steps to the tower the gander stares at me and complains loudly from the other side of the pond. Janine is looking through closets and drawers, gathering warm clothes I will take to Moscow. Around us everything is tender, slow, and silent.

REFLECTIONS

As I complete my review of these edited notes, seeking to grasp the emergence of a general picture from a new perspective, I return to these pages with astonishment.

Without any doubt, our field work—including two extensive research trips to South America, and investigations in Europe and the U.S., reinforced my earlier conclusions (i) that the UFO phenomenon was physically real, (ii) that it rested on an unknown, possibly non-human, possibly dangerous or hostile technology with extraordinary psychic components, and (iii) that governments—through their military intelligence channels—were aware of its reality.

But that is not what the public was told.

Instead, throughout the decade, the media were inundated with false information, hoaxed images and lurid reports that garnered high ratings on television. The weirdness came from a rogues gallery of individuals who presented themselves as researchers but told very strange stories of Alien invasion suggestive of a quasi-governmental, conspiratorial enigma. **(1)**

A decade before such a campaign would have failed, its whackiness exposed by eminent investigators and a skeptical public. But Allen Hynek died in 1986 and researcher Coral Lorenzen two years later, leaving the field without clear leadership among an increasingly gullible audience.

We now know that this campaign, clearly coordinated at some high level, used tricks of disinformation (notably the carefully crafted, true/fake MJ12 documents) and a bizarre collection of official and non-official agents.

Was this done to pick up some tidbits from independent researchers like Paul Bennewitz and Linda Howe who were hoping to catch real UFOs? Or to make sure that they didn't stumble on secret projects (such as classified prototypes) that used ufology as a convenient cover? Or to confuse the agents of some other nation? Or, in an even more extreme hypothesis, was there really some secret vault where captured craft were kept, perhaps alongside the bodies of Aliens, a hidden truth to be protected at all cost, as some of my colleagues were coming to believe?

I was not able to determine the reason for this extensive charade, which polluted the public's perception of the real phenomenon and discouraged many witnesses from reporting genuine observations. It created spurious belief systems or "memes" that further discredited the scientific study of UFOs. But what was the point of planting these false stories? When I left for Russia in 1990 to meet witnesses of the Voronezh case, that question continued to haunt me. I was still "on the trail of hidden truths," a very long trail indeed.

During the decade of the 1980s other facts influenced my own life and threw some light on these challenges. First, the opportunity to work on the "remote viewing" project at SRI and SAIC with psychically gifted experimenters taught me a novel approach to the paranormal aspects of UFO experiences. Second, the tightly classified nature of the remote viewing work opened my eyes to the complexities of secrecy and the machinations it entailed.

I am aware that these diaries contradict some cherished ideas about UFOs. During the 1980s it became obvious to me that the special services of the U.S., France and the U.K. (and perhaps others) were actively collaborating in research about the microwave effects of UFOs. Several laboratories worked towards the development of "non-lethal weapons" that, like UFOs, destroyed crops and paralyzed humans at a distance and even distorted their perceptions. There were exchanges of classified and confidential material between France, Great Britain and the U.S. about such devices, even as all three governments, in public, denied the reality of the phenomenon.

The deception did not stop there: There were renewed projects to secretly gather UFO information—not by funding a genuine, honest study—but by eavesdropping on the civilian researchers themselves. The goal was not scientific research but weaponization, away from public eyes. At this writing (2013) the results are still secret.

As I became aware of these facts, the narrative of this third volume developed greater maturity, gradually replacing the breathless excitement of my earlier work. This didn't come without new tensions, however: my growing interest in the paranormal factors widened the gap between me and the true believers among ufologists: They had reached absolute certainty that UFOs were spacecraft piloted by Aliens exploring our planet, a simplistic theory that fails to explain all the facts as reported by witnesses.

While both sides of the ufological debate viewed me as a heretic, I was fortunate to be grounded in a professional environment that was economically nurturing and intellectually free: venture capital, which I embraced with enthusiasm, gave me access to some of the brightest minds and most revolutionary technological ideas at a time when Silicon Valley was becoming a new Athens: the cradle of an innovative culture that would change human communications, medicine and intellectual life itself. It was an environment that recognized no limits and no taboos, where I learned something new every day—as I still do. The love of my children and the luminous presence of Janine, as always, made the explorations worthwhile and the varied experiences of our life even more precious.

NOTES AND REFERENCES

Part Nine: Deals and Ordeals

1. The venture fund that invested in InfoMedia was managed by the Page Mill Group, led by Jack Melchor, one of the earliest Silicon Valley venture organizations. Several senior executives participated, notably Phil Young and Paul Ely of Hewlett-Packard, Herb Dwight, CEO of Spectraphysics and Robert Noyce of Intel, the co-inventor of the microprocessor. Peter Wolken was the venture manager who handled the deal.

2. About Chris Boyce see *The Falcon and the Snowman*, by Robert Lindsey (NY: Simon & Schuster, 1979)

3. Bradley Earl Ayers, *The War that Never Was*. (Canoga Park: Major Books, 1979)

4. Jeannie Mills' book was entitled *Six Years with God: Life inside Jim Jones' People's Temple.* (New York: A&W Publishers, May 1979)

5. The Vidals were never found and may not have existed. Fabio Zerpa told me he had abandoned the idea of ever finding them because he could never interview a first-hand witness who actually knew them.

6. The case of Venado Tuerto is described in more detail in *Confrontations* (NY: Ballantine 1990, 153-157).

7. That scenario was used in the prologue to my novel, *FastWalker* (Berkeley: Frog, 1996).

8. Jimmy Guieu's book was entitled *Contacts OVNI Cergy-Pontoise* (Paris: Editions du Rocher, 1980)

9. I was not able to track down this rumor.

10. In *New Scientist* for 17 December 1994 Glenn Krawczyk of Queensland, Australia, expanded on the work of Michael Persinger for the U.S. national security establishment under project *Sleeping Beauty* in a paper entitled *Possible Cardiac Driving by an External Rotating Magnetic Field* (1973). Captain Paul Tyler, the director of the US Armed Forces radiobiology research institute, wrote in 1986 of a technique employed to disrupt "the electrical signal in cardiac muscle" to produce "complete asystole with a resultant fatal outcome," an ominous statement.

11. OTA was the Office of Technology Assessment, an agency of the legislative branch of the U.S. government tasked with advising Congress regarding pending legislation.

12. "Sir" Arthur Lundahl was director of the Armed Forces Photo Interpretation Center (APIC) in Washington, D.C. A legendary developer of advanced reconnaissance devices used in airplanes, balloons and satellites, he played a key role at the time of the U-2 crash and the Cuban missile crisis. The movie *Thirteen Days* makes a reference to a character named "Arthur" in his honor. He was one of very few Americans knighted by the Queen of England, which led his colleagues to refer jokingly to him as "Sir Arthur of the Light Table."

13. The title of "DCI" or director of Central Intelligence was given the director of the CIA in his role as the coordinator among the numerous agencies composing the Intelligence Community.

14. *Le Pays où l'on n'arrive jamais*, by André Dhotel (Paris: Gallimard 1973).

15. Carlos Castañeda raised much controversy with his books on the wisdom of Native American shamans in Mexico and the Southwest. An anthropology student, he is thought to have invented most of the events in his works, which sold millions of copies in the 1970s and 1980s.

16. Arthur-Maria Rener, a Belgian artist, was a favorite of French Rosicrucian expert Serge Hutin. Janine and I own several of his paintings.

17. Dr. Price-Williams hypnotized me to try and retrieve details of my 1955 sighting of a flying disk over Pontoise related in Volume One of *Forbidden Science*.

18. *Alintel* was published in Paris by *Mercure de France* in 1986.

19. *Nuclear Notepad* was the name of this massive software application that linked 72 nuclear power plants in 12 countries, including EDF sites in France and Japanese plants. At the time it was the only cross-border computer application authorized by the Japanese government.

20. The three witnesses of the Cash-Landrum case did not die from their exposure to the mysterious object, whose nature remained unexplained. Researcher John Schuessler, an aerospace engineer, devoted considerable effort to analyzing and documenting the case.

21. The psychic conference referred to here had taken place over the Tymnet network in May and June 1975.

22. The Crisis Management Hearings transcripts were edited by Robert Chartrand of the Congressional Research Service and published by the U.S. Government Printing Office under the title *Information Technology for Emergency Management.* (Subcommittee on Investigation and Oversight of the Science and Technology Committee, House of Representatives, 98th Congress, second Session, Serial HH, October 9, 1984).

23. RuAnn Pengov went on to serve as an executive at Hewlett-Packard and later as the CEO of Digital Island, an Internet company specialized in virtual private networks, which she took public during the Internet "Bubble" of the late 1990s. She later joined the Board of the Institute for the Future, where I met her again (as Mrs. RuAnn Ernst) in 2003.

24. The remarkable work of Croiset is documented in the book *Croiset the Clairvoyant* by Jack Harrison Pollack (Garden City, NJ: Doubleday, 1964).

25. *Holy Blood, Holy Grail* by Michael Baigent, Richard Leigh, and Henry Lincoln (NY: Delacorte, 1982) built a complex legend around the local story of a priest who dabbled in politics and secret societies of the *Belle Epoque* in the small town of Rennes-le-Château. The book launched a veritable cottage industry among New Age believers.

26. One would love to know if the young Einstein grew up in an environment where he was told fairy tales where the relativity of time was a factor, as in the theme of "Rip van Winkle." Who was his nanny?

27. Michael Murphy, *An End to Ordinary History*. Los Angeles: Tarcher, 1982.

28. Dr. Keith Harary and Ms. Hella Hammid were among the early, most successful experimenters in the SRI remote viewing program.

29. This AIAA paper appeared under the title *Basic Patterns in UFO Observations* by Poher, Claude and Vallee, Jacques (American Institute of Aeronautics and Astronautics, 13th Aerospace Sciences Meeting, Pasadena, California, 20 January 1975. AIAA Paper 75-42).

30. In reality the epidemic in question, ravaging the population of Haïti, was the beginning of sexually-transmitted AIDS and was not directly caused by the polluted environment.

31. "Monsieur Pellat" referred to René Pellat, scientific director of Cnes, a plasma physicist. He served on the Gepan oversight committee but maintained a negative bias towards the subject. He went on to be high commissioner for atomic energy.

32. Dr. Cheryl Weiner edited my book *Computer Message Systems* (NY: McGraw-Hill, 1983) the first textbook on groupware.

33. Videotext was an early attempt at interactive text and information retrieval on television. The technique, first developed in the U.K. and Scandinavia, used the vertical blanking interval to retrieve and process information. It was rapidly superseded by the rise of the Internet.

34. *Network Revolution* was never published in France. I was repeatedly told by French pundits that since France was implementing the Minitel, computer networks like the Internet had no future!

35. Ambroise Roux, a powerful executive at *Compagnie Générale des Eaux* in the 1980s, faded into the background as he retired. The company, a major Utility and construction business in France, eventually became known as Vivendi and made an unsuccessful foray into the information technology field under Jean-Marie Messier during the Internet "bubble."

36. Pierre Plantard (1920-2000) claimed to be the true King of France and the mastermind behind the French esoteric world, including the so-called Priory of Sion. He was exposed as a marginal right-wing character with a criminal record.

37. French researcher Jean-François Boëdec claimed that M. Dumonteil had confirmed to him that the Pontoise abduction of Franck Fontaine was part of an aborted military intelligence experiment.

38. Jacques Bergier: *La Guerre Secrète de l'Occulte* (Paris: J'Ai Lu 1978)

39. The Glomar Explorer project was a massive industrial effort aimed at secretly retrieving a Soviet nuclear submarine from the bottom of the ocean. This extraordinary feat of technology and naval espionage is (partially) documented in the book *Citizen Hughes* by Michael Drossin (NY: Holt 1985).

40. Rugged Digital Systems, Inc. was eventually acquired by Datametrics.

41. The "Philip" ghost was a remarkable experiment by a parapsychology research group in Toronto who "invented" an imaginary character and successfully invoked his ghost. See *Conjuring Up Philip* by Margaret Sparrow and Iris Owen (NY: Pocket 1977).

42. This book was published in the U.S. as *Psychic Spy—the Story of an Astounding Man* by Clifford L. Linedecker (NY: Doubleday 1976).

43. The *Blues Brothers* movie, for which Robert K. Weiss was producer, later received an award as the best musical sound track of all time.

44. As "NIO/Warning," Dave McManis was one of 12 National Intelligence Officers who form the National Intelligence Council.

45. Dr. David Saunders conducted psychological tests for SRI subjects. See *Remote Viewers, the Secret History of America's Psychic Spies* by James Schnabel (NY: Bantam Dell 1997).

Part Ten: Venture Capital

1. The French "smart card," consisting of a plastic credit card with an embedded chip, was invented by Roland Moreno and widely distributed in France under the auspices of various government projects. It was slow in being adopted elsewhere because of the required investment in additional equipment at the point-of-sale.

2. The "Sniffer plane" hoax may have started as an attempt to detect minerals from the air. The French government under Giscard d'Estaing was ridiculed for its gullibility in funding full-scale deployment of the equipment in question, which never worked. The press nicknamed the planes "*avions renifleurs*" and had much fun with the resulting scandal.

3. Dr. Forward was also approached by John Meier, Howard Hughes' trusted manager, to help with an ongoing classified study of UFO propulsion. John Meier died in 1972.

4. Actually the Nobel Prize for the transistor was shared among three inventors: William Shockley, John Bardeen and Walter Brattain. Microcomputers were invented by Robert Noyce and Federico Faggin. I had the opportunity to work with both of them in the 1970s and beyond.

5. All these cases are documented in my "Blue Files." See *Confrontations* (New York: Ballantine, 1990).

6. *Digital Productions* came into this potential market too early, with very expensive techniques. It did not survive as an independent company.

7. *Silicon Solutions*, another investment I made for the Sofinnova group, was acquired by Zycad, Inc.

8. Unfortunately my impression was tragically misleading. Dr. Hynek already had prostate cancer at that time, but was unaware of it.

9. George Adamski was an early contactee whose international best-seller *Inside the Spaceships* (Abelard-Schumann, 1955) caused a sensation. It served as the first introduction to the field for numerous people, including scientists who later recognized the story was a hoax.

10. The *Church of All Worlds* was an imaginary religious group preaching universal love in the classic 1962 Hugo award winner *Stranger in a Strange Land*, by Robert Heinlein. Inspired by the story, a group of gifted hippies under the direction of Timothy "Otter" Zell (later known as Oberon Ravenheart) actually incorporated a *Church of All Worlds* and established it as a major Pagan group throughout the United States.

11. The Bentwaters-Rendlesham case involved military personnel on a U.S. Air Force base on the North coast of England. See *Confrontations*, op.cit., pp.153-157.

12. The book *Prelude to the Landing on Planet Earth* by Stuart Holroyd (London: W.H.Allen, 1977) details the absurdity of the search for Hoova by followers of Uri Geller and Andrija Puharich. The author of the book is a wealthy Englishman who financed wild excursions around the world for a band of New Age believers convinced they were saving the planet.

13. San Francisco *Chronicle*, 12 August 1985.

14. Enrique Castillo Rincon later published his story in the book *OVNI, Gran Alborada Humana: La Historia Verdadera de un Contactado* (Lightning Source, December 1995).

15. The Bogota specimen was subjected to extensive analysis at the University of Texas. Its major component was aluminum, and it had clearly been exposed to extremes of temperature. The results were published in *Confrontations*, op.cit, pp. 42-45.

16. Tachyons are hypothetical elementary particles that travel faster than light.

17. Weinberg, Stephen. *Gravitation and Cosmology*, NY: Wiley 1972, p.78.

18. « L'Age de Raison du Venture Capital Américain ». *La Vie Française*, 9 Décembre 1985.

19. Méheust, Bertrand: *Soucoupes Volantes et Folklore* (Paris: Mercure de France, 1985).

20. Joe Dante (*Gremlins* 1984, *The Howling* 1981) and John Landis (*Kentucky Fried Movie* 1977, *Animal House* 1978) are two Hollywood directors who often worked together and with Robert K. Weiss, notably on the science fiction comedy *Amazon Women on the Moon* (1987).

21. The "Face on Mars" captured the imagination of many New Age believers well into the next century, even after actual exploration by robot probes and detailed imaging satellites had made it obvious the appearance of the face was an illusion created by light effects on a rocky outcrop.

22. The *Ovnibase* software technique was described in a paper entitled *Towards the use of Artificial Intelligence Techniques in the Screening of Reports of Anomalous Phenomena.* It was given before the American Institute of Aeronautics and Astronautics meeting in Los Angeles, 19 April 1986. A free copy of the software was given to Jean-Jacques Velasco of Gepan-Sepra but was never used within Cnes.

23. Seagrave, Sterling: *Yellow Rain – A Journey through the Terror of Chemical Warfare* (Natl. Book Network, 1981).

24. Among other works, Jacques Foccart wrote *Le Général en Mai – Chronique de l'Elysée 1968-69* (Paris : Fayard Jeune Afrique 1998)

25. Sitchin's theories about ancient astronauts became very popular in the 1990s, even eclipsing the earlier success of Von Daniken. See for example *The Twelfth Planet* (Book I of the *Earth Chronicles*).

26. Gilbert Payan, a graduate (1948) of *Ecole Polytechnique* and a specialist in power lasers, pursued parallel careers in industry and on the fringes of French secret military services. After post-graduate studies in Germany (1951-52) and at Cornell University (1952-53) Payan worked as a civil engineer, joining ENSA (now Technip) in 1959, developing a petro-chemical plant in Shiraz (Iran). From 1964 to 1971 he worked at Creusot-Loire as project leader on the Rapsodie nuclear plant, becoming head of R&D in the Mechanical department. In 1976 he was president of the Mechanics division of the DGRST (a military research center). From 1978 to 1981 he served as Chief Operating Officer, then CEO of *Instruments SA*, a company developing military optics. He became president of a franco-soviet group for scientific instrumentation in industry.

In 1982 Payan was director of the Mechanics-robotics-optics department at the Ministry of Research and Technology, a position he left in 1985 to become advisor on power laser developments under the Eureka program. He became CEO of Jobin & Yvon about 1986. After 1990 he continued to work as a private consultant.

Part Eleven: Dark Science

1. "Pentacle Memorandum" was the codeword Fred Beckman, Allen Hynek, and I used for this classified Battelle document I had discovered in Dr. Hynek's copy of the Blue Book project files. I had given Dr. Hynek the document when I left the U.S. in 1967, as described in Volume One of *Forbidden Science*. He never revealed its existence.

2. In February 2011 Colonel Alexander published a book (*UFOs: Myths, Conspiracies, and Realities.* NY: Macmillan) describing his efforts to obtain funding for this top-secret project. It has become known that the key meetings took place under DoE supervision on May 20-25, 1985 in the secure facility of the BDM Corporation in McLean, Virginia. The group called itself the "Advanced Theoretical Physics Conference" or ATP. Alleged participants were Samuel Finch, Oke Shannon and John Kink of Los Alamos National Laboratory; Bill Wilkinson from CIA; Howell McConnell from NSA (whom I had met in October 1972); Hal Puthoff and Jack Houck; Ed Speakman of INSCOM (Army Intelligence); Bill Souder and Bob Wood of McDonnell Douglas; Jake Stewart of the Undersecretary of Defense for Research and Engineering; Bert Stubblebine of BDM; Ron Blackburn, Milt Janzen and Don Keuble of Lockheed; Ralph Freeman,

Gary Bright, radiologist Paul Tyler, Ed Dames and Lt.Col. Mike Neery. Ron Pandolfi of CIA also claims to have been involved.

3. The Costa Rica photograph and its analysis appeared in articles I published jointly with Dr. Richard Haines in the *Journal of Scientific Exploration*. See *Photo Analysis of an Aerial Disk over Costa Rica* (JSE vol.3 no.2 pp.113-132, 1989) and *New Evidence* (JSE vol.4 no.1 pp.71-74, 1990).

4. The "Mars Effect" discovered by Michel Gauquelin and his wife caused major turmoil among skeptical scientists who tried to account for it by every means, including some very biased, even dishonest statistics. See *Is there a Mars Effect?* by Gauquelin in *Journal of Scientific Exploration* vol.2 no.1 (1988) pp.29-52. See further: *Biased Data Selection in Mars Effect Research*, by Suitbert Ertel and Kenneth Irving and *Is the Mars Effect Genuine?* by Paul Kurtz et al., *Journal of Scientific Exploration* vol.11, no.1 pp.1-40. The bitter fight largely contributed to Gauquelin's despair and depression, which led to his suicide.

5. Nellis Air Force Base, near Las Vegas, Nevada, is also the site of Area 51 that became a celebrated focus for New Age pilgrimages in the 1990s.

6. *Acid Dreams*, the complete social history of LSD: The CIA, the Sixties and Beyond by Martin A. Lee, Bruce Shlain. (NY:Grove, March 1986).

7. Neuron Data Corporation, which I helped finance through Sofinnova Ventures, had a long and tortured career under various managers until its acquisition by Blaze software, which was financially successful in 1999 but collapsed during the Internet debacle that followed. The company had invented a very clever scheme for rule-based artificial intelligence.

8. Jack Vorona, a top manager for the Defense Intelligence Agency, was a major source of funding for Hal Puthoff's remote viewing projects at SRI International.

In an email message posted to a parapsychology group in August 2010 Joe McMoneagle clarified the project's history after the initial study at SRI: "Study program, US Army INSCOM, called *Gondola Wish* began in late 1978 and ended after only a few months. This was replaced with the first operational INSCOM program called *Grill Flame* some time in mid-1979. This was changed to program *Center Lane* after President Carter exposed the original program during a press briefing when we found the missing Russian Intelligence bomber. It was subsequently changed again to program *Sun Streak* when DIA assumed managerial authority over the US Army personnel in the program. As of that time (1988) INSCOM was no longer the manager. It became *Star Gate* when joint management was assumed by DIA/CIA at the tail end of the program. *Star Gate* is how it is known today because everyone thinks it's a cool name."

Joe goes on to write: "NSA, CIA, DIA, DEA, DoD, FBI, NSC, White House, Secret Service and others were tasking agencies throughout its existence. Since the CIA was not directly associated with the program except as a tasking agency, they monitored what was going on with support to the other agencies. The only people who knew what was going on across the board, due to the fact that it was a black program and few had direct access, were at the Senate Select Committee on Intelligence through three of its oversight sub-committees."

9. Billy Meier is the New Age guru, based in Switzerland, who claimed to be in contact with Aliens from the Pleiades. His sensational photographs were accepted as factual by many New Age believers around the world, in spite of their rather obvious lack of authenticity.

10. Butler, E.M. *Ritual Magic*. Cambridge University Press, 1949.

11. Pierre Gordon: *L'Initiation Sexuelle et l'Evolution Religieuse* (Paris: Presses Universitaires de France, 1945).

12. The Crash of 1987 dropped the Dow Jones average by more than 500 points in one day and had a devastating effect on global financial development.

13. Richard Doty, who became notorious among ufologists when he leaked fake documents to Linda Howe and others during this period, was born February 15, 1950 in New York State. After basic training in security at Lackland Air Force Base in 1968, he volunteered for special duty at Indian Springs AFB in Nevada, a position that required a top-secret clearance. After Vietnam, Doty served at McChord AFB, Washington in 1971. After a period of overseas duty he was assigned to Ellsworth AFB, South Dakota with the 44th Security Squadron. In the spring of 1978, Doty says he was recruited by the Air Force Office of Special Investigations as an agent. After graduating the AFOSI Academy in Washington, D.C. he was sent to District 17 at Kirtland AFB in Albuquerque, New Mexico.

According to long-time researcher Barry Greenwood, Doty's public UFO connection began in 1978 with the alleged leak of an Ellsworth AFB document claiming a fire fight between Base security and Aliens. "While not known at the time, William Moore had informed Dr. Bruce Maccabee in March 1986 that Doty had confessed to faking the document." (*Saucer Smear*, by James W. Moseley, Vol.54 no.9, October 2007).

In August 1979 Doty became involved in the disinformation of physicist Paul Bennewitz, according to William Moore, a murky situation that led to a flurry of fake documents, false revelations about an "Aviary" of supposed experts on the Alien presence on Earth, and the 1983 attempts by Doty to get ufologists Linda Howe and Peter Gersten to disseminate the false information he supplied to them.

On August 15, 1986 Doty lost his clearance in Germany, apparently through illegal counterintelligence activities. A supervisor asked that he be reassigned to Kirtland where his son lived (Doty letter to Philip Klass, May 24, 1989). In October 1988 he appeared on the "UFO Cover-up Live!" television show as a mysterious character called "Falcon," part of a presentation that included statements that Aliens liked strawberry ice cream and Tibetan music (!) He left the Air Force the following month and became a New Mexico State Patrolman. In 2003 he was the co-author of a book called *Exempt from Disclosure* with Robert Collins (who was "Condor" in the same TV show) and Tim Cooper, the man suspected of having faked thousands of pages of the so-called "MJ-12 documents."

It was never clear to me how much of these activities were part of Doty's official disinformation assignments under AFOSI.

14. Dr. Bernard Veyret worked on French military research projects at Bordeaux University. See Part Twelve, note 11 below.

15. *Man Facing Southeast* (Hombre Mirando al Sudeste) FilmDallas Pictures, 1986, directed by Eliseo Subiela.

16. It later came to light that Russian authorities had tried to track me down to gain access to the Notepad global conferencing software in connection with the Chernobyl disaster. Renwick Breck, who was in charge of Infomedia corporation at the time, did not have the resources (either technically or financially) to restart the Nuclear Notepad software.

Part Twelve: The Observatory

1. Philip Dick is an American science-fiction novelist who wrote the classic story that inspired the movie *Bladerunner*. In the last few years of his life he felt certain he was in contact with a powerful psychic force of cosmic origin that he called VALIS or ZEBRA.

2. Arkady and Boris Strugatsky are brilliant soviet writers living in Leningrad. Some of their novels have appeared in English translation, notably *Definitely Maybe* (MacMillan 1978), *Escape Attempt* (1982), *Roadside Picnic* and *Tales of the Troika*.

3. Groupware is the name given to a family of group communication software products ranging from electronic mail and bulletin boards to conferencing. They are designed to enhance the productivity of social networks. Robert Johansen's book by that title (*Groupware: Computer support for business teams*) was published by The Free Press, a division of Macmillan, in 1988.

4. Gulf Breeze is a small Florida town that became celebrated as the focus of multiple claims of UFO encounters during 1988. Mr. Ed Walters, who called himself "Mr. Ed," was a local contractor who snapped a series of photographs of the alleged saucer. It came to light that he had previously spent time in State prison for forgery, a fact never disclosed by his ufological supporters, although they were aware of it.

5. Sobeps, the Belgian Society for the Study of Spatial Phenomena, was one of the best-organized civilian research groups in the world. It owned a building in Brussels with space for a well-stocked library and meeting rooms. It was disbanded in 2009.

6. The official report on plant pathology at Trans-en-Provence, describing the effects of the event on alfalfa plants, was published as GEPAN Technical Note 16: *Enquête 81/01, Analyse d'une Trace* (document CT/GEPAN-00013 by professor Bounias.

7. *Remote Viewing and Computer Communications: An Experiment*, by Jacques Vallee. *Journal of Scientific Exploration* vol.2, no.1 (1988) 13-28.

8. In 2008 Steven Spielberg used this multi-dimensional concept, and other elements of the *FastWalker* story, in the movie "Indiana Jones and the Mystery of the Crystal Skull." Universal Pictures had bought the rights to my novel.

9. *The Fifty-Minute Hour* is a very interesting book published by psychiatrist Robert Lindner. It is subtitled "A Collection of true psychoanalytical Tales": NY, Rinehart, 1954.

10. Ref: *Technique des Arts* no.18, May-June 1989: "Jean-François Deluol, nephew of André Deluol, sculptor specialized in direct cutting, is a great admirer of Veronese, Titian, Derain and Chirico whom he met in 1966 in his Roman workshop. He owes to (Chirico) his inspiration in this painting entitled *The Interrupted Journey,* finished in 1983 and dedicated to French scientist Jacques Vallée."

11. In 2010 John Schuessler confirmed he was acquainted with Dr. Ron Weiss: "I knew Dr. Ron Weiss very well. He was the brain behind the electrophoresis project that was tested on the Space Shuttle. We used to meet and update each other in very clandestine spots at McD. I was one of the references leading to his new job at Aberdeen. Ron had a strong interest in humanoids. He was a physiologist."

12. *Mercury Interactive* went public four years later (Nasdaq: MERQ) and became a member of the S&P 500. It was one of my most successful venture investments on behalf of Euro-America funds. In 2006 Mercury was acquired by Hewlett-Packard for $5.6 billion.

13. The SGDN report in question (on physiological effects of weak microwaves) is entitled *Effets Biologiques des micro-ondes de faible puissance*, authored by A. Caristan, M. Geffard and Bernard Veyret, laboratoire de bio-electromagnétisme, ENSCPB, Université de Bordeaux.

14. See the article by K. Florig in *IEEE Spectrum* for March 1988 and the article in "Défense et Armement - Héracles International" by J. Tennenbaum, May 1988.

15. *Five Arguments against the Extraterrestrial Origin of Unidentified Flying Objects* – presented at the 8th Annual Conference of the Society for Scientific Exploration (Boulder, Colorado, June 1989). The paper was reprinted as an appendix to my book *Revelations: Alien Contact and Human Deception* (NY: Ballantine, 1991).

16. The 1989 San Francisco earthquake was recorded at 7.1 on the Richter scale. It caused significant devastation, notably in the low-lying Marina district of San Francisco, where it was amplified by liquefaction of the unstable soil. It resulted in dozens of deaths as sections of the Bay Bridge and connecting freeways collapsed.

Reflections

1. This "rogues gallery" included paid agents like Bill Moore and Rick Doty, ex-military figures we have met in these pages like Bill Cooper, John Lear and Bill English, and bizarre informers like Bob Lazar and Dan T. Smith.

INDEX

Lightning Source UK Ltd.
Milton Keynes UK
UKHW050000200220
358982UK00007BA/1282